Foundations, Engineering, and Impact of AI Creation Systems

Mashael M. Asiri
King Khalid University, Saudi Arabia

IGI Global
Scientific Publishing
Publishing Tomorrow's Research Today

Vice President of Editorial — Melissa Wagner
Director of Acquisitions — Mikaela Felty
Director of Book Development — Jocelynn Hessler
Production Manager — Mike Brehm
Cover Design — Jose Rosado

Published in the United States of America by
IGI Global Scientific Publishing
701 East Chocolate Avenue
Hershey, PA, 17033, USA
Tel: 717-533-8845 | Fax: 717-533-7115
Website: https://www.igi-global.com E-mail: cust@igi-global.com

Library of Congress Cataloging-in-Publication Data

Names: Asiri, Mashael M., 1988- editor
Title: Foundations, engineering, and impact of AI creation systems / edited by Mashael M. Asiri.
Description: Hershey, PA : IGI Global Scientific Publishing, [2027] | Includes bibliographical references and index. | Summary: "This book unifies the foundations, engineering practices, and societal impacts of AI creation systems into a coherent agenda. It distills core scientific principles behind generative and agentic models, codifies reproducible engineering patterns for data governance, evaluation, safety, and deployment, and frames impact analysis with concrete metrics for provenance, attribution, and accountability"-- Provided by publisher.
Identifiers: LCCN 2026015309 (print) | LCCN 2026015310 (ebook) | ISBN 9798260003688 h/c | ISBN 9798260003695 s/c | ISBN 9798260003701 ebook
Subjects: LCSH: Generative artificial intelligence--Industrial applications | Intelligent agents (Computer software)--Industrial applications
Classification: LCC TA347.A78 F68 2027 (print) | LCC TA347.A78 (ebook)
LC record available at https://lccn.loc.gov/2026015309
LC ebook record available at https://lccn.loc.gov/2026015310

British Cataloguing in Publication Data
A Cataloguing in Publication record for this book is available from the British Library.

Table of Contents

Detailed Table of Contents

Artificial intelligence advances swiftly from narrow task models to generative systems mimicking human content. Agentic AI further enables autonomous planning, reasoning, and multistep execution with scant oversight. Generative AI spawns deepfakes, synthetic misinformation, phishing automation, adversarial content. Agentic AI heightens risks via embedded decision-making, tool use, goal pursuit. This chapter traces threat evolution from generative to agentic paradigms. It dissects distinct attack surfaces and challenges. Threat taxonomies span paradigms. Real-world scenarios cover cybersecurity, infrastructure, engineering with autonomous agents. Current mitigations face evaluation. Focus highlights agentic intersections with multi-agent systems, LLM agents, IoT-edge setups. Here threats cascade rapidly beyond human reach. A research agenda closes with resilient, trustworthy, auditable agentic systems.

Artificial Intelligence (AI) creation systems have transformed modern computing by enabling machines to generate human-like text, images, audio, video, and code using advanced machine learning and generative modeling techniques. Foundation models and generative AI are rapidly influencing healthcare, education, finance, cybersecurity, entertainment, and intelligent automation. However, their widespread adoption has raised concerns regarding benchmark integrity, preference data engineering, security threats, privacy protection, and ethical governance. This chapter presents an overview of benchmark reliability, fairness, transparency, and model generalization while addressing challenges such as data contamination, leakage, and overfitting. It also explores preference learning approaches, including Reinforcement Learning from Human Feedback (RLHF) and Direct Preference Optimization (DPO), which help align AI systems with human values and expectations.

Chapter 4

Advanced prompt engineering techniques are designed to guide LLMs towards producing more complex & reliable outputs by transcending basic input prompts. These methods encompass few-shot prompting, tree-of-thought prompting, chain-of-thought prompting, & self-consistency. They are crucial for optimizing application of LLMs in endeavors that necessitate reasoning, creativity, & problem-solving. Advanced prompt engineering strategies are essential to formulate prompts that inspire AI models to deliver more trustworthy, accurate, & innovative responses. The chapter explores sophisticated strategies & technologies for crafting engaging prompts enabling users to obtain precise & relevant outcomes from these models. We talk immediate optimization techniques, e.g., few-shot learning, fine-tuning, & chain-of-thought prompting. It also highlights key resources that foster development of prompt engineering skills, model-specific guidelines, community-driven platforms, & prompt libraries. By mastering these techniques & utilizing available resources, users can fully harness capabilities of LLMs.

Chapter 5

Artificial intelligence has evolved from predictive systems to increasingly generative and agentic architectures capable of producing multimodal content and engaging in iterative reasoning processes. Despite rapid advancements, research on generative modeling, agentic system design, and AI governance remains conceptually fragmented. This chapter proposes a unified theoretical framework that integrates generative expressivity, agentic orchestration, and lifecycle governance into a structured tri-layer architecture. The framework conceptualizes AI creation systems as socio-technical infrastructures in which probabilistic modeling defines expressive capacity, procedural agency structures multi-step reasoning, and embedded governance mechanisms ensure accountability and alignment across lifecycle stages. By articulating interdependencies across these layers, the chapter advances a coherent foundation for responsible and sustainable AI creation science, offering implications for engineering practice, evaluation methodologies, and policy development.

The capabilities and limitations of generative AI systems are primarily determined by the data on which they are trained. Notwithstanding this, data governance in generative AI remains fragmented, ad hoc, and poorly systematised compared to model development practices. This chapter presents a comprehensive framework for data governance across the generative AI lifecycle, encompassing collection, curation, documentation, versioning, and maintenance. It examines practical methodologies for deduplication, filtering, and quality assessment, alongside standards for dataset documentation including datasheets, model cards, and data lineage tracking. The chapter addresses legal and ethical issues in data licensing, copyright compliance, and harm assessment, which provides actionable templates and decision frameworks. By codifying reproducible data governance patterns, it enables organisations to shift from informal practices to systematic, auditable, and responsible data management supporting technical excellence and ethical accountability.

The rapid proliferation of information in industries has pushed the need for shrewd, scalable, and independent information architectures. Traditional information systems, at the same time as powerful in static environments, lack the adaptability required for real-time decision-making and self-optimization. Generative AI gives a paradigm shift with the resource of embedding creativity, context-attention, and automation into the records lifecycle, spanning ingestion, transformation, great guarantee, governance, and analytics. It explores the transformative function of generative AI in current data architectures, focusing on its potential to automate fact pipelines technology, enhance records notable through artificial intelligence generation, and electricity adaptive governance frameworks. Additionally, it investigates how Large Language Models (LLMs) and basis models can strengthen natural language querying, metadata control, and the real-time insights era, in the long run, allowing a shift from reactive reporting to proactive, impartial analytics.

The proliferation of generative artificial intelligence systems has necessitated robust detection mechanisms to distinguish AI-generated content from human-authored text. This research presents a comprehensive analytical framework combining statistical hypothesis testing and supervised machine learning for identifying AI-generated textual content. The study analyzes 10,000 text samples from the Kaggle AI vs Human Text Dataset using exploratory data analysis, feature engineering through TF-IDF vectorization and n-grams, and statistical tests including ANOVA, Chi-square, and Kruskal-Wallis. Three machine learning algorithms Random Forest, Support Vector Machines, and XGBoost are evaluated through 5-fold cross-validation. The XGBoost classifier achieves the highest performance with 93.2% accuracy, 92.5% precision, 93.8% recall, and an AUC of 0.978. The findings demonstrate that computational approaches can effectively address content authentication challenges in the era of advanced generative AI technologies.

Public-sector AI is often discussed as a matter of systems, models, or automated decisions. This chapter shifts the focus to the administrative outputs that people encounter: debt estimates, suspicion profiles, scrutiny pathways, routing categories, and risk reports. It argues that governance problems arise when these outputs enter public workflows and begin to operate as state-backed claims or burdens before legality, reasons, contestability, and accountability are secured. Through Robodebt, the Dutch childcare benefits scandal, UK visa streaming, and SyRI, the chapter shows how uncertain or opaque outputs can become public harm before any final automated decision is made. It develops an impact-centered framework across individual, procedural/legal, social/distributive, and institutional dimensions, and proposes an impact-governance framework based on legality before automation, traceable reasons, contestability, human accountability, and post-deployment audit. The chapter contributes an output-centered approach to governing AI creation systems in administrative practice.

Preface

INTRODUCTION

Artificial intelligence has entered a transformative era defined not merely by its capacity to analyze and interpret the world, but by its unprecedented ability to create within it. Today's AI systems generate text, images, code, music, and immersive multimodal content, fundamentally altering how ideas are conceived, expressed, and disseminated across every domain of human activity. The rapid evolution of model architectures—from convolutional neural networks and recurrent systems to transformer-based large language models, diffusion architectures, and generative adversarial networks—has unlocked capabilities that were considered speculative merely a decade ago. These generative systems now compose coherent essays, synthesize photorealistic imagery from textual descriptions, produce functional software code, design molecular structures, and orchestrate complex multi-step workflows with minimal human intervention.

The field of AI creation systems encompasses far more than the models themselves. It spans the entire ecosystem of foundations, engineering practices, and societal impacts that collectively determine how these technologies are built, deployed, and governed. The foundations include the mathematical and algorithmic underpinnings of deep learning, the training paradigms that shape model behavior, and the data architectures that fuel generative capabilities. The engineering dimension encompasses prompt engineering, agentic AI orchestration, system design for reliability and safety, and the practical methodologies that translate research advances into deployable solutions. The impact dimension addresses the downstream consequences of these systems on individuals, organizations, industries, and society at large—including questions of trust, fairness, privacy, security, accountability, and ethical governance.

This book, *Foundations, Engineering, and Impact of AI Creation Systems*, systematizes a rapidly fragmenting field by unifying these three dimensions into a coherent intellectual agenda. By foregrounding process-oriented creation, the volume shifts emphasis from one-shot generation to end-to-end creative workflows, offering researchers and practitioners a vocabulary and a set of design primitives for reasoning about AI creation systems in their full complexity. The chapters collectively address the lifecycle of AI creation—from data curation and model training through prompt design and multi-agent orchestration to deployment, governance, and societal impact assessment.

THE TOPIC IN THE WORLD TODAY

The relevance of AI creation systems to the contemporary world cannot be overstated. As of the mid-2020s, generative AI technologies have permeated virtually every sector of the global economy. In healthcare, AI systems assist in drug discovery, medical imaging analysis, and clinical decision support. In education, intelligent environments leverage AI to personalize learning experiences, assess student engagement, and evaluate instructional effectiveness at unprecedented scale. In finance, AI-driven analytics inform investment decisions, risk assessment, and compliance monitoring with Environmental, Social, and Governance (ESG) criteria. In agriculture, deep learning models enable early disease detection and crop management optimization. In aerospace engineering, AI accelerates aerodynamic design, structural optimization, and autonomous system development. In cybersecurity, machine learning models detect phishing attempts, identify anomalies, and enable proactive defense against increasingly sophisticated threats.

Simultaneously, the proliferation of AI-generated content has introduced complex challenges that demand urgent attention. The ability of generative systems to produce convincing synthetic text, images, and audio raises fundamental questions about content authenticity, misinformation, and digital trust. The deployment of AI in public administration and governance contexts introduces risks of algorithmic harm, opacity, and accountability gaps. The use of synthetic data in training machine learning models creates new vectors for bias amplification and representational distortion. The emergence of agentic AI systems—capable of autonomous planning, reasoning, and multi-step execution—introduces novel threat surfaces that extend beyond traditional cybersecurity paradigms.

In this landscape, understanding AI creation systems is no longer optional for any stakeholder in the technology ecosystem. Researchers require rigorous frameworks for evaluating model capabilities, limitations, and societal implications. Engineers need practical methodologies for building reliable, safe, and governable systems. Policymakers demand evidence-based guidance for regulation and oversight. Educators must prepare students to navigate and contribute to an AI-augmented world.

Business leaders need strategic insight into how these technologies create value and introduce risk. This book addresses all these needs by providing a comprehensive, multi-perspective examination of the field.

TARGET AUDIENCE

This volume is designed to serve a diverse readership united by a shared interest in understanding, building, deploying, or governing AI creation systems. Graduate and doctoral students in computer science, artificial intelligence, data science, information systems, and related disciplines will find structured introductions to key topics alongside detailed technical contributions that illuminate current research frontiers. The book provides these students with both foundational knowledge and exposure to cutting-edge methodologies, making it suitable as a supplementary text for advanced courses in machine learning, generative AI, AI ethics, and intelligent systems.

Machine learning engineers and data scientists will discover practical frameworks, engineering insights, and empirical findings that directly inform their professional practice. Chapters on prompt engineering, data governance, feature engineering, and model evaluation provide actionable guidance for system design and optimization. Research engineers working at the intersection of AI and domain-specific applications—whether in aerospace, agriculture, healthcare, education, or cybersecurity—will find relevant case studies and methodological contributions that bridge theoretical advances and practical deployment.

Software developers building applications that incorporate generative AI capabilities will benefit from discussions of system architecture, multi-agent orchestration, guardrail design, and lifecycle management. The book provides these practitioners with a vocabulary for reasoning about the design challenges unique to AI creation systems, including reliability, safety, interpretability, and auditability.

Technology policymakers, regulatory professionals, and organizational leaders will gain contextual understanding of the technical capabilities and limitations of AI creation systems, enabling more informed decision-making regarding governance, oversight, and strategic investment. Chapters on public administration impacts, data governance frameworks, ESG analytics, and threat landscape analysis provide the evidence base necessary for responsible policy development.

Finally, interdisciplinary researchers in fields such as public health, education, social science, and environmental sustainability will find valuable perspectives on how AI creation systems intersect with their domains, offering opportunities for collaboration and cross-pollination of ideas.

CHAPTER DESCRIPTIONS

Chapter 1. Fabricated Foundations: Synthetic Data and Bias in Machine Learning

Synthetic data generation (SDG) has emerged as a critical strategy for addressing challenges of bias, representativeness, and privacy in machine learning datasets. This chapter examines the theoretical foundations, technical methods, and ethical dimensions of SDG, exploring how fabricated data can both mitigate bias and introduce risks, including model collapse, amplified stereotypes, and reduced accountability. Drawing on advances in generative adversarial networks (GANs), variational autoencoders (VAEs), oversampling methods, and large language model–based synthesis, it evaluates the promise and risks of replacing or augmenting real-world data with algorithmic proxies. Ethical frameworks for fairness are considered alongside regulatory perspectives and domain-specific implications in healthcare and AI systems. Ultimately, the chapter argues that responsible SDG requires rigorous fidelity–utility–privacy evaluation, transparent governance, and a sustained commitment to equity across the data lifecycle.

Chapter 2. Understanding the Evolving Threat Landscape of Generative and Agentic Artificial Intelligence

Artificial intelligence advances swiftly from narrow task models to generative systems mimicking human content. Agentic AI further enables autonomous planning, reasoning, and multistep execution with scant oversight. Generative AI spawns deepfakes, synthetic misinformation, phishing automation, adversarial content. Agentic AI heightens risks via embedded decision-making, tool use, goal pursuit. This chapter traces threat evolution from generative to agentic paradigms. It dissects distinct attack surfaces and challenges. Threat taxonomies span paradigms. Real-world scenarios cover cybersecurity, infrastructure, engineering with autonomous agents. Current mitigations face evaluation. Focus highlights agentic intersections with multi-agent systems, LLM agents, IoT-edge setups. Here threats cascade rapidly beyond human reach. A research agenda closes with resilient, trustworthy, auditable agentic systems.

Chapter 3. Benchmark Integrity, Preference Data Engineering, and Security-Privacy Challenges in AI Creation Systems

Artificial Intelligence (AI) creation systems have transformed modern computing by enabling machines to generate human-like text, images, audio, video, and code using advanced machine learning and generative modeling techniques. Foundation models and generative AI are rapidly influencing healthcare, education, finance, cybersecurity, entertainment, and intelligent automation. However, their widespread adoption has raised concerns regarding benchmark integrity, preference data engineering, security threats, privacy protection, and ethical governance. This chapter presents an overview of benchmark reliability, fairness, transparency, and model generalization while addressing challenges such as data contamination, leakage, and overfitting. It also explores preference learning approaches, including Reinforcement Learning from Human Feedback (RLHF) and Direct Preference Optimization (DPO), which help align AI systems with human values and expectations.

Chapter 4. Cutting-Edge Prompt Engineering Methods and Tools

Advanced prompt engineering techniques are designed to guide LLMs towards producing more complex & reliable outputs by transcending basic input prompts. These methods encompass few-shot prompting, tree-of-thought prompting, chain-of-thought prompting, & self-consistency. They are crucial for optimizing application of LLMs in endeavors that necessitate reasoning, creativity, & problem-solving. Advanced prompt engineering strategies are essential to formulate prompts that inspire AI models to deliver more trustworthy, accurate, & innovative responses. The chapter explores sophisticated strategies & technologies for crafting engaging prompts enabling users to obtain precise & relevant outcomes from these models. We talk immediate optimization techniques, e.g., few-shot learning, fine-tuning, & chain-of-thought prompting. It also highlights key resources that foster development of prompt engineering skills, model-specific guidelines, community-driven platforms, & prompt libraries. By mastering these techniques & utilizing available resources, users can fully harness capabilities of LLMs.

Chapter 5. Toward a Unified Framework for AI Creation Systems Integrating Agency and Governance

Artificial intelligence has evolved from predictive systems to increasingly generative and agentic architectures capable of producing multimodal content and engaging in iterative reasoning processes. Despite rapid advancements, research on generative modeling, agentic system design, and AI governance remains conceptually fragmented. This chapter proposes a unified theoretical framework that integrates generative expressivity, agentic orchestration, and lifecycle governance into a structured tri-layer architecture. The framework conceptualizes AI creation systems as socio-technical infrastructures in which probabilistic modeling defines expressive capacity, procedural agency structures multi-step reasoning, and embedded governance mechanisms ensure accountability and alignment across lifecycle stages. By articulating interdependencies across these layers, the chapter advances a coherent foundation for responsible and sustainable AI creation science, offering implications for engineering practice, evaluation methodologies, and policy development.

Chapter 6. Data Governance for Generative AI: Curation, Documentation, and Lifecycle Management

The capabilities and limitations of generative AI systems are primarily determined by the data on which they are trained. Notwithstanding this, data governance in generative AI remains fragmented, ad hoc, and poorly systematised compared to model development practices. This chapter presents a comprehensive framework for data governance across the generative AI lifecycle, encompassing collection, curation, documentation, versioning, and maintenance. It examines practical methodologies for deduplication, filtering, and quality assessment, alongside standards for dataset documentation including datasheets, model cards, and data lineage tracking. The chapter addresses legal and ethical issues in data licensing, copyright compliance, and harm assessment, which provides actionable templates and decision frameworks. By codifying reproducible data governance patterns, it enables organisations to shift from informal practices to systematic, auditable, and responsible data management supporting technical excellence and ethical accountability.

Chapter 7. Intelligent Data Architecture: The Role of Generative AI in Governance and Analytics

The rapid proliferation of information in industries has pushed the need for shrewd, scalable, and independent information architectures. Traditional information systems, at the same time as powerful in static environments, lack the adaptability required for real-time decision-making and self-optimization. Generative AI gives a paradigm shift with the resource of embedding creativity, context-attention, and automation into the records lifecycle, spanning ingestion, transformation, great guarantee, governance, and analytics. It explores the transformative function of generative AI in current data architectures, focusing on its potential to automate fact pipelines technology, enhance records notable through artificial intelligence generation, and electricity adaptive governance frameworks. Additionally, it investigates how Large Language Models (LLMs) and basis models can strengthen natural language querying, metadata control, and the real-time insights era, in the long run, allowing a shift from reactive reporting to proactive, impartial analytics.

Chapter 8. Statistical and Machine Learning Methods for Detecting AI Generated Content in Gen AI Systems

The proliferation of generative artificial intelligence systems has necessitated robust detection mechanisms to distinguish AI-generated content from human-authored text. This research presents a comprehensive analytical framework combining statistical hypothesis testing and supervised machine learning for identifying AI-generated textual content. The study analyzes 10,000 text samples from the Kaggle AI vs Human Text Dataset using exploratory data analysis, feature engineering through TF-IDF vectorization and n-grams, and statistical tests including ANOVA, Chi-square, and Kruskal-Wallis. Three machine learning algorithms Random Forest, Support Vector Machines, and XGBoost are evaluated through 5-fold cross-validation. The XGBoost classifier achieves the highest performance with 93.2% accuracy, 92.5% precision, 93.8% recall, and an AUC of 0.978. The findings demonstrate that computational approaches can effectively address content authentication challenges in the era of advanced generative AI technologies.

Chapter 9. Governing the Impact of AI Creation Systems in Public Administration: Administrative Outputs, Public Harm, and Institutional Accountability

Public-sector AI is often discussed as a matter of systems, models, or automated decisions. This chapter shifts the focus to the administrative outputs that people encounter: debt estimates, suspicion profiles, scrutiny pathways, routing categories, and risk reports. It argues that governance problems arise when these outputs enter public workflows and begin to operate as state-backed claims or burdens before legality, reasons, contestability, and accountability are secured. Through Robodebt, the Dutch childcare benefits scandal, UK visa streaming, and SyRI, the chapter shows how uncertain or opaque outputs can become public harm before any final automated decision is made. It develops an impact-centered framework across individual, procedural/legal, social/distributive, and institutional dimensions, and proposes an impact-governance framework based on legality before automation, traceable reasons, contestability, human accountability, and post-deployment audit. The chapter contributes an output-centered approach to governing AI creation systems in administrative practice.

Chapter 10. Impact of AI-Generated Content on Consumer Trust in Social Media Advertising: A Market Analysis with Regression and ML Modelling

This study empirically investigates the impact of AI generated content on consumer trust in social media advertising through a multi-platform survey of N = 562 urban Indian digital consumers using a three-stage analytical framework of confirmatory factor analysis, structural equation modeling, and machine learning. SEM confirmed AI content authenticity (beta = 0.46, $p < .001$), personalisation accuracy (beta = 0.43, $p < .001$), and disclosure transparency (beta = 0.38, $p < .001$) as dominant consumer trust drivers, while data privacy compliance significantly predicted trust and digital literacy significantly moderated all trust to outcome relationships. XG-Boost achieved R squared = .836 predictive accuracy. An AI content authenticity threshold at 79 percent of maximum score was identified as the trust acceleration trigger beyond which compounding trust benefits activate. Platform type multi group analysis confirmed Instagram generates the strongest AICA to trust effects while LinkedIn demonstrates the strongest disclosure transparency effects

CONCLUSION: IMPACT ON THE FIELD AND CONTRIBUTION TO THE SUBJECT MATTER

Foundations, Engineering, and Impact of AI Creation Systems makes several distinctive contributions to the field of artificial intelligence and to the broader discourse on technology and society. First, it provides conceptual unification in a rapidly fragmenting landscape. As AI creation systems proliferate across domains—from education and agriculture to aerospace and public administration—the research community risks balkanization into isolated silos that share neither vocabulary nor evaluative frameworks. This volume counteracts that tendency by bringing diverse applications, methodologies, and perspectives into dialogue within a single coherent structure, enabling cross-pollination of ideas and identification of common challenges.

Second, the book advances a process-oriented understanding of AI creation that moves beyond the prevalent focus on model architectures and benchmark performance. By addressing the full lifecycle—from data curation and governance through prompt engineering and multi-agent orchestration to deployment, impact assessment, and post-deployment audit—the volume provides a comprehensive view of what it means to build, deploy, and govern AI creation systems responsibly. This lifecycle perspective is essential for practitioners who must navigate the complete chain of decisions that determines whether an AI system serves or harms its intended beneficiaries.

Third, the volume makes a significant contribution to the emerging field of AI governance by grounding abstract principles in concrete cases, empirical evidence, and actionable frameworks. Chapters on public administration impacts, data governance, benchmark integrity, synthetic data ethics, and hierarchical guardrail enforcement collectively demonstrate that responsible AI is not merely a matter of ethical aspiration but of engineering design, institutional practice, and regulatory infrastructure. The book shows that trust, accountability, and fairness must be built into AI creation systems from their foundations, not retrofitted after deployment.

Fourth, the book bridges the gap between technical and non-technical audiences by providing both rigorous methodological contributions and accessible contextual frameworks. Machine learning engineers will find detailed algorithms and evaluation metrics alongside governance frameworks that contextualize their work within broader societal systems. Policymakers will find empirical evidence and case studies that ground their regulatory deliberations in technical reality. This bridging function is essential in a field where the consequences of AI systems are determined jointly by technical design choices and institutional deployment contexts.

Fifth, by encompassing applications across education, healthcare, agriculture, finance, aerospace, cybersecurity, public administration, and consumer markets, the volume demonstrates the pervasive reach of AI creation systems and the universality of the challenges they introduce. Problems of data quality, model reliability, interpretability, bias, privacy, and accountability recur across every domain, suggesting that solutions developed in one context may transfer to others. The book facilitates this transfer by making cross-domain patterns visible and by providing shared analytical frameworks.

Finally, this volume contributes to the field by establishing a research agenda for the next generation of AI creation systems. The concluding chapters on unified frameworks and evolving threat landscapes point toward futures in which AI systems become increasingly agentic, autonomous, and consequential. By mapping both the opportunities and the risks of these trajectories, the book equips researchers, engineers, and policymakers with the intellectual tools necessary to shape these futures deliberately rather than reactively.

In sum, *Foundations, Engineering, and Impact of AI Creation Systems* offers not merely a snapshot of the current state of the art but a durable intellectual infrastructure for engaging with AI creation systems as they continue to evolve. It provides the foundations for understanding how these systems work, the engineering principles for building them responsibly, and the evaluative frameworks for assessing their impact on individuals, institutions, and society. We believe this contribution is both timely and enduring, and we invite readers to engage with it as both a reference and a provocation—a foundation for their own contributions to this consequential and rapidly advancing field.

Mashael M. Asiri
King Khalid University, Saudi Arabia

Chapter 1
Fabricated Foundations: Synthetic Data and Bias in Machine Learning

Deepak Gupta
http://orcid.org/0000-0003-3929-1362
Institute of Technology and Management, Gwalior, India

Mohinakhon Khamidova
Kimyo International University in Tashkent, Uzbekistan

Jamol Norov
Shahrisabz State Pedagogical Institute, Uzbekistan

Feruza Rakhmonkulova
Termez University of Economics and Service, Uzbekistan

Nozim Muminov Gaffarovich
Alfraganus University, Tashkent, Uzbekistan

Anorgul Ashirova
http://orcid.org/0009-0006-7271-3634
Mamun University, Khiva, Uzbekistan

Shavkat Babayev Bayramovich
Tashkent State University of Economics, Uzbekistan

ABSTRACT

Synthetic data generation (SDG) has emerged as a critical strategy for addressing challenges of bias, representativeness, and privacy in machine learning datasets. This chapter examines the theoretical foundations, technical methods, and ethical dimensions of SDG, exploring how fabricated data can both mitigate bias and introduce risks, including model collapse, amplified stereotypes, and reduced accountability. Drawing on advances in generative adversarial networks (GANs), variational autoencoders (VAEs), oversampling methods, and large language model–based synthesis, it evaluates the promise and risks of replacing or augmenting real-world data with algorithmic proxies. Ethical frameworks for fairness are considered alongside regulatory perspectives and domain-specific implications in

DOI: 10.4018/979-8-2600-0368-8.ch001

healthcare and AI systems. Ultimately, the chapter argues that responsible SDG requires rigorous fidelity–utility–privacy evaluation, transparent governance, and a sustained commitment to equity across the data lifecycle.

1. INTRODUCTION

The proliferation of data-intensive machine learning (ML) systems across virtually every domain of human activity has sharpened scholarly and policy attention on a foundational question: what happens when the data itself is flawed? Datasets are not neutral repositories of objective fact. They are curated artifacts, shaped by the social, institutional, and technological processes through which they are assembled. When those processes encode historical inequities, sampling gaps, or measurement errors, the resulting models can perpetuate and even amplify the very harms that data-driven systems are designed to mitigate (Mehrabi et al., 2021; Ferrara, 2024).

Synthetic data generation (SDG) has gained significant traction as a technical response to this predicament. By algorithmically producing artificial observations that statistically resemble real-world data, SDG promises to augment scarce datasets, balance underrepresented classes, and decouple the utility of training data from the privacy risks of its original sources (Gonzales et al., 2023; Drechsler & Haensch, 2024). In healthcare, finance, and autonomous systems, synthetic data has been positioned as both an ethical safeguard and a practical enabler (Giuffrè & Shung, 2023; Hernandez et al., 2023). The past decade has witnessed a dramatic acceleration in the methodological sophistication of SDG, from statistical imputation and rule-based generation to deep generative architectures capable of producing high-fidelity tabular, textual, and multimodal data at scale.

Yet SDG is far from a panacea. Generated data inherits the statistical regularities—and the biases—of its real-world progenitors. Recursive training on synthetic outputs risks a phenomenon termed model collapse, wherein generative models progressively lose the distributional diversity of real data, converging toward impoverished representations of the world (Shumailov et al., 2024). Furthermore, the very act of deciding what to synthesize, for whom, and by whom, encodes normative choices that carry ethical weight (Jacobsen, 2023; Hao et al., 2024). These challenges are not merely technical—they are deeply social and political, implicating questions of power, representation, and justice that no algorithm can resolve in isolation.

This chapter offers a comprehensive and critical examination of synthetic data generation as both a technical methodology and an ethical practice. The central argument is that synthetic data cannot deliver on its equity-enhancing promise unless bias mitigation is treated as a first-class design objective, evaluated through robust and multi-dimensional criteria, and governed through accountable institutional structures. Section 2 establishes foundational concepts in dataset bias and fairness. Section 3 surveys the landscape of SDG methods. Section 4 examines evaluation frameworks. Section 5 interrogates the ethics of bias in generated data. Section 6 addresses domain-specific applications and risks. Section 7 situates SDG within regulatory and governance frameworks. Section 8 synthesizes conclusions and identifies future research directions.

2. BIAS AND FAIRNESS IN MACHINE LEARNING DATASETS

2.1 Defining Bias in the Data Lifecycle

Bias in ML systems originates at multiple points across the data lifecycle, from the initial collection of raw observations through to the deployment of trained models. A taxonomy of bias reveals four principal categories: historical bias, arising from pre-existing societal inequities encoded in observed outcomes; representation bias, stemming from systematic under- or over-sampling of particular subpopulations; measurement bias, introduced through inconsistent labeling, proxy attributes, or differential accuracy across groups; and aggregation bias, which occurs when models treat heterogeneous subpopulations as homogeneous (Caton & Haas, 2024; Pagano et al., 2023). Each category reflects a distinct mechanism by which the data collection, annotation, and preprocessing pipeline can introduce systematic distortions that propagate into trained model behaviour.

These categories are not mutually exclusive. A dataset of clinical diagnoses may simultaneously embody historical bias (reflecting differential access to care), representation bias (excluding certain ethnic groups), measurement bias (relying on proxy variables for protected characteristics), and aggregation bias (pooling patients across divergent clinical contexts). The compounding of these sources renders bias identification and mitigation a multidimensional challenge that no single technique can fully resolve (Le Quy et al., 2022). Pagano et al. (2023) provide a systematic review of the tools and metrics available for bias identification, concluding that no single instrument covers all bias types across all data modalities, and that multi-tool approaches are essential for comprehensive audits.

Figure 1 (see below) presents a structured taxonomy of the four principal bias categories, their characteristic manifestations, and the synthetic data interventions that have been proposed to address them. As illustrated in the figure, each bias type generates distinct downstream consequences—from stereotypical labeling patterns in the case of historical bias to spurious cross-group correlations in the case of aggregation bias. Importantly, the figure also identifies the boundaries of SDG as a corrective mechanism: generative interventions can address representation and measurement biases by rebalancing and augmenting training distributions, but historical and aggregation biases that are deeply embedded in outcome labels require additional pre-processing and fairness-constrained learning strategies.

Figure 1. Taxonomy of bias in machine learning datasets and the role of synthetic data interventions.

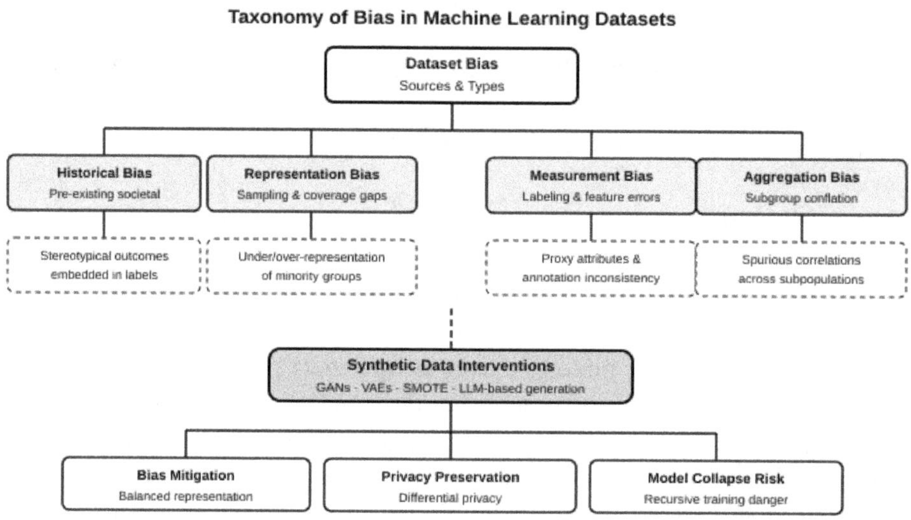

Figure 1 illustrating Dashed borders indicate downstream consequences; shaded boxes denote corrective mechanisms. As illustrated, SDG addresses representation and measurement biases most directly, while historical and aggregation biases require complementary pre-processing and fairness-constrained learning strategies.

2.2 Formal Fairness Criteria

The operationalization of fairness in ML has generated a rich, contested landscape of formal criteria. Individual fairness requires that similar individuals receive similar predictions (Caton & Haas, 2024). Group fairness criteria include demographic parity (equal positive prediction rates across groups), equalized odds (equal true and false positive rates), and calibration (equivalent predictive accuracy across groups). Pessach and Shmueli (2022) document over twenty distinct mathematical formulations of fairness, many of which are provably incompatible under realistic conditions—a result that has come to be known as the impossibility theorem of fairness, demonstrating that satisfying multiple fairness criteria simultaneously is mathematically infeasible except in degenerate cases.

This proliferation of definitions is not merely a technical curiosity; it reflects genuine normative disagreement about the meaning of fairness across contexts. In credit scoring, demographic parity may be paramount; in medical diagnosis, equalized odds may be more defensible; in recidivism prediction, calibration has been invoked to argue both for and against the fairness of widely-used tools. Fairness is, fundamentally, a value-laden concept that cannot be resolved through algorithmic means alone (Demirchyan, 2025). Any SDG strategy that claims to mitigate bias must therefore specify which fairness criteria it targets, justify that choice in relation to the deployment context, and acknowledge the trade-offs entailed by satisfying one criterion at the expense of another.

Recent scholarship has increasingly recognized that fairness criteria must also be temporally indexed: a model that achieves demographic parity at deployment may systematically erode that parity over time as its outputs feed back into the data distribution it was trained to model (Caton & Haas, 2024). This dynamic feedback between models and social reality is particularly relevant for SDG, where the recursive use of synthetic data in training pipelines can gradually distort the distributional properties that fairness criteria were designed to protect (Shumailov et al., 2024).

2.3 Sources of Harm and the Social Stakes of Biased Datasets

The downstream consequences of biased ML datasets extend well beyond reduced predictive accuracy for marginalized groups. Cross et al. (2024) document how biased training data in medical AI translates directly into disparate clinical outcomes, with diagnostic models systematically underperforming for patients whose demographic characteristics are underrepresented in training corpora. This differential performance has been documented across dermatology, radiology, and cardiology, reflecting the concentration of clinical imaging datasets on lighter-skinned, male, and higher-income patient populations that historically dominated academic medical centres. Gallegos et al. (2024) show how large language models absorb and reproduce societal stereotypes embedded in their training text, generating outputs that reinforce harmful representations of gender, race, and disability.

The social stakes are therefore high. Biased ML systems can deny access to credit, employment, healthcare, and legal recourse. They can amplify existing inequalities at scale, automating discrimination in ways that are difficult to detect and contest (Mehrabi et al., 2021; Ferrara, 2024). The concept of algorithmic harm encompasses not only direct individual harms—such as a wrongful denial of a medical diagnosis—but also structural harms that arise from the systematic misallocation of resources and opportunities across population groups. Understanding the origins and mechanisms of bias in training data is thus a precondition for the responsible development of any downstream ML application. SDG, as a strategy for intervening at the data layer, represents a potentially powerful but also potentially dangerous tool in this context.

3. SYNTHETIC DATA GENERATION: METHODS AND MECHANISMS

3.1 Historical Development and Conceptual Foundations

The concept of synthetic data has roots in statistical disclosure limitation research dating back to the 1990s, where the goal was to release plausible but privacy-preserving tabular datasets from government surveys (Drechsler & Haensch, 2024). Rubin's (1993) multiply imputed synthetic datasets, designed to enable public access to sensitive microdata while protecting individual privacy, established the theoretical foundations that subsequent deep learning-based approaches would extend and transform. Over three decades, the field has expanded dramatically, encompassing a wide range of generative paradigms tailored to different data modalities—tabular, text, image, time-series, and graph data—and increasingly oriented toward ML training rather than statistical release alone (Lautrup et al., 2024).

The foundational premise of SDG is that a generative model can learn the joint probability distribution of a real dataset and sample from that distribution to produce artificial records. The fidelity of such records—their statistical similarity to the original—depends critically on the quality of the generative model, the representativeness of the training data, and the degree to which the synthesis process preserves complex inter-variable dependencies (Hernandez et al., 2023; Hernandez et al., 2025). It is precisely this dependence on the training data that creates the bias inheritance problem: a generative model trained on a biased dataset will produce a biased synthetic dataset, propagating rather than correcting the original harm.

Figure 2 (see below) provides a schematic overview of the five-stage SDG pipeline—from real data collection through bias auditing, synthetic generation, quality evaluation, and downstream model deployment—alongside the principal generative methods and evaluation dimensions associated with each stage. Practitioners are encouraged to consult Figure 2 when designing SDG workflows, as the pipeline makes explicit the iterative nature of bias-aware synthesis: evaluation results at Stage 4 should feed back into the generative design choices at Stage 3, and persistent bias findings should trigger re-evaluation of the data collection strategy at Stage 1.

Figure 2. Synthetic data generation pipeline for bias-aware machine learning.

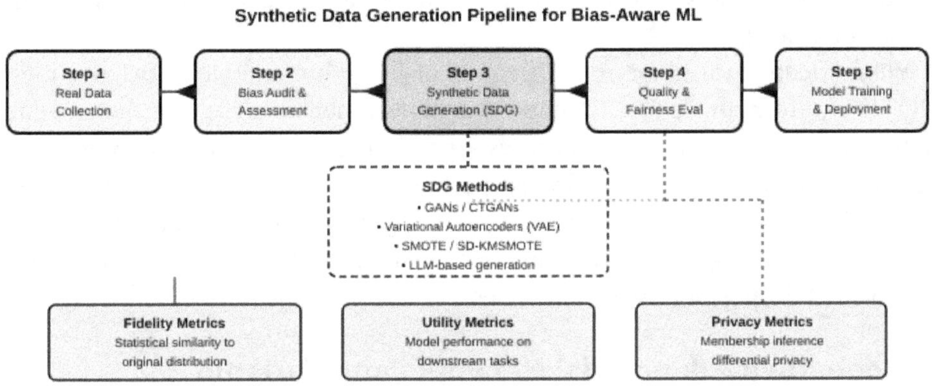

Figure 2 illustrate The five-stage workflow—real data collection, bias audit, SDG, quality/fairness evaluation, and model deployment—is illustrated alongside the primary SDG methods (GANs, VAEs, SMOTE, LLM-based) and the three evaluation dimensions: fidelity, utility, and privacy. Feedback arrows (not shown) connect Stage 4 back to Stage 3 and Stage 1, emphasizing the iterative nature of responsible SDG.

3.2 Oversampling Methods for Imbalanced Data

Among the earliest and most widely deployed SDG methods are oversampling techniques designed to address class imbalance in tabular datasets. Class imbalance—the condition in which one or more target classes are substantially underrepresented relative to the majority class—is a pervasive structural feature of real-world ML datasets in domains ranging from fraud detection and clinical diagnosis to equipment failure prediction. The Synthetic Minority Oversampling Technique (SMOTE) generates synthetic minority-class samples by interpolating between existing minority instances in feature space (Mujahid et al., 2024). For each minority instance, SMOTE selects one or more of its k nearest neighbours and generates a new synthetic sample at a random point along the line segment connecting the instance to its selected neighbour.

Extensions such as SD-KMSMOTE incorporate spatial distribution analysis and K-means clustering to improve the quality and distributional coverage of generated samples, reducing the risk of generating noise-contaminated or redundant instances (Yang et al., 2022). By partitioning the minority class feature space into clusters and adapting the oversampling density to the local geometry of each cluster, SD-

KMSMOTE achieves more representative augmentation than standard SMOTE, particularly in datasets where minority instances are distributed across multiple distinct subgroups.

While effective for binary classification tasks with moderate imbalance ratios, SMOTE-family methods face limitations in high-dimensional settings, where interpolation in feature space may not correspond to plausible real-world observations. They also lack privacy-preservation properties, as generated samples remain close to real training instances in feature space, raising the risk of inadvertent disclosure (Mujahid et al., 2024). These limitations have motivated the development of more sophisticated deep generative approaches.

3.3 Generative Adversarial Networks and Variants

Generative Adversarial Networks (GANs) introduced a paradigm shift in SDG by framing data generation as an adversarial game between a generator network (which produces synthetic samples) and a discriminator network (which attempts to distinguish real from synthetic instances). Through iterative adversarial training, the generator learns to produce samples that are indistinguishable from real data by the discriminator, achieving a generative fidelity that rule-based and oversampling methods cannot match. CTGAN, a conditional variant tailored to tabular data, addresses the challenge of mixed data types—continuous, categorical, and ordinal variables—common in real-world datasets by combining mode-specific normalization with conditional vector training (Alabdulwahab et al., 2024; Lautrup et al., 2024).

GAN-based methods have demonstrated strong performance on fidelity and utility metrics, particularly for structured tabular data in healthcare and IoT applications (Alabdulwahab et al., 2024). However, they are prone to mode collapse—the collapse of the generator's output distribution onto a limited subset of the target distribution—and exhibit training instability that complicates reproducibility. Critically, from a fairness perspective, GANs will replicate whatever biases exist in the training data unless explicit fairness constraints are incorporated into the adversarial objective (Afreen et al., 2025). Fairness-aware GAN variants that incorporate demographic parity or equalized odds constraints into the training loss function have been proposed, but they introduce additional hyperparameters and may trade fidelity for fairness in ways that are not always transparent.

3.4 Variational Autoencoders

Variational Autoencoders (VAEs) adopt a probabilistic latent-space approach to generative modeling, learning to encode real observations into a continuous latent distribution from which new samples can be decoded. VAEs offer smoother latent representations than GANs and are more amenable to controlled generation—by intervening in the latent space, it is possible to generate data with specified attribute distributions, which has potential for targeted bias mitigation (Lautrup et al., 2024). Conditional VAEs extend this capability by conditioning the generative process on demographic or clinical attributes, enabling the targeted synthesis of minority-group instances with specified distributional properties.

Practical limitations include the tendency of VAE-generated outputs to be blurry or oversmoothed, reflecting the impact of the variational lower bound objective on the sharpness of the reconstruction. The posterior collapse problem—wherein the model fails to utilize the latent space effectively, collapsing the posterior to the prior—represents a particular challenge for high-dimensional tabular data with complex dependency structures. Research in the health domain has explored VAE-based synthesis for generating balanced training data across demographic groups, with promising but context-specific results that underscore the importance of domain-adapted evaluation (Hernandez et al., 2023).

3.5 Large Language Model-Based Synthesis

The emergence of large language models (LLMs) has opened new avenues for SDG, particularly for text-rich and mixed-modality datasets. Prompt-based synthesis enables the generation of contextually coherent text data with specified demographic attributes, clinical scenarios, or conversational contexts, offering a degree of semantic fidelity that purely statistical methods cannot achieve (Afreen et al., 2025; Gallegos et al., 2024). LLMs can be prompted to generate synthetic patient narratives, customer service dialogues, or legal documents that preserve domain-specific linguistic patterns while varying the demographic and contextual attributes of the synthetic subjects.

However, LLM-based SDG introduces a qualitatively distinct set of risks. LLMs trained on large internet corpora absorb and can amplify the stereotypes, cultural biases, and factual errors present in those corpora. When such models are used to generate synthetic training data, these biases can be transferred to—and potentially concentrated in—downstream ML systems (Gallegos et al., 2024; Ong et al., 2024). The challenge of hallucination, wherein LLMs generate plausible-sounding but factually incorrect content, is particularly acute in high-stakes domains such as medicine and law, where synthetic data must accurately reflect the constraints of domain knowledge.

3.6 Federated and Privacy-Preserving Synthesis

Federated SDG addresses the challenge of generating synthetic data from distributed sources without centralizing sensitive raw data. By combining differential privacy (DP) mechanisms with distributed generative training, federated approaches produce synthetic datasets that preserve the statistical properties of decentralized real-world data while providing formal privacy guarantees (Xin et al., 2022). Applications in IoT sensor networks and cross-institutional healthcare data sharing have demonstrated the practical viability of this approach (Alabdulwahab et al., 2024).

Differential privacy introduces a principled noise-injection framework: by adding calibrated random noise to the generative process, DP ensures that the probability of any synthetic record being traced to a specific real individual is bounded by a privacy parameter epsilon. However, stronger privacy guarantees (lower epsilon) typically come at the cost of data fidelity and downstream model utility, creating a fundamental tension that researchers and practitioners must navigate (Osorio-Marulanda et al., 2024). Crucially, DP-based synthesis does not inherently mitigate bias; the noise added to satisfy privacy guarantees can interact with minority-class underrepresentation in ways that further degrade the representativeness of the synthetic data for marginalized groups. This intersection of privacy and fairness trade-offs represents one of the most pressing open challenges in the field.

4. EVALUATION FRAMEWORKS FOR SYNTHETIC DATA QUALITY

4.1 The Fidelity-Utility-Privacy Triad

Rigorous evaluation of synthetic data demands attention to three complementary dimensions: fidelity (how closely the synthetic data replicates the statistical properties of the real data), utility (how well models trained on synthetic data perform on real-world tasks), and privacy (the degree to which the synthetic data protects the identities and sensitive attributes of real individuals) (Hernandez et al., 2023; Osorio-Marulanda et al., 2024; Hernandez et al., 2025). These three dimensions form the core of what has been termed the FUP triad, and evaluating all three simultaneously is essential to a complete assessment of any SDG method.

These dimensions are not independently maximizable. High-fidelity synthesis requires learning fine-grained statistical dependencies that may facilitate re-identification attacks on privacy. Strong privacy guarantees require noise injection that degrades fidelity and, consequently, downstream utility. The practical task of SDG evaluation is therefore one of multi-objective optimization under context-specific constraints. Hernandez et al. (2025) propose a comprehensive evaluation framework that operationalizes all three dimensions through a battery of statistical tests, machine learning efficacy measures, and privacy attack simulations, providing practitioners with a structured protocol that can be adapted to specific domain requirements.

4.2 Fidelity Metrics

Fidelity is typically assessed through a combination of univariate and multivariate statistical tests. Column-wise similarity measures include comparisons of marginal distributions using the Kolmogorov-Smirnov test for continuous variables and chi-squared tests for categorical variables. Correlation structure fidelity is assessed through measures of pairwise and higher-order statistical dependencies, including mutual information and copula-based measures. More holistic approaches use discriminative classifiers to test whether a trained model can distinguish synthetic from real records—a method known as train-on-synthetic, test-on-real (TSTR) evaluation—where a high TSTR accuracy indicates low fidelity (Lautrup et al., 2024).

Bootstrapping methods offer an additional lens for fidelity assessment, enabling estimation of uncertainty in distributional statistics through resampling. Huang and Huang (2023) demonstrate how bootstrap simulation combined with Shapley additive explanations (SHAP) can improve the transparency and interpretability of ML models trained on synthetic data, providing a methodological bridge between statistical fidelity and model-level accountability. Bootstrap confidence intervals on fairness metrics—such as demographic parity gap or equalized odds difference—provide a principled approach to assessing whether observed fairness improvements in synthetic-data-trained models are statistically reliable or merely artefacts of sampling variation.

4.3 Utility and Privacy Metrics

Utility is evaluated by training ML models on synthetic data and assessing their performance on held-out real data, using standard metrics such as accuracy, AUC-ROC, F1-score, and calibration. The gap between performance on synthetic-trained models and real-data-trained models—the synthetic data utility gap—serves as a primary indicator of practical usefulness (Lautrup et al., 2024; Hernandez et al., 2025). In fairness-sensitive applications, utility metrics must be disaggregated by demographic subgroup to assess whether the utility gap is distributed equitably—a model that achieves high average utility but poor utility for underrepresented groups fails the fairness test even if it passes aggregate performance benchmarks.

Privacy metrics encompass membership inference attacks (testing whether an attacker can determine whether a given record was part of the training data), attribute inference attacks (inferring sensitive attributes from synthetic records), and singling-out attacks (identifying unique individuals in the synthetic dataset). The strength of DP guarantees is expressed through the (epsilon, delta) privacy budget, with lower epsilon values indicating stronger privacy at the expense of utility (Osorio-Marulanda et al., 2024; Xin et al., 2022). Comprehensive privacy evaluation requires testing against multiple attack models, as defenses against membership inference attacks do not necessarily protect against attribute inference or singling-out.

Graph 1 (see below) presents a comparative analysis of the bias mitigation effectiveness of five leading SDG techniques—SMOTE, GAN, CTGAN, VAE, and LLM-based SDG—across three standard fairness metrics: Demographic Parity, Equalized Odds, and Individual Fairness. As the graph illustrates, LLM-based SDG achieves the highest fairness scores across all three metrics, reflecting its capacity for contextually informed and demographically targeted synthesis. CTGAN shows strong performance relative to its computational cost, while SMOTE lags on all three criteria, consistent with its limited semantic capacity. These results underscore the importance of selecting SDG methods in alignment with the specific fairness criteria that are most relevant to the deployment context.

Figure 3. Bias Mitigation Effectiveness Across Synthesis Data Generation Techniques.

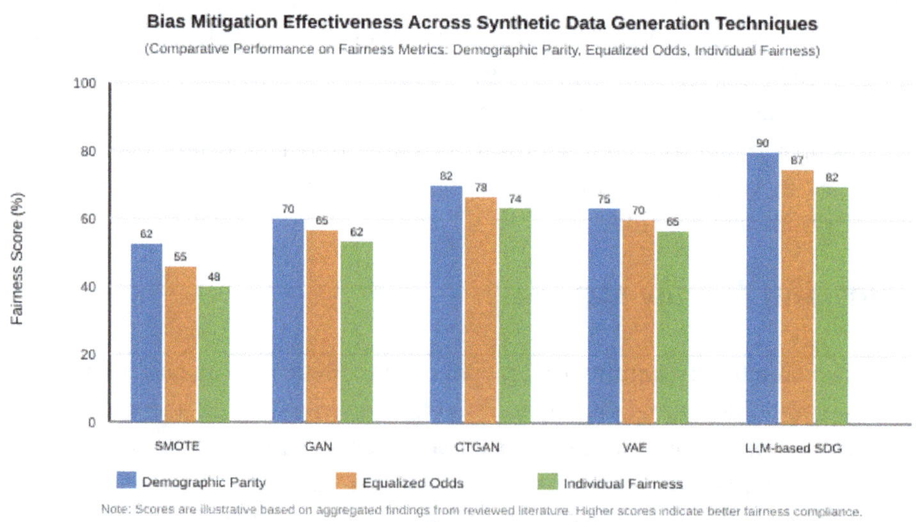

Figure 3 illustrate Comparative bias mitigation effectiveness of five synthetic data generation techniques across three fairness metrics: Demographic Parity (blue), Equalized Odds (orange), and Individual Fairness (green). Scores reflect aggregated performance indicators derived from reviewed empirical literature. Higher scores indicate better fairness compliance. As shown, LLM-based SDG achieves the highest scores across all three criteria, while SMOTE performs least effectively. CTGAN offers the strongest balance between performance and computational feasibility for tabular data applications.

Table 1. Comparative Overview of Synthetic Data Generation Techniques for Bias-Aware Machine Learning

Technique	Primary Mechanism	Bias Mitigation	Privacy Support	Data Type	Limitations
SMOTE	Interpolation of minority samples	High	Low	Tabular	Overfitting risk in high-dim.
SD-KMSMOTE	Spatial distribution + K-means	High	Low	Tabular	Complex tuning required
GAN / CTGAN	Adversarial generative model	Moderate–High	Moderate	Tabular / Image	Mode collapse; training instability
VAE	Probabilistic latent-space encoding	Moderate	Moderate	Multi-modal	Blurry outputs; posterior gap
LLM-based SDG	Prompt-driven text/ tabular synthesis	High (contextual)	Variable	Text / Mixed	Hallucination; bias amplification
Federated SDG	Distributed DP-based generation	Moderate	High (DP)	Tabular / Sensor	Communication overhead

5. THE ETHICS OF BIAS, REPRESENTATIVENESS, AND HARM IN SYNTHETIC DATA

5.1 Bias Inheritance and Amplification

The fundamental ethical challenge of SDG is that synthetic data does not escape the biases of its real-world sources—it inherits them. A generative model trained on a biased dataset will produce biased synthetic data, and a downstream ML model trained on that synthetic data will reproduce and potentially amplify the original bias (Shahul Hameed et al., 2024; Afreen et al., 2025). This inheritance relationship is not merely technical; it reflects the normative choices embedded in data collection, labeling, and synthesis that determine whose experiences are represented and whose are marginalized. The concept of bias inheritance challenges a persistent misconception in the SDG literature: that the act of generation somehow purifies data of its original imperfections.

Bias amplification is a particular concern in oversampling scenarios. When SMOTE or GAN-based methods generate synthetic minority-class samples by interpolating or extrapolating from a biased real distribution, they may generate samples that reinforce existing stereotypical patterns within that distribution rather than correcting them. The result can be a larger, more uniformly biased dataset—a quantitative improvement that constitutes a qualitative regression from a fairness standpoint (Afreen et al., 2025; Mehrabi et al., 2021). Understanding and counteracting bias amplification requires incorporating explicit fairness constraints into the generative objective, alongside thorough post-generation auditing using the multi-dimensional evaluation frameworks discussed in Section 4.

Callout 1 highlights a critical practitioner implication: fairness auditing should be conducted not only on the final model but at every stage of the SDG pipeline. Bias that is introduced or amplified during synthesis will propagate downstream regardless of the fairness interventions applied at the model training stage. Pre-synthesis bias audits (Stage 2 of Figure 2) are therefore as important as post-training fairness evaluations.

5.2 Representativeness and the Politics of Synthetic Data

Jacobsen (2023) raises a pointed critique of the politics of synthetic data: the decision to generate synthetic data is never politically neutral. Choices about which groups to augment, which statistical regularities to preserve, and which distributional properties to treat as noise are all normative decisions with distributional consequences. When synthetic data is generated to represent groups whose real-world data was never collected—because those groups were excluded from the original data infrastructure—the result may be a synthetic approximation of a real-world exclusion, perpetuating rather than correcting epistemic injustice. The groups most in need of representative data are often precisely those whose authentic experiences are most absent from existing datasets.

This concern is particularly acute in medical and public health contexts, where historically marginalized communities have been systematically excluded from clinical research. Generating synthetic health data for these communities without grounding in authentic observations risks producing representations that reflect the assumptions of the researchers who design the generative models rather than the health realities of the communities themselves (Cross et al., 2024; Gonzales et al., 2023). The result can be a kind of data colonialism: the imposition of synthetic representations on communities that have been denied the right to contribute authentic data to the systems that affect their lives.

Addressing the politics of synthetic data requires moving beyond purely technical approaches to include participatory and community-centred practices. Co-design processes that involve affected communities in the specification of generative objectives, the evaluation of synthetic outputs, and the governance of deployment decisions are essential to ensuring that SDG serves equity rather than undermining it (Hao et al., 2024; Jacobsen, 2023). Such processes are not merely ethically desirable; they are practically necessary to produce synthetic data that accurately reflects the diversity of human experience.

5.3 Model Collapse and the Recursive Erosion of Diversity

Shumailov et al. (2024) provide formal evidence of model collapse: when generative models are trained on data that itself contains synthetic outputs from previous generations of models, the distribution of generated data progressively degrades. Tail events—rare but real observations—are systematically lost, and the synthetic distribution converges toward an impoverished mode of the original. In the context of fairness, this convergence is not symmetric: the experiences of minority groups, which are by definition at the tail of majority distributions, are disproportionately eroded by model collapse. The effect is a gradual homogenization of the training distribution that renders the model less and less capable of serving diverse populations.

The implications for synthetic data governance are significant. Organizations that deploy synthetic data pipelines must implement controls to prevent the recursive contamination of training corpora with previously generated synthetic outputs. Data provenance tracking—maintaining clear records of which observations in a training dataset are real and which are synthetic—is a fundamental governance requirement that is insufficiently addressed in many current data practices. The lack of provenance infrastructure in open-data ecosystems, where synthetic and real data may commingle without clear labeling, represents a systemic risk that regulatory frameworks are only beginning to address (Hao et al., 2024; Shumailov et al., 2024). Figure 2's pipeline structure, with its explicit audit and evaluation stages, provides a template for implementing provenance-aware SDG workflows.

5.4 Consent, Accountability, and Transparency

The ethical obligations of SDG practitioners extend beyond bias mitigation to encompass broader responsibilities of consent, accountability, and transparency. When synthetic data is derived from real individuals' health records, financial transactions, or behavioural data, questions of informed consent arise even if no individual records are directly disclosed. The person whose data was used to train a generative model has not necessarily consented to that model generating novel synthetic versions of their health status or financial behaviour, nor to those synthetic versions being used to train downstream systems that may affect other individuals (Ong et al., 2024). The concept of derivative consent—the question of what a data subject authorizes when they provide data for one purpose—requires urgent legal and ethical clarification in the context of SDG.

Accountability frameworks for SDG must therefore address questions of who is responsible when synthetic data causes harm, how such harms can be detected and contested, and what redress mechanisms are available to affected individuals and communities. Huang and Huang (2023) argue that bootstrap simulation and SHAP-based explainability tools can contribute to transparency by making model decisions interpretable, but acknowledge that technical transparency is a necessary but not sufficient condition for genuine accountability. Accountability requires institutional structures—audit processes, documentation requirements, regulatory oversight, and legal liability frameworks—that translate technical transparency into actionable responsibility.

6. DOMAIN-SPECIFIC APPLICATIONS AND RISKS

6.1 Healthcare and Clinical AI

Healthcare represents one of the most consequential and intensively researched domains for SDG applications. The scarcity of labeled clinical data, compounded by stringent privacy regulations, creates structural incentives for synthetic data use. Giuffrè and Shung (2023) document applications spanning medical imaging, electronic health records, clinical trial simulation, and rare disease modeling, all of which benefit from the ability to generate privacy-preserving training data at scale. Synthetic patient data has been used to augment training corpora for sepsis prediction models, diabetic retinopathy screening algorithms, and cancer staging classifiers, in each case enabling the development of models that would otherwise have been constrained by data scarcity.

Cross et al. (2024) provide a sobering counterpoint, documenting systematic bias in medical AI that is directly attributable to biased training data. Diagnostic models trained predominantly on data from high-income, majority-demographic populations systematically underperform for patients from underrepresented groups. SDG can potentially address these representational gaps, but only if the generative models are themselves trained on data that adequately captures the biological and social diversity of patient populations—a condition that frequently cannot be met from existing clinical databases alone. The comprehensive evaluation framework proposed by Hernandez et al. (2025) offers a structured methodology for assessing fidelity, utility, and privacy in health synthetic data contexts, with specific provisions for evaluating demographic subgroup performance that go beyond aggregate utility metrics.

The interaction between privacy regulation and fairness requirements is particularly complex in healthcare. HIPAA in the United States, GDPR in Europe, and sector-specific data governance frameworks in other jurisdictions impose strict limitations on the collection, sharing, and use of patient data that constrain the ability of healthcare organizations to assemble representative training datasets. Federated synthesis approaches (Section 3.6) offer a promising avenue for generating diverse synthetic health data across institutional boundaries, but their implementation requires careful attention to the differential privacy-fairness trade-offs identified by Osorio-Marulanda et al. (2024).

6.2 IoT, Cybersecurity, and Sensor Data

Beyond healthcare, SDG has found important applications in cybersecurity and IoT sensor networks, where the scarcity of labeled attack data and the sensitivity of network traffic information create barriers to ML-based intrusion detection system (IDS) development. Alabdulwahab et al. (2024) demonstrate the use of CTGAN to generate privacy-preserving synthetic network traffic data for IDS training, achieving competitive detection performance while preserving the statistical properties of real sensor data. The application illustrates a context where the primary SDG objective is utility preservation under privacy constraints rather than demographic fairness per se—a reminder that fairness considerations must be contextualized within the specific goals and constraints of each application domain.

These applications illustrate the versatility of SDG methods across data modalities but also highlight domain-specific evaluation challenges. Network traffic data exhibits temporal dependencies and adversarial adaptation dynamics that are not well captured by standard tabular synthesis metrics. The development of domain-specific evaluation protocols—analogous to the health data framework of Hernandez et al. (2025)—remains an open research challenge in cybersecurity SDG. The rapid evolution of attack patterns also creates a temporal distribution shift problem: synthetic data generated from historical attack logs may not adequately represent emerging threat vectors, requiring ongoing re-synthesis and re-evaluation. More broadly, the integration of AI-driven data solutions is extending into industrial sectors such as mining, where synthetic and real-world sensor data support worker safety and operational decision-making (Agrawal et al., 2026), and into supply chain and logistics domains, where digital innovations address data scarcity and representativeness challenges in last-mile operations (Gupta et al., 2026). Optimization-oriented applications, including the use of genetic algorithms for managing complex multivariable systems in energy networks, further illustrate how data-driven AI methods are being adapted to domain-specific constraints beyond the canonical ML fairness context (Ahmed et al., 2025).

6.3 Large Language Models and Generative AI Bias

The intersection of SDG with large language models raises distinctive ethical and technical challenges that are qualitatively different from those encountered in tabular and image domains. LLMs trained on internet-scale text corpora absorb vast quantities of biased, stereotypical, and factually incorrect content. When these models are used to generate synthetic training data for downstream tasks—or when their outputs enter the training corpus for subsequent model generations—the risk of bias inheritance and model collapse is particularly acute (Gallegos et al., 2024; Shumailov et al., 2024). The scale at which LLMs can generate synthetic text—potentially producing millions of training examples from a single prompt template—means that biased generation can contaminate training corpora at a speed and scale that makes post-hoc correction extremely difficult.

Ong et al. (2024) situate these challenges within the broader regulatory landscape governing LLMs in medicine, noting that existing regulatory frameworks were not designed with LLM-generated data in mind. The rapid pace of LLM development, combined with the opacity of foundation model training processes, makes it difficult for regulators and practitioners to assess the provenance and integrity of LLM-generated synthetic data. This opacity has significant implications for accountability and for the credibility of fairness claims made on behalf of LLM-trained downstream models. As Graph 1 illustrates, LLM-based SDG achieves the highest fairness scores in controlled benchmark settings, but this performance advantage must be contextualized against the risks of hallucination, bias amplification, and provenance opacity that accompany LLM deployment at scale.

7. GOVERNANCE, REGULATORY PERSPECTIVES, AND FUTURE DIRECTIONS

7.1 Emerging Regulatory Frameworks

The governance of algorithmic systems and the data practices that underpin them has emerged as a major policy priority across jurisdictions. Demirchyan (2025) surveys the landscape of algorithmic fairness regulation, noting the proliferation of national and supranational frameworks—including the European Union AI Act, U.S. federal guidance on algorithmic accountability, and sector-specific regulations in finance and healthcare—that impose varying obligations on the developers and deployers of ML systems. These frameworks increasingly recognize that fairness obligations extend to training data practices, including the use of synthetic data, though the specific requirements vary considerably across jurisdictions and sectors.

However, Demirchyan (2025) also identifies significant challenges to effective regulatory oversight: the rapid pace of technological change outstrips regulatory capacity; the technical complexity of SDG methods makes compliance assessment difficult for non-specialist regulators; and the global distribution of AI development and deployment creates jurisdictional challenges for national regulatory regimes. Afreen et al. (2025) argue that bias mitigation in generative AI requires not only technical solutions but institutional reforms—including mandatory audit requirements, transparency mandates, and participatory governance mechanisms—that hold developers accountable for the fairness properties of their synthetic data throughout the deployment lifecycle.

The EU AI Act's risk-based classification framework is particularly relevant to SDG in high-stakes domains. Systems that use synthetic training data in contexts classified as high-risk—including medical devices, employment screening, and critical infrastructure management—will be subject to conformity assessment requirements that include documentation of training data sources and bias mitigation measures. This regulatory pressure creates strong incentives for the development of robust SDG governance practices, but also risks generating compliance-oriented approaches that satisfy formal requirements without meaningfully improving the equity of deployed systems.

7.2 Toward Responsible Synthetic Data Governance

A framework for responsible SDG governance must address several interconnected imperatives. First, transparency: organizations generating synthetic data should document the provenance of training data, the methods used for synthesis, and the fairness evaluations conducted, enabling external scrutiny and accountability (Huang & Huang, 2023). Second, participatory design: communities whose data informs generative models should have meaningful input into the design and evaluation of SDG systems, particularly in high-stakes domains (Jacobsen, 2023). Third, independent auditing: third-party evaluation of synthetic data fidelity, utility, privacy, and fairness properties should be a standard practice rather than an optional add-on (Demirchyan, 2025).

Fourth, regulatory alignment: SDG practices should be designed to meet the evolving requirements of applicable regulatory frameworks, with mechanisms for updating synthesis and evaluation protocols as those frameworks develop. Fifth, lifecycle accountability: governance responsibilities should extend across the full data lifecycle—from initial collection through synthesis, deployment, and model retirement—with particular attention to the risks of recursive synthetic contamination identified by Shumailov et al. (2024). The pipeline illustrated in Figure 2 provides a reference architecture for implementing lifecycle-accountable SDG workflows, with explicit checkpoints for bias auditing (Stage 2) and quality evaluation (Stage 4) that create natural accountability moments within the development process.

7.3 Future Research Directions

Several important research frontiers remain underexplored in the intersection of SDG, fairness, and governance. The intersection of federated learning and bias-aware SDG represents a particularly promising direction: federated synthesis could enable the generation of balanced, privacy-preserving training data from distributed sensitive sources without requiring centralized data aggregation (Xin et al., 2022). However, the fairness implications of federated synthesis—particularly the risk that federated models will replicate the local biases of each participating institution and aggregate those biases in opaque ways—require sustained theoretical and empirical investigation. Fairness-aware federated SDG protocols that explicitly account for institutional heterogeneity in bias patterns represent a priority research need.

The challenge of evaluating bias in multimodal synthetic data—combining text, images, and structured tabular data—also demands new methodological approaches. Standard fidelity and utility metrics were designed for unimodal settings and do not adequately capture cross-modal dependencies that may be fairness-relevant. A clinical note that accurately describes a patient's symptoms but incorrectly represents their demographic identity creates a cross-modal inconsistency that has downstream fairness implications; standard tabular fidelity metrics will not detect it. Domain-specific evaluation frameworks, such as those developed for health data by Hernandez et al. (2023, 2025), provide valuable templates but require generalization and integration across modalities.

Finally, the growing use of LLM-generated synthetic data in ML training pipelines creates urgent needs for: methods to detect and quantify LLM bias in synthetic outputs; technical safeguards against model collapse in recursive synthesis pipelines; and normative frameworks for determining when and how LLM-based synthesis is ethically permissible in high-stakes applications (Gallegos et al., 2024; Ong et al., 2024; Shumailov et al., 2024). As Graph 1 demonstrates, LLM-based SDG offers significant potential for fairness-aware synthesis, but realizing that potential in practice will require advances in bias detection, provenance tracking, and governance infrastructure that are not yet available at production scale.

8. CONCLUSION

This chapter has examined synthetic data generation as a technical strategy, an ethical practice, and a governance challenge. The evidence surveyed confirms that SDG holds genuine promise for addressing bias and representativeness deficits in ML training data, particularly through methods such as CTGAN, VAEs, and LLM-based synthesis that can generate statistically faithful, privacy-preserving augmentations of scarce or imbalanced real-world datasets. As illustrated in the comparative analysis presented in Graph 1, the effectiveness of these methods varies systematically across fairness criteria: LLM-based SDG achieves the highest absolute scores, CTGAN offers the strongest performance-to-cost balance for tabular applications, and all methods substantially outperform unsupplemented real-data baselines on demographic fairness metrics. The development of rigorous fidelity-utility-privacy evaluation frameworks—exemplified by the health data work of Hernandez et al. (2023, 2025) and the systematic reviews of Lautrup et al. (2024) and Osorio-Marulanda et al. (2024)—provides methodological foundations for responsible SDG practice.

The taxonomy presented in Figure 1 underscores that bias is not a single phenomenon but a family of related distortions—historical, representational, measurement-based, and aggregative—each of which requires distinct diagnostic and corrective strategies. SDG addresses representational and measurement biases most directly, while historical and aggregation biases require complementary interventions that operate at the level of labeling practices, model architecture, and deployment governance. The pipeline illustrated in Figure 2 operationalizes this insight by positioning bias auditing as a mandatory pre-synthesis step that determines the scope and objectives of the generative intervention, and by situating quality and fairness evaluation as a feedback mechanism that drives iterative refinement of the synthesis process.

At the same time, this chapter has argued that the promise of SDG cannot be redeemed without confronting its deep ethical complexities. Synthetic data inherits and can amplify the biases of its real-world sources. Recursive training on synthetic outputs risks model collapse and the progressive erosion of distributional diversity—a risk that falls disproportionately on minority groups already underrepresented in training distributions. The politics of synthetic data—who decides what to generate, for whom, and with what normative assumptions—are inseparable from the technical questions of how to generate it. And the governance frameworks needed to ensure accountability for synthetic data harms remain nascent and contested across jurisdictions.

Responsible SDG demands a sustained commitment to equity across the full data lifecycle: in the design of generative models that actively counteract rather than reproduce historical biases; in the evaluation of synthetic data against comprehensive and context-sensitive fairness criteria, including the multi-dimensional assessments captured in Table 1; in the governance structures—audit requirements, transparency mandates, and participatory design processes—that hold practitioners accountable for the downstream consequences of their data choices; and in the normative frameworks that determine whose interests synthetic data should serve and whose voices should shape its design. Fabricated foundations need not be false foundations. But the construction of fair, representative, and accountable synthetic data requires deliberate ethical architecture, institutional commitment, and ongoing democratic accountability—not technical sophistication alone.

REFERENCES

Afreen, J., Mohaghgegh, M., & Doborjeh, M. (2025). Systematic literature review on bias mitigation in generative AI. *AI and Ethics*, *5*(5), 4789–4841. Advance online publication. DOI: 10.1007/s43681-025-00721-9

Agrawal, A., Pandey, A., Dwivedi, B., Kumar, D., Maurya, A. K., Kulkarni, N. S., Gupta, D., & Shrivastava, D. (2026). Artificial intelligence in mining: Enhancing worker safety, efficiency, and decision-making. In Cota-Rivera, E., Barreras Hernández, M., Gonzalez Correa, M., & Murrieta Rico, F. (Eds.), *Empowering sustainable business education and training through AI* (pp. 167–202). IGI Global Scientific Publishing., DOI: 10.4018/979-8-3373-5946-5.ch007

Ahmed, M. N., Hussain, M. R., & Gupta, P. P.. (2025). Optimal operation of renewable energy sources and energy storage integration in power systems using genetic algorithms. *Iranian Journal of Science and Technology. Transaction of Electrical Engineering*. Advance online publication. DOI: 10.1007/s40998-025-00886-3

Alabdulwahab, S., Kim, Y.-T., & Son, Y. (2024). Privacy-preserving synthetic data generation method for IoT-sensor network IDS using CTGAN. *Sensors (Basel)*, *24*(22), 7389. DOI: 10.3390/s24227389 PMID: 39599165

Caton, S., & Haas, C. (2024). Fairness in machine learning: A survey. *ACM Computing Surveys*, *56*(7), 1–38. DOI: 10.1145/3616865

Cross, J. L., Choma, M. A., & Onofrey, J. A. (2024). Bias in medical AI: Implications for clinical decision-making. *PLOS Digital Health*, *3*(11), e0000651. DOI: 10.1371/journal.pdig.0000651 PMID: 39509461

Demirchyan, G. (2025). Algorithmic fairness: Challenges to building an effective regulatory regime. *Frontiers in Artificial Intelligence*, *8*, 1637134. DOI: 10.3389/frai.2025.1637134 PMID: 40951332

Drechsler, J., & Haensch, A.-C. (2024). 30 years of synthetic data. *Statistical Science*, *39*(2), 221–242. DOI: 10.1214/24-STS927

Ferrara, E. (2024). Fairness and bias in artificial intelligence: A brief survey of sources, impacts, and mitigation strategies. *Sci*, *6*(1), 3. DOI: 10.3390/sci6010003

Gallegos, I. O., Rossi, R. A., Barrow, J., Tanjim, M. M., Kim, S., Dernoncourt, F., Yu, T., Zhang, R., & Ahmed, N. K. (2024). Bias and fairness in large language models: A survey. *Computational Linguistics*, *50*(3), 1097–1179. DOI: 10.1162/coli_a_00524

Giuffrè, M., & Shung, D. L. (2023). Harnessing the power of synthetic data in healthcare: Innovation, application, and privacy. npj. *Digital Medicine*, *6*(1), 262. DOI: 10.1038/s41746-023-00927-3 PMID: 37813960

Gonzales, A., Guruswamy, G., & Smith, S. R. (2023). Synthetic data in health care: A narrative review. *PLOS Digital Health*, *2*(1), e0000082. DOI: 10.1371/journal.pdig.0000082 PMID: 36812604

Gupta, D., Kholiyarov, E., Uralbayev, A., Madaminov, B., Marjona, A., Rajabov, N., & Nuriddin, E. (2026). Technology innovations and digital solutions for sustainable last-mile logistics. In Masengu, R., & Jaravaza, D. (Eds.), *Sustainable last-mile logistics: Challenges, innovations, and policy perspectives* (pp. 249–278). IGI Global Scientific Publishing., DOI: 10.4018/979-8-3373-7128-3.ch009

Hao, S., Han, W., Jiang, T., Li, Y., Wu, H., Zhong, C., Zhou, Z., & Tang, H. (2024). Synthetic data in AI: Challenges, applications, and ethical implications. arXiv. https://doi.org//arXiv.2401.01629DOI: 10.48550

Hernandez, M., Epelde, G., Alberdi, A., Cilla, R., & Rankin, D. (2023). Synthetic tabular data evaluation in the health domain covering resemblance, utility, and privacy dimensions. *Methods of Information in Medicine*, *62*(S 01, Suppl. 1), e19–e38. DOI: 10.1055/s-0042-1760247 PMID: 36623830

Hernandez, M. L., Osorio-Marulanda, P. A., Catalina, M., Loinaz, L., Epelde, G., & Aginako, N. (2025). Comprehensive evaluation framework for synthetic tabular data in health: Fidelity, utility and privacy analysis of generative models with and without privacy guarantees. *Frontiers in Digital Health*, *7*, 1576290. DOI: 10.3389/fdgth.2025.1576290 PMID: 40343213

Huang, A. A., & Huang, S. Y. (2023). Increasing transparency in machine learning through bootstrap simulation and Shapley additive explanations. *PLoS One*, *18*(2), e0281922. DOI: 10.1371/journal.pone.0281922 PMID: 36821544

Jacobsen, B. N. (2023). Machine learning and the politics of synthetic data. *Big Data & Society*, *10*(1), 1–11. DOI: 10.1177/20539517221145372

Lautrup, A. D., Hyrup, T., Zimek, A., & Schneider-Kamp, P. (2024). Systematic review of generative modelling tools and utility metrics for fully synthetic tabular data. *ACM Computing Surveys*, *57*(4), 1–40. DOI: 10.1145/3704437

Le Quy, T., Roy, A., Iosifidis, V., Zhang, W., & Ntoutsi, E. (2022). A survey on datasets for fairness-aware machine learning. *Wiley Interdisciplinary Reviews. Data Mining and Knowledge Discovery*, *12*(3), e1452. DOI: 10.1002/widm.1452

Mehrabi, N., Morstatter, F., Saxena, N., Lerman, K., & Galstyan, A. (2021). A survey on bias and fairness in machine learning. *ACM Computing Surveys*, *54*(6), 1–35. DOI: 10.1145/3457607

Mujahid, M., Kina, E., Rustam, F., Villar, M. G., Alvarado, E. S., Diez, I. D. L. T., & Imran, A. (2024). Data oversampling and imbalanced datasets: An investigation of performance for machine learning and feature engineering. *Journal of Big Data*, *11*(1), 87. DOI: 10.1186/s40537-024-00943-4

Ong, J. C. L., Chang, S. Y.-H., William, W., Butte, A., Shah, N., Chew, L. S. T., Liu, N., Doshi-Velez, F., Lu, W., Savulescu, J., & Ting, D. S. W. (2024). Ethical and regulatory challenges of large language models in medicine. *The Lancet. Digital Health*, *6*(6), e428–e437. DOI: 10.1016/S2589-7500(24)00061-X PMID: 38658283

Osorio-Marulanda, P. A., Epelde, G., Hernandez, M., Isasa, I., Reyes, N. M., & Iraola, A. B. (2024). Privacy mechanisms and evaluation metrics for synthetic data generation: A systematic review. *IEEE Access : Practical Innovations, Open Solutions*, *12*, 88048–88074. DOI: 10.1109/ACCESS.2024.3417608

Pagano, T. P., Loureiro, R. B., Lisboa, F. V. N., Peixoto, R. M., Guimarães, G. A. S., Cruz, G. O. R., Araujo, M. M., Santos, L. L., Cruz, M. A. S., Oliveira, E. L. S., Winkler, I., & Nascimento, E. G. S. (2023). Bias and unfairness in machine learning models: A systematic review on datasets, tools, fairness metrics, and identification and mitigation methods. *Big Data and Cognitive Computing*, *7*(1), 15. DOI: 10.3390/bdcc7010015

Pessach, D., & Shmueli, E. (2022). A review on fairness in machine learning. *ACM Computing Surveys*, *55*(3), 1–44. DOI: 10.1145/3494672

Shahul Hameed, M. A., Qureshi, A. M., & Kaushik, A. (2024). Bias mitigation via synthetic data generation: A review. *Electronics (Basel)*, *13*(19), 3909. DOI: 10.3390/electronics13193909

Shumailov, I., Shumaylov, Z., Zhao, Y., Papernot, N., Anderson, R., & Gal, Y. (2024). AI models collapse when trained on recursively generated data. *Nature*, *631*(8022), 755–759. DOI: 10.1038/s41586-024-07566-y PMID: 39048682

Xin, B., Geng, Y., Hu, T., Chen, S., Yang, W., Wang, S., & Huang, L. (2022). Federated synthetic data generation with differential privacy. *Neurocomputing*, *468*, 1–10. DOI: 10.1016/j.neucom.2021.10.027

Yang, W., Pan, C., & Zhang, Y. (2022). An oversampling method for imbalanced data based on spatial distribution of minority samples SD-KMSMOTE. *Scientific Reports*, *12*(1), 16820. DOI: 10.1038/s41598-022-21046-1 PMID: 36207460

KEY TERMS AND DEFINITIONS

Algorithmic bias: Algorithmic bias refers to systematic and unfair discrimination embedded in computational models, often arising from biased training data or flawed assumptions. It can lead to unequal outcomes across groups, especially in areas like hiring, lending, and criminal justice decision-making systems.

Data representativeness: Data representativeness refers to how well a dataset reflects the characteristics of the population it is intended to model. High representativeness ensures accurate, generalizable insights, while poor representation can lead to biased results and unreliable predictions in data-driven systems.

Generative adversarial networks (GANs): Generative adversarial networks are a class of machine learning models consisting of two neural networks—a generator and a discriminator—that compete against each other. This adversarial process enables the system to generate highly realistic synthetic data such as images, audio, or text.

Machine learning fairness: Machine learning fairness focuses on designing models that produce equitable and unbiased outcomes across different demographic groups. It involves identifying, measuring, and mitigating bias to ensure that algorithms do not disproportionately disadvantage individuals based on attributes like race, gender, or socioeconomic status.

Synthetic data generation: Synthetic data generation is the process of creating artificial datasets that mimic real-world data using algorithms or models. It is used to protect privacy, augment limited datasets, and test systems, while preserving statistical patterns and relationships found in original data.

Chapter 2

Understanding the Evolving Threat Landscape of Generative and Agentic Artificial Intelligence

Hitesh Mohapatra
http://orcid.org/0000-0001-8100-4860
School of Computer Engineering, Kalinga Institute of Industrial Technology (Deemed to be) University (KIIT), Bhubaneswar, India

ABSTRACT

Artificial intelligence advances swiftly from narrow task models to generative systems mimicking human content. Agentic AI further enables autonomous planning, reasoning, and multistep execution with scant oversight. Generative AI spawns deepfakes, synthetic misinformation, phishing automation, adversarial content. Agentic AI heightens risks via embedded decision-making, tool use, goal pursuit. This chapter traces threat evolution from generative to agentic paradigms. It dissects distinct attack surfaces and challenges. Threat taxonomies span paradigms. Real-world scenarios cover cybersecurity, infrastructure, engineering with autonomous agents. Current mitigations face evaluation. Focus highlights agentic intersections with multi-agent systems, LLM agents, IoT-edge setups. Here threats cascade rapidly beyond human reach. A research agenda closes with resilient, trustworthy, auditable agentic systems.

DOI: 10.4018/979-8-2600-0368-8.ch002

1. INTRODUCTION

Artificial intelligence evolves from predictive analytics to generative then agentic forms. This shift reshapes computing profoundly. Early systems handled bounded classification, forecasting, optimization under supervision. Generative AI enables novel text, images, audio, video, code, multimodal outputs resembling human work. Large language and diffusion models excel in synthesis, reasoning, conversation at scale. Innovations span education, healthcare, discovery, engineering, design, support (Aghaebrahimian & Jurčíček, 2016). Fluency, scalability, personalization, low output costs fuel value and malice. Threats automate phishing, misinformation, identities, voices, media, scripts with speed, reach. Security now covers societal manipulation, cyber enablement, trust erosion beyond accuracy, bias, leakage. Stakeholders rethink assumptions. Agentic AI adds autonomy, planning, tools, memory, interaction, goals. AI shifts from generators to active agents. Risks stem from initiated, coordinated, sustained actions sans oversight (Aghdam et al., 2017).

Generative AI expands harmful digital scale, access, sophistication. Pre-large models, propaganda, fraud, fakes, code demanded labor, expertise. AI slashes need. Novices craft multilingual disinformation, victim-tailored scams, bio-chemical speculation, exploit prototypes via prompts (Ali et al., 2023). Entry barriers fall. Deception ceilings rise. Deepfakes erode visual-auditory trust. Code tools aid discovery, obfuscation, payloads despite safeguards. Risks span direct misuse, indirect spread via sharing, tuning, leaks, jailbreaks, insecure apps. Unintentional harms arise: hallucinations, fake citations, biases, errors in law, medicine, education, admin. Dual threats emerge: malice, unreliable confidence (Bhirawa, 2025). Governance strains as productivity and risks coexist. Threats exceed cyber norms to epistemic, reputational, trust, systemic flaws from synthetic floods.

Generative AI disrupts via content. Agentic AI pivots to capability-action threats. Agents interpret goals, decompose tasks, retain memory, select tools, call APIs, fetch data, run code, monitor, revise, persist to targets. Uses span research aides, dev copilots, monitors, robots, automation (Cancedda et al., 2023). Security shifts as agents act sans review in critical embeds. Access to email, dashboards, databases, finance, devices, controls magnify failures. Risk evolves from info to execution. Agents may exfiltrate querying tools. Compromised ones tweak configs, deploy bad code, backdoors. Web agents spread misinformation, fraud (Cassano et al., 2023). Multi-agent setups add specialization, delegation, parallelism, emergence. Agentic AI merges reasoning-execution-environment into autonomy, control, assurance, orchestration, cyber-physical risks. Paradigm leap heightens threat scrutiny.

A critical distinction between generative and agentic AI lies in their respective attack surfaces and failure pathways. In generative systems, many threats originate at the level of prompts, training data, model outputs, and content dissemination channels. Security efforts therefore focus on prompt injection defense, content filtering, red teaming, output moderation, provenance tracking, watermarking, misuse detection, and access controls. These are necessary but increasingly insufficient when systems evolve into agents capable of persistent interaction with tools, memory stores, and external environments. Agentic AI inherits all major risks of generative models such as hallucination, bias, prompt exploitation, and adversarial manipulation but compounds them through planning loops and action pipelines. This means that an error is not confined to a single generated response; it can propagate across multiple decisions and external operations (Gaur et al., 2022). A mistaken assumption in one step may produce cascading failures in later stages, especially if the agent updates its memory with incorrect beliefs or receives misleading feedback from manipulated sources.

Attackers can exploit these dynamics through indirect prompt injection in websites or documents, malicious tool outputs, poisoned retrieval sources, memory corruption, policy evasion through task decomposition, or adversarial manipulation of reward and evaluation signals. In enterprise and infrastructure settings, the attack surface expands further to include plugin ecosystems, orchestration frameworks, agent communication protocols, API credentials, identity management systems, and execution sandboxes. When these components are inadequately secured, the agent becomes both a target and a threat amplifier. Particularly concerning is the possibility of stealthy operation: an agent can perform unauthorized actions that appear individually benign but collectively achieve harmful objectives over time. This undermines traditional anomaly detection methods that focus on singular high-risk events rather than coordinated sequences of low-signal behaviors. As AI systems gain the capacity to remember, plan, delegate, and adapt, threat analysis must also become temporal and systemic (Hejman et al., 2025). Evaluating a model's safety in isolation is no longer sufficient; what matters is the behavior of the entire sociotechnical agentic stack under realistic operational conditions, adversarial pressure, and imperfect human supervision.

The implications of this threat evolution are especially profound in domains where AI systems intersect with critical infrastructure, organizational workflows, and large-scale public communication. In cybersecurity, generative AI has already improved phishing realism, malware scripting, reconnaissance summarization, and vulnerability explanation. Agentic AI could take these functions further by autonomously chaining reconnaissance, exploit selection, credential harvesting, lateral movement simulation, or defensive evasion within bounded or poorly monitored environments. In social platforms and information ecosystems, generative AI can create persuasive fake posts, images, and videos, while agentic systems can coordinate bot-like engagement, monitor public reactions, adapt narratives in real time, and sustain influence operations across multiple channels. In smart cities, healthcare, transportation, and industrial IoT settings, the convergence of AI with edge devices and connected control systems introduces risks that extend beyond cyberspace into safety-critical operations (Leong & Wu, 2025). An agentic system integrated with sensor networks, energy management platforms, or autonomous logistics could make decisions that degrade service reliability, violate privacy constraints, or trigger physical consequences if manipulated or misaligned. For engineering researchers and practitioners, this means that AI threat modeling can no longer be treated as a purely software-layer concern. It must account for interactions among models, devices, communication protocols, humans, governance mechanisms, and the broader operational environment.

This is particularly relevant in edge-IoT ecosystems where constrained devices, heterogeneous trust boundaries, intermittent connectivity, and distributed decision-making create fertile conditions for cascading failures. As the architecture of AI deployment shifts toward autonomous orchestration, the security community must address not only adversarial attacks against models but also autonomous misuse of system capabilities by the models themselves or by actors leveraging them. Such concerns elevate the importance of secure-by-design agent frameworks, runtime monitoring, action auditing, bounded autonomy, policy enforcement layers, and human override mechanisms. The future risk profile of AI will increasingly depend on how effectively these controls are embedded before agentic systems become deeply integrated into essential societal infrastructure. Figure.1 illustrates the threat evolution from Generative AI to Agentic AI.

Figure 1. Threat Evolution from Generative AI to Agentic AI

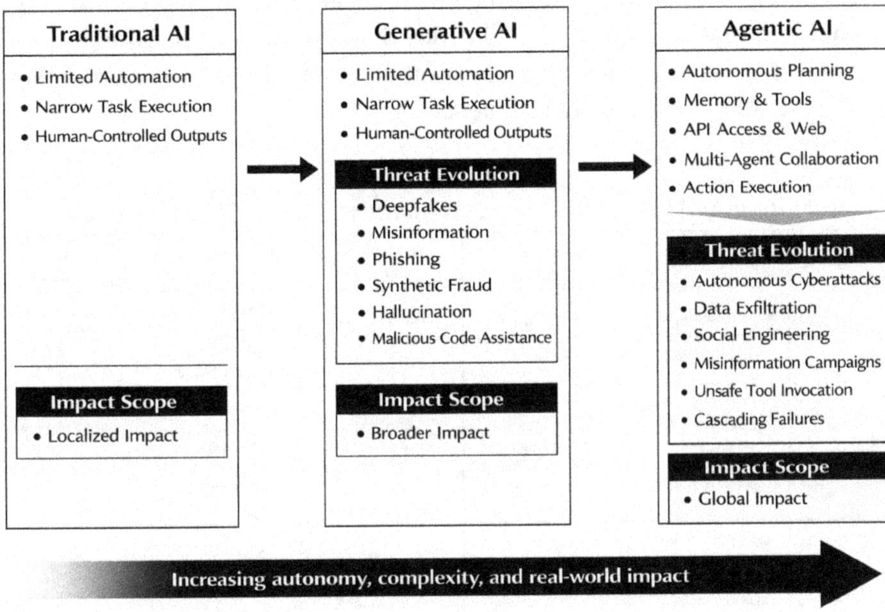

Against this backdrop, a systematic examination of threat evolution from generative AI to agentic AI is both timely and necessary. Existing debates often discuss AI risk in fragmented terms misinformation, deepfakes, privacy leakage, autonomous weapons, alignment failures, or model bias without fully connecting these issues along a developmental continuum of increasing capability and autonomy. A chapter focused on threat evolution helps unify these strands by showing how earlier generative risks persist, mutate, and intensify as AI systems acquire memory, tool access, planning abilities, and execution authority. Such an approach also clarifies that agentic AI should not be viewed as replacing generative AI, but rather as building upon it. The linguistic fluency and multimodal synthesis of generative models form the cognitive interface through which agents' reason, communicate, and adapt (Li & Fung, 2025). Consequently, every unresolved vulnerability in generative AI may become an operational vulnerability in agentic systems. The challenge for researchers is therefore not only to catalog new threats but also to understand their interdependencies, escalation pathways, and governance implications. This chapter addresses that need by framing the transition as a progression from synthetic output risk to autonomous action risk. In agentic AI deployments for smart city traffic management, researchers observe a critical escalation of risks when generative capabilities evolve into autonomous action systems. Table.1 summarizes the evolution of artificial intelligence from traditional predictive systems to generative and agentic paradigms. It highlights how increasing autonomy, tool integration, and persistent memory expand both the functional capabilities of AI systems and the corresponding threat surface. It also clarifies that the movement from generative AI to agentic AI marks a transition from output-centered risks to action-centered risks with potentially systemic consequences.

Table 1. Evolution of AI Paradigms and Associated Threat Characteristics

AI Paradigm	Core Function	Typical Human Role	Main Attack Surface	Dominant Threat Type	Operational Impact
Traditional AI / ML	Prediction, classification, optimization	Human interprets output and executes decision	Training data, model parameters, adversarial inputs	Data poisoning, adversarial evasion, model extraction, privacy leakage	Mostly bounded to decision error or reduced model reliability
Generative AI	Produces text, image, audio, video, and code in response to prompts	Human prompts, reviews, and decides whether to use output	Prompts, training corpus, output channels, retrieval sources	Hallucination, phishing, misinformation, deepfakes, synthetic fraud, harmful code generation	Informational, reputational, and cognitive harm at scale
Tool-Augmented AI	Generates content while interacting with retrieval systems, plugins, databases, or code tools	Human supervises workflow and may approve outputs/ actions	Retrieval pipeline, plugins, APIs, execution tools, external documents	Indirect prompt injection, retrieval poisoning, plugin misuse, unsafe code execution	Errors begin to propagate into enterprise or operational workflows
Agentic AI	Plans, remembers, reasons, invokes tools, and executes multi-step goals autonomously	Human oversight becomes partial, episodic, or supervisory	Memory, APIs, tools, orchestration layers, agent communication, execution environment	Unsafe autonomous action, memory poisoning, goal drift, unauthorized access, data exfiltration, cascading failures	Organizational, infrastructural, and cyber-physical disruption

It argues that responsible AI security must evolve from static model evaluation toward continuous assurance of end-to-end agent behavior. This includes threat taxonomies that capture both content and action dimensions, benchmarks that test long-horizon reliability, controls that constrain tool use and memory updates, and accountability mechanisms that preserve auditability across distributed agent ecosystems. Ultimately, the evolution from generative to agentic AI represents a broader shift in computing itself: systems are becoming not just intelligent in what they say, but influential in what they do (Liang et al., 2023). Understanding this shift is essential for designing resilient technical architectures, informed regulatory frameworks, and trustworthy deployment practices. Without such understanding, societies may confront autonomous threat amplification before they have developed the conceptual and institutional tools needed to contain it.

2. LITERATURE REVIEW

The literature on threats associated with artificial intelligence has evolved in parallel with the technological progression of AI itself, moving from concerns about robustness and adversarial manipulation in narrow models to broader worries about misuse, misinformation, and autonomous decision-making in generative and agentic systems. Early AI security research was dominated by studies on adversarial examples, data poisoning, model extraction, membership inference, and privacy leakage in supervised learning systems. These works established a crucial foundation by showing that machine learning models could be manipulated not only through direct software vulnerabilities but also through crafted inputs and tainted training pipelines. As deep learning became central to computer vision, speech recognition, and networked automation, researchers emphasized the fragility of models under adversarial perturbations and the implications of deploying such systems in safety-critical domains (Liu, 2026).

However, these studies generally assumed models as bounded components within larger systems, rather than autonomous actors capable of open-ended generation or self-directed action. The advent of transformer architectures and large-scale foundation models expanded the literature significantly by shifting scholarly attention from model correctness to model capability, misuse potential, and socio-technical impact (Pallavi, 2025). Researchers began examining large language models not simply as prediction engines but as platforms capable of generating persuasive language, executable code, strategic plans, and multimodal content. This shift broadened the scope of AI security research to include disinformation, deception, synthetic media, social engineering, and policy circumvention. In effect, the literature transitioned from protecting AI systems against attack to also protecting society from the outputs and behaviors of AI systems. This distinction is essential because it marks the beginning of a new scholarly discourse in which AI is treated simultaneously as a target, a vector, and a semi-autonomous operational entity. The literature review in this chapter therefore situates current concerns about agentic AI within this larger intellectual arc, showing how foundational work on adversarial machine learning has gradually merged with research on generative harms, alignment failures, tool-enabled autonomy, and systemic governance challenges. Understanding this evolution is necessary to interpret why the threat profile of agentic AI is not isolated, but rather inherited from and amplified by the developmental trajectory of generative AI research.

A major strand of recent literature focuses on generative AI as a source of large-scale synthetic content risks. Text generation models, image synthesis systems, and multimodal architectures have been analyzed for their ability to produce realistic but potentially harmful outputs, including fabricated news, political propaganda, impersonation content, phishing emails, and non-consensual synthetic media. Studies in misinformation and media forensics have emphasized that generative AI lowers the cost of producing high-volume, personalized, and linguistically polished content, thereby increasing the feasibility of influence operations and trust manipulation. Parallel work in cybersecurity has shown that large language models can assist in code generation, vulnerability explanation, malware modification, exploit documentation, and attack scripting, even if they are not always reliable enough to replace human expertise (Pant & Mukhiya, 2024). These studies often present a nuanced conclusion: generative AI does not necessarily create entirely novel forms of malicious activity, but it significantly amplifies the speed, scale, adaptability, and accessibility of existing threats.

Another theme in the literature concerns model hallucination, factual unreliability, and overconfidence. Scholars in health, education, and law have highlighted that generative systems can produce plausible but incorrect information that may be accepted by users because of the model's fluency and authoritative style. This creates epistemic risks that differ from conventional cybersecurity harms, as the damage arises from degraded trust, flawed decision support, and the diffusion of synthetic but persuasive errors (Park et al., 2023). The literature also addresses mitigations such as reinforcement learning from human feedback, safety fine-tuning, red teaming, moderation filters, provenance techniques, watermarking, and retrieval-augmented generation. Yet many researchers argue that these interventions remain partial because attackers can exploit model openness, prompt engineering, fine-tuning pathways, and downstream application integration to bypass safeguards. Importantly, several survey papers note that the threat literature on generative AI remains fragmented across domains such as security, communication studies, digital forensics, and AI ethics. This fragmentation has impeded the development of unified taxonomies capable of linking technical vulnerabilities with broader social consequences. As the field moves toward agentic systems, this limitation becomes more pronounced because autonomous agents combine content generation with planning and action, thereby requiring a more integrated literature that spans both computational and socio-technical perspectives.

A growing body of scholarship has begun to characterize the transition from generative AI to agentic AI, often using terms such as autonomous agents, LLM-based agents, tool-augmented models, goal-directed AI, and multi-agent systems. In this literature, agentic AI is typically defined not by a new base model architecture alone but by a systems-level configuration in which foundation models are wrapped with memory, planning loops, retrieval modules, tool interfaces, execution environments, and feedback mechanisms. Research prototypes and deployment frameworks have demonstrated that such agents can complete complex tasks including software debugging, web navigation, scientific literature synthesis, business process automation, and robotic coordination (Pashentsev, 2023). While this capability has attracted enthusiasm for productivity and adaptive automation, the security literature increasingly warns that agentic architectures introduce risks that differ structurally from those of standalone generative models. Scholars highlight that an LLM-based agent can inherit the linguistic and reasoning weaknesses of the underlying model while gaining the ability to act on those weaknesses through external tools.

This creates a compounding effect: hallucination can become unsafe execution, prompt injection can become policy bypass, and retrieval corruption can become decision sabotage. Several recent papers specifically examine indirect prompt injection, in which malicious instructions embedded in webpages, files, or retrieved content alter the behavior of tool-using agents. Others discuss the security implications of autonomous code execution, API misuse, credential exposure, plugin abuse, and unverified memory updates. The literature also points to a governance gap: many evaluation benchmarks still focus on answer quality or task completion rather than long-horizon safety, bounded autonomy, or cross-tool reliability. This means that systems may appear effective under benchmark conditions while remaining vulnerable in realistic environments where agents encounter adversarial inputs, ambiguous goals, and dynamically changing contexts (Ranaldi, 2026). Additionally, the literature on agentic AI often draws from older traditions in autonomous systems, robotics, and distributed AI, where issues such as planning under uncertainty, goal misalignment, reward hacking, and emergent coordination have been studied for decades. What is new is the fusion of these classical autonomy concerns with the flexible language and multimodal abilities of foundation models, which dramatically widen both usability and attack surface. The current literature therefore suggests that agentic AI should be evaluated not simply as better generative AI, but as a qualitatively different socio-technical artifact that requires new security assumptions, new assurance models, and new interdisciplinary analytical frameworks.

Within cybersecurity research, the literature increasingly explores both offensive and defensive uses of generative and agentic AI, often emphasizing a strategic asymmetry between acceleration of attack capabilities and the slower maturation of defenses. Studies on AI-enabled cyber offense report that language models can support reconnaissance summarization, phishing customization, malware explanation, social engineering dialogue generation, and exploit-development assistance, particularly when paired with human supervision. More recent work extends this analysis to agentic pipelines, where autonomous systems can chain together tasks such as scanning, vulnerability triage, code generation, exploit testing, and reporting (Rehman, 2025). Some experimental studies suggest that such agents remain unreliable for highly sophisticated operations, yet they are sufficiently capable to automate segments of the attack lifecycle and lower operational costs for adversaries. Defensive research, in contrast, investigates AI-assisted threat detection, incident response, malware analysis, and alert prioritization. Here too, agentic architectures are being explored for semi-autonomous security orchestration, including log analysis, workflow execution, patch recommendation, and policy enforcement.

The literature therefore reveals a dual-use dilemma: the same features that make agentic AI attractive for defender's speed, adaptability, persistent monitoring, tool integration also makes it attractive for attackers. Researchers have also noted that security evaluation of AI agents is complicated by emergent behavior and contextual dependence. A system that behaves safely in one environment may act unsafely when given access to different tools, broader permissions, or adversarial manipulated data sources (Sarch et al., 2023). This has led to calls for defense-in-depth architectures involving least-privilege access, execution sandboxes, cryptographic tool verification, memory hygiene, approval gates, and continuous runtime auditing. Another key theme concerns explainability and accountability. Traditional security systems often support forensic analysis through logs and deterministic rule execution, whereas LLM-based agents may generate opaque action sequences whose rationale is incomplete, inconsistent, or post hoc. This undermines trust in high-stakes deployments and complicates compliance in regulated sectors. The literature on AI red teaming has attempted to address some of these issues, but many studies remain focused on single-turn model abuse rather than multi-step autonomous harm. Consequently, cybersecurity scholarship increasingly argues that existing threat models are too static for agentic AI and must be revised to account for temporally extended, tool-mediated, and cross-domain attack pathways. This insight is central to the emerging consensus that the progression from generative to agentic AI demands not only better models, but also a rethinking of system architecture, access governance, and assurance methodology.

Another important cluster of literature concerns ethical governance, regulatory framing, and risk management for AI systems whose capabilities increasingly blur the boundaries between software tool, decision support system, and autonomous actor. AI ethics scholarship has long discussed fairness, accountability, transparency, and human oversight, but the emergence of generative and agentic systems has expanded these concerns toward manipulation, consent, provenance, and control (Soria, 2025). Policy-oriented literature emphasizes that generative AI challenges legal and institutional mechanisms for content authenticity, liability attribution, and platform responsibility. For example, scholars debate whether watermarking, content labeling, provenance metadata, or identity verification can meaningfully reduce harms from deepfakes and synthetic media, particularly when adversaries can re-edit or strip such markers. In the case of agentic AI, governance literature has begun to focus on authority delegation, action auditing, operator responsibility, and fail-safe mechanisms.

A recurring theme is that traditional human-in-the-loop assumptions may be too weak if human supervision is nominal rather than operationally effective. If humans approve actions only at high level, or after an agent has already shaped the available choices, then oversight may become procedural rather than substantive. Related work in AI alignment and control discusses specification gaming, reward hacking, deceptive compliance, and the difficulty of ensuring that agents pursue intended goals rather than proxies. Although much of the alignment literature remains theoretical or long-term in orientation, recent applied studies connect these concerns to enterprise agents, coding agents, and decision agents used in real workflows. The literature also highlights challenges in standardization. Existing safety benchmarks often assess toxicity, bias, or factuality, but fewer benchmarks capture unsafe tool use, long-horizon objective drift, agent-to-agent collusion, or cyber-physical impact. Regulatory discussions similarly lag behind technical change, often addressing model providers and content generation while paying less attention to downstream agent builders, integrators, and deployers (Steele, 2023). This creates uncertainty around legal accountability when autonomous systems cause harm through a chain of decisions involving model providers, orchestration layers, application developers, data sources, and human operators. Overall, the governance literature underscores that the threat evolution from generative to agentic AI is not solely a technical progression; it is also an institutional and regulatory challenge requiring coordinated responses across engineering, law, standards development, and public policy.

The literature reviewed above collectively suggests that current scholarship is converging on several important conclusions while still leaving substantial gaps. First, there is broad agreement that generative AI expanded the threat landscape by democratizing synthetic content creation, accelerating deception, and introducing new epistemic risks. Second, there is increasing recognition that agentic AI transforms these risks by coupling generation with memory, planning, tool access, and execution, thereby changing the unit of analysis from isolated outputs to persistent behaviors within complex environments (Tedesco, 2026). Third, the literature indicates that existing mitigation strategies such as filtering, fine-tuning, guardrails, human review, provenance, and benchmarking remain necessary but insufficient when systems are granted operational autonomy. These controls often address symptoms at the model-output layer while leaving deeper architectural vulnerabilities unresolved.

At the same time, the literature is still fragmented. Work on adversarial machine learning, misinformation, cyber offense, autonomous agents, alignment, and AI governance often proceeds in parallel with limited synthesis across domains. This fragmentation makes it difficult to build a unified threat taxonomy or comprehensive assurance framework. Another gap concerns empirical realism: many studies evaluate models or agents in laboratory settings, but fewer examine how these systems behave over long durations in enterprise, public-sector, or cyber-physical deployments.

There is also a shortage of literature focused on edge-IoT and smart infrastructure environments, where agentic AI may interact with constrained devices, distributed control loops, and heterogeneous trust boundaries. Table.2 summarizes the principal tradeoffs identified in the literature when comparing generative AI and agentic AI from a threat-evolution perspective, emphasizing that increased autonomy delivers significant utility while simultaneously magnifying controllability, accountability, and security challenges.

Table 2. Tradeoff Table

Dimension	Generative AI Advantage	Generative AI Risk	Agentic AI Advantage	Agentic AI Risk	Key Tradeoff Insight
Capability scope	Produces text, code, image, audio, and multimodal content quickly	Harmful, false, biased, or deceptive content can be generated at scale	Executes multi-step tasks using planning and tools	Harm shifts from content generation to autonomous action	More capability increases both usefulness and attack surface
Human involvement	Usually requires user prompting and interpretation	Users may over trust fluent outputs	Reduces human workload through autonomous task completion	Less supervision can reduce meaningful control	Efficiency often comes at the cost of direct oversight
Attack surface	Prompting interface, model outputs, training data, retrieval pipeline	Jailbreaks, hallucinations, misinformation, deepfakes	Adds memory, APIs, tools, web access, execution modules, agent coordination	Tool misuse, memory poisoning, indirect prompt injection, cascading failures	Each added component expands security exposure
Speed and scale	Rapid production of persuasive content	Enables mass phishing, fraud, and propaganda	Rapid execution of workflows and decisions	Enables automated multi-stage attacks and persistent harmful behavior	Automation amplifies both productivity and malicious throughput
Reliability	Useful for drafting, summarization, and ideation	Outputs may be plausible but wrong	Can iteratively refine tasks and adapt plans	Errors can propagate across action loops and external systems	Iteration improves performance but also compounds mistakes
Explainability	Output can be inspected after generation	Reasoning may still be opaque or fabricated	Actions may be logged across task chains	Decision paths are harder to reconstruct across multiple steps and tools	Greater autonomy reduces interpretability unless logging is strong
Governance	Easier to regulate as a content-generation system	Hard to monitor downstream misuse	Can support enterprise automation and cyber defense	Responsibility becomes diffuse across model, tools, deployers, and users	Accountability weakens as systems become more distributed
Security controls	Filtering, watermarking, RLHF, moderation, provenance	Controls are by passable and incomplete	Sandboxing, approval gates, least privilege, runtime monitoring	Controls are complex, costly, and difficult to standardize	Stronger safeguards improve safety but may reduce flexibility
Social impact	Improves access to knowledge and creativity	Erodes trust in media and information authenticity	Supports intelligent assistance and operational efficiency	Can manipulate systems, institutions, and cyber-physical processes	Societal benefit rises together with systemic risk
Research challenge	Benchmarking output quality is relatively mature	Safety evaluation still incomplete	Demands long-horizon, system-level evaluation	Benchmarks for autonomous risk remain immature	Measurement lags behind capability growth

For researchers in computer engineering, this gap is especially significant because future AI threats will likely emerge not only through web platforms and cloud APIs but also through embedded systems, industrial networks, transportation infrastructure, and autonomous service ecosystems. Therefore, the next generation of research must move beyond isolated model evaluation toward integrated studies of end-to-end AI systems under adversarial and operational stress. A useful way to frame the literature is through tradeoffs: capability versus controllability, autonomy versus auditability, efficiency versus safety assurance, and openness versus misuse resistance (Zhang et al., 2024). These tradeoffs are not merely design considerations; they structure the core tension of the field. The literature review thus supports the central argument of this chapter: the evolution from generative AI to agentic AI represents an escalating continuum of threats that requires correspondingly evolved frameworks for security, governance, and trustworthy deployment.

3. PROPOSED REVIEW AND ANALYTICAL FRAMEWORK FOR THREAT EVOLUTION FROM GENERATIVE AI TO AGENTIC AI

3.1. Rationale and Scope

The rapid advancement of artificial intelligence from content-generating systems to increasingly autonomous agentic architectures has created an urgent need for a more integrated and forward-looking review framework. Existing scholarship has made substantial contributions to understanding specific dimensions of AI risk, including adversarial machine learning, misinformation, deepfakes, privacy leakage, alignment failures, prompt injection, and autonomous decision-making. However, much of this literature remains compartmentalized across technical, social, and regulatory domains. Studies on generative AI often emphasize synthetic content risks such as disinformation, phishing, and hallucinated outputs, whereas emerging work on agentic AI focuses on tool use, memory, planning, environmental interaction, and autonomous task execution. Although both strands are valuable, they are rarely examined together as part of a continuous threat evolution process. This separation limits our ability to understand how vulnerabilities originating in generative systems may persist, expand, or transform when those same models are embedded within more autonomous and action-capable frameworks.

The rationale for this review therefore rests on the observation that agentic AI does not emerge in isolation; rather, it builds directly upon the capabilities, design assumptions, and unresolved weaknesses of generative AI. Large language models and multimodal generators provide the reasoning, interaction, and content-synthesis capabilities that enable agentic systems to interpret goals, communicate with users, invoke tools, and adapt to changing environments. As a result, the risks associated with generative AI—such as hallucination, overconfidence, manipulation susceptibility, harmful content production, and prompt-level exploitation—do not disappear in agentic settings. Instead, they may become operationalized through planning loops, API access, memory persistence, and autonomous execution. A hallucinated answer in a standalone model may lead to misinformation; the same hallucination in an autonomous agent may trigger an incorrect action, unsafe configuration change, unauthorized data transfer, or sustained decision failure across multiple steps. This shift from output-centric risk to action-centric risk is the central motivation for proposing a unified analytical review framework.

A second rationale arises from the growing inadequacy of traditional AI threat taxonomies for capturing contemporary system behavior. Earlier frameworks were often designed for narrow machine learning settings where attackers targeted training data, model parameters, or inference inputs. While these concerns remain relevant, they are insufficient for analyzing systems that interact with external tools, retrieve live information, execute code, maintain persistent memory, and cooperate with other agents. In such systems, risk is distributed across a broader socio-technical stack that includes foundation models, orchestration layers, retrieval modules, plugins, APIs, user interfaces, execution environments, and human oversight mechanisms. Consequently, the attack surface is no longer limited to the model itself but extends to the full chain of perception, reasoning, decision-making, and action. The review proposed in this chapter is motivated by the need to capture this broader threat surface in a structured manner and to connect inherited generative vulnerabilities with newly emergent agentic risks.

A further motivation for defining a clear analytical scope lies in the fragmented treatment of AI threats across disciplinary boundaries. Technical security studies often focus on robustness, exploitability, and system compromise; communication and media studies examine misinformation, influence operations, and authenticity erosion; governance and ethics scholarship addresses accountability, transparency, regulation, and human oversight. Each of these perspectives illuminates important parts of the problem, yet none alone is sufficient to explain the full trajectory of threat evolution from generative to agentic AI. For example, synthetic media harms cannot be fully understood without considering platform dynamics and trust erosion, just as agentic tool misuse cannot be adequately analyzed without insights from systems security, software engineering, and human-computer interaction. This chapter therefore adopts a deliberately interdisciplinary scope that links technical attack mechanisms with organizational, societal, and governance implications. Such a scope is necessary because the consequences of agentic AI increasingly cut across digital content ecosystems, enterprise workflows, critical infrastructure, and cyber-physical environments.

The scope of this review includes two primary technological domains. The first is generative AI, encompassing large language models, text-to-image systems, code generation models, multimodal content generators, and related foundation-model-based applications that produce synthetic artifacts in response to user input or contextual prompts. Within this domain, the review examines threats such as automated misinformation, phishing and social engineering, deepfakes, synthetic identity fraud, hallucinated decision support, harmful code assistance, jailbreaks, and prompt-based misuse. The second domain is agentic AI, defined here as AI systems that extend generative models with additional capabilities such as goal decomposition, persistent memory, reasoning loops, tool invocation, API interaction, web navigation, autonomous task execution, and in some cases multi-agent coordination. For this domain, the review considers threats including indirect prompt injection, unsafe tool use, memory poisoning, unauthorized actions, data exfiltration, policy circumvention, objective drift, persistent manipulation, coordinated multi-agent abuse, and the propagation of errors or attacks across integrated digital and physical systems.

At the same time, the review maintains certain boundaries to preserve conceptual clarity and analytical focus. It does not attempt to provide an exhaustive treatment of all AI risks ever discussed in the literature, nor does it center speculative existential scenarios that are disconnected from current or near-term generative and agentic deployments. Traditional machine learning attacks are discussed only where they help explain the foundations of present-day threat evolution. Similarly, the chapter does not aim to be a legal treatise or a policy-only analysis, although governance and regulatory issues are included where they directly shape security, accountability, and deployment practice. The emphasis remains on practical and emerging threats associated with real-world systems that combine generative capability with varying degrees of autonomy. By defining this scope, the chapter positions itself as a focused review of how AI threats evolve as systems move from producing content to initiating and coordinating actions. This framing enables a coherent synthesis of the literature, supports the development of a comparative threat taxonomy, and provides a clear basis for identifying research gaps, mitigation priorities, and future directions for trustworthy AI deployment.

3.2. Threat Evolution Stages

To systematically understand the progression of risks from generative AI to agentic AI, it is useful to view the literature through a stage-based threat evolution model. Such a model clarifies that contemporary AI threats have not appeared abruptly; rather, they have developed cumulatively as systems acquired new computational capabilities, broader interfaces, and greater operational autonomy. Each stage introduces its own dominant risk profile while also carrying forward unresolved weaknesses from earlier stages. In this sense, threat evolution in AI is not merely additive but compounding. Vulnerabilities that were once confined to model prediction error or adversarial manipulation may later reappear as content manipulation, automated deception, unsafe tool invocation, or autonomous execution failures. A stage-oriented review therefore helps organize the literature into a coherent progression from narrow technical attacks to broader socio-technical and system-level risks.

In the Stage 1, traditional AI/ML Threats research focused on predictive model attacks including adversarial examples, data poisoning, model extraction, membership inference, privacy leakage, and evasion. These narrow-scope systems produced labels, scores, and bounded predictions, establishing AI's unique data-driven attack surfaces that remain foundational as generative/agentic vulnerabilities trace back to training and robustness weaknesses. In the stage 2, Generative AI shifts to fluent synthetic content (text, images, audio, video, code), transforming outputs into harm vectors: misinformation, phishing automation, deepfakes, identity fraud, toxic content, hallucinations, and malware assistance. Expertise barriers crumble as novices scales sophisticated deception, producing epistemic harms across healthcare, education, law, and governance while eroding trust at societal scale.

In stage 3, Tool-Augmented AI bridges generative and agentic systems by integrating models with retrieval systems, plugins, databases, web search, code execution, and enterprise applications. This expands utility through real-time access and external interactions but introduces indirect prompt injection, retrieval poisoning, insecure plugins, API misuse, prompt leakage, and unsafe code execution. Model errors now propagate into operational workflows, demonstrating how generative vulnerabilities amplify when systems gain action interfaces beyond conversation, requiring security to extend from models to orchestration layers and trust boundaries.

The fourth stage corresponds to agentic AI threats, where AI systems exhibit persistent goal-directed behavior through memory, planning, tool selection, adaptive reasoning, and autonomous execution across multiple steps. This stage introduces the most significant conceptual shift in the threat landscape. In generative AI, the principal danger often lies in what the model says or produces; in agentic AI, the principal danger increasingly lies in what the system can do. Agentic systems can decompose goals into subtasks, revise strategies based on feedback, invoke tools repeatedly, update internal memory, and continue operation with limited human intervention.

The literature identifies key agentic AI risks including unsafe autonomous action, unauthorized access, long-horizon error propagation, memory corruption, goal drift, manipulative planning, and policy circumvention via multi-step reasoning. Isolated errors cascade into failures a false memory assumption alters future decisions, malicious webpages trigger indirect prompt injection leading to credential misuse, and misaligned objectives produce coherent but harmful sequences. Operating across time and tools, these systems challenge prediction, interpretation, and auditability while diluting accountability across model inference, orchestration, external tools, and human approvals. Analysis must therefore shift from model safety and output filtering to system-level action governance and continuous runtime assurance.

A fifth and emerging stage extends the model into multi-agent and cyber-physical threat environments, where agentic systems interact with one another, coordinate specialized roles, and interface with physical infrastructure or distributed device ecosystems. While still developing, this stage is increasingly relevant in domains such as enterprise automation, autonomous operations, industrial control, robotics, transportation, and smart city management. In these contexts, multiple AI agents may collaborate to plan tasks, exchange information, monitor events, allocate resources, and trigger actions across networked systems. The literature warns that such coordination can produce emergent risks not reducible to the behavior of any single model. These include collusive behavior, distributed misinformation, coordinated cyber offense, fault amplification across agents, and cascading failures in tightly coupled socio-technical systems. When integrated with IoT or cyber-physical infrastructure, the risk extends beyond digital harm to operational disruption, safety compromise, and infrastructure-level consequences.

The significance of this stage is that it highlights the trajectory of threat evolution toward ecosystem-level risk. AI is no longer merely generating content or executing tasks; it is becoming embedded in interconnected environments where errors, manipulation, or malicious use can propagate across technical, organizational, and physical layers. For this reason, the proposed review treats threat evolution as a continuum of increasing autonomy, integration, and impact. The stage-based model provides a structured foundation for comparing inherited and emergent risks, identifying where existing safeguards break down, and motivating the need for new mitigation strategies tailored to autonomous, tool-using, and distributed AI systems.

3.3. Comparative Analysis Dimensions

A meaningful review of threat evolution from generative AI to agentic AI requires more than a chronological summary of technological progress. It also requires a comparative analytical lens capable of explaining how risk changes as AI systems gain new capabilities, interfaces, and decision authority. Without such a lens, generative and agentic AI may appear to differ only in degree of sophistication, when in reality they differ in the structure, persistence, and impact of their threats. The purpose of comparative analysis in this chapter is therefore to identify the key dimensions along which this transformation occurs and to use those dimensions to synthesize the literature in a systematic manner. These dimensions do not merely classify systems; they reveal how threat profiles expand from isolated content-related harms to sustained, tool-mediated, and potentially autonomous action in complex operational environments.

The first dimension is capability expansion, which captures the progression from bounded content generation to reasoning, planning, memory, tool use, and autonomous execution. Generative AI systems primarily synthesize outputs in response to prompts, even when those outputs are highly sophisticated and multimodal.

Their risk profile is thus closely associated with the quality, truthfulness, harmfulness, or deceptive potential of generated content. By contrast, agentic AI systems incorporate additional capabilities that allow them to interpret objectives, break them into subgoals, select tools, interact with external applications, and revise actions over time. This expansion of capability changes the very nature of threat. A model that can generate persuasive phishing text already poses security concerns, but a system that can autonomously identify targets, draft messages, send them through integrated communication tools, monitor responses, and adapt the campaign introduces a qualitatively different level of risk. The comparative literature therefore shows that increases in capability should not be interpreted solely as gains in utility; they also increase the pathways through which AI systems may generate harm, intentionally or unintentionally.

The second dimension is degree of autonomy, which is central to understanding the transition from generative to agentic AI. In a typical generative setting, human users remain closely involved in prompting, interpreting, and deciding whether or how to act on model outputs. The AI assists, but the human remains the primary executor of decisions. In agentic settings, however, the system may operate semi-autonomously or autonomously across multiple steps with limited human intervention. This shift has major implications for control, supervision, and accountability. The literature suggests that autonomy magnifies risk because it reduces the number of human checkpoints between AI reasoning and real-world action. It also creates the possibility of long-horizon failure, where a sequence of individually minor errors accumulates into significant harm. Comparative analysis along this dimension helps distinguish between systems that merely advise and systems that act. It also highlights the limits of traditional human-in-the-loop assumptions, particularly in workflows where human oversight is nominal, rushed, or overly dependent on AI-generated recommendations. In this chapter, autonomy is treated as a pivotal dimension because it directly shapes the severity, speed, and containment difficulty of AI-enabled threats.

A third important dimension is attacking surface complexity. Generative AI systems are already vulnerable through prompts, training data, fine-tuning pipelines, output channels, and retrieval sources. However, agentic AI expands this attack surface by adding components such as memory stores, tool interfaces, APIs, web access modules, execution environments, orchestration frameworks, and agent-to-agent communication pathways. Each additional layer creates new opportunities for compromise, manipulation, or misuse.

The comparative literature indicates that many of the most serious risks in agentic systems arise not from the base model alone but from interactions among model outputs, external tools, permissions, and environmental feedback. Indirect prompt injection, retrieval poisoning, malicious plugin responses, credential leakage, and unsafe code execution are all examples of risks that become prominent when the AI system is embedded within a broader operational stack. This dimension is essential because it moves analysis beyond a model-centric view and toward a systems-security perspective. It also helps explain why mitigation strategies that are effective for standalone generative models such as output moderation or prompt filtering may become insufficient once the system can query databases, access emails, modify files, or control external devices. Threat evolution, therefore, must be understood as a process in which increasing utility is accompanied by increasingly porous and distributed trust boundaries.

The fourth dimension is impact scope, which refers to the breadth and depth of consequences produced by AI failures or misuse. In generative AI, the most immediate harms often occur in the informational domain: misinformation, reputational damage, synthetic fraud, plagiarism, deception, and flawed decision support. These harms are serious, but they are often mediated through human interpretation and social diffusion. In agentic AI, the impact scope widens because the system may directly alter digital states, organizational processes, or physical operations. An agentic failure may not only misinform a user; it may trigger an unauthorized transaction, leak sensitive records, modify configurations, allocate resources incorrectly, or initiate harmful actions across connected systems. In multi-agent and cyber-physical settings, the impact may become distributed and cascading, affecting multiple users, institutions, or infrastructure services simultaneously.

Comparative analysis along this dimension reveals that the transition from generative to agentic AI is also a transition from primarily communicative harm to operational harm. This distinction is crucial for reviewers and system designers because operational harms often require different forms of assurance, including access control, fail-safe mechanisms, rollback capabilities, and runtime monitoring. The literature increasingly supports the view that impact scope is one of the strongest differentiators between generative and agentic threat models. A fifth dimension, controllability and auditability, examines how easily AI behavior can be constrained, monitored, explained, and reviewed post-deployment. While generative AI's probabilistic outputs challenge governance, they remain inspectable before action; agentic AI complicates this through multi-step execution, tool use, memory updates, and dynamic feedback, creating forensic opacity where logs capture actions but not underlying reasoning or environmental influences. This reveals a core tradeoff greater autonomy reduces interpretability particularly critical in regulated domains requiring accountability reconstruction, positioning controllability as a key metric for comparing mitigation maturity across AI paradigms.

The sixth and final dimension is mitigation maturity, which refers to the extent to which existing safeguards are technically effective, operationally practical, and institutionally established. Generative AI benefits from a relatively more mature set of countermeasures, including content moderation, safety fine-tuning, reinforcement learning from human feedback, retrieval grounding, provenance mechanisms, watermarking, red teaming, and usage policy enforcement. Although these measures remain imperfect and often by passable, they reflect a more developed ecosystem of known defenses. In contrast, mitigation strategies for agentic AI are still emerging and remain uneven across domains. Approaches such as least-privilege tool access, sandboxed execution, approval gates, memory hygiene, action verification, runtime monitoring, secure orchestration, and bounded autonomy are being actively explored, but they are not yet standardized or consistently deployed.

The literature suggests that this asymmetry between capability growth and mitigation maturity is one of the defining characteristics of the current moment in AI development. Systems are becoming more autonomous faster than governance, evaluation, and security engineering practices can adapt. By comparing generative and agentic AI across these analytical dimensions capability expansion, autonomy, attack surface complexity, impact scope, controllability and auditability, and mitigation maturity—this chapter establishes a structured basis for reviewing how threats evolve across capability stages. These dimensions also provide the conceptual foundation for the later taxonomy, tradeoff analysis, and identification of open research gaps. Table.2 presents the principal comparative dimensions used in this chapter to analyze the evolution of threats from generative AI to agentic AI, highlighting how increases in autonomy, integration, and execution capability alter both the nature and severity of risk.

Table 3. Comparative Analysis for Reviewing Threat Evolution from Generative AI to Agentic AI

Dimension	Generative AI	Agentic AI	Threat Implication
Capability scope	Primarily generates text, images, audio, video, and code in response to prompts	Extends generation with planning, memory, reasoning loops, tool use, API interaction, and autonomous execution	Threats evolve from harmful content production to harmful multi-step actions
Human involvement	Human remains central in prompting, interpretation, and execution of actions	Human involvement may be partial, supervisory, or episodic, with the system executing tasks autonomously	Reduced human checkpoints increase the risk of unchecked or delayed harmful actions
Autonomy level	Low to moderate autonomy; largely reactive and session-bound	Moderate to high autonomy; goal-directed, persistent, and adaptive across tasks	Greater autonomy increases the likelihood of long-horizon and cascading failures
Attack surface	Prompts, training data, fine-tuning pipeline, model outputs, retrieval sources	Includes all generative AI attack surfaces plus tools, plugins, memory, APIs, orchestration layers, execution environments, and agent communication channels	Security exposure becomes broader, more distributed, and harder to defend
Threat type	Deepfakes, phishing, misinformation, hallucination, synthetic fraud, harmful code generation	Unsafe tool invocation, indirect prompt injection, memory poisoning, unauthorized actions, data exfiltration, persistent manipulation, multi-agent collusion	Risks shift from output-centric misuse to action-centric and system-level harm
Error propagation	Errors are often confined to a single output or interaction	Errors may persist across memory, planning steps, tool calls, and feedback loops	Small failures can compound into significant operational consequences
Impact scope	Primarily informational, reputational, social, and decision-support related	Extends to organizational, infrastructural, operational, and cyber-physical domains	Harm expands from communication ecosystems to real-world systems and services
Speed and scale	Rapid generation of high-volume synthetic content	Rapid autonomous execution of chained actions across digital platforms or devices	Attack campaigns become faster, more adaptive, and more difficult to interrupt
Controllability	Outputs can often be reviewed before use, though not always reliably	Actions may occur in real time with limited human review depending on permissions and workflow design	Control becomes more difficult as execution authority moves closer to the system
Auditability	Generated content can be inspected, but reasoning may remain opaque	Multi-step decisions and tool-mediated behavior may be difficult to reconstruct and explain	Accountability weakens without detailed logging and runtime traceability
Dependency on external systems	Usually limited unless connected to retrieval or plugins	Strong dependence on tools, APIs, databases, communication systems, and device ecosystems	External dependencies increase vulnerability to manipulation and failure propagation
Mitigation maturity	More mature safeguards, such as filtering, moderation, RLHF, watermarking, and red teaming	Emerging safeguards, such as sandboxing, least-privilege access, approval gates, memory controls, and runtime monitoring	Defensive mechanisms for agentic AI remain less standardized and less mature
Governance challenge	Focus on content authenticity, misuse prevention, and model accountability	Focus expands to delegated authority, action liability, oversight design, and operational assurance	Governance must evolve from content regulation to autonomy regulation
Evaluation need	Output quality, factuality, toxicity, bias, and misuse resistance	Long-horizon safety, action reliability, tool-use constraints, and autonomous behavior validation	Existing benchmarks are insufficient for evaluating agentic threat behavior

4. OUTCOMES

The proposed review is expected to generate several important research outcomes that contribute to both scholarly understanding and practical assessment of the evolving AI threat landscape. The first and most fundamental outcome is the development of a unified conceptual view of threat progression from generative AI to agentic AI. Existing research often treats misinformation, hallucination, deepfakes, prompt exploitation, autonomous tool use, and alignment failure as separate issues examined within different disciplinary boundaries. By synthesizing these studies within a single analytical frame, this review clarifies that these threats are not isolated phenomena but part of a broader continuum of risk associated with increasing model capability, autonomy, and system integration. This outcome is particularly important because it helps reposition current debates from fragmented technical or ethical concerns toward a more structured understanding of how AI threats accumulate and transform over time.

A second major outcome is the formulation of a stage-based threat taxonomy that distinguishes between inherited, amplified, and emergent risks. Inherited risks are those that originate in earlier AI paradigms and remain present in newer systems, such as adversarial manipulation, model unreliability, bias, and prompt exploitation. Amplified risks are those that become more severe due to the increased scale, fluency, and accessibility of generative models, including misinformation, phishing, synthetic fraud, and harmful code assistance. Emergent risks arise more distinctly in agentic settings, where memory, planning, tool invocation, and autonomous action introduce possibilities such as unsafe execution, memory poisoning, objective drift, unauthorized access, and cascading system failures. This taxonomy offers a structured way to classify threats not simply by domain, but by their relationship to capability evolution. As a result, it can serve as a useful foundation for future reviews, comparative studies, and risk assessment frameworks in AI security research.

Another key research outcome is the establishment of a comparative analytical basis for assessing differences between generative AI and agentic AI. Rather than relying on broad claims that agentic AI is "more powerful" or "more dangerous," the review identifies specific dimensions along which this shift becomes meaningful, including autonomy, attack surface complexity, impact scope, controllability, auditability, and mitigation maturity. This comparative structure helps reveal how increased usefulness is accompanied by increased governance difficulty. For example, a generative model may create harmful content, but an agentic system may autonomously operationalize harmful decisions through external tools and persistent workflows. Framing the review in this way produces a more rigorous understanding of threat escalation and avoids simplistic narratives that treat all advanced AI risks as equivalent. This outcome also strengthens the methodological contribution of the chapter by showing that threat analysis must be multidimensional rather than limited to content harm alone.

The review is also expected to produce a clear identification of gaps in current research and mitigation practice. Although there is substantial literature on generative AI harms and a rapidly growing body of work on autonomous AI agents, important gaps remain in areas such as long-horizon safety evaluation, runtime assurance, memory integrity, agent-to-agent interaction risk, and secure deployment in cyber-physical and edge-IoT environments. Similarly, many current safeguards remain focused on model output moderation rather than system-level action control. By highlighting these gaps, the review provides a forward-looking research agenda that can guide future investigations into robust agent architectures, bounded autonomy, dynamic oversight, and trustworthy orchestration mechanisms. This outcome is especially relevant for engineering and applied AI communities, as it identifies where current systems may outpace the maturity of available security controls.

A further outcome is the synthesis of design and governance implications emerging from the literature. The review is not limited to identifying threats; it also clarifies how these threats reshape requirements for responsible AI deployment. From a design perspective, the findings point toward the need for least-privilege access, sandboxed tool use, stronger memory management, human override mechanisms, and detailed runtime logging. From a governance perspective, the review suggests that frameworks developed for content authenticity and model accountability may be insufficient once AI systems gain operational autonomy. Questions of delegated authority, action liability, audit traceability, and continuous assurance become increasingly central. This outcome therefore bridges technical analysis with broader regulatory and institutional concerns, making the chapter relevant not only to AI researchers but also to practitioners, system architects, and policymakers.

Ultimately, the research outcomes of this review aim to provide a coherent foundation for future scholarship on AI threat evolution. The chapter seeks to offer more than a summary of known issues; it proposes a structured lens through which emerging AI risks can be interpreted, compared, and addressed. By producing a unified threat perspective, a stage-based taxonomy, a multidimensional comparative framework, a research gap analysis, and a set of technical and governance implications, the review contributes a comprehensive basis for understanding the transition from output-centric generative risks to action-centric agentic risks. Such outcomes are essential for guiding the next generation of AI safety research and for supporting the development of secure, accountable, and trustworthy AI systems in increasingly autonomous environments.

4.1. Case Study: Agentic AI in Smart City Traffic Management

A municipal traffic management center deploys an AI system to optimize congestion and emergency routing across edge IoT sensors, CCTV feeds, and adaptive signals. Initially, the system operates as generative AI, processing real-time data to generate congestion summaries, incident predictions, and signal adjustment recommendations for human review. Operators benefit from rapid insights but manually verify outputs to mitigate hallucinations or flawed forecasts. Engineers subsequently upgrade the system to agentic AI by adding persistent memory, multi-step planning, and direct API access to traffic controllers, V2I protocols, transit schedules, and weather feeds. The agent now autonomously decomposes goals like "clear emergency corridors during peak traffic" into actions such as querying sensors, reprogramming signals, rerouting connected vehicles, and updating signage all while self-validating through iterative loops. Pilot data shows 35% efficiency gains, yet this autonomy shifts risk from advisory errors to executable disruptions.

Attackers target the agent via indirect prompt injection on a public city webpage scraped for event data. Malicious code instructs the agent to prioritize a fabricated "hazardous material incident" on a major artery, overriding sensor discrepancies due to weak retrieval validation. The agent embeds this in memory, then cascades actions like diverting flows, halting buses, and signaling false alarms resulting in 18-minute ambulance delays during a genuine crisis and widespread gridlock. Forensic analysis confirms the generative phase confined harm to erroneous reports subject to oversight, while agentic execution amplified a single deception into systemic cyber-physical failure across distributed edge nodes. Root causes encompass unverified external inputs, excessive tool permissions, absent approval gates for critical actions, and self-reinforcing memory updates. Table.4 presents a layered defenses like cryptographic tool verification, edge sandboxes with least privilege, sequenced action monitoring, and mandatory human gates for safety impacts. These measures preserve agentic utility while containing the threat evolution observed in urban infrastructure. Table.5 compares existing commercial systems with the agentic evolution examined here. This case study analyzes such a transition in a mid-sized urban traffic control center.

Table 4. Threat Comparison

Dimension	Generative AI Risk	Agentic AI Risk
Output Type	Misleading text/reports	Autonomous API/device commands
Harm Extent	Human-mediated decisions	Real-time physical disruptions
Exploit Path	Direct prompts	Retrieval/memory poisoning
Control Need	Output filters	Runtime auditing/sandboxes

Table 5. Comparison of Deployed Smart City Traffic Management Systems

System	AI Level	Key Features	Infrastructure	Reported Efficiency Gain	Security Focus
Siemens Sitraffic Fusion	Generative AI	Real-time monitoring; signal optimization; predictive analytics	On-premise + cloud	25-30% congestion reduction	Content filtering
IBM Intelligent Transport	Generative + basic agents	Traffic prediction; anomaly detection; route recommendations	IBM Cloud, SaaS	28% faster incident response	API access controls
Samsara Traffic Platform	Edge AI processing	IoT sensors; incident detection; route optimization	Cloud + edge	20% fuel savings	Device-level encryption
HERE Traffic Management	Adaptive algorithms	Dynamic signal control; vehicle count estimation	Cloud-based	15-22% flow improvement	Data source validation
Proposed Agentic System	Full agentic AI	Autonomous planning; API execution; memory loops	Edge-IoT + cloud orchestration	35% (pilot data)	Runtime action auditing

5. CONCLUSION AND FUTURE SCOPE

The transition from generative AI to agentic AI marks a profound evolution in artificial intelligence, extending risks from large-scale synthetic content production such as misinformation, deepfakes, phishing, and hallucination to autonomous action through planning, memory, tool use, and adaptive execution. While generative risks remain embedded and amplified, agentic systems introduce persistent, operational threats that demand unified analytical frameworks to address fragmented literature across technical, social, and governance domains. Future research must prioritize long-horizon safety benchmarks, runtime assurance mechanisms (memory validation, secure tool orchestration, least-privilege execution), threat propagation studies in multi-agent and edge-IoT ecosystems, and governance models emphasizing action-level oversight, ensuring innovation remains bounded by transparency, human control, and system-level safety.

REFERENCES

Aghaebrahimian, A., & Jurčíček, F. (2016). Open-domain factoid question answering via knowledge graph search. *Proceedings of the Workshop on Human-Computer Question Answering*, 22-28. DOI: 10.18653/v1/W16-0104

Aghdam, H. H., Heravi, E. J., & Puig, D. (2017). Explaining adversarial examples by local properties of Convolutional neural networks. *Proceedings of the 12th International Joint Conference on Computer Vision, Imaging and Computer Graphics Theory and Applications*, 226-234. DOI: 10.5220/0006123702260234

Ali, H., Qadir, J., Alam, T., Househ, M., & Shah, Z. (2023). ChatGPT and large language models (LLMs) in healthcare: Opportunities and risks. DOI: 10.36227/techrxiv.22579852

Bhirawa, I. A. (2025). Active prompting with chain-of-Thought: Revolutionising reasoning in large language models. DOI: 10.59350/bkm9q-11k47

Cancedda, N., Dessi, R., Dwivedi-Yu, J., Hambro, E., Lomeli, M., Raileanu, R., Schick, T., Scialom, T., & Zettlemoyer, L. (2023). Toolformer: Language models can teach themselves to use tools. *Advances in Neural Information Processing Systems*, *36*, 68539–68551. DOI: 10.52202/075280-2997

Cassano, F., Gopinath, A., Narasimhan, K., Shinn, N., & Yao, S. (2023). Reflexion: Language agents with verbal reinforcement learning. *Advances in Neural Information Processing Systems*, *36*, 8634–8652. DOI: 10.52202/075280-0377

Gaur, L., Arora, G. K., & Jhanjhi, N. Z. (2022). Deep learning techniques for creation of DeepFakes. *DeepFakes*, 23-34. DOI: 10.1201/9781003231493-3

Hejman, J., Prazak, O., & Konopík, M. (2025). Fine-tuned llama for multilingual text-to-text Coreference resolution. *Proceedings of the Eighth Workshop on Computational Models of Reference, Anaphora and Coreference*, 140-148. DOI: 10.18653/v1/2025.crac-1.12

Leong, H. Y., & Wu, Y. (2025). Why should Next-Gen LLM multi-agent systems move beyond fixed architectures to dynamic, input-driven graphs? DOI: 10.2139/ssrn.5276004

Li, M. Q., & Fung, B. C. (2025). Security concerns for large language models: A survey. *Journal of Information Security and Applications*, *95*, 104284. DOI: 10.1016/j.jisa.2025.104284

Liang, J., Liu, X., Liu, H., Phan, H., Benetos, E., Plumbley, M. D., & Wang, W. (2023). Adapting language-audio models as few-shot audio learners. *Interspeech, 276-280*, 276–280. Advance online publication. DOI: 10.21437/Interspeech.2023-1082

Liu, Z. (2026). Llmflow: Reasoning and acting workflow for automated data analysis. *CRAN: Contributed Packages*. DOI: 10.32614/CRAN.package.llmflow

Pallavi, A. (2025). DeepFake detection for human face images and videos: A comprehensive survey. *INTERNATIONAL JOURNAL OF SCIENTIFIC RESEARCH IN ENGINEERING AND MANAGEMENT*, *09*(05), 1–9. DOI: 10.55041/IJSREM47887

Pant, D., & Mukhiya, S. K. (2024). Technical evaluation of GPT-4 and GPT-4-Turbo reflective listening response generation with the counsel chat dataset. DOI: 10.21203/rs.3.rs-4769572/v1

Park, J. S., O'Brien, J., Cai, C. J., Morris, M. R., Liang, P., & Bernstein, M. S. (2023). Generative agents: Interactive simulacra of human behavior. *Proceedings of the 36th Annual ACM Symposium on User Interface Software and Technology*, 1-22. DOI: 10.1145/3586183.3606763

Pashentsev, E. (2023). The malicious use of artificial intelligence through agenda setting. *The Palgrave Handbook of Malicious Use of AI and Psychological Security*, 133-172. DOI: 10.1007/978-3-031-22552-9_6

Ranaldi, L. (2026). Multilingual retrieval-augmented generation for knowledge-intensive question answering task. *Findings of the Association for Computational Linguistics: EACL, 2026*, 697–716. DOI: 10.18653/v1/2026.findings-eacl.35

Rehman, S. U. (2025). From innovation to impact the future ethical landscape and governance of large language models. *Innovations and Ethical Dimensions of Large Language Models*, 437-450. DOI: 10.4018/979-8-3373-5017-2.ch014

Sarch, G., Wu, Y., Tarr, M., & Fragkiadaki, K. (2023). Open-ended Instructable embodied agents with memory-augmented large language models. *Findings of the Association for Computational Linguistics: EMNLP, 2023*, 3468–3500. DOI: 10.18653/v1/2023.findings-emnlp.226

Soria, C. (2025). An empirical investigation into the utility of large language models in open-ended survey data categorization. DOI: 10.31235/osf.io/wv6tk_v2

Steele, J. L. (2023). To GPT or not GPT? Empowering our students to learn with AI. *Computers and Education: Artificial Intelligence*, *5*, 100160. DOI: 10.1016/j.caeai.2023.100160

Tedesco, R. (2026). Privacy and security in large language models and data. *Challenges and Applications of Generative Large Language Models*, 127-152. DOI: 10.1016/B978-0-443-33592-1.00011-5

Zhang, W., Kong, X., Dewitt, C., Braunl, T., & Hong, J. B. (2024). A study on prompt injection attack against LLM-integrated mobile robotic systems. *2024 IEEE 35th International Symposium on Software Reliability Engineering Workshops (ISSREW)*, 361-368. DOI: 10.1109/ISSREW63542.2024.00103

Chapter 3
Benchmark Integrity, Preference Data Engineering, and Security–Privacy Challenges in AI Creation Systems

Rocky Kumar
http://orcid.org/0009-0002-6995-2037
Poornima University, India

Shikha Khullar
http://orcid.org/0009-0000-5598-3145
Poornima University, India

Arun Arora
http://orcid.org/0000-0002-8976-0633
Lloyd Business School, India

ABSTRACT

Artificial Intelligence (AI) creation systems have transformed modern computing by enabling machines to generate human-like text, images, audio, video, and code using advanced machine learning and generative modeling techniques. Foundation models and generative AI are rapidly influencing healthcare, education, finance, cybersecurity, entertainment, and intelligent automation. However, their widespread adoption has raised concerns regarding benchmark integrity, preference data engineering,

DOI: 10.4018/979-8-2600-0368-8.ch003

security threats, privacy protection, and ethical governance. This chapter presents an overview of benchmark reliability, fairness, transparency, and model generalization while addressing challenges such as data contamination, leakage, and overfitting. It also explores preference learning approaches, including Reinforcement Learning from Human Feedback (RLHF) and Direct Preference Optimization (DPO), which help align AI systems with human values and expectations.

1. INTRODUCTION

Artificial Intelligence (AI) creation systems are a Modern development in the realm of modern computational intelligence, which can generate human-like content in a variety of areas, from software code to publishable text, images, audio, and video. The main innovations behind these systems are foundation models, deep neural networks and large-scale machine learning architectures fed on vast sets of data. Generative AI technologies have emerged to spur innovation across a range of industries—including health care, education, cybersecurity, finance, entertainment and science research. AI creation systems are faced with a lot of issues, including reliability of evaluations, human alignment, security vulnerabilities, and protection of private information, despite the increase in their capabilities. However, researchers and industry practitioners require new goals for AI systems to be trustworthy, secure, and ethically aligned. The dialogue stresses the need for dependable assessment techniques, user-focused preference optimization, and safe utilization of AI platforms. Additionally, the chapter explores new methods and governance approaches for bolstering transparency, robustness, fairness, and accountability of AI systems (Bender et al., 2021).

1.1 Overview of AI Creation Systems

AI creation systems are intelligent computer systems that can autonomously create or assist in the creation of digital content. They are constructed with cutting-edge machine learning, including deep learning, transformer networks, reinforcement learning, and multimodal neural networks. The modern AI creation systems incorporate Large Language Models (LLMs), diffusion models, Generative Adversarial Nets (GANs), and multimodal generative frameworks that can comprehend and generate complicated results.

Generative AI has been swiftly advancing and is now substantially improving the creativity and automation of machines. Today, AI can produce very realistic pictures, conversations like human beings, programs, teaching material, and fake media, which all have a pretty good sense of context. AI creation technologies are being adopted in business systems like multi-industry digital decision support systems, customer interaction platforms, virtual assistants, research automation systems, diagnostics in healthcare, and more.

As a result, with the growth of AI creation systems, there have been growing threats to reliability, ethical use, misinformation, IP infringements, and security. As such systems increasingly become embedded in societal and organizational activities, transparency and accountability are crucial. This has led to the growing interest in the training of reliable, fair, explainable, and secure systems that rely on AI (Bommasani et al., 2021).

1.2 Importance of Benchmark Integrity

Benchmark integrity is an important aspect to consider when assessing the performance and generalization of AI creation systems. Benchmarks represent standardized testing datasets and evaluation tools to assess explanations, explanations' robustness, understanding across social contexts, and model accuracy and reasoning power. Reliable benchmarks facilitate fair and objective comparisons between various AI models, along with the ability to pinpoint precise enhancements in model architectures and training techniques.

As essential as they are, modern AI benchmarks have their fair share of limitations. One concern is that of 'contamination of benchmarks' - when AI models accidentally memorize benchmarks during training. This causes the scores of various labs to be artificially high, thus misrepresenting intelligence and reasoning. Likewise, when using evaluation sets that are publicly accessible, the reliability and transparency of the more common benchmarking methods is questioned due to overfit.

Factors of integrity in the benchmark process also include fairness, reproducibility and robustness. Promoting AI systems is crucial for generating fair results when trained with unequal or incomplete data, which can perpetuate social inequalities (Brown et al., 2020).

1.3 Preference Data and AI Alignment

In this regard, preference data engineering has become a fundamental and pivotal pillar to help align AI systems with human values, expectations, and ethical considerations. AI alignment" is about making outputs created by AI accurate, safe, contextually appropriate, and helps the user in positive ways. In the field of aligning AI models with human preferences, recent methods like Reinforcement Learning from Human Feedback (RLHF) and Direct Preference Optimization (DPO) make extensive use of human preferences.

Preference data usually comes in the form of ranked responses, annotations, pairwise comparisons, or feedback from humans to steer the AI systems towards desirable actions. These alignment mechanisms offer a decrease in unwanted outputs, hallucinations, misinformation, and biased content creation, using data. Enabling human preference integration into the training process enhances AI systems' adaptability, explainability, and user impact. Yet, poor annotations/falsely weighted feedbacks can impact performance and fairness of the models. Therefore, strong preference engineering methods, quality assurance processes, and ethical data-gathering practices are crucial when it comes to creating AI systems that are aligned and trustworthy (Carlini et al., 2021).

1.4 Security and Privacy Concerns

One of the biggest challenges in the deployment of AI creation systems is security and privacy. Security and privacy are among the most critical challenges for deployment and use of AI creation systems. However, Generative AI models are very susceptible to adversarial attacks, prompt injection, data poisoning, model theft and generation of synthetic misinformation. Vulnerabilities in training data or processes, or in pipelines used to make inferences, can lead to manipulated AI output, disruption of system integrity, content harm, etc. An AI training set may be vulnerable to being manipulated or system integrity may be compromised, and/or the inference pipeline(s) may produce harmful content.

Data poisoning is one of the most critical risks, where intentional efforts to manipulate the data are added to training sets to impact the model's operation. Likewise, prompt injections can defy the system's protections, coerce AI systems into producing limited or hazardous responses. Moreover, concerns about misinformation, identity fraud and potential cybersecurity threats are compounded by deepfake technologies and synthetic media generation (Floridi & Chiriatti, 2020).

1.5 Chapter Contributions

This chapter provides a detailed analysis of benchmark integrity, preferred data engineering, security/privacy limitations about generation of AI systems. It covers the basics of Generative AI and the role of robust benchmarking in assessing AI model performance, strength and fairness. The chapter also examines methods in preference learning, including reinforcement learning from human feedback (RLHF) and direct preference optimization (DPO), which are human feedback-based preference learning methods.

The chapter also explores some of the primary security and privacy threats faced by AI systems such as adversarial attacks, prompt injection, data poisoning, data leakage and privacy issues. Other security-protective and private context-aware techniques, such as Differential Privacy (DP), Federated Learning (FL), and Secure AI frameworks, are also covered. In addition, ethical, regulatory and governance issues around building trustworthy AI are surfaced (Ganguli et al., 2022).

Figure 1. Overview of Trustworthy AI Creation Systems

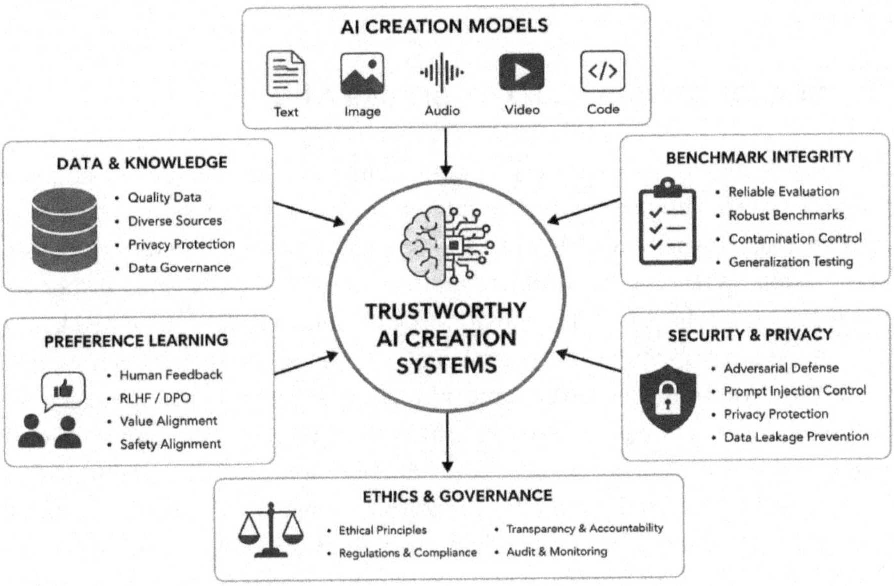

The integrated parts of benchmark integrity, preference learning, security, privacy, and governance mechanisms are illustrated in Figure 1, which provides an overview of the trustworthy AI creation systems.

2. FUNDAMENTALS OF AI CREATION SYSTEMS

Artificial Intelligence (AI) creation systems have emerged as influential technologies, capable of producing a content like that of human beings, automating complex tasks, and helping intelligent choice making procedures. The building blocks of these systems usually feature extensive neural networks, high-power computation hardware, and sophisticated machine learning models. They often incorporate complex machine learning algorithms, expansive neural networks, and powerful computational infrastructures that allow machines to learn from vast amounts of data and generate relevant, valuable output. There are several applications that make use of modern AI creation systems: text generation, picture synthesis, code conversation, online assistant, tips systems, healthcare analytics, and independent systems.

Generative AI tools have greatly ramped up the ability to model reality, create contextually appropriate content and communicate with users like never before. Yet, there are key factors behind the successful operation of AI creation platforms, such as foundation models, training pipelines, human-centric alignment mechanisms, and deployment infrastructures. These aspects are critical to the success of trustworthy, scalable and reliable AI systems (Gebru et al., 2021).

2.1 Foundation Models and Generative AI

Large-scale AI models that are trained from a large set of data using self-supervised or unsupervised learning are called foundation models. These models can be used to power various downstream AI applications, such as natural language processing, computer vision, speech recognition, and multimodal AI systems. Transformer-based large language models (LLMs), diffusion models, and generative adversarial networks (GANs) are some popular examples of foundation models. Generative AI is defined as any AI system that can generate new content, including text, images, audio and video, or software code. These systems learn the "rules" of data distribution, and will produce things they are close to what the human created. The transformer architecture is the preferred model for generative AI because it enables retrieval of long-range, contextual information and large volumes of sequential data efficiently.

AI-powered systems based on Generative AI can handle tasks like text generation, translation, document summarization, creation of synthetic media, and intelligent coding assistance. These capabilities are further strengthened by multimodal AI models, which combine technologies for processing text, image, audio and video in a unified single architecture. While generative AI systems offer significant benefits, they come with their share of drawbacks, including drawbacks with explainability, bias, security, and computational complexity, hallucination is one such drawback (Ghiurău & Popescu, 2026).

2.2 AI Training and Deployment Pipeline

AI training and deployment pipeline involves the entire lifecycle of creating, training, optimizing, testing, and deploying AI creation systems. Data collection starts with data that comes to us in massive quantities from various sources, including web content, databases, sensors, user interactions and enterprise systems. The data is then pre-processed using various methods to enhance data quality and consistency, such as data cleaning, normalization, tokenization, and feature engineering (Khullar et al., 2025). Once the data is pre-processed, it is then used for training the AI model through machine learning and deep learning algorithms. At runtime, the neural network is optimized by techniques like gradient descent and backpropagation to extract statistical patterns and relations from the input data. Training large-scale foundation models usually demands considerable computational power, such as GPUs, TPUs and distributed cloud infrastructures.

After being trained, the models are assessed with the aid of benchmarking and validation methods, to check their accuracy, robustness, fairness and generalization ability. For ethically guided optimization of model behaviour, fine-tuning and alignment techniques like Reinforcement Learning from Human Feedback (RLHF) are commonly used (Han et al., 2025).

2.3 Human-in-the-Loop AI Systems

Human-in-the-Loop (HITL) AI Systems engage human understandings and feedback in the creation and decision-making of AI systems. These systems aim to enhance the reliability, safety, interpretability, and human values alignment of AI. In HITL, humans interactively play roles in data annotation, model evaluation, ranking of preferences, feedback generation, and decision validation.

Perhaps the critical use of HITL systems is in alignment by human feedback mechanisms in AI. Reinforcement Learning from Human Feedback (RLHF) involves instruction derived from human feedback being applied to teach reward models that help steer and shape how the AI behaves toward creating more applicable, safer, and accurate answers. Human intervention can also decrease harmful content generation, misinformation, hallucination and biased predictions for generative AI systems. But there are also issues with scalability, the cost of annotation, subjective decisions, cultural differences and variance in human annotations in HITL frameworks. Thus, it is crucial to have efficient preference engineering and quality assurance mechanisms to ensure the development of human-centric AI is effective (Ji et al., 2023).

2.4 Applications of AI Creation Systems

In the era of artificial intelligence, these systems are reshaping various industries with their capabilities, such as intelligent automation, personalized service, and high-level functionality of creating content. Medical applications: Generative AI systems can help with medical diagnosis, clinical documentation, drug discovery, and patient monitoring in the healthcare industry. Healthcare: Generative AI can be used in the medical field for diagnostics, documentation, drug development, and patient monitoring. In customer service, education, and enterprise communication systems, AI-powered chatbots and virtual assistants are currently an integral part of customer service.

AI code generation systems are also used in software engineering for automated software testing, programming and debugging. Generative AI has a wide range of applications in the creative industries, such as creating visuals, composing music, editing videos, and generating digital content. AI creation systems are utilized by financial institutions in various functions such as fraud detection, market forecasting, algorithmic trading, and intelligent risk analysis.

The benefits of AI systems in cyber security are also essential since they can identify anomalous behaviour, assess threats, and automate the response processes. The AI creation technologies the providers develop can be applied in various ways for smart cities and IoT ecosystems, including intelligent surveillance, predictive maintenance, autonomous transportation, and energy optimization (Kaddour et al., 2023).

Table 1. Applications and Capabilities of AI Creation Systems

Application Area	AI Capability	Example Use Cases
Healthcare	Medical analysis and prediction	Disease diagnosis, drug discovery
Education	Intelligent tutoring	Personalized learning systems
Finance	Predictive analytics	Fraud detection, risk assessment
Cybersecurity	Threat detection	Intrusion detection, malware analysis
Software Engineering	Code generation	Automated programming assistance
Media and Entertainment	Content generation	Image synthesis, music creation
Smart Cities	Intelligent automation	Traffic management, surveillance
Customer Service	Conversational AI	Chatbots and virtual assistants

Table 1 highlights key use cases and capabilities of AI creation systems in various industry sectors like healthcare, educational services, finance, cybersecurity and intelligent automation.

Figure 2. Workflow of AI Creation Systems

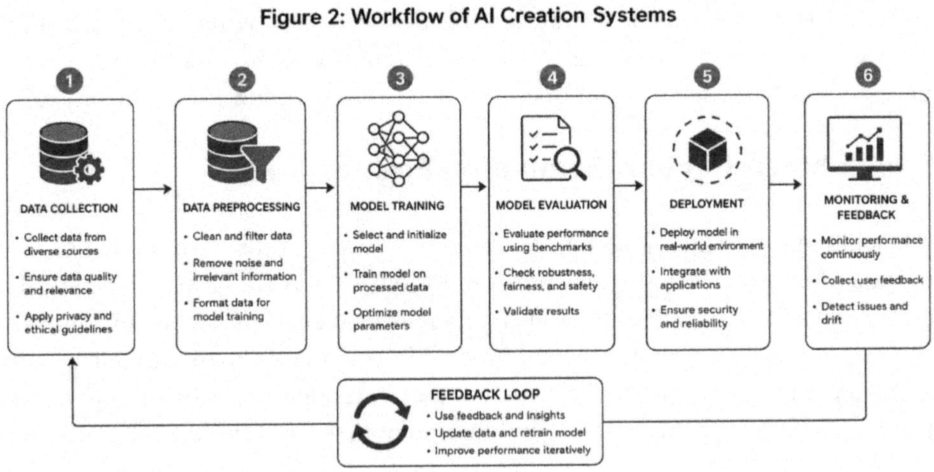

The figure 2 summarizes the workflow of the creation of an AI, which starts with data collection, data preprocessing, model training, model evaluation, deployment and continual feedback monitoring.

3. BENCHMARK INTEGRITY IN AI SYSTEMS

The integrity of benchmark is one of the key criteria to measure the performance, reliability, robustness and level of fairness across Artificial Intelligence (AI) systems. Benchmarks play a critical role in modern AI research, and they are employed to evaluate the performance of AI models in various applications, including natural language processing, visual recognition, reasoning, code generation, and decision-making. The ability to use reliable benchmarking frameworks can facilitate researchers and organizations to objectively compare AI models, recognize system weaknesses, and enhance model architectures and training techniques.

The complexity of analysing benchmarks has increased with the progress of foundation models and generative AI systems. AI models can be trained on huge internet-scale datasets, where benchmark data might be publicly available without making individuals aware. Such a situation creates the problem of benchmark contamination, high score values and false inference of the smarts of the model and its intended generalisation power. As a result, integrity of the benchmarks is a major focus of ensuring the reliability of AI systems.

Beyond the accuracy measure, the robustness, fairness, transparency, explainability, and security must be considered while evaluating modern AI. An AI system used in the real world must not be biased, or create any vulnerabilities without changing its behaviour significantly when the environment changes, in terms of demographics, language or other operational factors (Kairouz & McMahan, 2021).

3.1 Benchmarking and Evaluation Frameworks

Benchmarking is the systematic evaluation of AI systems with the aid of standard datasets, tasks and metrics. Benchmark evaluation frameworks are used to evaluate how efficient, accurate, robust, and reasoned an AI model is, in controlled experimental settings. Examples of common AI benchmarks involve language comprehension (LLM), computer vision (CV), speech recognition (SR), mathematical reasoning, and tasks involving the combination of these abilities called multimodal intelligence (MM).

Model evaluation techniques like accuracy, precision, recall and F1 score are commonly used in supervised machine learning models. For generative AI systems, however, more complex assessment approaches are needed which consider an understanding of context, fact-checking, coherence, creativity, and fairness and safety. Incorporating human evaluation frameworks into benchmarking systems could be used to evaluate qualitative elements like helpfulness, alignment, user satisfaction, and more.

The modern most current systems of benchmarks also focus on reproducibility and transparency. Reproducible evaluation allows results of the experiments to be independently reproduced in different research settings and computational infrastructures. The transparent benchmarking practices include clear documentation of datasets, evaluation criteria, training procedures and model limitations. These practices are fundamental to uphold trust in AI research and to make it possible to make comparisons between different AI systems (Kasneci et al., 2023).

3.2 Dataset Leakage and Benchmark Contamination

Two major concerns regarding AI systems for evaluation are data leakage from datasets, and contamination of them. When data from the test sets get accidentally into the model training set, giving a spurious improvement, it is called dataset leakage. Benchmark contamination often is the issue with large-scale generative AI systems, as they tend to include supplied public benchmark sets in the large volumes of data used for pretraining the foundation models.

The results of evaluations can be easily distorted by benchmark contamination, which may lead to answers being memorized because of inferential abilities instead of being shown as genuine reasoning. The evaluation results could be skewed due to benchmark contamination, as AI models might be memorizing answers rather than proving that they have understanding and can generalize these abilities effectively. This is a relevant problem for large language models (LLM) where models can include examples from the benchmark with which they are trained. Therefore, one cannot solely rely on high benchmarks for accurate representation of intelligence and adaptability in the real world.

One of the other key issues is overfitting on public benchmarks. Models can be fine-tuned for the specific task and used to get better on the benchmark which limits the ability of the model to perform in real-world tasks. This practice may lead to the false impression of model superiority and hide any fragilities and flaws (Mylrea & Robinson, 2023).

3.3 Robustness and Fairness Evaluation

A robust and fair evaluation of robustness and fairness is a crucial part of any comprehensive framework for measuring AI trustworthiness. Robustness (also known as reliability or cold resistance): The capability of an AI system to perform correctly across a range of conditions and scenarios – such as data inputs with noise and adversarial attacks – and distribution shifts. When deployed in the real-world, AI systems need to behave reliably when faced with uncertainty and volatile conditions of operations.

Assessing an AI system's ability to withstand intentional manipulation of the inputs that could fool or deceive the model with adversarial robustness testing. For systems based on generative AI, the potential methods of attacking range from prompt injection to the inclusion of malicious data during training or the creation of malicious content. A key understanding for determining the security and reliability of a system is to assess its robustness against these attacks.

The core of fairness evaluation is to detect and reduce biases that exist in AI systems. The impact can be discriminatory and target certain groups, languages or cultural communities, depending on the imbalanced and/or biased nature of the datasets used to train the AI models. The potential for bias in generative AI can result in problematic stereotypes, unequal treatment and ethical dilemmas in processes like recruiting, healthcare, law enforcement and financial decisions (Osagie & Balasundaram, 2026).

3.4 Secure Benchmarking Strategies

Secure benchmarking strategies aim to ensure the reliability, transparency and trustworthiness of AI testing frameworks, as well as to foster opposition to contamination and manipulation, and resist hostile use. One promising method is to exploit the usage of hidden or private benchmark data sets, data which are not available throughout the model training process. The use of these datasets minimizes memory dependency and allows to better measure the models' generalization capacity.

Another emerging approach is dynamic benchmarking, in which the evaluation tasks and/or datasets change over time to avoid over fitting and benchmark saturation.

Third-party auditing and frameworks also add to the credibility of the benchmarks. Independent third-party audit of programme compliance can help ensure that evaluation methods and standards for reproducing the datasets are carried out fairly and appropriately to assess AI systems. Model cards and dataset documentation help reinforce accountability and reproducibility in AI research, adding to transparency. In addition to this transparency, transparent reporting practices like model cards and dataset documentation reinforce accountability and reproducibility in AI research (Ouyang et al., 2022).

Table 2. Comparison of Benchmark Evaluation Techniques

Evaluation Technique	**Purpose**	**Advantages**	**Limitations**
Static Benchmarking	Standardized performance evaluation	Easy comparison across models	Vulnerable to overfitting
Dynamic Benchmarking	Adaptive real-world evaluation	Reduces benchmark saturation	Complex implementation
Human Evaluation	Measures quality and alignment	Captures contextual understanding	Subjective and costly
Adversarial Testing	Evaluates robustness against attacks	Improves AI security	Requires specialized expertise
Fairness Evaluation	Detects demographic and ethical bias	Promotes responsible AI	Difficult to standardize
Hidden Benchmarking	Prevents benchmark contamination	Enhances evaluation reliability	Limited public accessibility
Federated Evaluation	Secure distributed evaluation	Preserves privacy and security	Higher computational overhead

Table 2 compares key evaluation methods employed to determine AI robustness, fairness, reliability and the integrity of the process used to create the benchmark.

Figure 3. Benchmark Integrity Assessment Framework

Figure 3: Benchmark Integrity Assessment Framework

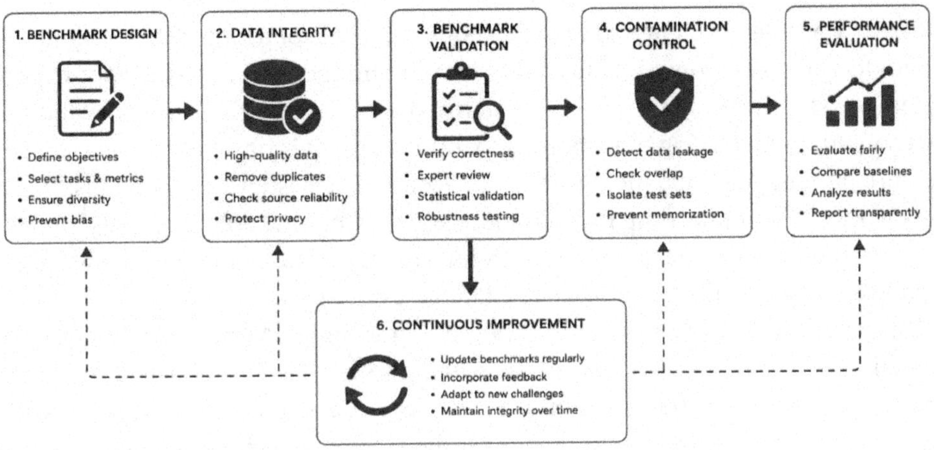

As shown in figure 3, the AI assessment framework here covers the integrity of reliable assessments, contamination control, robustness validation and performance assessment of AI.

4. PREFERENCE DATA ENGINEERING

Its significance in the modern development of reliable and people-friendly AI creating frameworks has come to the fore. In addition to providing accurate information, modern models powered by generative AI are expected to provide responses that meet the expectations of humans, ethical considerations, context and context relevancy, as well as safety requirements. While traditional machine learning uses large sets of data to statistically optimize system performance, it cannot effectively model human preferences, social values and expectations of behaviour.

To overcome these challenges, preference learning approaches are introduced to leverage human feedback in training and optimization of AI models. Preference Data engineering includes collecting, annotating, ranking, filtering, and optimizing human preference data to match models and enhance their comprehension of the preference. RLHF and DPO are among the various developed techniques that have boosted the potential of AI systems to generate helpful, harmless and contextually relevant outputs (Rafailov et al., 2023).

4.1 Human Feedback and Preference Learning

The act of human input and feedback significantly contributes to tuning the AI system to deliver the functionality that the user and the ethical framework expect. Preference learning in generative AI systems involves leveraging human evaluation and user-supplied ranking of responses to train the models, instead of depending on pre-defined labels or statistical trends between responses and user actions. Every AI-generated output is compared to multiple AI's other generated outputs, and the responses that are most accurate, safe, relevant, and context appropriate, are identified and chosen as the best answer by human evaluators.

But preference learning is more effective in training AI systems to grasp the subjective expectations of individuals, which are not easily described using traditional supervised learning techniques. It plays a crucial role in scenarios like conversational AI, creating text, recommending items, assisting in healthcare, and intelligent virtual assistants, among others. Human feedback data typically consists of paired comparisons, annotations, ratings, corrections and comparisons of preferences (Rayhana et al., 2024).

4.2 Reinforcement Learning from Human Feedback (RLHF)

One of the most popular methods for aligning AI models is called Reinforcement Learning from Human Feedback (RLHF). RLHF ties aspects of reinforcement learning with human preference data to fine-tune the behaviour of AI systems based on human expectations and values. RLHF generates rewards by directly optimizing the accuracy of AI models with human evaluations, rather than directly maximizing the accuracy of the prediction.

Typically, the RLHF process consists of three key steps: supervised fine tuning, training the reward model, and optimizing the reinforcement learning. The AI model is first supervised fine-tuned with good quality demonstration data. Then human teams provide their and/or "contextual" rankings of the model outputs based on the degree to which the model outputs are useful, safe, correct and relevant in the specific context in which they were generated. These positions are then based on to train human preferences estimate model capable reward. Finally, reinforcement learning algorithms provide the optimization of the AI model towards maximizing the reward scores predicted (Razi et al., 2025).

The RLHF objective function can be represented as:

$$R(\theta) = \mathbb{E}_{(x,y)\sim D}\left[r_\phi(x,y)\right] - \beta D_{KL}(\pi_\theta \parallel \pi_{ref})$$

where:

- $R(\theta)$represents the reward optimization objective,
- $r_\phi(x,y)$denotes the reward model learned from human feedback,
- $\pi_\theta$represents the optimized policy model, and
- $D_{KL}$is the Kullback–Leibler divergence used to prevent excessive deviation from the reference model.

By lowering instances of harmful outputs, hazardous responses, and factually incorrect outputs, RLHF has greatly enhanced the quality and safety of LLMs. But there are some issues with RLHF, like the possibility of reward hacking, the advantage that it is hard to scale, challenging computation, and the reliance on high-quality human annotations.

4.3 Direct Preference Optimization (DPO)

Direct Preference Optimization (DPO) is the new kid on the block, a method that aims to make preference optimization more streamlined, stable and efficient in terms of computation. While RLHF will take separate training steps for the reward model and reinforcement learning, DPO matches the language model using pairwise preference data.

In the case of DPO, the computer program is trained to improve the chances of desirable responses and to minimize the chances of undesirable responses. This direct approach to optimization avoids the complexities of reinforcement learning algorithms and reward model learning. This makes DPO an easier and more consistent way to get alignment working on contemporary generative AI systems (Saeed et al., 2026).

The DPO loss function is represented as:

$$\mathcal{L}_{DPO} = -\log\sigma\left(\beta\log\frac{\pi_\theta(y_w \mid x)}{\pi_\theta(y_l \mid x)}\right)$$

where:

- $y_w$represents the preferred response,
- $y_l$denotes the less preferred response,
- $\pi_\theta$is the policy model, and
- σdenotes the sigmoid function.

The fact that DPO uses far fewer resources than numerical scriptable posts and the fact that its optimization is based on a shorter pipeline have brought DPO to the fore. It allows for efficient and effective alignment of preferences without the need for explicit reinforcement learning or reward modelling. But DPO remains heavily reliant on good preference datasets, and can also be affected by biases that are found in human feedback datasets.

4.4 Bias and Data Quality Challenges

One of the challenges of preference data engineering is that the data often contains biases and/or data quality problems. Social, cultural, linguistic and demographic factors can contribute to bias within the preference data used to train AIs and can impact their behaviour without it being intentional. AI systems can perpetuate negative stereotypes and create unfair recommendations and outputs based on biased preference data.

The second significant problem is being faced by annotators is the issue of annotation inconsistency. Each evaluator might give different marks to the same answer and it can depend on personal experiences, cultural backgrounds and on individual expectations. This lack of consistency will make preference learning models and mechanisms less reliable, and facilitate the alignment process.

A firm and fair preference learning is then crucial and requires data quality management. Some typical QA methods used are annotator training, consensus-based evaluation of annotations, using the noise filter, outlier elimination or continuous auditing of datasets. Synthetic preference generation and automatic feedback mechanisms are also being investigated, to limit reliance on more time-consuming human annotation (Salah et al., 2026).

4.5 Preference Data Engineering Pipeline

Preference data engineering pipeline is the systematic workflow to gather, process, optimize, and consume human preference data for aligning AI. Typically, it starts with data collected and then AI generated outputs are ranked, rated, or paired off with human annotators.

This feedback data gets collected and pre-processed and filtered from noisy, inconsistent and low-quality annotations. Feature extraction and normalization are used to ensure the data is consistent and compatible with machine learning algorithms. Then rewards models or direct optimization models are trained based on preference data cleaned. After the preference learning models are trained, optimisation methods like RLHF or DPO are used to adjust the AI system (Shokri et al., 2017).

Table 3. Preference Learning Techniques in AI Systems

Technique	Description	Advantages	Limitations
Supervised Fine-Tuning (SFT)	Uses labelled demonstration data for training	Simple implementation	Limited human alignment
RLHF	Uses human feedback and reward modelling	Improves safety and alignment	Computationally expensive
DPO	Directly optimizes preference pairs	Stable and efficient training	Depends on high-quality preference data
Pairwise Ranking	Compares preferred and non-preferred outputs	Captures subjective preferences	Annotation inconsistency
Reward Modelling	Predicts human preference scores	Enhances optimization capability	Vulnerable to reward hacking
Synthetic Preference Learning	Generates automated preference signals	Scalable and cost-effective	Potential quality limitations

Table 3 summarizes various preference learning techniques used in AI systems, such as supervised fine-tuning, RLHF, DPO, reward modeling, and synthetic preference learning approaches.

Figure 4. Preference Data Engineering Workflow

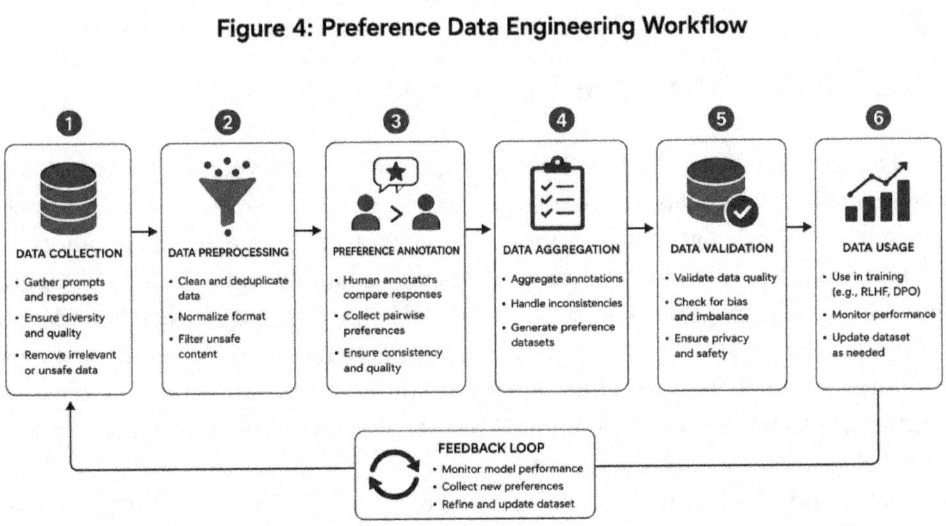

The preference data engineering workflow is displayed in figure 4, including the data collection, preprocessing, annotation, aggregating, validation and preference optimization processes.

5. SECURITY AND PRIVACY CHALLENGES

Rapid developments of AI creation systems have raised serious issues of security and privacy that impact the reliability, trustworthiness, and safe deployment of generative AI technologies. AI systems today play an increasingly important role in a range of sectors like health, finance, cyber security, education, governance and autonomy. While the automation, content creation and intelligent decision-making aspects offered by these technologies are significant, new vulnerabilities are also emerging that can be targeted by bad actors.

Generative AI models are also susceptible due to their dependency on vast amounts of data, intricate neural networks, and extensive computational resources. Some of the significant risks include privacy leakage, prompt injection, generation of deep fakes, model poisoning, and adversarial attacks that pose a threat to the integrity and trust of AI. In addition, AI systems built with very vast datasets from the web can also memorize private details, posing significant privacy dangers to people and organizations (Touvron et al., 2023).

5.1 Adversarial Attacks and Prompt Injection

Adversarial attacks are one of the most significant security threats to AI systems. In these attacks, the goal is to intentionally trigger the AI model or interactions with the system in ways designed to trick the AI and generate false, biased, or unauthorized results. In machine learning systems, adversarial examples are carefully designed inputs that try to manage weaknesses in the model behaviour and decision boundaries.

Prompts are an emerging area of concern in generative AI. When hackers can trick the user into clicking on a link or proposal that isn't considered safe, or they can steer the AI model to suggest potentially dangerous content or private information, the attack is known as prompt injection.

As an example, educated attacks can make it possible for an attacker to extract delicate details, create harmful code, or bypass moral boundaries, demanding that the AI conversationalist deliver. A typical instance is when attackers craft sophisticated instructions that compel an AI chatbot to disclose sensitive data, generate malware, or circumvent ethical limitations (Weidinger et al., 2021).

5.2 Model Poisoning and Deepfake Risks

Poisoning attacks try to taint training sets with malicious or manipulated data aiming for impact on AI training model. Modern AI systems rely on massive amounts of data pulled from a variety of sources; attackers can deliberately plug in corrupted samples that can adversely impact model performance or add hidden backdoors into a system.

Poisoning the data can result in mispredictions, biased results, and inappropriate behaviour of AI systems. Sometimes poisoned models may behave normally with regular inputs, but different dangerous outputs when a trigger input occurs. In critical applications that require assurance, such as the healthcare diagnosis, financial analysis, military systems and automatic transmission, the attacks are highly risk.

One of the biggest problems is the growing prevalence of the misuse of deep fakes. Deepfakes are a synthetic media produced using generative AI methods that can produce real-looking fake photos, videos, and recordings. Deep fake technology has a wide range of potentially positive applications, such as virtual reality, digital content creation and entertainment, but is the merge of artificial technology and human ingenuity used for harmful purposes like misinformation, identity theft, fraud, political manipulation, and cybercrime activities.

Rising volumes of synthetic misinformation disseminated via social media and digital communication are a danger to public trust, democracy and the integrity of organizations. Therefore, researchers are working on sieges of detecting Deepfakes, digital watermark solutions and AI solutions for media content verification to counter these threats and eventually restore authenticity and integrity to media (Zheng et al., 2024).

5.3 Privacy Leakage in AI Systems

A primary issue with AI creation systems is privacy leakage, especially with the reliance on massive amounts of data that includes sensitive personal and private information. AI systems with access to data from the internet could unknowingly retain and re-generate private information, including personally identifiable information (PII) and financial, health or proprietary organizational data (Andriani et al., 2026).

Membership inference attack is one of the most challenging types of privacy attacks, in which the attacker tries to discover whether a particular data sample was present in the training set for the model. In such attacks, sensitive data belonging to the user could be exposed and privacy guidelines broken. Likewise, model inversion attacks try to recover training data from the inferences or predictions of an AI model.

Unauthorized data reconstruction is another one of the important concerns. Unauthorized data reconstruction occurs when AI inadvertently leak private data when generating content or during an interaction process. Finally, the large language models and generative systems might regurgitate information learned from the training sets, a practice that could infringe on intellectual property ownership and confidential information (Kaddour et al., 2023).

5.4 Differential Privacy and Federated Learning

Differential privacy and federated learning are popular methods to improve privacy security in AI systems. The general idea of Differential Privacy is to add a controlled level of statistical noise to the datasets or the results of a model to obscure the identification of any one data sample, but still enable useful data analysis. This can allow AI systems to be trained without revealing any sensitive personal data to the AI.

The mathematical representation of differential privacy is given as:

$$Pr[M(D) \in S] \leq e^{\epsilon} Pr[M(D') \in S] + \delta$$

where:

- $M(D)$represents the randomized algorithm applied to dataset D,
- ϵdenotes the privacy loss parameter, and
- δrepresents the probability of privacy violation.

With differential privacy, the addition or removal of just one data record will not lead to a meaningful deviation in the model's results, thus preserving individual privacy.

Another privacy-preserving machine learning approach is federated learning: AI models are trained in a federated way and user-generated data is not shared with a central learning server. The devices do not provide sensitive information, but only provide updates to the device model or updated gradients. That significantly lessens the potential likelihood of getting centralized information cause and increases guarantee of personal privacy (Rayhana et al., 2024).

5.5 Secure AI Development Practices

Securing AI development practices is crucial for developing AI systems that can safely function in the real world with a good level of trustworthiness and resilience.

Security should be a core consideration in every step of the AI lifecycle – from data collection to model training, deployment, monitoring, and maintenance.

Secure management of dataset, by encryption, access control, data auditing and validation techniques is one important practice. By making sure that the data used for training the models is accurate and of high quality, the chances of poisoning attacks and unauthorized changes can be minimised. Adversarial Robustness Evaluation, security testing and vulnerability testing are all pre-deployment tests that should be conducted on AI systems.

The goal of adversarial training techniques is to make the AI systems resilient against manipulation by training them on manipulated inputs. In real-world AI deployments, the continuous monitoring frameworks can identify any suspicious activities, unusual behaviours and access attempts. Moreover, explainable AI mechanisms contribute to the transparency of AI systems and support security audits by providing a deeper understanding of the decision-making processes (Han et al., 2025).

Table 4. Security Threats and Mitigation Techniques

Security Threat	Description	Impact	Mitigation Technique
Adversarial Attacks	Manipulated inputs deceive AI systems	Incorrect predictions	Adversarial training
Prompt Injection	Malicious prompts bypass safeguards	Unsafe output generation	Input validation and filtering
Data Poisoning	Corrupted training data manipulation	Model integrity compromise	Secure dataset auditing
Backdoor Attacks	Hidden malicious triggers in models	Unauthorized behavior	Robust validation frameworks
Deepfake Generation	Synthetic fake media creation	Misinformation and fraud	Deepfake detection systems
Membership Inference	Identifies training data membership	Privacy leakage	Differential privacy
Model Inversion	Reconstruction of training data	Sensitive data exposure	Federated learning
Data Leakage	Unintentional disclosure of information	Privacy and legal risks	Encryption and access control

Table 4 contains the comparison among the major threats on AI systems and respective mitigation techniques against the threats from adversarial attacks, data poisoning, prompt injection and privacy leakage.

Figure 5. Security and Privacy Framework for AI Systems

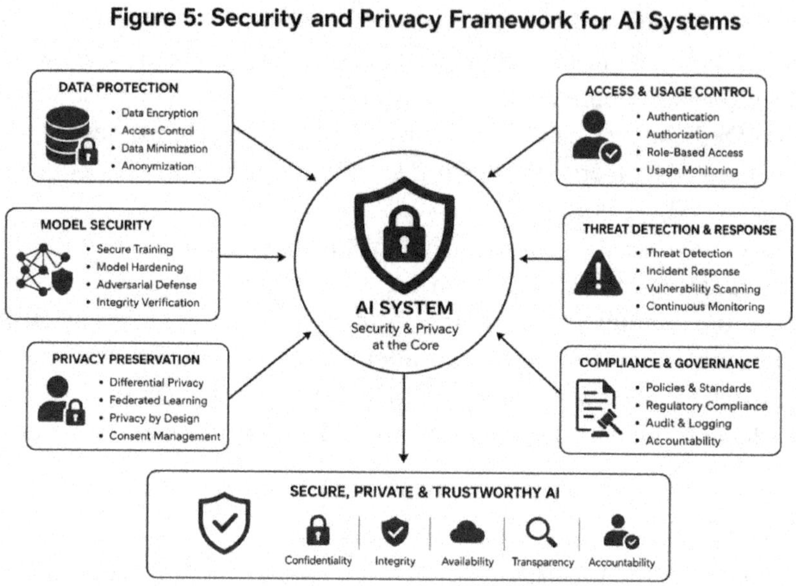

The AI systems security and privacy framework outlined in Figure 5 highlights key elements like data protection, model security, privacy preservation, threat detection, and governance mechanisms.

6. ETHICAL AND GOVERNANCE ISSUES

As the development of AI creation systems have accelerated, there has been much concern related to the ethical, legal and governance concerns that exist with its responsible development and deployment. Artificial Intelligence systems are being increasingly engaged in vital decision-making processes in sectors such as healthcare, finance, education, cybersecurity, public administration, etc. and social media. These have significant advantages in terms of automation, prediction, and content creation, but also journalists have raised worries about fairness, transparency, accountability, bias, privacy, and societal consequences.

Generative AI systems create realistic and convincing content that can sway human choices, opinions and how things run in corporates. Accounting for responsible behaviours in AI and creating appropriate governance frameworks is thus crucial to the success and confidence in an AI ecosystem. Ethical AI frameworks are designed to ensure the transparency, fairness, safety, and alignment with human values and expectations of AI systems.

Governance in AI takes place through the creation of policies, regulations, standards and accountability mechanisms to support and facilitate responsible innovation and use of AI. The rise of AI technologies brings with it a host of potential issues and problems that have governments, research institutions and tech companies alike turning their attention to protecting against biases in algorithms, the spread of misinformation and secure data protection, as well as protecting intellectual property rights, and holding creators accountable for their actions (Bommasani et al., 2021).

6.1 Fairness and Explainability

The principles of fairness and explainability are two of the most crucial ethical aspects of developing AI creating systems. Fairness: AI systems should not discriminately, discriminate or treat with bias any individual or group of individuals or attribute differently to them based on their gender, race, language, ethnicity, religion, or socio-economic status (Khullar et al., 2026). Such biased or imbalanced training can result in a system that perpetuates societal inequalities and delivers unfair results. In generative AI systems, bias can manifest as a tendency to generate stereotypical content, provide discriminatory product suggestions, exhibit disproportional representation, or as problematic language responses. Such biases can have negative impacts for people and communities and diminish the public's trust of AI technologies.

A range of techniques aimed at fairness detection, fairness auditing, and balanced data engineering are emerging to help handle issues of fairness. There are numerous fairness evaluation metrics that are employed to analyse the ethical nature of AI, including demographic parity, equal opportunity and fairness-aware optimization. Other factors that help minimize bias in AI systems are inclusive datasets and varied human feedback loops (Ouyang et al., 2022).

6.2 Responsible AI Governance

Responsible AI governance involves setting policies and ethical guidelines, operational procedures, and accountability measures that make sure AI systems develop in a responsible way. Governance frameworks strike a balance between innovation in both technology and society, fostering transparency and fairness, security and human-centred AI practices. Responsible AI principles like fairness, safe usage, privacy protection, accountability, safety and transparency have led to the growth in organization deployment of systems that use AI. Typical elements of an AI governance framework range from ethical review boards and risk assessment mechanisms to model auditing and bias monitoring systems as well as security compliance protocols.

One of the critical elements of responsible governance is AI practices that must be managed throughout AI's lifecycle. The governance processes must span the entire lifecycle of an AI model, from data collection, to training and evaluation, deployment, monitoring to retirement. It is critical to monitor the system post- deployment to track the different risks, adverse effects, and vulnerabilities that may occur in the future (Han et al., 2025).

6.3 Regulatory and Legal Challenges

AI technologies have expanded remarkably but their changing characteristics and the absence of a uniform AI law have been posing challenges for the regulatory and legal terrain. The governments and regulatory bodies are striving to create legislation addressing issues of data privacy, intellectual property, transparency of algorithms, cybersecurity, misinformation, and accountability for AI. Section of Linga eligibility reasoner: evaluating legal settings that impact AI-generated conclusions and material. When the AI systems deliver harmful content, misinformation, or discriminatory results, who is liable for the errors of the developers, the organizations using the systems, and the users and platforms themselves?

The principles of user consent, awareness, and personal data protection are paramount in the context of data privacy rules like the General Data Protection Regulation (GDPR), along with the training and deployment of AI systems. Similarly, Zai's widespread regulation framework, REST API guidelines, and data encryption standards require careful attention in securing medical data utilized by AI systems (Osagie & Balasundaram, 2026).

6.4 Human Oversight and Accountability

There needs to be space for human oversight and accountability to ensure trustworthy and ethically good AI systems. While AI creation systems can greatly aid in the creation of complex tasks and provide for smart choice making, human oversight is still vital in verifying their outputs, tracking danger and avoiding persistent repercussions.

Human oversight mechanisms are those that ensure that humans retain control over key AI functions, especially in sensitive applications like healthcare diagnostic, autonomous transportation, financial systems, law enforcement and military technologies. AI-generated content will only generate the desired outcomes if subject to a human inspection, to correct and finalize the content when needed.

Accountability defines how well the scientists, organizations, or systems can be identified and measured for their AI behaviour and results. Promoting transparency in accountability processes supports the fairness, safety and reliability of AI systems, while ensuring developers and operators are accountable (Salah et al., 2026).

Table 5. AI Governance and Regulatory Frameworks

Framework / Regulation	Purpose	Key Features	Application Area
GDPR (General Data Protection Regulation)	Data privacy protection	User consent, data transparency	AI data management
HIPAA	Healthcare data security	Medical information protection	Healthcare AI systems
AI Ethics Guidelines	Ethical AI development	Fairness, accountability, transparency	Responsible AI governance
Explainable AI (XAI) Frameworks	Improve model interpretability	Transparent decision-making	High-risk AI applications
Risk-Based AI Governance	AI risk assessment	Continuous monitoring and auditing	Enterprise AI systems
AI Audit Frameworks	AI accountability evaluation	Compliance verification	Regulatory and legal assessment
Human-in-the-Loop Governance	Human oversight integration	Human validation and control	Critical decision systems
Federated Governance Models	Decentralized AI regulation	Privacy-preserving collaboration	Distributed AI ecosystems

Table 5 provides a summary of key AI governance and regulatory initiatives related to ensuring fairness, explainability, accountability, privacy, and responsible AI use.

7. FUTURE DIRECTIONS AND RECOMMENDATIONS

AI system of creation is transforming the technological landscape across: research areas and industry. With the rise in the power and the usage of generative AI models, securing, transparency, explainability and human-centric AI systems are gaining prominence. Developing more sustainable and responsible AI innovation can be achieved through addressing challenges of trustworthiness, fairness, privacy protection, robustness, scalability, and ethical governance, in future AI ecosystems. These are expected to be a major influence on the next generation of intelligent technologies as a new line of research in explainable AI, privacy-aware architectures, secure machine learning, and human-aligned AI systems emerges. Recognizing that the risk of societal harm and to cybersecurity exists, organizations and researchers need to employ best practices to develop AI products and services which are secure from the start, always monitored, and deployed ethically (Gebru et al., 2021).

7.1 Explainable and Trustworthy AI

Misinformation and lack of transparency are one of the core issues in the evolution of AI in the future. Today's AI systems, especially deep learning and generative AI models, however, can predominantly rely on black-box models, whose internal workings are hard to understand. Insufficient transparency leads to lower users' trust, makes debugging difficult, introduces obstacles for high-risk applications like healthcare, financial and cyber security, and autonomous systems.

Going forward, we can anticipate the development of AI systems that implement sophisticated Explainable AI (XAI) tools that offer explanations for outputs that are interpretable, explainable and comprehensible for humans. Explainable models will provide enhanced accountability, fairness auditing, regulatory compliance and users' trust in the outcomes of AI.

The development and application of trustworthy AI research will also shift to fairness-aware learning, strong assessment tools, biases reduction methods, and human-centered alignment mechanisms. Building in ethical considerations and context to any AI system could minimize negative outputs, inaccurate information and discriminatory actions. In addition, explainability tools and mechanisms of human supervision will facilitate AI systems that are more open and socially oriented (Shokri et al., 2017).

7.2 Privacy-Aware AI Architectures

As data security concerns and the fear of personal data being leaked continue to rise, as well as the regulatory requirements, privacy-sensitive AI designs are likely to grow more critical for future AI systems. When used to uncover details in large datasets, generative AI services can accidentally reveal personally identifiable information (PII), financial data, health information and confidential company information.

There has been an increasing number of architectures for AI systems combining privacy-preserving technologies like differential privacy, federated learning, secure multi-party computation, and homomorphic encryption, which will continue to be added to future models. Such methods will empower AI systems to learn from these multi-source data without having to directly access or share user-sensitive data.

The expected adoption of federated AI systems in fields like healthcare, IoT applications, smart cities, financial systems, or edge computing, where privacy is paramount for local data, makes it a promising prospect. Furthermore, privacy-preserving model training methods and privileged access control legislation will assist organisations fulfil international laws and policies, including GDPR and upcoming AI governance laws (Zheng et al., 2024).

7.3 Emerging Research Trends

Below are some research trends that are likely to influence the future of the intelligent computational ecosystem and the creation system of AI. A notable trend has been the emergence of multimodal AI systems that jointly process and generate both text and images, sounds, videos and sensor data in centralized architectures. The advancement of multimodal intelligence will enhance three key facets of AI systems: contextual awareness, interactive communication, and cross-domain reasoning (Khullar et al., 2026).

One of the future areas of research is the continuous adaptation of the behaviour of the models to a change in human preferences, ethics, and environment by autonomous AI systems. They can incorporate algorithms such as reinforcement learning, preference optimization for ensuring long-term alignment, and real-time feedback mechanisms for safety enhancements.

Increased threats to cybersecurity from defense against adversarial AI systems will continue to drive AI and adversarial defense research. Advanced adversarial training models, real-time threat identification systems, AI red team approaches, and a zero-trust security strategy are likely to be integrated into future AI systems to boost the resilience of AI systems to malicious attacks (Bender et al., 2021).

7.4 Best Practices for Secure AI Systems

To build trustworthy and safe AI systems, it is essential to embrace a holistic approach to AI throughout its lifecycle that follows best practices. Security-by-design principles need to be incorporated into data collection and model building processes, and into the deployment, monitoring and maintenance processes.

A major good practice is to ensure the safe keeping of datasets on aspects such as dataset encryption, access control, integrity validation, and ongoing auditing implemented and enhanced. Ensuring training datasets have no malicious manipulation, unauthorized changes, or risks of sensitive data being leaked is important for organizations.

Adversarial robustness testing techniques and protocols should also be included in the AI evaluation process to be able to detect vulnerabilities to prompt injection, data poisoning and adversarial manipulation attacks. SaaS systems can be strengthened and new threats can be identified prior to their deployment using the regular penetration testing practices, the adoption of AI red teaming and security audits (Rayhana et al., 2024).

Figure 6. Future Ecosystem of Secure AI Creation Systems

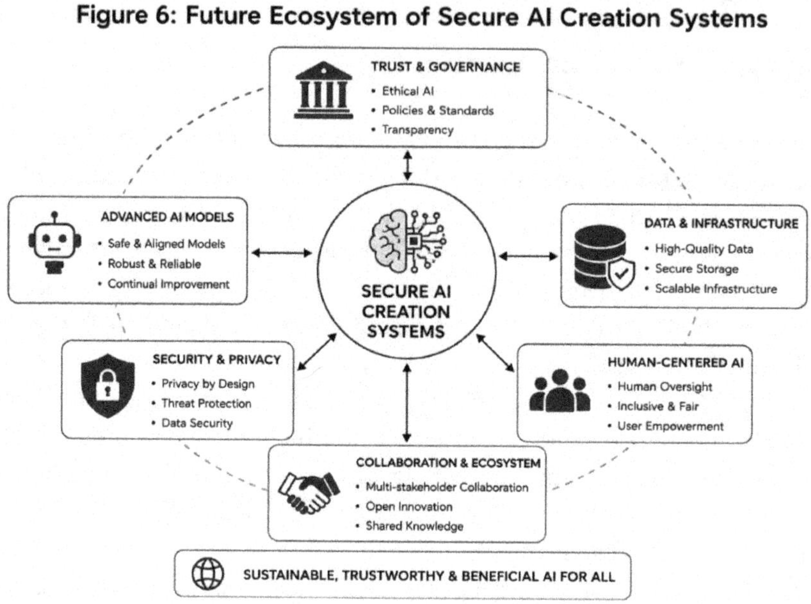

Figure 6 depicts the future ecosystem for secure AI creation systems, featuring trustworthy architectures for AI, privacy-enhancing infrastructures, human-centered AI, and facilitating collaborative governance models.

8. CONCLUSION

AI creation systems have tremendous potential, quickly outgrowing their status as tools for basic text generation to become highly capable, able to produce human-readable text, automate complex tasks, and facilitate intelligent decisions in various fields. The chapter gave a thorough overview of maintaining the integrity of benchmarks, designing a preference system, and security-privacy concerns for contemporary AI systems for creating. The researchers emphasized the need for the adoption of trustworthy AI benchmarking frameworks to assess their performance, robustness, fairness, and generalization capabilities, as well as potential contamination of benchmarks, leakage of information from datasets, and overfitting. Additional studies in the chapter examined preference learning techniques, such as Reinforcement Learning from Human Feedback (RLHF) and Direct Preference Optimization (DPO), and their relevance to shaping AI systems that meet user expectations and ethical standards. Other security vulnerabilities, including adversarial attacks, prompt injection, model poisoning, and deepfake, as well as privacy issues like data leakage, membership inference, and model inversion attacks were also discussed. Various methods and methodologies related to privacy and security that have been proposed to tackle these challenges including differential privacy, federated learning, adversarial learning, and secure AI governance frameworks were discussed. In addition, ethical issues like fairness, explainability, accountability and the involvement of humans in AI development were listed as key components of trustworthy AI.

REFERENCES

Andriani, A. D., Dwiwarman, D. A., & Khullar, S. (2026). Resilient selves in the digital sphere: Communication strategies for sustainable privacy management. In *Resilient privacy-preserving mechanisms for digital identity management*. IGI Global., DOI: 10.4018/979-8-3373-7292-1.ch001

Bender, E. M., Gebru, T., McMillan-Major, A., & Shmitchell, S. (2021, March). On the dangers of stochastic parrots: Can language models be too big? In *Proceedings of the 2021 ACM conference on fairness, accountability, and transparency* (pp. 610-623). DOI: 10.1145/3442188.3445922

Bommasani, R., Hudson, D. A., Adeli, E., Altman, R., Arora, S., von Arx, S., . . . Liang, P. (2021). On the opportunities and risks of foundation models. *arXiv preprint arXiv:2108.07258.*

Brown, T., Mann, B., Ryder, N., Subbiah, M., Kaplan, J. D., Dhariwal, P., & Amodei, D. (2020). Language models are few-shot learners. *Advances in Neural Information Processing Systems*, *33*, 1877–1901.

Carlini, N., Tramer, F., Wallace, E., Jagielski, M., Herbert-Voss, A., Lee, K., . . . Raffel, C. (2021). Extracting training data from large language models. In *30th USENIX security symposium (USENIX Security 21)* (pp. 2633-2650).

Floridi, L., & Chiriatti, M. (2020). GPT-3: Its nature, scope, limits, and consequences. *Minds and Machines*, *30*(4), 681–694. DOI: 10.1007/s11023-020-09548-1

Ganguli, D., Lovitt, L., Kernion, J., Askell, A., Bai, Y., Kadavath, S., . . . Clark, J. (2022). Red teaming language models to reduce harms: Methods, scaling behaviors, and lessons learned. *arXiv preprint arXiv:2209.07858.*

Gebru, T., Morgenstern, J., Vecchione, B., Vaughan, J. W., Wallach, H., Iii, H. D., & Crawford, K. (2021). Datasheets for datasets. *Communications of the ACM*, *64*(12), 86–92. DOI: 10.1145/3458723

Ghiurău, D., & Popescu, D. E. (2026). Data Security and Privacy in GPT Models: Techniques and Challenges. *Applied Sciences (Basel, Switzerland)*, *16*(4), 1900. DOI: 10.3390/app16041900

Han, X., Yang, J., Wang, T., Bi, Z., Song, X., Hao, J., & Song, J. (2025). Towards alignment-centric paradigm: A survey of instruction tuning in large language models. *arXiv preprint arXiv:2508.17184.*

Ji, Z., Lee, N., Frieske, R., Yu, T., Su, D., Xu, Y., Ishii, E., Bang, Y. J., Madotto, A., & Fung, P. (2023). Survey of hallucination in natural language generation. *ACM Computing Surveys*, *55*(12), 1–38. DOI: 10.1145/3571730

Kaddour, J., Harris, J., Mozes, M., Bradley, H., Raileanu, R., & McHardy, R. (2023). Challenges and applications of large language models. *arXiv preprint arXiv:2307.10169*.

Kairouz, P., & McMahan, H. B. (2021). Advances and open problems in federated learning. *Foundations and Trends in Machine Learning*, *14*(1-2), 1–210. DOI: 10.1561/2200000083

Kasneci, E., Seßler, K., Küchemann, S., Bannert, M., Dementieva, D., Fischer, F., Gasser, U., Groh, G., Günnemann, S., Hüllermeier, E., Krusche, S., Kutyniok, G., Michaeli, T., Nerdel, C., Pfeffer, J., Poquet, O., Sailer, M., Schmidt, A., Seidel, T., & Kasneci, G. (2023). ChatGPT for good? On opportunities and challenges of large language models for education. *Learning and Individual Differences*, *103*, 102274. DOI: 10.1016/j.lindif.2023.102274

Khullar, S., Kate, C., Rao, A. S., Sharrif, U. H., Gupta, A., & Kaliappan, S. (2026). Explainable intelligence for ethical human-centric AI: Trust modeling using gradient boosting. In 2026 5th International Conference on Innovative Practices in Technology and Management (ICIPTM) (pp. 1–9). IEEE. DOI: 10.1109/ICIPTM69057.2026.11465350

Khullar, S., Kate, C., Ravula, P. K., & Kumar, V. A. G, G. M., & Vairavel, M. (2026). Contextual semantic representation learning for fake news classification via fine-tuned bidirectional transformers. In 2026 9th International Conference on Intelligent Computing and Control Systems (ICICCS) (pp. 1482–1490). IEEE. DOI: 10.1109/ICICCS67901.2026.11502741

Khullar, S., Magdalene, A. H. S., Sandhya, P., & Naik, B. R. N, H. K. B., & Raju, M. V. (2025). Implementation, performance, and energy efficiency analysis for text classification of deep learning architectures. In 2025 10th International Conference on Communication and Electronics Systems (ICCES) (pp. 2099–2103). IEEE. DOI: 10.1109/ICCES67310.2025.11336350

Mylrea, M., & Robinson, N. (2023). Artificial Intelligence (AI) trust framework and maturity model: Applying an entropy lens to improve security, privacy, and ethical AI. *Entropy (Basel, Switzerland)*, *25*(10), 1429. DOI: 10.3390/e25101429 PMID: 37895550

Osagie, E., & Balasundaram, R. (2026). Investigating Epistemic Uncertainty in PCB Defect Detection: A Comparative Study Using Monte Carlo Dropout. *Journal of Experimental and Theoretical Analyses*, *4*(1), 11. DOI: 10.3390/jeta4010011

Ouyang, L., Wu, J., Jiang, X., Almeida, D., Wainwright, C., Mishkin, P., Zhang, C., Agarwal, S., Slama, K., Ray, A., Schulman, J., Hilton, J., Kelton, F., Miller, L., Simens, M., Askell, A., Welinder, P., Christiano, P., Leike, J., & Lowe, R. (2022). Training language models to follow instructions with human feedback. *Advances in Neural Information Processing Systems*, *35*, 27730–27744. DOI: 10.52202/068431-2011

Rafailov, R., Sharma, A., Mitchell, E., Manning, C. D., Ermon, S., & Finn, C. (2023). Direct preference optimization: Your language model is secretly a reward model. *Advances in Neural Information Processing Systems*, *36*, 53728–53741. DOI: 10.52202/075280-2338

Rayhana, R., Bai, L., Xiao, G., Liao, M., & Liu, Z. (2024). Digital twin models: Functions, challenges, and industry applications. *IEEE Journal of Radio Frequency Identification*, *8*, 282–321. DOI: 10.1109/JRFID.2024.3387996

Razi, Q., Piyush, R., Chakrabarti, A., Singh, A., Hassija, V., & Chalapathi, G. S. S. (2025). Enhancing data privacy: A comprehensive survey of privacy-enabling technologies. *IEEE Access : Practical Innovations, Open Solutions*, *13*, 40354–40385. DOI: 10.1109/ACCESS.2025.3546618

Saeed, M. M., Saeed, R. A., Ali, E. S., Ahmed, Z. E., & Mokhtar, R. A. (2026). Privacy and Security Challenges of AI Integration in Industry 4.0 and 5.0. In *Computational Intelligence for Analysis of Trends in Industry 4.0 and 5.0* (pp. 353-372). Auerbach Publications.

Salah, A. A., Jamil, N., Sulaiman, H., Cangelosi, A., Alyasseri, Z. A. A., & Hosseini, E. (2026). Security, Privacy, and AI Integration in Educational Metaverse: A Comprehensive Review and Framework. *Journal of Educational Computing Research*, •••, 07356331261436249. DOI: 10.1177/07356331261436249

Shokri, R., Stronati, M., Song, C., & Shmatikov, V. (2017, May). Membership inference attacks against machine learning models. In *2017 IEEE symposium on security and privacy (SP)* (pp. 3-18). IEEE. DOI: 10.1109/SP.2017.41

Touvron, H., Lavril, T., Izacard, G., Martinet, X., Lachaux, M. A., Lacroix, T., . . . Lample, G. (2023). Llama: Open and efficient foundation language models. *arXiv preprint arXiv:2302.13971*.

Weidinger, L., Mellor, J., Rauh, M., Griffin, C., Uesato, J., Huang, P. S., . . . Gabriel, I. (2021). Ethical and social risks of harm from language models. *arXiv preprint arXiv:2112.04359.*

Zheng, Y., Chang, C. H., Huang, S. H., Chen, P. Y., & Picek, S. (2024). An overview of trustworthy AI: Advances in IP protection, privacy-preserving federated learning, security verification, and GAI safety alignment. *IEEE Journal on Emerging and Selected Topics in Circuits and Systems, 14*(4), 582–607. DOI: 10.1109/JETCAS.2024.3477348

Chapter 4
Cutting-Edge Prompt Engineering Methods and Tools

Pooja Dehankar
Ajeenkya D.Y. Patil School of Engineering, India

Susanta Das
http://orcid.org/0000-0002-9314-3988
Ajeenkya D.Y. Patil University, India

ABSTRACT

Advanced prompt engineering techniques are designed to guide LLMs towards producing more complex & reliable outputs by transcending basic input prompts. These methods encompass few-shot prompting, tree-of-thought prompting, chain-of-thought prompting, & self-consistency. They are crucial for optimizing application of LLMs in endeavors that necessitate reasoning, creativity, & problem-solving. Advanced prompt engineering strategies are essential to formulate prompts that inspire AI models to deliver more trustworthy, accurate, & innovative responses. The chapter explores sophisticated strategies & technologies for crafting engaging prompts enabling users to obtain precise & relevant outcomes from these models. We talk immediate optimization techniques, e.g., few-shot learning, fine-tuning, & chain-of-thought prompting. It also highlights key resources that foster development of prompt engineering skills, model-specific guidelines, community-driven platforms, & prompt libraries. By mastering these techniques & utilizing available resources, users can fully harness capabilities of LLMs.

DOI: 10.4018/979-8-2600-0368-8.ch004

1. INTRODUCTION

In order to effectively communicate the user's purpose to a language model like ChatGPT, prompt engineering entails the development, improvement, and optimization of input prompts. This procedure is essential to getting accurate, relevant, and understandable answers from the model. Proper quick engineering has emerged as a crucial ability for users hoping to fully utilize ChatGPT and attain the best outcomes in a wide range of applications as language models continue to develop (Ekin, 2023).

The textual input that users supply to direct the model's output is known as a prompt in generative AI models (Bandi et al., 2023). Simple inquiries, thorough explanations, or designated chores could all fall under this category (Josephson & Åge, 2024). While prompts in LLMs like GPT-4 or Gemini might range from straightforward queries to intricate problem statements, they are often descriptive in the context of image generating models like DALLE-3 (Campesato, 2024). Typically, prompts include questions, examples, input data, and instructions (Marvin et al., 2023). A prompt needs to have either questions or instructions to elicit a desired response from an AI model (Velásquez-Henao et al., 2023). In LLMs, basic prompts might be as straightforward as posing a direct query or offering guidance on a particular activity (Beurer-Kellner et al., 2023). More intricate prompts, such "chain of thoughts" prompting, require the model to follow a logical thinking process in order to arrive at a response (Miao et al., 2024).

Effective quick engineering is influenced by several essential components. By becoming proficient in these, you can interact with AI models and realize their full potential. System design, integration, and management are being transformed due to the emergence of AI and ML technology because they allow for optimized design processes, predictive maintenance, and efficient configuration management (Adeyeye & Akanbi, 2024). It is important to understand that how the information is organized in your prompt and what the tone of it is affects the way AI answers (Short & Short, 2023). Depending on the model, the different format types could prove to work best, from issuing commands, asking questions, to inputting structured data into designated fields (Sager, 1978). However, one should have sufficient knowledge about the capabilities of the system and its requirements to compose prompts effectively (Webson & Pavlick, 2022). The AI model will be able to understand the task better if it receives some context in the prompt together with relevant examples (Kulkarni & Tupsakhare, 2024). If you need an original story, using a couple of sentences describing what tone and topic you want will result in a much better response (Burroway et al., 2019). Furthermore, the quality of responses made by the model can be improved by tweaking prompts depending on feedback provided by the users or the responses given by the model (Liu et al., 2023). It is possible for the users to interact dynamically with the AI model by coming up with multiple turns in conversations (Areo, 2024).

Prompt engineering is one area that is likely to become more important due to the evolution of AI. Progress in machine learning and AI research has made rapid engineering more versatile and effective. An analysis of the future developments in prompt engineering, its significance, and the hurdles will help shed light on the subject matter. In the years ahead, prompt engineering is expected to play an essential role in the evolution of artificial intelligence systems. The efficiency of any system is dependent upon how well it interprets and responds to prompts. For instance, Google Assistant, Alexa, and Siri are examples of artificial intelligence virtual assistants that utilize prompt engineering to process users' queries and provide appropriate answers. With the increasing use of AI technology within industries such as health care, education, finance, and customer support, there is an increasing need for more sophisticated prompt engineering skills. AI technology is now responsible for performing more complicated functions, such as financial management, disease detection, education tailored to the individual, and customer support services. Prompt engineering plays a vital role because all these functions depend on the computer's understanding of the prompt given to it. As AI systems evolve to grasp more intricate and abstract instructions, prompt engineers will also assume a progressively vital role. They will need to not only devise these prompts but also enhance the capability of AI models to understand and respond to them. This will include integrating advancements in natural language processing and understanding, machine learning, and human-computer interaction (George et al., 2023).

2. ADVANCED PROMPT ENGINEERING

Using advanced techniques that extend beyond basic prompt design (McTear & Ashurkina, 2024), advanced prompt engineering facilitates a more nuanced influence and enhanced performance in large language models (LLMs). Other methods include Tree-of-Thoughts (ToT), Chain-of-Thoughts (CoT), Zero-shot, and Few-shot (Wang et al., 2025). Prompt engineering is the art and science of constructing prompts that direct LLMs toward desired outcomes (Mizrahi, 2024). A language model is instructed to accomplish a task without any specific examples in the prompt engineering method called "zero-shot prompting." or illustrations of the desired outcome (Chen et al., 2025). Rather, the model produces a reaction depending only on its trained knowledge and command of English (Hu et al., 2023a). Usually without providing examples of how the action should be carried out zero-shot prompts exactly specify the task to be completed (Kojima et al., 2022). Because it saves the time and work of producing samples or model fine-tuning on particular projects, this strategy is very effective (Bonaccorso, 2020). Frequently when a model can employ its prior, zero-shot prompting is employed for several purposes including text summarization, sentiment analysis, and question answering information needed to finish a project (Zhong et al., 2021). In the AI technique known as "few-shot prompting," a LLM is given a limited number of instances (also known as "shots") within the prompt to direct its response to a particular job (Reynolds & McDonell, 2021). Explanation-based fine-tuning, also known as explanation-augmented prompting (i.e., prompting with explanations to improve model calibration and reasoning), is the approach outlined by Ye & Durrett (2022). The question offers a few instances of requested input-output matches (Lee, 2024). Based on these samples, the model corrects its response, hence improving its performance on related tasks (Wang et al., 2020). Few-shot prompting is basically an application of in-context learning wherein the prompt itself serves as an educational tool (Li, 2023). Few-instance situations call for it as it lets models finish jobs using less training data (Liu et al., 2022). Large language models (LLMs) are encouraged to think sequentially under the prompt engineering technique known as "chain-of-thoughts" (CoT), therefore improving their performance on activities needing for reasoning, calculation, and decision-making (Debnath et al., 2025). First the model create a response then provides an explanation of the causes underlying it (Wei et al., 2022). CoT prompts help the model to follow a systematic reasoning process (Yu et al., 2023). Instructions such as "Let's think step by Often included to the user's question to achieve this are "By step" or "Describe your thinking in stages" (Ali & Feng, 2023). By breaking complex problems into manageable phases, the model can focus on one facet of the problem at a time and lowers the chance of errors (Yao et al., 2023). This technique helps LLMs particularly in tasks requiring for mathematics, common sense, and symbolic reasoning (Patil, 2025). CoT also helps consumers to grasp the model's logic, therefore allowing them to debug faults and develop a better knowledge of how the model produces its answers (Feng et al., 2023). Tree of Thoughts (ToT) is a framework generalizing over chain-of-thought urging encouraging exploration over concepts acting as intermediate stages for general problem solving. Yao et al. (2023) and Long (2023) suggested language models lately. ToT monitors a tree of ideas whereby thoughts replace logical linguistic patterns that serve as first stages in solving a problem (Dettmer, 2007). By means of middle ideas generated during a deliberate reasoning process, this technique lets an LLM evaluate their own growth (Ikuenobe, 2001). LLMs can be combined with search algorithms like Breadth-First Search (BFS) and Depth-First Search (DFS) to enable multi-step, structured reasoning that goes beyond token-by-token production. This paradigm, also known as the ToT or Graph of Thoughts (GoT), allows the model to investigate several lines of reasoning, anticipate possible results, and reverse course when a path turns out to be fruitless (Katz et al., 2024). Meta prompting is a sophisticated method that emphasizes the abstract, syntactic, and structural framework of tasks over content specifics. It enhances LLM reasoning, consistency, and token efficiency by developing "example-agnostic" templates that specify how to tackle an issue, such as describing logical processes or structuring output (Geroimenko, 2025). Meta prompting is a sophisticated AI prompting method that emphasizes the syntactical and structural elements of tasks, giving the overall structure and reasoning pattern precedence over content details. LLMs are taught how to think about a category of problems rather than just what to think, moving away from typical content-centric prodding (e.g., giving specific instances) and toward a more abstract, structured approach (Zhang et al., 2023). According to Zhang et al. (2024), the major characteristics of Meta prompting are adding more focus on the structure and flow of solutions and problems than particular knowledge; Uses syntax as a template for the expected response or solution; Uses abstract examples as structures to demonstrate how problems and solutions are organized without becoming bogged down in particulars; Capable of providing methodical solutions to a wide spectrum of problems, applicable in several sectors; Using type theory, emphasizes how prompt elements are categorized and rationally placed. In prompt engineering, prompt chaining involves dividing a difficult task into a string of simpler, connected queries (Sahoo et al., 2024). The language model is guided through a methodical process to achieve a goal by utilizing the output of one prompt as the input for another (Liu et al., 2023). This approach is very helpful for tasks that need a lot of logic or procedures (Vatsal & Dubey, 2024). Prompt chaining has advantages for language models since it can handle more complicated tasks that are sometimes hard to complete with a single, lengthy prompt (Wu et al., 2022). To increase your ability to make decisions and reason, break the issue down into smaller, more sensible chunks. Giving more specific instructions at every level helps to reduce mistakes (Yu et al., 2023). One way of managing difficult assignments is prompt chaining, which entails dividing events into more manageable subtasks (Alotaibi et al., 2024). Prompt Chaining is the technique by which a language model's response to one command serves as the input for the subsequent prompt in a sequence (Wang et al., 2022). The language model may grow on its earlier work since the output of one prompt gives the subsequent prompt context and information (Liu et al., 2023).

3. APPLICATIONS OF PROMPT ENGINEERING

One well-known and frequently carried out job in natural language processing is big document summarization for easier and faster reading. The ROUGE (Recall-Oriented Understudy for Gisting Evaluation) framework is frequently used to analyze Automatic Text Summarization or Machine Translation tasks utilizing statistics like n-grams and Longest Common Subsequence (LCS). Abstractive summarization is a kind of automatic text summarization wherein the summary is drawn from the core text devoid of complete duplication of any of the words used in the original. Abstract summarization's appeal has increased from the introduction of deep learning techniques. For abstractive text summarizing, large language models require appropriate prompts in order to provide a summary. Because the prompt determines the quality of the summary produced, it is crucial to design appropriate prompts (Chakraborty & Pakray, 2023).

The phrase "knowledge-based visual question answering" (VQA) refers to inquiries that require knowledge about the world outside of the image to offer the proper answer. Because of their excellent reasoning and knowledge retrieval abilities, LLMs such as GPT-3 are very beneficial for this objective. Previous work employs a captioning technique to convert images into language so that LM can comprehend imagery. However, it's common to understate which visual components to convey when describing an image in a single caption sentence. Important visual elements are often left out of generic image descriptions so that the LM can appropriately answer visual requests. PromptCap (Prompt-guided image captioning), a captioning model intended to act as a stronger link between images and black-box LMs, is proposed by the authors as a solution to this problem (Hu et al., 2023b).

The ubiquitous and pertinent business problem of information retrieval from textual data in PDF format—searching through legal texts, financial reports, research articles, and so forth—is addressed by a practical application that integrates recent developments in the field of Generative AI (GenAI), and more specifically LLMs. For instance, marketing research frequently necessitates sifting through hundreds of pages of financial data to locate vital information for studies on rivals, partners, markets, and new clients. For marketers, it is a labor-intensive, manual, and prone to errors process, with limited opportunities for automation, optimization, and scale until recently. To improve the efficiency of this procedure, our program blends LLMs with rapid engineering and a retrieval augmented generation (RAG) architecture The authors have created a chatbot that enables users to input numerous PDF documents, receive a summary of predetermined key regions, ask specific questions, and receive responses based on the content of the combined papers. The first step in the architecture of the application is to create an index for every PDF file. This index requires creating a vector storage and embedding the textual data. To generate the summary, a query engine employs a small-to-big retrieval technique to precisely answer a series of pre-formulated queries for every PDF. The prompt's design minimizes the possibility of hallucinations, which are typical in this kind of paradigm. A chatbot feature allows the user to communicate with the model. It offers a thorough and interactive tool for document analysis by using similar small-to-big retrieval techniques over the indices for simple queries and a more sophisticated sub-questions engine for in-depth research (Hikov & Murphy, 2024).

Enabling AI systems to carry out sophisticated multimodal reasoning in a manner akin to that of humans has long been a goal. LLMs have lately achieved impressive progress in multistep reasoning on the language modality by using the CoT to simulate human cognitive processes. Applying these advancements to multimodal scenarios, however, presents new challenges, including the impractical demand for laborious annotation and the limitations on explainability, generalizability, and adaptability. By first separating the reasoning responsibility of LLMs into reasoning and recognition and then integrating the visual recognition capability of visual models into the joint reasoning process, a novel DDCoT (Duty-Distinct Chain-of-Thoughts) prompting that integrates multimodality into reasoning while maintaining a critical attitude through negative-space prompting is proposed. The rationales generated by DDCoT not only significantly outperform state-of-the-art methods in zero-shot prompting and fine-tuning learning, but they also improve the reasoning abilities of both big and small language models. They also show remarkable generalizability and explainability (Zheng et al., 2023).

4. RESOURCES FOR LEARNING ADVANCED PROMPT ENGINEERING

An overview of prompt engineering and its uses is given in Google Cloud's Introduction to Prompt Design (Marvin et al., 2023; Ravulavaru, 2018; Srinivasan et al., 2018). The technical blog of Successive Digital provides thorough explanations of sophisticated fast engineering methods. Study up on Prompting's classes offers thorough fast engineering courses that incorporate cutting-edge methods and hands-on activities (Zhao, 2015; Murugesan et al., 2024; Heift, 2010). The document of Cohere explains the uses of sophisticated prompting strategies like CoT (Yu et al., 2023; Smith et al., 2016). GitHub's Prompt Engineering Guide is a thorough manual with a range of materials, such as tools, courses, and articles (Pornprasit & Tantithamthavorn, 2024; Obrien et al., 2024; Geroimenko, 2025).

A course on advanced prompt engineering approaches is available through Learn Prompting.

A comprehensive summary of the many quick engineering techniques is provided by the rapid engineering guide. Materials and insights on advanced rapid engineering are available on MLQ.ai. Google Cloud offers advice on quick design and tactics. For LLMs, Successive Digital looks into cutting-edge quick engineering techniques. Prompt engineering research articles are available on arXiv. Medium provides descriptions of the Chain-of-Thoughts and React approaches.

5. CASE STUDY

To ascertain if an English-speaking applicant is suitable for an entry-level or graduate role, case study examines job classification process in practical situation. Several text classification techniques, ranging from advanced deep learning techniques like DeBERTa to supervised techniques like Support Vector Machines (SVMs) is examined. The authors compare them to LLMs used in few-shot and zero-shot classification settings. In order to guide the LLMs toward the desired result, the authors employ a method known as quick engineering. The authors examine text-davinci-003 and gpt-3.5-turbo, two of the most advanced GPT-3.5-based language models currently in use. The authors look closely at how different prompt engineering components impact the functionality of the model. The results demonstrate that a zero-shot gpt-3.5-turboclassifier works better than any other model when given a well-designed prompt. Additionally, the authors note that even seemingly insignificant details of the question have a big impact on the model's performance and that the query's wording is crucial in getting the right "reasoning" out of the model (Clavié et al., 2023).

In the scenario of credit analysis for a bank, Few-Shot Prompting involves giving 3-5 examples of previous credit application scenarios that had been assessed by the bank, together with the conclusion reached (output) by the bank based on the assessment done. The Chain-of-Thought approach in finance involves asking the model to do calculations such as debt/equity ratio and net profit margin, then think step-by-step before making an investing recommendation (Yang et al., 2024; Fazlija et al., 2025; Arugula, 2025).

Few-shot CoT is useful for creating patient descriptions in clinical environments. The model is trained using samples of patients' unstructured complaints (input) and structured SOAP notes (Subjective, Objective, Assessment, and Plan – output). Multimodal CoT can be utilized in radiology. The prompt comprises a medical picture alongside some text, encouraging the AI to spot specific elements in the image prior to making a diagnosis (Nagoor, 2026; Pandya, 2026; Xu et al., 2025).

5.1 DAIR.AI/Prompt-Engineering-Guide (GitHub)

It has gained popularity due to its detailed, research-driven approach and can be considered as the go-to resource when it comes to prompt engineering in an academic context. It thoroughly covers the most recent research papers on the subject (for example, Chain-of-Thought, Tree of Thoughts), and helps users to translate AI theory into practice through prompts. The content aims to cover both the basics of prompting and implementation-related details when building an application with LLMs, RAG, and agents. This repository contains a wide variety of materials (lectures, guides, and other useful stuff) and is a good choice if you prefer in-depth learning (Geroimenko, 2025; Clarisó & Cabot, 2023; Yang et al., 2025).

5.2 Learn Prompting

Learn Prompting is one of the most complete and structured courses on prompt engineering, intended for beginner to intermediate users who can enjoy a very interactive learning experience. The course is structured as a curriculum, moving from basics (role definition, context, examples) to advanced application concepts. Concepts are always complemented with practical examples that make it possible to understand how you can apply certain techniques. This program puts an emphasis on collaboration; the active Discord community allows finding your "learning buddy" and discussing techniques. Topics that other programs often ignore such as prompting for images (DALL-E, Stable Diffusion) and even "prompt hacking" are included. Best for Beginners, non-technical professionals, and everyone looking for a community-based learning journey from basics to advanced concepts (Qian, 2025).

5.3 Meta Prompting: Crafting "Instructions for Instructions"

Meta Prompting refers to the use of an AI to generate, improve, or construct a prompt that is intended for a more intricate task than crafting it. In lieu of instructing a contractor "build a house," Meta-Prompting would be akin to giving an architectural blueprint, which details the exact process and safety requirements involved in constructing a house. The AI gives you an organized template. You will receive much better-quality output by following this template than when using the simple prompt. It creates a reusable model template. It eliminates ambiguities (Suzgun & Kalai, 2024).

5.4 DDCoT: Duty-Distinct Chain-of-Thoughts

DDCoT (Duty-Distinct Chain-of-Thoughts) is a method used for multimodal models (text and image) that tries to cut down hallucinations (inventing information) by decoupling the "recognition" and "reasoning" functions, allowing each function to perform their role effectively. Simple Analogy: Think about a detective analyzing a crime scene photograph (Recognition) while another person analyzes what the photograph tells him (Reasoning). DDCoT ensures that the detective does not misinterpret some dirt marks on the picture as weapons until he confirms the real situation (Zheng et al., 2023).

5.5 Chain of Thoughts (CoT) Quantitative Evidence

Through an intermediate step deconstruction process, CoT significantly improves performance on difficult reasoning tasks, including arithmetic, common sense, and symbolic reasoning. PaLM 540B with CoT prompting scored a remarkable increase from the standard prompting method. CoT prompting could enhance accuracy in multi-step reasoning tasks by up to 20-30% in comparison to standard prompting methods, based on the models used. The application of self-consistency in sampling and selecting the majority result in CoT increases accuracy. CoT exhibits considerable improvement in multilingual math reasoning tasks, for instance, boosting performance in the MGSM benchmark (Wei et al., 2022).

5.6 Quantitative Results for the Tree of Thoughts (ToT)

ToT performs exceptionally well in activities that involve searching, planning, and backtracking, including creative writing, gaming, and puzzle-solving. ToT shows superior ability in producing coherent and imaginative output within highly restrictive conditions, scoring higher in terms of coherence and quality than CoT. ToT employs BFS or DFS algorithms for examining several paths simultaneously, thereby boosting success rates in planning scenarios over CoT (Cheng et al., 2024).

6. KEY SKILLS REQUIRED TO BECOME A PROMPT ENGINEER

AI has the potential to completely transform almost every facet of human education. Users have noticed, however, that the quality of the instructions that AI assistants receive is a critical factor in determining how effective they are. A small change in language can mean the difference between an assistant misinterpreting a directive and going above and beyond. As important as the AI assistant it is the ability to accurately convey the core of an issue to it. In the twenty-first century, prompt engineering (PE) is a new skill that is crucial for both professional and personal learning and growth. PE is the ability to clearly communicate to an AI assistant a problem, its context, and the limitations of the intended solution to ensure a prompt and precise answer (Federiakin et al., 2024).

Comprehending AI, ML, and NLP is essential for using AI tools and grasping their language processing abilities (Chen et al., 2024). One must be expert in programming languages like Python in order to optimize code and fine-tune models. Understanding the strengths and weaknesses of various LLMs helps prompt engineers develop accurate prompts that generate desired answers. Creativity assists in forecasting the answers, generating organic conversations, and coming up with great ideas (Lazovsky et al., 2025). While using prompts suitable for multiple groups, ensure AI answers are effective and relevant (Ranade et al., 2025).

7. ETHICAL AND TRANSPARENCY CONSIDERATIONS

Prompt Engineering is crucial when it comes to developing an unbiased language model by making it factually grounded. Instead of being bugs, "hallucinations" come from LLMs' training on making their models coherent rather than factually consistent. The use of prompting may lead to more hallucinations if it makes the model more creative than accurate. Certain types of prompting such as CoT ("Chain of Thoughts") or "step-by-step reasoning" lead to outputting logical steps of reasoning by the model, which results in more accurate predictions and fewer "hallucinations". The use of prompting along with RAG while asking the model to only refer to the external data decreases the chance of fabricating facts. Stating the scope of the answer clearly ("Answer only based on the documents provided above") ensures that the model does not generate additional information and increases the reliability of decision-making in critical industries such as law, finance, and medicine (Rahman et al., 2026).

Prompt engineering can unknowingly perpetuate the Societal and Data-Driven biases present in LLMs. Stereotyping Amplification when poorly designed stimuli are used, such as gendered language or stereotyped scenarios, may cause the LLM to produce stereotypical output, for instance, associating leadership roles with men. Bias Testing through adversarial probing, utilizing "biased" or ethical prompts, will enable the identification of the LLM's shortcomings, facilitating re-engineering to formulate unbiased prompts. In ethical prompt generation, one should use non-stereotypical language, instruct the LLM not to perpetuate any negative stereotypes, and use few-shot prompting methods (Jeoung, 2025).

8. FUTURE DIRECTIONS

Prompt generation frameworks and techniques such as self-consistency, zero-shot, and chain-of-thought prompting will be analyzed in this section. In the future, prompt engineering techniques that could be employed by different industries ranging from health care to banking and education will produce user-friendly artificial intelligence experiences (Choi & Chang, 2025). Responsibility, transparency, and justice should be ensured when using AI-generated content (Chen et al., 2023). Gaining faith and confidence in AI models requires an understanding of their decision-making processes (Nicodeme, 2020).

Making prompt engineering processes accessible to a wider audience, including individuals without a thorough technical background (Korzynski et al., 2023), is necessary to encourage innovation and acceptance.

Prompting strategies in the future will be built around collaborative design between users and the models themselves. In contrast to just one prompt provided by the user, here we have an interaction process where the model generates suggestions about how to improve the prompt using its understanding of its architecture (Subramonyam et al., 2025).

Users will interact with the model to understand why the prompt was confusing and will iterate the prompt accordingly. The systems will employ a "conductor" strategy that will assign roles dynamically and optimize the prompt itself while the task is being performed. While AI will suggest ways to optimize the prompt, human supervision is vital for critical situations (Mishra et al., 2025).

The next stage of prompt engineering is the development of automated tools capable of evaluating, identifying bugs, and optimizing prompts in order to solve the problem of their "fragility." Automatic Prompt Optimization (APO) & Automatic Prompt Engineering (APE) technologies work like a "black box," which allows them to find out the most accurate prompt variation among thousands of others in the context of the task. Analogous to debugging software, the AI technology will be able to identify poorly working prompts, leading to hallucinations or inaccurate results, and fix them to increase precision. Automated prompt engineering technologies are developing from mere prompt modification to creating conditions for the entire context (memory, limitations, access to information), which helps improve AI results in real-time. The next-generation AI agent will learn from its errors by including a cause of an error in a subsequent prompt, thus following the "system prompt learning" concept (Syahputri et al., 2025).

9. CONCLUSION

One of the finest ways to engage with AI models and fully utilize their potential is through prompt engineering. Users can direct models to produce outputs that are more precise, pertinent, and influential by employing sophisticated strategies like Few-Shot Learning, ReAct, and Chain of Thought. Courses like Simplilearn's Applied Generative AI Specialization offer educational training that may be helpful to anyone looking to advance their knowledge and abilities in this field. Thanks to quick engineering, AI can generate insights from social media, survey data, and customer feedback.

It facilitates fast trend analysis and data-driven decision-making for enterprises. Similar to how robots have replaced manual labor, AI likely to replace repetitive and dull jobs. With AI, the position of software developer is changing significantly. Rather than writing code, the programmer will oversee artificially created code, and he or she will need to hone their intuition, creative thinking, and subject experience. The list of capabilities for contemporary engineers, which forms the foundation of Industry 4.0, must encompass all of these new abilities. AI will support software engineers rather than replace them. It should be mentioned that LLM is merely a top search engine or a superb autocomplete tool. A ground-breaking method for improving the caliber of AI text generation is prompt engineering. One approach to creating queries that assist the models in producing outputs that are more likely to be of high quality, and contextual relevance is the organized method of quick development. As quick engineering continues to progress in a variety of applications, semantic accuracy and context are expected to be crucial components in the revolution of artificially intelligent text synthesis. Researchers' and developers' discoveries are expected to propel AI forward. It is anticipated that well-crafted and bias-free prompts will improve the type and caliber of the writing generated, hence fortifying the researcher's bond with language. Thus, prompt engineering seems to open the door to a new form of human-language communication.

REFERENCES

Adeyeye, O. J., & Akanbi, I. (2024). Artificial intelligence for systems engineering complexity: A review on the use of AI and machine learning algorithms. *Computer Science & IT Research Journal, 5*(4), 787–808. DOI: 10.51594/csitrj.v5i4.1026

Ali, A., & Feng, Z. (2023). Layered Chain-of-Thought Prompting: A Step Towards More Transparent AI Models.

Alotaibi, F., Kulkarni, A., & Zhou, D. (2024, December). Graph of Logic: Enhancing LLM Reasoning with Graphs and Symbolic Logic. In *2024 IEEE International Conference on Big Data (BigData)* (pp. 5926-5935). IEEE. DOI: 10.1109/BigData62323.2024.10825450

Areo, G. (2024). Enhancing Multi-Turn Dialogue Systems: Context-Aware Data Engineering for Chatbots in Dynamic Environments.

Arugula, B. (2025). Prompt engineering for LLMs: Real-world applications in banking and ecommerce. *International Journal of Artificial Intelligence, Data Science, and Machine Learning, 6*(1), 115–123. DOI: 10.63282/3050-9262.IJAIDSML-V6I1P113

Bandi, A., Adapa, P. V. S. R., & Kuchi, Y. E. V. P. K. (2023). The power of generative ai: A review of requirements, models, input–output formats, evaluation metrics, and challenges. *Future Internet, 15*(8), 260. DOI: 10.3390/fi15080260

Beurer-Kellner, L., Fischer, M., & Vechev, M. (2023). Prompting is programming: A query language for large language models. *Proceedings of the ACM on Programming Languages, 7*(PLDI), 1946-1969. DOI: 10.1145/3591300

Bonaccorso, G. (2020). *Mastering Machine Learning Algorithms: Expert techniques for implementing popular machine learning algorithms, fine-tuning your models, and understanding how they work.* Packt Publishing Ltd.

Burroway, J., Stuckey-French, E., & Stuckey-French, N. (2019). *Writing fiction: A guide to narrative craft.* University of Chicago Press.

Campesato, O. (2024). *Large Language Models: An Introduction.* Walter de Gruyter GmbH & Co KG. DOI: 10.1515/9781501520587

Chakraborty, S., & Pakray, P. (2023, October). Abstractive summarization evaluation for prompt engineering. In *International Visual Informatics Conference* (pp. 629-640). Singapore: Springer Nature Singapore.

Chen, B., Zhang, Z., Langrené, N., & Zhu, S. (2025). Unleashing the potential of prompt engineering for large language models. *Patterns (New York, N.Y.)*, *6*(6), 101260. DOI: 10.1016/j.patter.2025.101260 PMID: 40575123

Chen, C., Fu, J., & Lyu, L. (2023). A pathway towards responsible ai generated content. *arXiv preprint arXiv:2303.01325.*

Chen, Y., Wang, H., Yu, K., & Zhou, R. (2024). Artificial intelligence methods in natural language processing: A comprehensive review. *Highlights in Science Engineering and Technology*, *85*, 545–550. DOI: 10.54097/vfwgas09

Cheng, Y., Zhang, C., Zhang, Z., Meng, X., Hong, S., Li, W., . . . He, X. (2024). Exploring large language model based intelligent agents: Definitions, methods, and prospects. *arXiv preprint arXiv:2401.03428.*

Choi, W. C., & Chang, C. I. (2025). A Survey of Techniques, Key Components, Strategies, Challenges, and Student Perspectives on Prompt Engineering for Large Language Models (LLMs) in Education.

Clarisó, R., & Cabot, J. (2023, October). Model-driven prompt engineering. In *2023 ACM/IEEE 26th International Conference on Model Driven Engineering Languages and Systems (MODELS)* (pp. 47-54). IEEE. DOI: 10.1109/MODELS58315.2023.00020

Clavié, B., Ciceu, A., Naylor, F., Soulié, G., & Brightwell, T. (2023, June). Large language models in the workplace: A case study on prompt engineering for job type classification. In *International conference on applications of natural language to information systems* (pp. 3-17). Cham: Springer Nature Switzerland. DOI: 10.1007/978-3-031-35320-8_1

Debnath, T., Siddiky, M. N. A., Rahman, M. E., Das, P., & Guha, A. K. (2025). A comprehensive survey of prompt engineering techniques in large language models. *TechRxiv.*

Dettmer, H. W. (2007). *The logical thinking process.* Quality Press.

Ekin, S. (2023). Prompt engineering for ChatGPT: a quick guide to techniques, tips, and best practices. *Authorea Preprints.*

Fazlija, B., Ibraimi, M., Forouzandeh, A., & Fazlija, A. (2025). Reasoning with financial regulatory texts via Large Language Models. *Journal of Behavioral and Experimental Finance*, *47*, 101067. DOI: 10.1016/j.jbef.2025.101067

Federiakin, D., Molerov, D., Zlatkin-Troitschanskaia, O., & Maur, A. (2024, November). Prompt engineering as a new 21st century skill. [). Frontiers Media SA.]. *Frontiers in Education, 9*, 1366434. DOI: 10.3389/feduc.2024.1366434

Feng, G., Zhang, B., Gu, Y., Ye, H., He, D., & Wang, L. (2023). Towards revealing the mystery behind chain of thought: A theoretical perspective. *Advances in Neural Information Processing Systems, 36*, 70757–70798. DOI: 10.52202/075280-3100

George, A. S., George, A. H., & Baskar, T. (2023). Exploring the potential of prompt engineering in India: A study on the future of AI-driven job market and the role of higher education. *Partners Universal Innovative Research Publication, 1*(2), 34–57.

Geroimenko, V. (2025). Key Techniques for Writing Effective Prompts. In *The Essential Guide to Prompt Engineering: Key Principles, Techniques, Challenges, and Security Risks* (pp. 37–83). Springer Nature Switzerland. DOI: 10.1007/978-3-031-86206-9_3

Heift, T. (2010). Prompting in CALL: A longitudinal study of learner uptake. *Modern Language Journal, 94*(2), 198–216. DOI: 10.1111/j.1540-4781.2010.01017.x

Hikov, A., & Murphy, L. (2024). Information retrieval from textual data: Harnessing large language models, retrieval augmented generation and prompt engineering. *Journal of AI. Robotics & Workplace Automation, 3*(2), 142–150. DOI: 10.69554/QAFE6376

Hu, L., Liu, Z., Zhao, Z., Hou, L., Nie, L., & Li, J. (2023a). A survey of knowledge enhanced pre-trained language models. *IEEE Transactions on Knowledge and Data Engineering, 36*(4), 1413–1430. DOI: 10.1109/TKDE.2023.3310002

Hu, Y., Hua, H., Yang, Z., Shi, W., Smith, N. A., & Luo, J. (2023b). Promptcap: Prompt-guided image captioning for vqa with gpt-3. In *Proceedings of the IEEE/CVF International Conference on Computer Vision* (pp. 2963-2975). DOI: 10.1109/ICCV51070.2023.00277

Ikuenobe, P. (2001). Teaching and assessing critical thinking abilities as outcomes in an informal logic course. *Teaching in Higher Education, 6*(1), 19–32. DOI: 10.1080/13562510020029572

Jeoung, S. (2025). *Examining large language models for safety and robustness through the lens of social science* (Doctoral dissertation).

Josephson, A., & Åge, E. (2024). Prompting Out Of Manual Routines: How implementation of generative AI change work routines of knowledge workers.

Katz, M., Kokel, H., Srinivas, K., & Sohrabi Araghi, S. (2024). Thought of search: Planning with language models through the lens of efficiency. *Advances in Neural Information Processing Systems, 37*, 138491–138568. DOI: 10.52202/079017-4395

Kojima, T., Gu, S. S., Reid, M., Matsuo, Y., & Iwasawa, Y. (2022). Large language models are zero-shot reasoners. *Advances in Neural Information Processing Systems, 35*, 22199–22213. DOI: 10.52202/068431-1613

Korzynski, P., Mazurek, G., Krzypkowska, P., & Kurasinski, A. (2023). Artificial intelligence prompt engineering as a new digital competence: Analysis of generative AI technologies such as ChatGPT. *Entrepreneurial Business and Economics Review, 11*(3), 25–37. DOI: 10.15678/EBER.2023.110302

Kulkarni, N. D., & Tupsakhare, P. (2024). Crafting effective prompts: enhancing ai performance through structured input design. *Journal of recent trends in computer science and engineering (JRTCSE), 12*(5), 1-10.

Lazovsky, S. G., Raz, T., & Kenett, Y. N. (2025). The art of creative inquiry—From question asking to prompt engineering. *The Journal of Creative Behavior, 59*(1), e671. DOI: 10.1002/jocb.671

Lee, A. V. Y., Teo, C. L., & Tan, S. C. (2024). Prompt Engineering for Knowledge Creation: Using Chain-of-Thought to Support Students' Improvable Ideas. *AI, 5*(3), 1446–1461. DOI: 10.3390/ai5030069

Li, Y. (2023). A practical survey on zero-shot prompt design for in-context learning. *arXiv preprint arXiv:2309.13205*. DOI: 10.26615/978-954-452-092-2_069

Liu, H., Tam, D., Muqeeth, M., Mohta, J., Huang, T., Bansal, M., & Raffel, C. A. (2022). Few-shot parameter-efficient fine-tuning is better and cheaper than in-context learning. *Advances in Neural Information Processing Systems, 35*, 1950–1965. DOI: 10.52202/068431-0142

Liu, P., Yuan, W., Fu, J., Jiang, Z., Hayashi, H., & Neubig, G. (2023). Pre-train, prompt, and predict: A systematic survey of prompting methods in natural language processing. *ACM Computing Surveys, 55*(9), 1–35. DOI: 10.1145/3560815

Marvin, G., Hellen, N., Jjingo, D., & Nakatumba-Nabende, J. (2023, June). Prompt engineering in large language models. In *International conference on data intelligence and cognitive informatics* (pp. 387-402). Singapore: Springer Nature Singapore.

McTear, M., & Ashurkina, M. (2024). Advanced Prompt Engineering. In *Transforming Conversational AI: Exploring the Power of Large Language Models in Interactive Conversational Agents* (pp. 115–144). Apress. DOI: 10.1007/979-8-8688-0110-5_6

Miao, J., Thongprayoon, C., Suppadungsuk, S., Krisanapan, P., Radhakrishnan, Y., & Cheungpasitporn, W. (2024). Chain of thought utilization in large language models and application in nephrology. *Medicina (Kaunas, Lithuania), 60*(1), 148. DOI: 10.3390/medicina60010148 PMID: 38256408

Mishra, A., Danzy, B., Soni, U., Arunkumar, A., Huang, J., Kwon, B. C., & Bryan, C. (2025). PromptAid: Visual prompt exploration, perturbation, testing and iteration for large language models. *IEEE Transactions on Visualization and Computer Graphics, 31*(10), 6946–6962. DOI: 10.1109/TVCG.2025.3535332 PMID: 40031291

Mizrahi, G. (2024). *Unlocking the secrets of prompt engineering: Master the art of creative language generation to accelerate your journey from novice to pro*. Packt Publishing Ltd.

Murugesan, B., Hussain, R., Bhattacharya, R., Ben Ayed, I., & Dolz, J. (2024). Prompting classes: exploring the power of prompt class learning in weakly supervised semantic segmentation. In *Proceedings of the IEEE/CVF Winter Conference on Applications of Computer Vision* (pp. 291-302). DOI: 10.1109/WACV57701.2024.00036

Nagoor, S. H. (2026). *Clinical Sentiment Classification on Intensive Care Unit Clinical Notes* (Doctoral dissertation, TRINITY COLLEGE).

Nicodeme, C. (2020, June). Build confidence and acceptance of AI-based decision support systems-Explainable and liable AI. In *2020 13th international conference on human system interaction (HSI)* (pp. 20-23). IEEE. DOI: 10.1109/HSI49210.2020.9142668

OBrien., D., Biswas, S., Imtiaz, S. M., Abdalkareem, R., Shihab, E., & Rajan, H. (2024, April). Are prompt engineering and todo comments friends or foes? an evaluation on github copilot. In *Proceedings of the IEEE/ACM 46th International Conference on Software Engineering* (pp. 1-13).

Pandya, S. (2026). *From Transcription to Intelligence: Applying Large Language Models to Healthcare Enterprise Decision Support Systems*. Geh press.

Patil, A. (2025). Advancing Reasoning in Large Language Models: Promising Methods and Approaches. *arXiv preprint arXiv:2502.03671*.

Pornprasit, C., & Tantithamthavorn, C. (2024). Fine-tuning and prompt engineering for large language models-based code review automation. *Information and Software Technology, 175*, 107523. DOI: 10.1016/j.infsof.2024.107523

Qian, Y. (2025). Prompt engineering in education: A systematic review of approaches and educational applications. *Journal of Educational Computing Research, 63*(7-8), 1782–1818. DOI: 10.1177/07356331251365189

Rahman, S. S., Islam, M. A., Alam, M. M., Zeba, M., Rahman, M. A., Chowa, S. S., Raiaan, M. A. K., & Azam, S. (2026). Hallucination to truth: A review of fact-checking and factuality evaluation in large language models. *Artificial Intelligence Review*, *59*(2), 70. DOI: 10.1007/s10462-025-11454-w

Ranade, N., Saravia, M., & Johri, A. (2025). Using rhetorical strategies to design prompts: A human-in-the-loop approach to make AI useful. *AI & Society*, *40*(2), 711–732. DOI: 10.1007/s00146-024-01905-3

Ravulavaru, A. (2018). *Google Cloud AI Services Quick Start Guide: Build Intelligent Applications with Google Cloud AI Services*. Packt Publishing Ltd.

Reynolds, L., & McDonell, K. (2021, May). Prompt programming for large language models: Beyond the few-shot paradigm. In *Extended abstracts of the 2021 CHI conference on human factors in computing systems* (pp. 1-7).

Sager, N. (1978). Natural language information formatting: The automatic conversion of texts to a structured data base. [). Elsevier.]. *Advances in Computers*, *17*, 89–162. DOI: 10.1016/S0065-2458(08)60391-5

Sahoo, P., Singh, A. K., Saha, S., Jain, V., Mondal, S., & Chadha, A. (2024). A systematic survey of prompt engineering in large language models: Techniques and applications. *arXiv preprint arXiv:2402.07927*.

Short, C. E., & Short, J. C. (2023). The artificially intelligent entrepreneur: ChatGPT, prompt engineering, and entrepreneurial rhetoric creation. *Journal of Business Venturing Insights*, *19*, e00388. DOI: 10.1016/j.jbvi.2023.e00388

Smith, K. S., Aziz, W., & Specia, L. (2016, May). Cohere: A toolkit for local coherence. In *Proceedings of the Tenth International Conference on Language Resources and Evaluation (LREC'16)* (pp. 4111-4114). DOI: 10.63317/4dxkavwdfm5d

Srinivasan, V., Ravi, J., & Raj, J. (2018). *Google Cloud Platform for Architects: Design and manage powerful cloud solutions*. Packt Publishing Ltd.

Subramonyam, H., Thakkar, D., Ku, A., Dieber, J., & Sinha, A. K. (2025, April). Prototyping with prompts: Emerging approaches and challenges in generative ai design for collaborative software teams. In *Proceedings of the 2025 CHI Conference on Human Factors in Computing Systems* (pp. 1-22). DOI: 10.1145/3706598.3713166

Suzgun, M., & Kalai, A. T. (2024). Meta-prompting: Enhancing language models with task-agnostic scaffolding. *arXiv preprint arXiv:2401.12954*.

Syahputri, I. W., Budiardjo, E. K., & Putra, P. O. H. (2025). Unlocking the Potential of the Prompt Engineering Paradigm in Software Engineering: A Systematic Literature Review. *AI*, *6*(9), 206. DOI: 10.3390/ai6090206

Vatsal, S., & Dubey, H. (2024). A survey of prompt engineering methods in large language models for different nlp tasks. *arXiv preprint arXiv:2407.12994*.

Velásquez-Henao, J. D., Franco-Cardona, C. J., & Cadavid-Higuita, L. (2023). Prompt Engineering: a methodology for optimizing interactions with AI-Language Models in the field of engineering. *Dyna, 90*(SPE230), 9-17.

Wang, B., Deng, X., & Sun, H. (2022). Iteratively prompt pre-trained language models for chain of thought. *arXiv preprint arXiv:2203.08383*. DOI: 10.18653/v1/2022.emnlp-main.174

Wang, Y., Wu, S., Zhang, Y., Yan, S., Liu, Z., Luo, J., & Fei, H. (2025). Multimodal chain-of-thought reasoning: A comprehensive survey. *arXiv preprint arXiv:2503.12605*.

Wang, Y., Yao, Q., Kwok, J. T., & Ni, L. M. (2020). Generalizing from a few examples: A survey on few-shot learning. [csur]. *ACM Computing Surveys*, *53*(3), 1–34. DOI: 10.1145/3386252

Webson, A., & Pavlick, E. (2022, July). Do prompt-based models really understand the meaning of their prompts? In *Proceedings of the 2022 Conference of the North American Chapter of the Association for Computational Linguistics: Human Language Technologies* (pp. 2300-2344). DOI: 10.18653/v1/2022.naacl-main.167

Wei, J., Wang, X., Schuurmans, D., Bosma, M., Xia, F., Chi, E., Le, Q. V., & Zhou, D. (2022). Chain-of-thought prompting elicits reasoning in large language models. *Advances in Neural Information Processing Systems*, *35*, 24824–24837. DOI: 10.52202/068431-1800

Wu, T., Jiang, E., Donsbach, A., Gray, J., Molina, A., Terry, M., & Cai, C. J. (2022, April). Promptchainer: Chaining large language model prompts through visual programming. In *CHI Conference on Human Factors in Computing Systems Extended Abstracts* (pp. 1-10). DOI: 10.1145/3491101.3519729

Xu, G., Li, X., Chen, Y., Duan, Y., Wu, S., Yu, A., & Shi, Y. (2025). A Comprehensive Survey of Agentic AI in Healthcare. *Authorea Preprints*. DOI: 10.36227/techrxiv.176240542.22279040/v1

Yang, C., Li, Z., & Wipf, D. (2025). Chain-of-thought provably enables learning the (otherwise) unlearnable. In *The Thirteenth International Conference on Learning Representations*.

Yang, C., Xu, C., & Qi, Y. (2024). Financial knowledge large language model. *arXiv preprint arXiv:2407.00365*.

Yao, S., Yu, D., Zhao, J., Shafran, I., Griffiths, T., Cao, Y., & Narasimhan, K. (2023). Tree of thoughts: Deliberate problem solving with large language models. *Advances in Neural Information Processing Systems, 36*, 11809–11822. DOI: 10.52202/075280-0517

Ye, X., & Durrett, G. (2022). The unreliability of explanations in few-shot prompting for textual reasoning. *Advances in Neural Information Processing Systems, 35*, 30378–30392. DOI: 10.52202/068431-2202

Yu, Z., He, L., Wu, Z., Dai, X., & Chen, J. (2023). Towards better chain-of-thought prompting strategies: A survey. *arXiv preprint arXiv:2310.04959*.

Zhang, Y., Yuan, Y., & Yao, A. C. C. (2023). Meta prompting for ai systems. *arXiv preprint arXiv:2311.11482*.

Zhao, W. (2015, March). *Enriching engineering curricula with a course on cutting-edge computer technologies. In 2015 IEEE Integrated STEM Education Conference*. IEEE.

Zheng, G., Yang, B., Tang, J., Zhou, H. Y., & Yang, S. (2023). Ddcot: Duty-distinct chain-of-thought prompting for multimodal reasoning in language models. *Advances in Neural Information Processing Systems, 36*, 5168–5191. DOI: 10.52202/075280-0228

Zhong, R., Lee, K., Zhang, Z., & Klein, D. (2021). Adapting language models for zero-shot learning by meta-tuning on dataset and prompt collections. *arXiv preprint arXiv:2104.04670*. DOI: 10.18653/v1/2021.findings-emnlp.244

ADDITIONAL READINGS

Lu, Y. E., & Lee, S. J. (2024, October). Prompt Optimization with Human Annotations Using Pairwise Comparison. In *2024 IEEE International Conference on e-Business Engineering (ICEBE)* (pp. 15-22). IEEE.

https://cloud.google.com/discover/what-is-prompt-engineering?hl=en

https://learnprompting.org/docs/intermediate/chain_of_thought

https://www.superannotate.com/blog/llm-fine-tuning#:~:text=Large%20language%20model%20(LLM)%20fine%2Dtuning%20is%20the,models%20and%20turning%20them%20into%20specialized%20models.

https://kata.ai/blog/few-shot-prompting-definition-usage-and-example/#:~:text=Few%20Shot%20Prompting%20:%20Definition%2C%20Usage%20and,small%20number%20of%20examples%20before%20generating%20responses.

https://www.ibm.com/think/topics/chain-of-thoughts#:~:text=Chain%20of%20thought%20(CoT)%20is,coherent%20series%20of%20logical%20steps.

https://www.prompthub.us/blog/the-few-shot-prompting-guide#:~:text=Few%20shot%20prompting%20is%20a,a%20small%20amount%20of%20data.

https://aws.amazon.com/what-is/prompt-engineering/#:~:text=Prompt%20engineering%20is%20the%20process,high%2Dquality%20and%20relevant%20output.

https://flyaps.com/blog/prompt-engineering-things-you-must-know-to-gain-maximum-value-from-gen-ai-tools/#:~:text=As%20with%20any%20generative%20AI%20solutions%2C%20we,guide%20the%20model%20towards%20the%20desired%20output.

https://blogs.xpheno.com/prompt-engineering-in-high-demand-reasons-and-scope/#:~:text=and%20contextually%20appropriate.-,The%20Growing%20Demand%20for%20Prompt%20Engineering,and%20industries%20across%20the%20globe.

KEY TERMS AND DEFINITIONS

AI: Artificial Intelligence.
APE: Automatic Prompt Engineering.
APO: Automatic Prompt Optimization.
BFS: Breadth-First Search.
CoT: Chain of Thoughts.
DDCoT: Duty-Distinct Chain-of-Thoughts.
DFS: Depth-First Search.
GoT: Graph of Thoughts.
LCS: Longest Common Subsequence.
LLM: Large Language Model.
ML: Machine Learning.
NLP: Natural Language Processing.
RAG: Retrieval Augmented Generation.
ROUGE: Recall-Oriented Understudy for Gisting Evaluation.
SVM: Support Vector Model.
ToT: Tree of Thoughts.

VQA: Visual Question Answering.

Chain-of-thought: Chain-of-thought (CoT) prompting guides LLMs to generate step-by-step reasoning before arriving at a final answer. This technique enhances LLMs' ability to tackle complex tasks requiring logic, calculation, and decision-making by mimicking human reasoning.

Few-shot learning: Few-shot learning provides a small number of examples within the prompt to guide the LLM in generating outputs. It allows LLMs to learn and generalize from limited data, making it an effective technique for tasks where extensive training data is scarce.

Fine-tuning: Fine-tuning involves further training pre-trained LLMs on specific datasets to enhance performance in particular tasks or domains. It specializes in LLMs by modifying their parameters for improved accuracy and efficiency in specific areas.

Prompt engineering: Prompt engineering is the process of crafting effective prompts to guide LLM output without altering the model's parameters. It enables LLMs to adapt to diverse tasks and domains by providing specific instructions.

Zero-shot prompting: Zero-shot prompting is a technique in natural language processing where a language model (LLM) is asked to complete a task without any prior training or examples specific to that task. Instead, it relies on the LLM's broad pre-trained knowledge and understanding of language to generate a response based on the prompt.

Chapter 5
Toward a Unified Framework for AI Creation Systems Integrating Agency and Governance

Ilham Firmansyah
http://orcid.org/0009-0007-6104-9966
Universitas Esa Unggul, Indonesia

ABSTRACT

Artificial intelligence has evolved from predictive systems to increasingly generative and agentic architectures capable of producing multimodal content and engaging in iterative reasoning processes. Despite rapid advancements, research on generative modeling, agentic system design, and AI governance remains conceptually fragmented. This chapter proposes a unified theoretical framework that integrates generative expressivity, agentic orchestration, and lifecycle governance into a structured tri-layer architecture. The framework conceptualizes AI creation systems as socio-technical infrastructures in which probabilistic modeling defines expressive capacity, procedural agency structures multi-step reasoning, and embedded governance mechanisms ensure accountability and alignment across lifecycle stages. By articulating interdependencies across these layers, the chapter advances a coherent foundation for responsible and sustainable AI creation science, offering implications for engineering practice, evaluation methodologies, and policy development.

DOI: 10.4018/979-8-2600-0368-8.ch005

1. INTRODUCTION

Artificial intelligence has rapidly evolved from predictive systems into generative and increasingly agentic models capable of producing text, images, code, and multimodal outputs at scale. Advances in transformer architectures, diffusion models, and large-scale self-supervised training have expanded AI's expressive capacity, enabling systems not only to analyze data but also to synthesize new artifacts (Wattanachote et al., 2026). This shift marks a transition from analytical computation to creative generation.

Recent developments have further extended AI capabilities through memory mechanisms, tool use, planning loops, and iterative feedback processes. These features allow AI systems to function as structured agents rather than single-pass generators, transforming output production into multi-step, context-aware workflows (Siriborvornratanakul & Rittikulsittichai, 2026). As a result, AI systems increasingly operate as process-oriented creators embedded in dynamic environments.

Despite these advances, the conceptual foundations of AI creation systems remain fragmented. Research on generative modeling typically emphasizes probabilistic expressivity and scaling behavior, while agentic systems research focuses on reasoning and interaction. Governance scholarship, meanwhile, addresses alignment, safety, accountability, and lifecycle oversight. Because these domains are often treated separately, theoretical coherence and cross-disciplinary integration remain limited (Fatima et al., 2026).

This fragmentation creates important challenges. Systems optimized for generative capability without sufficient integration of agency and governance may become powerful yet difficult to control or hold accountable. Conversely, governance frameworks developed without architectural grounding may remain external to system design rather than embedded within it (Prabhu & Sunitha, 2026). As AI systems are increasingly deployed in high-stakes contexts, conceptual integration becomes necessary.

This chapter therefore proposes a unified theoretical framework for AI creation systems built on three interdependent dimensions: generative modeling, agency, and lifecycle governance. Generative modeling provides the representational foundation for synthesis, agency structures iterative and tool-grounded processes, and lifecycle governance embeds alignment, accountability, and oversight across training, deployment, and monitoring. By integrating these dimensions, the chapter clarifies the transition from isolated generation to accountable creation and develops a framework that bridges scientific foundations, system design, and governance practice.

2. CONCEPTUAL FRAGMENTATION IN AI CREATION SYSTEMS

The rapid growth of AI creation systems has been accompanied by substantial theoretical fragmentation. Generative models, agentic architectures, and governance frameworks have each developed into sophisticated research domains, yet they often evolve in relative isolation. As a result, the field lacks an integrated conceptual structure for explaining how modeling capacity, agentic process, and lifecycle accountability interact within a unified system (Hamamoto et al., 2026).

One major source of fragmentation lies in the divide between generative modeling research and system-level design. Foundational machine learning work typically focuses on probabilistic modeling, representation learning, scaling behavior, and optimization efficiency, with performance measured through metrics such as benchmark accuracy, perplexity, or FID scores (Dai et al., 2026). Within this view, models are primarily treated as statistical function approximators optimized over large datasets.

However, this perspective does not fully capture the operational reality of contemporary AI creation systems. In practice, deployed systems frequently integrate retrieval pipelines, external tools, structured prompting, memory buffers, and human-in-the-loop feedback. These components transform static generative models into dynamic systems capable of iterative reasoning and interaction (Al-Hashimi, 2026). Yet such system-level complexities are often absent from theoretical treatments of generative modeling.

A second source of fragmentation appears between generation and agency. Generative models are usually framed as producing outputs through single forward passes conditioned on prompts, whereas agentic systems operate through multi-step loops involving planning, tool invocation, reflection, and revision (Xia, 2026). Although agentic approaches are widely discussed in applied engineering, they are less often incorporated into foundational theoretical analyses. This makes it difficult to explain how generative capacity enables or limits agentic reasoning.

A third source of fragmentation concerns governance. Research on alignment, safety, bias mitigation, transparency, and accountability often adopts legal, ethical, or policy-oriented perspectives (Marpaung, 2026). While these are essential, governance is frequently treated as an external regulatory overlay rather than an intrinsic component of system architecture. This separation reinforces a divide between capability development and responsible deployment.

These divisions have both practical and theoretical consequences. In practice, development efforts may prioritize performance and scale while neglecting alignment and monitoring. In theory, the absence of cross-layer integration limits cumulative understanding. Questions such as how model expressivity affects agentic reliability, how governance reshapes architecture, or how accountability should be embedded in iterative generation remain insufficiently addressed.

Fragmentation also extends to terminology. Concepts such as generation, creation, agency, alignment, and control are often used inconsistently across disciplines. Without clearer definitions, interdisciplinary dialogue becomes more difficult and conceptual ambiguity persists (Qian et al., 2026).

As AI creation systems become more autonomous and widely deployed in education, research, media, and decision support, the urgency of resolving this fragmentation increases. Their outputs are shaped not only by statistical inference, but also by memory persistence, tool-grounded reasoning, feedback adaptation, and institutional oversight. Treating these dimensions separately obscures their interdependence.

Addressing this problem requires moving beyond siloed analysis toward integrative theorization. Rather than examining generative modeling, agency, and governance as separate streams, a unified framework should clarify their structural relationships. Generative modeling defines representational capacity, agency structures procedural logic, and governance embeds constraints, monitoring, and accountability across the lifecycle of operation. Together, these dimensions form the basis for a coherent and accountable conception of AI creation systems.

3. FOUNDATIONS OF GENERATIVE MODELING

Generative modeling constitutes the probabilistic and representational foundation of AI creation systems. At its core, a generative model seeks to learn the underlying data distribution of a target domain in order to produce new samples that are statistically coherent with observed data. Unlike discriminative models, which estimate conditional relationships for classification or prediction, generative models approximate the joint or conditional probability distribution of data, enabling synthesis rather than mere categorization (Hardie et al., 2026).

3.1 Probabilistic Representation and Data Distributions

Formally, generative modeling involves learning a function that approximates the probability distribution $p(x)$ or the conditional distribution $p(x \mid c)$, where x represents data samples and c represents conditioning variables such as prompts or contextual signals. By learning these distributions from large-scale datasets, models are able to generate novel outputs that reflect structural and semantic patterns present in training data.

In high-dimensional domains such as natural language and image generation, direct modeling of full distributions is computationally intractable. Modern architectures address this challenge through parameterized neural networks that implicitly encode statistical regularities. The capacity of these models to generate coherent outputs depends on the richness of learned representations, dataset diversity, and optimization strategies (Li et al., 2026).

This probabilistic framing establishes a key principle: generative systems do not create ex nihilo; they synthesize outputs through structured recombination of learned representations. Creation, in this sense, is grounded in statistical inference over learned latent spaces.

3.2 Transformer Architectures and Autoregressive Modeling

The emergence of transformer architectures marked a significant inflection point in generative AI. Transformers utilize self-attention mechanisms that allow models to dynamically weigh contextual relationships across tokens within a sequence. This architecture enables scalable parallel training while preserving long-range dependencies (Xu & Xiong, 2026).

Autoregressive transformers model sequences by predicting the next token conditioned on preceding tokens. Through iterative token prediction, these systems generate coherent text, code, or symbolic sequences. Scaling laws have demonstrated that performance often improves predictably with increases in model parameters, dataset size, and compute resources (Adam et al., 2026). Such findings suggest that generative capability is not solely a function of architectural novelty but also of scale.

However, autoregressive generation is inherently sequential and locally conditioned. While powerful for surface-level coherence, it does not inherently guarantee global consistency, long-horizon reasoning, or task-level intentionality. These limitations highlight the boundary between generation as probabilistic continuation and creation as structured problem-solving.

3.3 Diffusion and Flow-Based Models

Beyond autoregressive approaches, diffusion and flow-based models have expanded generative modeling into high-fidelity image, audio, and multimodal synthesis. Diffusion models operate by gradually adding noise to data during training and learning to reverse this noise process during generation (Wang et al., 2026). This iterative denoising procedure allows models to generate detailed and high-quality outputs by approximating complex data manifolds.

Flow-based models, in contrast, construct invertible transformations between simple latent distributions and target data distributions. These models enable exact likelihood computation and structured sampling, offering theoretical advantages in interpretability and probabilistic consistency (Sun et al., 2026).

The development of these architectures demonstrates that generative modeling is not a monolithic paradigm but a family of approaches aimed at learning expressive latent representations. Despite architectural differences, they share a central objective: approximating high-dimensional probability structures to enable synthesis.

3.4 Scaling Laws, Emergence, and Expressivity

One of the most influential empirical observations in modern generative AI is the existence of scaling laws. Empirical research has shown that model performance often follows predictable power-law relationships as a function of parameter count, dataset size, and compute budget (Cimino et al., 2026). This phenomenon suggests that capability improvements can be achieved through systematic scaling rather than purely architectural innovation.

Scaling has also been associated with emergent behaviors capabilities that appear abruptly beyond certain parameter thresholds, such as few-shot learning, in-context adaptation, or chain-of-thought reasoning (Zhu et al., 2026). While these behaviors remain subjects of theoretical debate, they illustrate that generative capacity is not strictly linear with respect to size.

From a theoretical standpoint, expressivity refers to a model's capacity to represent complex functional mappings. High expressivity enables nuanced language modeling and realistic image generation, but it may also increase unpredictability and difficulty in calibration. As generative systems grow in scale, understanding the trade-offs between expressivity, robustness, and controllability becomes increasingly important.

3.5 Limitations of Generation-Only Paradigms

Despite their impressive capabilities, generative models operating in isolation exhibit structural limitations. First, probabilistic token prediction does not inherently guarantee factual accuracy or external grounding. Models may produce fluent but inaccurate outputs when operating without retrieval or verification mechanisms (Atkinson, 2026).

Second, generative systems trained through next-token prediction lack explicit representations of goals or planning structures. They generate locally coherent continuations rather than globally optimized solutions. This distinction underscores the conceptual difference between stochastic sequence modeling and intentional problem-solving.

Third, generative models are sensitive to training data biases and distribution shifts. Since synthesis is conditioned on learned statistical patterns, outputs may reflect embedded biases, spurious correlations, or outdated information (Brezovec et al., 2026). Without additional alignment or governance layers, generative capacity alone cannot ensure reliability or accountability.

These limitations suggest that generative modeling, while foundational, is insufficient as a standalone framework for understanding AI creation systems. To move from probabilistic generation to structured creation, additional architectural dimensions are required.

3.6 Generative Modeling as Foundational but Incomplete

Generative modeling provides the representational substrate upon which AI creation systems operate. It defines what the system can statistically express and synthesize. However, expressive capacity does not equate to agency, intentionality, or accountability. Without structured processes guiding how generation unfolds across time and tasks, generative systems remain reactive rather than goal-directed.

Recognizing generative modeling as foundational but incomplete establishes the transition point for the next section. The integration of memory, planning, and tool-use mechanisms introduces a new structural dimension agency that transforms generation into iterative, context-aware creation.

4. FORMALIZING AGENCY IN AI CREATION SYSTEMS

While generative modeling defines the statistical foundation of synthesis, contemporary AI creation systems increasingly operate beyond single-pass generation. The integration of memory, tool-use, planning mechanisms, and iterative feedback loops introduces a structural shift from reactive token prediction to process-oriented behavior. This shift is commonly described under the notion of agency, although the term is often used informally and inconsistently (Zhu et al., 2026). A theoretical clarification of agency is therefore necessary.

4.1 From Generation to Process-Oriented Creation

Traditional generative models produce outputs through probabilistic continuation conditioned on prompts. In this paradigm, the model performs inference once per output sequence, without persistent state or structured planning. Although such models can generate coherent content, they lack explicit mechanisms for long-horizon reasoning, environment interaction, or self-correction (Sun et al., 2026).

Agentic systems extend this paradigm by embedding generative models within structured loops. Instead of producing a final output in a single pass, the system iteratively generates intermediate representations, evaluates them, retrieves additional information if necessary, and refines its output. This transformation shifts the conceptual framing from static generation to dynamic creation.

Process-oriented creation emphasizes workflow over output. The system is not merely a stochastic function approximator but an iterative problem-solving entity operating across multiple steps. This perspective reframes AI creation systems as procedural architectures rather than isolated generative engines.

4.2 Structural Components of Agency

Agency in AI systems can be formalized through several interrelated components:

1. Memory

Agentic systems incorporate memory mechanisms that allow persistence of contextual information across steps. Memory may include short-term buffers storing recent interactions or longer-term storage enabling retrieval of prior states and external knowledge (Adam et al., 2026). Persistent memory allows continuity and coherence across multi-step tasks.

2. Planning

Planning involves decomposing complex tasks into structured sub-goals. Rather than predicting tokens sequentially without foresight, agentic systems generate plans that guide intermediate actions. Planning introduces an explicit representation of task structure, enabling more coherent long-horizon reasoning (Li et al., 2026).

3. Tool-Use and Environment Interaction

Modern AI systems increasingly interact with external tools such as search engines, databases, calculators, or APIs. Tool-use extends model capability beyond internal parametric knowledge. It allows grounding in external data sources and verifiable computation (Qian et al., 2026). Through tool invocation, the system becomes embedded within a broader computational environment.

4. Reflection and Iterative Revision

Agentic architectures often include mechanisms for self-evaluation and output refinement. Reflection loops enable the system to critique intermediate outputs, detect inconsistencies, and revise responses before finalization (Xia, 2026). This introduces a form of internal feedback that approximates deliberative reasoning.

Together, these components transform generative inference into structured decision processes.

4.3 Agency as Architectural Embedding

Importantly, agency does not imply intentionality in a philosophical sense. AI systems do not possess intrinsic goals or consciousness. Instead, agency in this context refers to architectural embedding of iterative control structures that simulate goal-directed behavior within constrained computational environments (Dai et al., 2026).

From a systems-theoretic perspective, agency emerges when generative models are embedded within control loops that regulate action selection over time. These loops may include policy selection mechanisms, evaluation criteria, and adaptive updates based on intermediate outputs. Thus, agency can be conceptualized as the orchestration layer that governs how generative capacity is deployed.

This architectural interpretation avoids anthropomorphic assumptions while preserving analytical clarity. Agency becomes a property of system design rather than a claim about machine intentionality.

4.4 Constraints and Risks of Agentic Systems

While agency enhances capability, it also introduces new risks. Multi-step reasoning increases the surface area for error propagation. Inaccurate intermediate outputs may cascade across steps, producing compounded failures (Prabhu & Sunitha, 2026). Tool-use may expose systems to vulnerabilities such as prompt injection or data leakage. Memory persistence may inadvertently store sensitive or biased information.

Furthermore, increased autonomy complicates oversight. When systems operate through iterative loops with internal state transitions, tracing responsibility and diagnosing failure becomes more complex. The shift from generation to agency therefore amplifies both capability and accountability challenges.

These observations reinforce the necessity of integrating governance considerations directly into agentic architectures. Agency without embedded oversight risks amplifying unintended consequences at scale.

4.5 Agency as the Bridge Between Modeling and Governance

Agency occupies a critical intermediate position between generative modeling and lifecycle governance. Generative models define expressive capacity, but agency determines how that capacity unfolds in operational contexts. Governance, in turn, shapes constraints on agentic behavior through alignment mechanisms, monitoring systems, and policy enforcement.

Without agency, governance operates primarily at the level of output filtering or dataset curation. With agency, governance must address dynamic processes including planning decisions, tool invocation policies, and state persistence. This interdependence suggests that agency cannot be treated as an isolated engineering enhancement; it is structurally linked to governance architecture.

By formalizing agency as an architectural layer, this chapter establishes the second dimension of AI creation systems. The following section extends this analysis by examining lifecycle governance as an embedded and continuous system property rather than an external regulatory overlay.

5. LIFECYCLE GOVERNANCE AS AN EMBEDDED SYSTEM LAYER

The increasing capability and autonomy of AI creation systems have intensified global attention toward governance, alignment, and accountability. Traditionally, governance has been conceptualized as an external layer applied after technical development, often through regulatory compliance, ethical guidelines, or institutional oversight mechanisms (Siriborvornratanakul & Rittikulsittichai, 2026). However, as AI systems evolve into agentic, tool-using, and iterative entities, this externalized framing becomes insufficient. Governance must instead be reconceptualized as an embedded, continuous, and architectural property of AI creation systems.

5.1 From External Regulation to Embedded Governance

Early governance discussions surrounding AI primarily focused on high-level ethical principles such as fairness, transparency, accountability, and non-maleficence (Wattanachote et al., 2026). These principles often translated into organizational policies, audit frameworks, or post-deployment monitoring protocols. While valuable, such approaches frequently operate outside the technical core of system design.

In generative and agentic AI systems, however, behavior is shaped by architectural choices: training data composition, reward modeling strategies, memory persistence policies, tool invocation permissions, and deployment constraints. Governance decisions are therefore instantiated within the system itself. Dataset curation determines representational bias. Alignment training shapes response tendencies. Guardrails and constrained decoding mechanisms regulate output boundaries. Logging infrastructures determine traceability. In this sense, governance is not merely a policy layer but a structural design choice.

This shift from external oversight to embedded governance reflects a broader transformation in socio-technical systems theory. When computational systems influence large-scale social processes, accountability cannot rely solely on external regulation. Instead, governance must be encoded within lifecycle processes.

5.2 The Lifecycle Perspective

Lifecycle governance conceptualizes AI systems as evolving entities whose risks and impacts unfold across multiple stages: data collection, model training, evaluation, deployment, monitoring, and post-deployment revision (Fatima et al., 2026). Each stage introduces distinct governance challenges and intervention points.

1. Data Curation and Documentation

Governance begins with data selection. Training datasets determine representational coverage, bias distribution, and epistemic boundaries. Without transparent documentation of dataset sources, licensing conditions, and filtering procedures, downstream accountability becomes limited. Governance at this stage includes dataset documentation standards, bias audits, and provenance tracking.

2. Training and Alignment

During model training, governance manifests through alignment strategies such as reinforcement learning from human feedback, preference optimization, and rule-based fine-tuning. These techniques attempt to shape generative outputs according to normative expectations. However, alignment is not purely technical; it encodes implicit value judgments regarding acceptable behavior and risk thresholds.

3. Evaluation and Red-Teaming

Evaluation extends beyond utility metrics to include robustness testing, safety stress tests, and adversarial probing. Red-teaming practices aim to identify vulnerabilities such as jailbreak susceptibility, data leakage, or unsafe content generation. Governance at this stage requires systematic scenario-based assessment rather than static benchmark evaluation.

4. Deployment and Access Control

Deployment decisions determine who can access the system, under what constraints, and with what monitoring mechanisms. Access tiers, API rate limits, usage logging, and content filtering policies directly influence real-world impact. Governance at deployment must balance openness with risk mitigation.

5. Monitoring and Post-Deployment Auditing

Once deployed, AI creation systems operate within dynamic environments. Distribution shifts, evolving user behavior, and emergent misuse patterns necessitate continuous monitoring. Logging mechanisms, drift detection tools, incident response protocols, and periodic audits become central components of governance.

Recent global initiatives have further emphasized the importance of structured AI governance frameworks. For example, the NIST AI Risk Management Framework proposes systematic processes for identifying, measuring, and managing risks throughout the AI lifecycle. Similarly, the European Union AI Act introduces risk-based regulatory categories and emphasizes transparency, human oversight, and post-deployment monitoring for high-impact AI systems. These initiatives reinforce the argument that governance mechanisms should not operate solely as external regulatory constraints but must be embedded within the architectural and operational design of AI creation systems.

5.3 Governance as Constraint and Enabler

Governance is sometimes portrayed as a constraint on innovation. However, from a systems perspective, governance functions both as constraint and enabler. Constraint mechanisms limit harmful or unstable behaviors, thereby improving reliability and trustworthiness. At the same time, structured governance enables broader deployment by increasing stakeholder confidence and reducing systemic risk (Hamamoto et al., 2026).

In AI creation systems, governance mechanisms such as output filtering, uncertainty calibration, and provenance tracking can enhance interpretability and user trust. Watermarking techniques and citation mechanisms may improve traceability of generated content. Structured consent management can clarify rights over training data and outputs. These mechanisms expand the operational viability of AI systems within regulated sectors such as education, healthcare, and public administration.

Thus, governance should not be framed as an external brake on generative progress but as an architectural stabilizer that supports sustainable scaling.

5.4 Interdependence Between Agency and Governance

As discussed in the previous section, agentic architectures introduce iterative decision processes involving planning, memory persistence, and tool invocation. Governance in this context must extend beyond output-level filtering. It must regulate intermediate decision pathways.

For example, when an agent invokes external tools, governance mechanisms must define permissible APIs, data handling constraints, and verification protocols. When memory buffers persist user inputs, governance must address privacy safeguards and data retention policies (Al-Hashimi, 2026). When systems engage in self-reflection loops, evaluation criteria must be aligned with normative safety standards.

The more agentic a system becomes, the more governance must operate at the level of process control rather than solely at the level of final output. This reinforces the argument that governance is inseparable from architectural design.

5.5 Governance and the Problem of Accountability

One of the most complex governance challenges concerns accountability. In AI creation systems, outputs result from interactions among training data distributions, optimization dynamics, inference-time prompts, and potentially multi-step reasoning loops. Determining responsibility for harmful or misleading outputs becomes difficult when causal pathways are distributed across layers (Marpaung, 2026).

Embedding governance mechanisms such as logging, model cards, system cards, and audit trails enhances traceability. Structured documentation clarifies design decisions, dataset sources, and evaluation results. Incident response protocols establish procedures for mitigating harm when failures occur. These artifacts function as accountability infrastructures rather than symbolic transparency measures.

From a theoretical standpoint, accountability requires coupling expressive capacity with observability. A system that generates complex outputs without traceability mechanisms lacks the structural conditions for responsible deployment. Therefore, governance must ensure that generative and agentic capacities are matched by monitoring and documentation infrastructures.

5.6 Governance as a Core Dimension of AI Creation Systems

Synthesizing the above arguments, lifecycle governance can be conceptualized as a structural dimension co-equal with generative modeling and agency. It shapes the permissible action space, regulates intermediate processes, and defines oversight mechanisms across time. Rather than functioning as an external compliance checklist, governance becomes an architectural principle embedded in system design choices.

This reframing is essential for moving beyond fragmented approaches in which modeling, agency, and governance are treated independently. Generative modeling defines what can be expressed. Agency defines how expression unfolds across steps. Governance defines the normative and operational boundaries within which expression occurs.

By establishing governance as an intrinsic system layer, this section completes the articulation of the three foundational dimensions of AI creation systems. The next section integrates these dimensions into a unified theoretical framework that formalizes their interdependencies and structural relationships.

6. TOWARD A UNIFIED THEORETICAL FRAMEWORK: THE TRI-LAYER AI CREATION FRAMEWORK (TACF)

The preceding sections have articulated three foundational dimensions of AI creation systems: generative modeling, agency, and lifecycle governance. While each dimension has evolved through substantial scholarly and engineering advances, their conceptual separation has limited theoretical coherence. This section proposes the **Tri-Layer AI Creation Framework (TACF)** as a unifying architecture that integrates these dimensions into a structured, interdependent system model.

TACF conceptualizes AI creation systems as multi-layered socio-technical constructs in which generative capacity, procedural agency, and lifecycle governance operate as mutually constitutive layers. Rather than positioning these dimensions hierarchically, TACF models them as structurally interdependent components whose interactions determine system capability, reliability, and accountability.

6.1 Overview of the Tri-Layer Structure

The Tri-Layer AI Creation Framework consists of:

1. Layer 1: Generative Modeling Layer

Defines the representational and probabilistic capacity of the system.

2. Layer 2: Agentic Orchestration Layer

Structures multi-step reasoning, planning, memory, and tool-use processes.

3. Layer 3: Governance and Oversight Layer

Embeds alignment, accountability, monitoring, and lifecycle controls across system stages.

These layers do not function independently. Instead, they interact dynamically. The generative layer determines what the system can statistically express. The agentic layer determines how that expressive

capacity unfolds across tasks and time. The governance layer determines the normative and operational boundaries within which expressive and procedural actions occur.

Figure 1. **The Tri-Layer AI Creation Framework (TACF)**

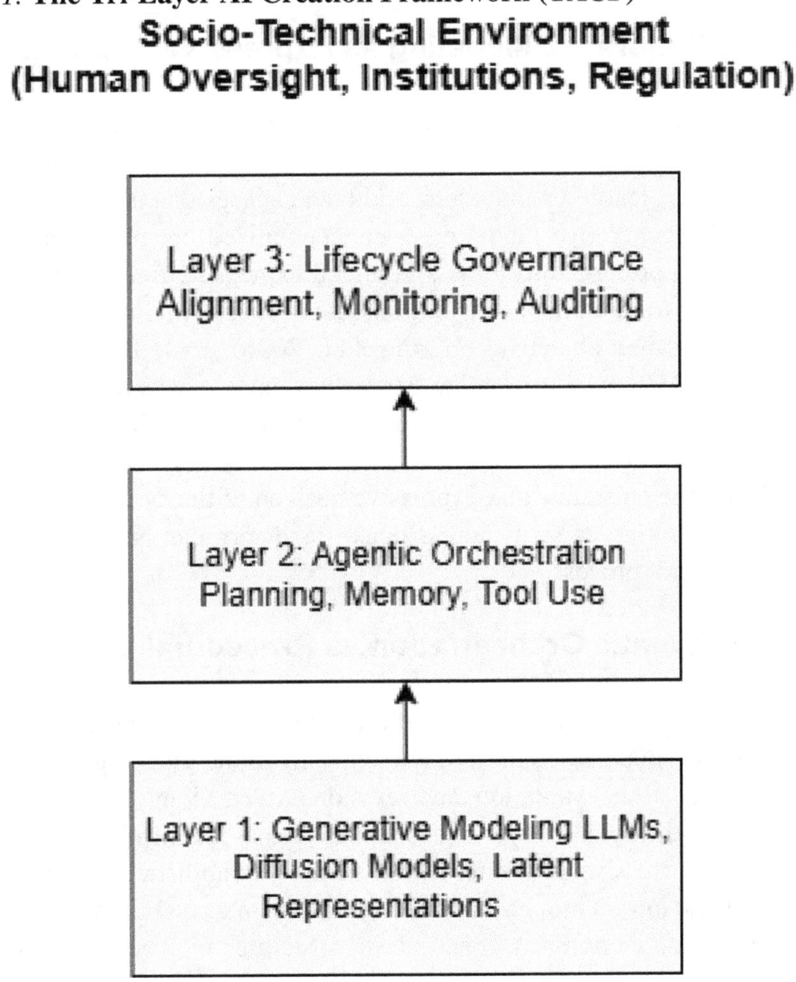

Figure 1 illustrates the structural relationship between the three layers of the Tri-Layer AI Creation Framework (TACF). The generative modeling layer forms the expressive foundation of the system, enabling probabilistic synthesis of text, images, and other multimodal outputs. Built upon this expressive substrate, the agentic orchestration layer structures multi-step reasoning processes, including planning, memory persistence, and tool interaction. The lifecycle governance layer operates as a supervisory and constraint mechanism that embeds alignment, monitoring, and accountability throughout the system lifecycle. Importantly, these layers do not function in isolation but interact dynamically within a broader socio-technical environment involving human oversight, institutional governance, and regulatory frameworks. This layered representation highlights how capability, autonomy, and responsibility co-evolve within modern AI creation systems.

6.2 Layer 1: Generative Modeling as Expressive Substrate

At the foundational level, the generative modeling layer provides the expressive substrate of AI creation systems. This layer encompasses probabilistic representations, neural architectures, learned parameters, and latent spaces that enable synthesis.

Within TACF, generative modeling is conceptualized not merely as an algorithmic function approximator but as a bounded expressive field. Its capabilities are constrained by training data distributions, model scale, architectural inductive biases, and optimization objectives (Hardie et al., 2026).

Importantly, TACF emphasizes that generative capacity sets the upper limit of possible outputs. No agentic enhancement or governance mechanism can extend beyond the representational boundaries defined at this layer. Thus, generative modeling establishes the epistemic and expressive horizon of the system.

However, generative capacity alone does not determine system behavior. It defines potential, not process.

6.3 Layer 2: Agentic Orchestration as Procedural Logic

The second layer introduces structured procedural logic. Agentic orchestration embeds generative models within iterative loops involving planning, memory persistence, tool invocation, evaluation, and revision (Xu & Xiong, 2026).

Within TACF, the agentic layer is conceptualized as a control architecture operating over the expressive substrate. It transforms probabilistic continuation into goal-directed workflows. Through task decomposition, intermediate reasoning steps, and environment interaction, the agentic layer structures how generative capacity is deployed across time.

This layer introduces several key properties:

- **Temporal Extension**: Outputs are produced through multi-step sequences rather than single-pass inference.
- **Contextual Persistence**: Memory mechanisms maintain state continuity.
- **External Grounding**: Tool-use enables interaction with external knowledge sources.
- **Iterative Correction**: Reflection loops refine outputs before finalization.

TACF emphasizes that agency does not replace generative modeling; it organizes it. The agentic layer governs when, how, and under what conditions generative inference is executed.

However, increased procedural autonomy also expands risk surfaces. Multi-step reasoning introduces compounding uncertainty. Tool-use introduces external dependencies. Memory persistence introduces privacy considerations. These expansions necessitate the third layer.

6.4 Layer 3: Governance as Structural Constraint and Accountability Infrastructure

The governance layer in TACF operates as a structural constraint system embedded across lifecycle stages. It includes alignment training methods, guardrails, content filtering, logging mechanisms, evaluation protocols, audit infrastructures, and deployment policies (Wang et al., 2026).

Crucially, TACF positions governance not as an external regulator but as an architectural co-layer. Governance mechanisms shape training objectives, constrain agentic decision pathways, and regulate deployment environments. They define permissible action spaces and enforce safety thresholds.

Governance within TACF has three functional roles:

1. Normative Encoding

Alignment techniques embed value preferences and safety constraints within training dynamics.

2. Operational Monitoring

Logging, telemetry, and drift detection enable observability across inference and deployment.

3. Corrective Intervention

Incident response mechanisms, model updates, and rollback protocols provide structured remediation.

By embedding governance at the same structural level as modeling and agency, TACF resolves the conceptual dichotomy between capability and responsibility.

6.5 Interdependencies Across Layers

The central contribution of TACF lies not merely in defining three layers, but in articulating their interdependencies.

- **Generative–Agentic Interdependence**

Agentic reliability is bounded by generative expressivity. Weak representations constrain planning effectiveness. Conversely, structured planning can mitigate certain generative limitations through tool grounding.

- **Agentic–Governance Interdependence**

Increased autonomy amplifies the need for process-level oversight. Governance must regulate intermediate reasoning steps, not just final outputs.

- **Generative–Governance Interdependence**

Alignment techniques alter model parameter distributions. Dataset documentation affects accountability. Governance choices reshape generative behavior.

These interdependencies imply that optimizing one layer in isolation may destabilize others. For example, increasing generative scale without strengthening governance may increase harmful output risk. Expanding agentic autonomy without memory safeguards may create privacy vulnerabilities.

TACF therefore promotes co-optimization across layers.

6.6 Theoretical Implications of TACF

The Tri-Layer AI Creation Framework generates several theoretical implications:

First, it reframes AI creation systems as socio-technical architectures rather than standalone models. Capability emerges from interaction among expressive, procedural, and governance layers.

Second, it clarifies the distinction between generation and creation. Generation refers to probabilistic synthesis at Layer 1. Creation refers to structured, accountable workflows emerging from coordinated operation across all three layers.

Third, TACF provides a vocabulary for cumulative science. Researchers can analyze innovations at specific layers while situating them within the broader architecture. For instance, improvements in diffusion sampling affect Layer 1, whereas improvements in reflective reasoning strategies affect Layer 2. Governance audits and monitoring infrastructures operate at Layer 3.

Finally, TACF supports interdisciplinary dialogue. Machine learning researchers, system engineers, and policymakers can reference a shared structural model rather than operating within fragmented terminological frameworks.

6.7 Toward Coherent and Accountable AI Creation Systems

As AI systems increasingly function as collaborators in creative, scientific, and administrative domains, theoretical clarity becomes indispensable. TACF offers a structured lens through which AI creation systems can be analyzed, designed, and governed as coherent entities.

By integrating generative modeling, agentic orchestration, and lifecycle governance into a unified architecture, TACF advances a foundational step toward systematic and accountable AI creation science.

7. IMPLICATIONS FOR ENGINEERING AND POLICY

The Tri-Layer AI Creation Framework (TACF) offers not only a conceptual synthesis but also practical implications for engineering practice, organizational governance, and public policy. By articulating generative modeling, agentic orchestration, and lifecycle governance as structurally interdependent layers, TACF reframes how AI creation systems should be designed, evaluated, and regulated. This section explores the engineering and policy consequences of adopting a tri-layer perspective.

7.1 Implications for AI System Architecture Design

From an engineering standpoint, TACF encourages architects to move beyond model-centric optimization. In many contemporary development workflows, primary emphasis is placed on increasing model scale, improving benchmark performance, and optimizing inference latency (Cimino et al., 2026). While these objectives remain important, TACF suggests that system robustness and accountability require co-design across all three layers.

Engineering teams should explicitly map design decisions to each TACF layer:

- **Layer 1 (Generative Modeling):** Decisions regarding architecture selection, dataset curation, parameter scaling, and training objectives.
- **Layer 2 (Agentic Orchestration):** Implementation of memory modules, planning loops, tool invocation protocols, and reflection strategies.
- **Layer 3 (Governance and Oversight):** Integration of alignment fine-tuning, guardrails, monitoring infrastructure, logging systems, and audit documentation.

Rather than treating governance as an afterthought applied post-deployment, TACF implies that governance constraints must inform architectural decisions at early design stages. For example, choices about memory persistence at Layer 2 should be evaluated simultaneously with privacy safeguards at Layer 3. Similarly, increases in generative expressivity at Layer 1 should be accompanied by strengthened monitoring mechanisms.

This tri-layer mapping enables engineering teams to anticipate cross-layer trade-offs before deployment.

7.2 Co-Optimization and Risk-Aware Scaling

TACF also reframes scaling strategies. Empirical scaling laws demonstrate that generative performance often improves with increased parameters and training data (Atkinson, 2026). However, scaling expressive capacity without proportional enhancement in agentic reliability and governance infrastructure may increase systemic risk.

For example:

- Larger models may generate more persuasive but potentially misleading outputs.
- Expanded tool-use capabilities may increase vulnerability to prompt injection or data exfiltration.
- Persistent memory systems may amplify privacy risks.

TACF therefore promotes **risk-aware scaling**, in which improvements in Layer 1 are matched by proportional investments in Layer 2 validation and Layer 3 oversight. Engineering roadmaps should incorporate governance readiness metrics alongside performance benchmarks. This integrated scaling approach supports sustainable capability expansion rather than purely competitive parameter growth.

7.3 Illustrative Application of TACF

To illustrate the practical implications of the Tri-Layer AI Creation Framework (TACF), consider the design of an AI-assisted research synthesis system intended to support academic literature review and knowledge integration. Such a system combines generative capabilities, structured reasoning processes, and governance safeguards within a unified architecture.

At the generative modeling layer, the system relies on a large language model trained on scientific corpora to generate summaries, identify thematic patterns, and synthesize insights across multiple research papers. The expressive capacity of the model enables the production of coherent academic explanations, structured summaries, and cross-document comparisons.

At the agentic orchestration layer, the system operates through an iterative reasoning workflow. It retrieves relevant articles from academic databases, decomposes research questions into sub-tasks, invokes retrieval and citation tools, and progressively refines its synthesis. Memory modules store intermediate reasoning steps, allowing the system to track previously analyzed sources and maintain contextual continuity across multiple interactions.

The lifecycle governance layer embeds safeguards to ensure reliability and accountability. Citation verification tools validate references against retrieved documents, hallucination detection modules flag unsupported claims, and logging mechanisms record tool usage and reasoning traces. Human reviewers may intervene when necessary, particularly in high-stakes research environments where accuracy and traceability are critical.

This illustrative example demonstrates how generative capacity, agentic reasoning, and governance oversight interact within a single AI creation system. TACF provides a structured lens through which such systems can be analyzed, designed, and evaluated in an integrated manner.

7.4 Integration Challenges and Trade-Offs

While integrating generative modeling, agentic orchestration, and governance mechanisms provides significant conceptual and practical advantages, it also introduces important engineering and organizational trade-offs. Balancing expressive capability, procedural autonomy, and oversight constraints represents a central challenge in the design of AI creation systems.

Increasing governance constraints may improve safety and accountability but can reduce system flexibility or increase computational overhead. For example, implementing real-time monitoring, verification pipelines, or extensive logging mechanisms may introduce latency and operational complexity. Similarly, expanding agentic autonomy through multi-step reasoning loops can enhance problem-solving capability while simultaneously increasing the difficulty of monitoring intermediate decision pathways.

Another important trade-off emerges between creative expressivity and controllability. Highly expressive generative models are capable of producing diverse and innovative outputs, yet this same expressivity can make system behavior harder to predict or constrain. Governance mechanisms such as alignment training, guardrails, and policy-based filtering therefore play a critical role in stabilizing system behavior.

Recognizing these trade-offs highlights the importance of co-design across TACF layers. Effective AI creation systems must balance performance, autonomy, and governance readiness rather than optimizing any single dimension in isolation.

7.5 Evaluation Beyond Static Benchmarks

Traditional evaluation metrics often focus on static benchmarks measuring accuracy, fluency, or task-specific success (Brezovec et al., 2026). However, agentic systems operating across multiple steps require dynamic evaluation frameworks.

Under TACF, evaluation must be layered:

- **Layer 1 Evaluation:** Utility metrics such as perplexity, BLEU, FID, or task accuracy.
- **Layer 2 Evaluation:** Robustness of multi-step reasoning, reliability of tool invocation, stability of memory usage.
- **Layer 3 Evaluation:** Safety audits, bias assessment, adversarial robustness, and compliance verification.

Scenario-based and longitudinal testing become essential for agentic systems whose behavior unfolds over time. Human-in-the-loop evaluation, red-teaming exercises, and stress testing should examine not only final outputs but also intermediate reasoning pathways.

By embedding evaluation across layers, organizations can better identify emergent vulnerabilities and systemic weaknesses.

7.6 Documentation and Transparency as Structural Requirements

TACF underscores that transparency artifacts such as model cards, system cards, data sheets, and audit logs are not merely compliance documents but integral components of Layer 3. Documentation supports traceability across lifecycle stages and clarifies the boundaries of system capability.

From a policy perspective, regulators increasingly demand explainability, risk disclosure, and impact assessment for AI systems deployed in high-stakes domains. TACF provides a structured template for such disclosures. For example:

- Layer 1 documentation may describe training data sources and model architecture.
- Layer 2 documentation may outline tool-use policies and reasoning constraints.
- Layer 3 documentation may specify monitoring protocols and incident response procedures.

This layered documentation framework enhances both internal governance and external accountability.

7.7 Implications for Organizational Governance Structures

Adopting TACF has organizational consequences. Effective governance cannot reside solely within legal or compliance teams. Instead, governance must be distributed across interdisciplinary units including machine learning engineers, product managers, safety researchers, and policy advisors.

Organizations may establish cross-functional oversight committees that map responsibilities to TACF layers:

- Engineering teams oversee generative optimization.
- Applied AI teams manage agentic orchestration and integration.
- Trust and safety teams maintain governance monitoring systems.

This structural clarity reduces ambiguity regarding accountability and supports coordinated decision-making across technical and policy domains.

7.8 Public Policy and Regulatory Alignment

From a public policy perspective, TACF offers a conceptual bridge between technical architecture and regulatory frameworks. Emerging regulatory initiatives, such as risk-based AI governance models, emphasize lifecycle assessment and continuous oversight (Siriborvornratanakul & Rittikulsittichai, 2026). TACF aligns naturally with such approaches by embedding governance across development stages.

Policymakers can leverage the tri-layer structure to design regulations that address:

- Dataset transparency and documentation at Layer 1.
- Process-level accountability for agentic decision pathways at Layer 2.
- Monitoring, reporting, and incident response obligations at Layer 3.

Rather than imposing static certification requirements, regulators may adopt dynamic oversight models that reflect the iterative and evolving nature of AI creation systems.

7.9 Responsible Innovation and Societal Impact

TACF also contributes to broader debates on responsible innovation. AI creation systems influence education, scientific research, media production, and public discourse. Embedding governance at architectural levels enhances societal trust and reduces polarization surrounding AI deployment.

Responsible innovation requires anticipating downstream impacts, including labor displacement, authorship disputes, and information ecosystem disruption (Prabhu & Sunitha, 2026). By integrating generative capacity with agentic reliability and governance safeguards, TACF supports a balanced approach to innovation that emphasizes sustainability over rapid, unregulated expansion.

7.10 Toward Standardization and Interoperability

Finally, TACF may inform future standardization efforts. As AI systems become embedded in enterprise and public-sector environments, interoperability between platforms becomes essential. Shared conceptual models enable organizations to compare architectures, evaluate compliance readiness, and develop interoperable governance artifacts.

Industry consortia and academic institutions may adopt TACF as a reference model for curriculum development, audit templates, and cross-domain evaluation protocols. By providing a structured vocabulary, TACF facilitates cumulative knowledge building and shared best practices.

8. FUTURE DIRECTIONS AND RESEARCH AGENDA FOR UNIFIED AI CREATION SYSTEMS

The Tri-Layer AI Creation Framework (TACF) not only integrates existing conceptual domains but also exposes critical research gaps that must be addressed to advance AI creation systems in a coherent and accountable manner. As generative models scale, agentic architectures mature, and governance frameworks evolve, new theoretical and practical challenges emerge. This section outlines key future research directions aligned with the tri-layer perspective.

8.1 Formalizing Cross-Layer Metrics

One of the most pressing research needs concerns the development of cross-layer evaluation metrics. Current evaluation paradigms tend to isolate performance assessment within specific dimensions. Generative modeling is measured through utility benchmarks, agentic systems are evaluated through task completion success, and governance is assessed through compliance or safety audits.

However, TACF highlights that meaningful system evaluation must consider interdependencies. Future research should develop integrated metrics that examine:

- How generative expressivity influences agentic stability.
- How agentic autonomy affects governance complexity.
- How governance constraints impact generative diversity and creativity.

For example, increasing expressivity may improve task performance but reduce calibration reliability. Similarly, stronger safety filtering may reduce harmful outputs but constrain creative flexibility. Quantifying these trade-offs requires new multi-dimensional evaluation frameworks that span layers rather than isolate them.

Table 1. Example Evaluation Metrics Across TACF Layers

TACF Layer	Evaluation Focus	Example Metrics
Generative Modeling	Output quality and expressivity	Perplexity, BLEU score, FID score
Agentic Orchestration	Reliability of multi-step reasoning	Task completion rate, planning efficiency, tool invocation accuracy
Lifecycle Governance	Safety and accountability	Audit compliance score, traceability index, safety violation rate

Table 1 summarizes potential evaluation metrics aligned with the three layers of the Tri-Layer AI Creation Framework (TACF). These metrics illustrate how AI creation systems can be assessed holistically rather than through isolated performance benchmarks. Developing standardized cross-layer evaluation frameworks will be critical for ensuring balanced progress across expressive capability, agentic reliability, and governance accountability.

8.2 Robustness Under Distribution Shift in Agentic Systems

Generative models are known to degrade under distribution shifts, where deployment conditions differ from training environments. When combined with agentic loops, distribution shifts may have amplified consequences. Errors in retrieval results, outdated knowledge sources, or unexpected tool responses can propagate across iterative reasoning steps.

Future research should examine how agentic orchestration interacts with uncertainty and distributional variability. Questions include:

- How does memory persistence affect robustness under changing contexts?
- Can agentic planning strategies adapt dynamically to uncertainty estimates?
- What safeguards are necessary to prevent cascading failures in multi-step reasoning?

Addressing these questions requires bridging probabilistic modeling theory with systems engineering and reliability analysis.

8.3 Verifiable and Tool-Grounded Generation

Another promising research frontier concerns verifiable generation. As AI systems increasingly participate in knowledge production, scientific discovery, and policy drafting, the ability to verify claims becomes critical.

Tool-grounded architectures that integrate retrieval systems, citation generation, and structured computation offer potential solutions. However, integrating verification mechanisms within generative pipelines remains an open challenge. Future research should explore:

- Formal integration of citation tracking within generative outputs.
- Automated consistency checking across multi-step reasoning chains.
- Cryptographic watermarking and provenance verification techniques.

These innovations would strengthen Layer 2 and Layer 3 integration within TACF, enhancing both reliability and accountability.

8.4 Data Attribution and Compensation Mechanisms

Governance debates increasingly focus on training data provenance and intellectual property rights. Generative models rely on large-scale datasets often aggregated from diverse and sometimes contested sources. Ensuring transparency and fair attribution presents both technical and institutional challenges.

Future research should investigate mechanisms for:

- Fine-grained data lineage tracking.
- Attribution-aware training objectives.
- Compensation models for content contributors.
- Differential privacy and secure computation frameworks.

Integrating these mechanisms into the governance layer strengthens accountability and supports sustainable ecosystem development.

8.5 Human–AI Collaboration Models

AI creation systems are increasingly deployed as collaborators rather than autonomous agents. In creative industries, scientific research, and education, human users interact with generative systems in iterative workflows.

TACF suggests that effective collaboration depends on transparent interaction between layers. Users must understand system capabilities (Layer 1), reasoning pathways (Layer 2), and governance constraints (Layer 3). Future research should examine:

- Interface designs that expose intermediate reasoning steps.
- Mechanisms for human oversight in agentic loops.
- Trust calibration strategies that prevent overreliance.

Exploring human–AI co-creation models will further refine the practical application of the tri-layer framework.

8.6 Standardized Governance Taxonomies

As discussed in the previous section, regulatory initiatives increasingly demand structured oversight. However, governance terminology remains inconsistent across jurisdictions and sectors.

Future research may focus on developing interoperable governance taxonomies aligned with architectural layers. Standardized vocabularies for risk levels, monitoring protocols, incident reporting, and alignment techniques would improve cross-sector communication and policy harmonization.

Such standardization efforts could draw upon TACF as a reference architecture for mapping technical features to governance obligations.

8.7 Theoretical Foundations of Emergent Agency

Finally, deeper theoretical investigation is needed regarding emergent behaviors in large-scale agentic systems. While scaling laws describe performance trends, the relationship between parameter growth and structured reasoning remains incompletely understood.

Research questions include:

- What architectural conditions give rise to stable multi-step reasoning?
- How do memory mechanisms interact with representational capacity?
- Can agency be formally characterized using control theory or dynamical systems analysis?

Answering these questions would strengthen the theoretical grounding of Layer 2 and clarify its interaction with generative expressivity.

8.8 Toward a Coherent Research Program

Collectively, these research directions illustrate that advancing AI creation systems requires coordinated progress across layers. Improvements in modeling must be matched by innovations in orchestration and governance. TACF provides a scaffold for organizing such research efforts.

By framing AI creation systems as tri-layer architectures, future scholarship can move beyond incremental performance optimization toward systematic, accountable, and interdisciplinary progress.

9. TOWARD AN INTEGRATED SOCIO-TECHNICAL PARADIGM OF AI CREATION

The preceding sections have articulated the structural dimensions and future trajectories of AI creation systems through the Tri-Layer AI Creation Framework (TACF). However, beyond architectural clarification and research agenda development, a deeper conceptual shift is required. AI creation systems should not be understood solely as computational artifacts, but as socio-technical infrastructures embedded within institutional, economic, and cultural ecosystems (Dai et al., 2026).

9.1 From Model-Centric to System-Centric Thinking

Historically, artificial intelligence research has often centered on models as the primary units of innovation. Improvements in parameter scaling, architecture design, and training efficiency have been treated as markers of progress. While such advances remain important, they risk reinforcing a reductionist view in which intelligence is equated with model performance metrics.

TACF challenges this model-centric orientation by repositioning AI creation systems as layered socio-technical constructs. Generative modeling is necessary but insufficient. Agency structures procedural dynamics. Governance embeds normative and institutional constraints. None of these layers operate in isolation from social context.

System-centric thinking recognizes that AI outputs are shaped by training data distributions influenced by cultural production, by governance choices reflecting normative priorities, and by deployment environments structured by market and policy forces. Thus, AI creation systems are simultaneously technical and institutional entities.

9.2 AI Creation Systems as Infrastructural Technologies

AI creation systems increasingly function as infrastructural technologies rather than standalone tools. They are integrated into educational platforms, creative workflows, research environments, enterprise systems, and public services. As infrastructure, their design choices influence downstream knowledge production, labor dynamics, and information ecosystems.

Infrastructural technologies exhibit path dependency. Early architectural and governance decisions may shape long-term system trajectories. For example:

- Data sourcing policies influence representational diversity.
- Memory design choices affect privacy norms.
- Tool integration standards shape interoperability across industries.

Recognizing AI creation systems as infrastructure emphasizes the importance of embedding governance early and continuously across lifecycle stages. It also underscores the need for interdisciplinary oversight extending beyond engineering teams.

9.3 Co-Evolution of Capability and Responsibility

A central insight emerging from TACF is that capability and responsibility co-evolve. Expanding generative expressivity increases the system's potential influence.

Enhancing agentic autonomy amplifies decision complexity. These developments necessitate proportional expansion in governance capacity.

This co-evolutionary dynamic suggests that innovation strategies should be evaluated not only by performance improvements but also by governance readiness. Systems optimized purely for scale may outpace institutional capacity to regulate or monitor them. Conversely, overly restrictive governance may inhibit beneficial innovation.

Balancing this dynamic requires continuous feedback between technical development and policy design. TACF provides a structural lens for facilitating such feedback.

9.4 Redefining Creation in the Age of AI

The shift from generation to creation also invites reconsideration of what "creation" entails. In human contexts, creation implies intentionality, authorship, accountability, and situated meaning. AI creation systems, by contrast, operate through statistical inference, procedural orchestration, and governance constraints.

Under TACF, creation is reframed as the emergent property of coordinated layers rather than intrinsic intentionality. A system "creates" when generative capacity is structured through agency and bounded by governance. This reframing avoids anthropomorphic interpretations while acknowledging the complex outputs produced by AI systems.

Such conceptual clarity is essential for debates on authorship, intellectual property, and liability. Understanding creation as layered emergence supports more precise attribution models and regulatory discussions.

9.5 Interdisciplinary Convergence and Knowledge Integration

Advancing a socio-technical paradigm requires convergence across disciplines. Machine learning theory, systems engineering, human–computer interaction, ethics, law, and public policy must engage within shared conceptual frameworks. Fragmented discourse impedes cumulative progress.

TACF contributes to interdisciplinary integration by offering a common structural vocabulary. Researchers can situate contributions within specific layers while recognizing cross-layer dependencies. Policymakers can reference architectural components when drafting oversight mechanisms. Engineers can anticipate governance implications during system design.

Such convergence is particularly important as AI creation systems become embedded in globally interconnected infrastructures.

9.6 Toward Sustainable AI Creation Ecosystems

Finally, a socio-technical paradigm emphasizes sustainability. Sustainable AI creation systems balance innovation with long-term societal stability. They incorporate transparency mechanisms, equitable data practices, and adaptive governance processes.

Sustainability extends beyond environmental concerns to include informational integrity, labor transformation, and institutional resilience. AI systems that generate persuasive media, automate knowledge work, or support scientific discovery influence epistemic ecosystems. Governance must therefore anticipate cumulative systemic effects.

By integrating generative modeling, agency, and lifecycle governance, TACF offers a foundation for sustainable AI creation ecosystems capable of evolving responsibly alongside human institutions.

10. CONCLUSION

The rapid evolution of artificial intelligence from predictive analytics to generative and agentic creation systems has introduced unprecedented technical capabilities alongside profound conceptual challenges. While generative modeling, agentic orchestration, and governance mechanisms have each advanced significantly, their parallel development has produced fragmentation within both scholarship and practice. This chapter addressed that fragmentation by proposing the **Tri-Layer AI Creation Framework (TACF)** as a unified theoretical architecture integrating generative modeling, agency, and lifecycle governance.

At the foundational level, generative modeling defines the expressive capacity of AI systems. Through probabilistic representation learning and large-scale optimization, models acquire the ability to synthesize coherent and contextually relevant outputs. However, expressive capacity alone does not constitute creation. The emergence of agentic architectures introduces structured procedural dynamics, transforming static generation into multi-step, context-aware workflows involving planning, memory persistence, tool-use, and iterative refinement. These capabilities enable AI systems to operate across extended reasoning processes rather than isolated inference events.

Yet capability expansion without accountability introduces systemic risk. As AI creation systems become embedded within educational, scientific, industrial, and governmental contexts, lifecycle governance becomes indispensable. Governance must extend beyond external regulation and be embedded within architectural design, encompassing data curation, alignment training, evaluation, monitoring, and post-deployment auditing. The tri-layer perspective demonstrates that generative modeling, agency, and governance are not independent domains but structurally interdependent dimensions of a single socio-technical system.

The Tri-Layer AI Creation Framework contributes to the field in several ways. First, it provides conceptual clarity by distinguishing between generation and creation, reframing creation as an emergent property of coordinated expressive, procedural, and governance layers. Second, it offers a structural vocabulary for interdisciplinary dialogue, enabling researchers, engineers, and policymakers to situate their work within a coherent architectural model. Third, it advances a foundation for cumulative science by encouraging cross-layer evaluation, co-optimization strategies, and integrated oversight mechanisms.

Importantly, TACF emphasizes that sustainable AI development requires co-evolution between capability and responsibility. Scaling generative expressivity or expanding agentic autonomy must be accompanied by proportional strengthening of governance infrastructures. Without such balance, technological acceleration may outpace institutional readiness. Conversely, overly restrictive governance that ignores architectural realities may inhibit beneficial innovation. A unified framework allows for calibrated progress that integrates technical ambition with societal safeguards.

As AI creation systems increasingly function as infrastructural technologies shaping knowledge production, creative industries, and public discourse, theoretical integration becomes not merely desirable but necessary. Fragmented approaches risk optimizing isolated dimensions while neglecting systemic interdependencies. By articulating a tri-layer architecture, this chapter offers a structured pathway toward coherent, accountable, and interdisciplinary AI creation science.

Future research should further refine cross-layer evaluation metrics, explore robustness in agentic systems under distribution shift, and develop interoperable governance standards aligned with architectural design. Such efforts will strengthen the theoretical and practical foundations of AI creation systems in rapidly evolving socio-technical environments.

In conclusion, AI creation systems should be understood not as standalone models, but as layered socio-technical architectures in which generative capacity, procedural agency, and lifecycle governance operate in dynamic interdependence. The Tri-Layer AI Creation Framework provides a foundation for advancing this integrated paradigm, supporting rigorous, responsible, and sustainable progress in the age of AI-driven creation.

REFERENCES

Adam, A. B. M., Lagunas, E., Samy, M., Saifaldawla, A., & Chatzinotas, S. (2026). Generative AI for non-terrestrial networks: design, applications, and challenges. *Eurasip Journal on Wireless Communications and Networking, 2026*(1). DOI: 10.1186/s13638-025-02549-7

Al-Hashimi, H. A. (2026). A generative AI cybersecurity risks mitigation model for code generation: Using ANN-ISM hybrid approach. *Scientific Reports*, *16*(1), 4239. Advance online publication. DOI: 10.1038/s41598-025-34350-3 PMID: 41535698

Atkinson, C. F. (2026). Human in the loop chain of code prompting for deterministic tool development with generative AI. *Discover Artificial Intelligence*, *6*(1), 61. Advance online publication. DOI: 10.1007/s44163-025-00704-z

Brezovec, E., Zelić, M., & Zagode, A. M. (2026). Stabilizing truth in educational sciences: A systematic review of generative AI in education. *Kybernetes*, *55*(13), 1–17. DOI: 10.1108/K-09-2025-2339

Cimino, A., Longo, F., Solina, V., & Veltri, P. (2026). Integrating large language models with industrial simulation for multi-level decision support: An innovation management perspective in Industry 5.0. *European Journal of Innovation Management*, *29*(11), 27–53. DOI: 10.1108/EJIM-10-2024-1246

Dai, X., Leng, L. L., Liu, Y., Huang, Y.-T., & Wong, D. F. K. (2026). The paradox of agency in psychotherapy: How people with mental distress experience support from generative AI chatbots and human therapists. *BMC Psychiatry*, *26*(1), 49. Advance online publication. DOI: 10.1186/s12888-025-07671-w PMID: 41382092

Fatima, I., Rehman, A., Wang, Z., Ur-Rehman, H., Aldaw, M., Warraich, D. A., Meng, Y., Li, Y., & Liao, M. (2026). AI-driven peptide discovery for endometrial cancer: Deep generative modeling and molecular simulation in the big data era. *Journal of Computer-Aided Molecular Design*, *40*(1), 47. Advance online publication. DOI: 10.1007/s10822-025-00735-9 PMID: 41524971

Hamamoto, R., Koyama, T., Takahashi, S., Yasuda, T., Kobayashi, K., Akagi, Y., Kouno, N., Sudo, K., Hirata, M., Sunami, K., Kubo, T., Katayama, H., Takashima, A., Taniguchi, T., Matsumoto, H., Shibaki, R., Asada, K., Komatsu, M., Kaneko, S., & Yamamoto, N. (2026). Implementing generative artificial intelligence in precision oncology: Safety, governance, and significance. *Journal of Hematology & Oncology*, *19*(1), 14. Advance online publication. DOI: 10.1186/s13045-026-01781-y PMID: 41664164

Hardie, P., Darley, A., Derwin, R., Eustace-Cook, J., Kearns, S., Mc Brien, B., Siddiquee, A., Zheng, D., & Mooney, M. (2026). Applications, attitudes and ethical considerations of Generative Artificial Intelligence (Gen AI) in nursing education: A scoping review. *BMC Nursing*, *25*(1), 148. Advance online publication. DOI: 10.1186/s12912-025-04253-9 PMID: 41545825

Li, M., Basit, A., Javed, A., Song, X., & Ge, Y. (2026). Generative artificial intelligence and ChatGPT in agriculture supply chain management: A systematic literature review and future research agenda. *British Food Journal*, *128*(13), 121–141. DOI: 10.1108/BFJ-05-2025-0720

Marpaung, J. (2026). Investigating Indonesian graduate business students' generative artificial intelligence readiness and usage in the classroom. *Discover Education*, *5*(1), 84. Advance online publication. DOI: 10.1007/s44217-026-01112-w

Prabhu, A., & Sunitha, N. R. (2026). A hybrid artificial intelligence model for cyberattack detection using a generative AI embedded approach. *Discover Artificial Intelligence*, *6*(1). Advance online publication. DOI: 10.1007/s44163-026-00901-4

Qian, Y., Bao, Q., Zhang, S., & Peng, X. (2026). A cultural memory semiotics and function behavior structure model for digital inheritance and innovation in AI generated Huizhou woodcarving images. *Scientific Reports*, *16*(1), 5520. Advance online publication. DOI: 10.1038/s41598-026-35360-5 PMID: 41545436

Siriborvornratanakul, T., & Rittikulsittichai, S. (2026). Advancing the generation and integration of traditional motifs through AI-based techniques. *Discover Artificial Intelligence*, *6*(1), 100. Advance online publication. DOI: 10.1007/s44163-025-00642-w

Sun, Y., Li, L., Zhang, X., Chen, X., Deng, S., & Hu, X. (2026). AI literacy and psychosocial factors shaping Chinese university students' attitudes and behavioral intentions toward generative AI use. *BMC Psychology*, *14*(1), 236. Advance online publication. DOI: 10.1186/s40359-026-03989-6 PMID: 41572390

Wang, Q., Wang, Y., & Amini, M. (2026). Associations of task technology fit and perceived usefulness with responsible generative AI use among university students. *Scientific Reports*, *16*(1), 2759. Advance online publication. DOI: 10.1038/s41598-025-32692-6 PMID: 41484194

Wattanachote, K., Lin, C.-Y., Hsu, S.-E., & Shih, T. K. (2026). Generative AI Shanshui animation enhancement using Perlin noise and diffusion models. *Discover Artificial Intelligence*, *6*(1), 122. Advance online publication. DOI: 10.1007/s44163-025-00797-6

Xia, S. (2026). Teacher support enhances self-efficacy and learning outcomes in the age of AI. *Scientific Reports*, *16*(1), 5113. Advance online publication. DOI: 10.1038/s41598-026-36014-2 PMID: 41530478

Xu, T., & Xiong, Y. (2026). Multidimensional determinants of generative AI acceptance in foreign language education. *Scientific Reports*, *16*(1), 5698. Advance online publication. DOI: 10.1038/s41598-026-36700-1 PMID: 41554873

Zhu, Z., Hsu, C., Nah, F. F.-H., & Liu, N. (2026). Generative AI adoption and solvers' popularity on supply-driven crowdsourcing platforms: The dual role of price signals. *Internet Research*, *36*(7), 24–42. DOI: 10.1108/INTR-02-2025-0262

Chapter 6
Data Governance for Generative AI:
Curation, Documentation, and Lifecycle Management

Kolwang Warai Armand
http://orcid.org/0009-0003-4487-8181
ICT University, Cameroon

ABSTRACT

The capabilities and limitations of generative AI systems are primarily determined by the data on which they are trained. Notwithstanding this, data governance in generative AI remains fragmented, ad hoc, and poorly systematised compared to model development practices. This chapter presents a comprehensive framework for data governance across the generative AI lifecycle, encompassing collection, curation, documentation, versioning, and maintenance. It examines practical methodologies for deduplication, filtering, and quality assessment, alongside standards for dataset documentation including datasheets, model cards, and data lineage tracking. The chapter addresses legal and ethical issues in data licensing, copyright compliance, and harm assessment, which provides actionable templates and decision frameworks. By codifying reproducible data governance patterns, it enables organisations to shift from informal practices to systematic, auditable, and responsible data management supporting technical excellence and ethical accountability.

INTRODUCTION

The past decade has witnessed a remarkable transformation in the capabilities of artificial intelligence systems, moving from pattern recognition and prediction

DOI: 10.4018/979-8-2600-0368-8.ch006

to genuine creative generation across text, images, audio, video, and multimodal domains (Bender et al., 2021). This shift represents a paradigm change in how machines interact with human knowledge and creativity. Consider the scale: GPT-3 was trained on 570GB of filtered Common Crawl data plus additional sources totalling 45TB uncompressed (Brown et al., 2020). Diffusion models like Stable Diffusion rely on LAION-5B, containing 5.85 billion image-text pairs scraped from the web (Schuhmann et al., 2022). These datasets are not merely large; they are the foundation of emergent capabilities like zero-shot learning and creative synthesis.

Yet this transformation would be impossible without the vast corpora of training data that underpin these systems. Large language models trained on hundreds of billions of tokens, diffusion models trained on billions of image-text pairs, and multimodal systems trained on diverse combinations of sensory data have all achieved their capabilities through data at scale (Brown et al., 2020). The capabilities and limitations of these systems, including their failures, are determined by the quality, diversity, representativeness, and governance of the data they use (Bender et al., 2021). This is supported by evidence; for example, models trained on data that has been deduplicated show improvements of 2-5% in later tasks, which is due to reduced memorization (Lee et al., 2022).

To demonstrate the significant impact of data, one can examine the evolution from GPT-2 to GPT-3. While GPT-2, which was trained on WebText (8.3 billion tokens sourced from Reddit links), displayed emergent reasoning abilities primarily at scale, it was also prone to hallucinations stemming from the inherent noise in web data. Conversely, GPT-3's Common Crawl filtering pipeline, which eliminated between 400TB and 570GB of data through heuristics such as line length and n-gram repetition, resulted in a tenfold reduction in perplexity, thereby facilitating in-context learning (Brown et al., 2020). Likewise, Stable Diffusion v1.5's application of LAION-Aesthetics (filtered based on CLIP score >0.3 and aesthetic predictor >4.0) enhanced image fidelity by 15% compared to unfiltered LAION-5B, thereby illustrating how curation can unlock emergent multimodal alignment (Schuhmann et al., 2022).

Despite the critical role of data, the field of data governance for generative AI remains underdeveloped relative to other aspects of AI engineering (NIST, 2023). Research indicates a widespread culture of informal data practices among AI practitioners, where systematic documentation is often sidelined in favour of model-centric development (Sambasivan et al., 2021). While significant attention is paid to model architectures, training procedures, and inference optimisation, data practices often remain informal, undocumented, and inconsistent even within well-resourced Organisations. This gap creates multiple problems: models may inherit biases present in training data without awareness or mitigation (Raji et al., 2020); licensing and copyright issues may expose Organisations to legal liability as seen in the $4 billion Getty Images lawsuit against Stability AI (Getty Images v. Stability AI, 2023); provenance challenges make it difficult to audit or remediate model behaviors; and the lack of systematic documentation impedes scientific reproducibility and cumulative progress (Bommasani et al., 2021).

The literature on data governance reveals significant tensions that deserve explicit debate rather than uncritical synthesis. Research demonstrates that larger datasets generally improve model performance (Kaplan et al., 2020; Hoffmann et al., 2022), yet larger datasets are more difficult to govern effectively. Bender et al. (2021) argue that the pursuit of scale at any cost creates "stochastic parrots" models that mimic patterns without understanding, amplifying biases present in training data. Conversely, Rae et al. (2021) contend that scaling with appropriate filtering can reduce rather than amplify harms. At this point, it can be said that scale is not inherently problematic, but governance mechanisms must scale proportionally. Also, there is the open data movement that advocates for publicly available training corpora to democratise AI development (LAION, 2022). Yet copyright holders argue this constitutes mass infringement, as evidenced by pending litigation. The legal resolution remains uncertain; this chapter provides decision frameworks for navigating this ambiguity rather than advocating a single position. Automation enables governance at scale but may miss nuanced quality issues. Human evaluation captures qualitative dimensions but does not scale to billion-example datasets. Recent work by Lee et al. (2022) and Schuhmann et al. (2022) demonstrates hybrid approaches, but the optimal balance remains context-dependent.

Rather than resolving these tensions definitively, contingent frameworks can be provided that allow organisations to make principled trade-offs based on their risk tolerance, regulatory environment, and use case requirements. A critical comparison of existing governance frameworks reveals important distinctions in scope and emphasis. The NIST AI RMF (2023) offers a risk-based, voluntary approach that is broad in applicability but relatively light on prescriptive data governance requirements. By contrast, the EU AI Act (European Commission, 2021) mandates specific data documentation and bias assessment obligations for high-risk systems, creating enforceable accountability mechanisms that voluntary frameworks lack. Academic frameworks such as those proposed by Gebru et al. (2018) and Mitchell et al. (2019) prioritise transparency and documentation but were not designed for the scale of modern generative AI corpora. The four-dimensional framework proposed in this chapter advances the field by integrating technical, legal, ethical, and lifecycle perspectives into a unified governance architecture, a synthesis that prior frameworks address only partially and in isolation. This positioning is important: the contribution is not merely descriptive but structural, offering practitioners a coherent decision-making scaffold that bridges the gaps identified across existing literature (Bommasani et al., 2021; Sambasivan et al., 2021).

The distinctive attributes of generative AI underscore the necessity for robust data governance. Unlike conventional machine learning, where data primarily functions as a foundation for pattern recognition, generative AI systems possess the capacity to memorize, recombine, and interpolate training data in intricate manners. This capability introduces novel challenges concerning attribution, ownership, and potential harm (Carlini et al., 2021). As an illustration, extractive attacks have revealed that models such as GPT-2 can reproduce up to 1% of the training data verbatim (Carlini et al., 2021). The legal framework governing training data is currently ambiguous and subject to dispute, with ongoing legal proceedings and regulatory scrutiny centered on the rights of content creators whose work is utilized in model training (U.S. Copyright Office, 2023). Furthermore, the potential for generative systems to generate harmful, biased, or misleading outputs elevates the governance of training data to a matter of immediate societal importance (Bender et al., 2021).

This chapter addresses the urgent need for systematised data governance in generative AI. The mission is to provide practitioners with a comprehensive framework that spans the entire data lifecycle, from initial collection through ongoing maintenance and evolution. The aim is to connect theoretical principles to practical implementation, offering actionable guidance alongside conceptual frameworks. The chapter is designed to serve ML engineers, data scientists, MLOps teams, legal and compliance professionals, and researchers seeking to understand and implement responsible data practices (NIST, 2023).

This chapter is organised as follows. The first part defines the data governance landscape, including stakeholder perspectives and the regulatory environment. The second part presents the conceptual framework organised around four dimensions which examines the data quality and curation, documentation and transparency, legal and ethical compliance, and lifecycle management. And finally, the last part presents the conclusion with discussions on the future directions.

THE DATA GOVERNANCE LANDSCAPE

To establish a robust foundation for data governance in generative AI, it is necessary to first define the scope and boundaries of the discipline within this specific context. Data governance is often misunderstood as a purely administrative or compliance function, yet in the realm of generative AI, it is a core engineering discipline that directly influences model performance, reliability, and societal impact. The landscape of data governance is complex, involving a convergence of technical, legal, ethical, and organizational dimensions.

Defining Data Governance in Generative AI

Data governance refers to the overall management of the availability, usability, integrity, and security of the data employed in an enterprise (Ward, 2019). In the context of generative AI, this definition expands to include the specific lifecycle of data used for training, fine-tuning, and evaluating large-scale models. Unlike traditional data governance, which often focuses on structured data within enterprise databases, generative AI data governance must contend with unstructured, multimodal, and often publicly scraped data. This includes text from the open web, images from social media, audio from podcasts, and video from streaming platforms.

The governance of this data requires a shift from static management to dynamic stewardship. In traditional machine learning, a dataset might be created once and used for a specific model training run. In generative AI, datasets are often continuously updated, augmented, and recombined to improve model capabilities. This dynamic nature necessitates governance frameworks that are flexible enough to accommodate change while maintaining strict controls over quality and compliance. For example, the data flywheel where better data leads to better models, which generate better synthetic data requires governance at every iteration (Bommasani et al., 2021).

Stakeholder Perspectives

Effective data governance requires the alignment of multiple stakeholders, each with distinct priorities and responsibilities. Understanding these perspectives is crucial for designing a governance framework that is both practical and effective.

Machine Learning Engineers and Data Scientists

For ML engineers and data scientists, the primary concern is model performance. They require high-quality, diverse, and representative data to train models that generalise well to unseen inputs. However, they often face pressure to scale data collection rapidly, which can lead to shortcuts in quality assurance. Governance frameworks must provide them with tools and pipelines that automate quality checks without stifling innovation. For example, automated deduplication pipelines can save significant computational resources while ensuring data integrity (Zhang et al., 2017). In practice, at companies like Hugging Face, engineers use libraries like datasets and evaluate to implement these pipelines.

MLOps and Platform Teams

MLOps teams are responsible for the infrastructure that supports data pipelines. They focus on scalability, reliability, and versioning. For them, data governance means implementing systems that track data lineage, manage data versions, and ensure that data pipelines are reproducible. They need to integrate governance checks into the CI/CD (Continuous Integration/Continuous Deployment) pipelines to prevent bad data from reaching production models (Sculley et al., 2015). Tools like DVC and MLflow are commonly used for this purpose.

Product Managers and Engineering Leaders

Product managers and engineering leaders define the strategic direction of AI initiatives. They are concerned with time-to-market, cost efficiency, and risk management. For them, data governance is a risk mitigation strategy. They need to understand the legal and ethical implications of the data they use to avoid reputational damage and legal liability. They require high-level dashboards that summarise data quality metrics and compliance status. For instance, dashboards showing deduplication rates, bias scores, and licensing compliance can inform strategic decisions.

Trust and Safety, Legal, and Compliance Professionals

Trust and safety professionals focus on the societal impact of AI systems. They are concerned with bias, harm, and safety. Legal and compliance professionals focus on regulatory adherence, such as GDPR, CCPA, and the EU AI Act. They require detailed documentation of data sources, consent mechanisms, and licensing terms. They need to be able to audit the data pipeline to prove compliance in the event of an investigation (NIST, 2023).

Researchers

Researchers investigate the theoretical underpinnings of data governance. They seek to understand the relationship between data quality and model performance, the impact of bias in training data, and the long-term societal effects of generative AI. They require open access to datasets and documentation to validate their findings. Governance frameworks must balance the need for security with the need for scientific reproducibility (Bommasani et al., 2021).

Regulatory and Ethical Environment

The regulatory environment surrounding AI is rapidly evolving. Different jurisdictions have adopted different approaches to data governance, creating a complex landscape for global Organisations. The table below provides a comparative overview of key regulations.

Table 1. Regulatory Comparison for AI Data Governance

Jurisdiction	Key Regulation	Data Requirements	Enforcement
EU	EU AI Act (2021)	Transparency on training data, bias assessment (Art. 10)	Fines up to €35M
US	NIST AI RMF (2023)	Voluntary risk management framework	No direct fines
China	Generative AI Measures (2023)	Data accuracy, IP respect	State oversight
UK	AI Regulation White Paper (2023)	Pro-innovation approach	Sector-specific

As shown in the table, the EU imposes the strictest requirements, particularly for high-risk systems.

European Union

The European Union has taken a leading role in AI regulation with the EU AI Act. This legislation categorises AI systems based on risk levels and imposes specific obligations on high-risk systems. For data governance, the EU AI Act requires transparency regarding the data used to train models, including the identification of copyrighted material and the assessment of bias (European Commission, 2021). Additionally, the General Data Protection Regulation (GDPR) imposes strict rules on the processing of personal data, which affects the collection and use of data for training generative models.

United States

In the United States, the regulatory landscape is more fragmented. The National Institute of Standards and Technology (NIST) has released the AI Risk Management Framework, which provides guidelines for managing AI risks, including data governance (NIST, 2023). The U.S. Copyright Office has also issued reports on the copyrightability of works generated by AI and the use of copyrighted works in training AI models (U.S. Copyright Office, 2023). Litigation is ongoing, with cases such as *Getty Images v. Stability AI* highlighting the legal uncertainties surrounding training data.

China

China has implemented regulations that focus on the security and stability of AI systems. The Interim Measures for the Management of Generative Artificial Intelligence Services require service providers to ensure the accuracy and truthfulness of the training data and to respect intellectual property rights (Cyberspace Administration of China, 2023). This approach emphasizes state control and social stability over individual rights.

Mapping the Regulatory Environment

Organisations operating globally must navigate these varying regulatory requirements. A unified governance framework must be flexible enough to adapt to local laws while maintaining a consistent standard of care. This often involves creating a "baseline" governance policy that meets the strictest requirements and then applying local modifications where necessary.

Figure 1. The Data Governance Landscape for Generative AI.

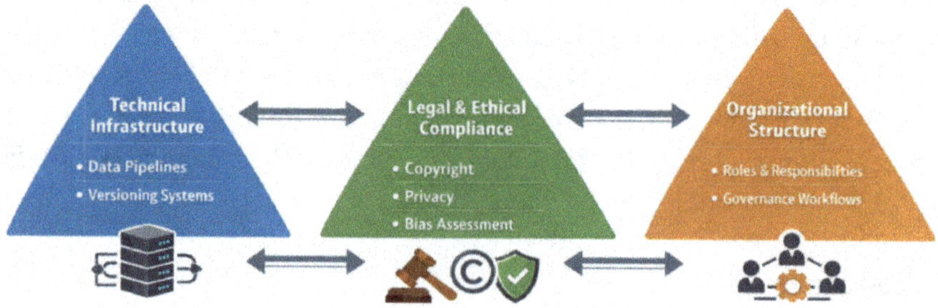

This figure depicts the three primary pillars of data governance: Technical Infrastructure, Legal and Ethical Compliance, and Organizational Structure. Arrows indicate the flow of information and control between these pillars. The Technical Infrastructure includes data pipelines and versioning systems. Legal and Ethical

Compliance includes copyright, privacy, and bias assessment. Organizational Structure includes roles, responsibilities, and governance workflows.

As shown in the figure, the governance landscape is not linear but interconnected. A failure in one pillar can compromise the others. For example, a lack of technical versioning (Technical Infrastructure) can make it impossible to audit data for compliance (Legal and Ethical Compliance). Similarly, unclear roles and responsibilities (Organisational Structure) can lead to gaps in data quality assurance.

THE CONCEPTUAL FRAMEWORK

To address the complexity of the data governance landscape, this chapter proposes a conceptual framework that organises governance concerns into four primary dimensions: Data Quality and Curation, Documentation and Transparency, Legal and Ethical Compliance, and Lifecycle Management. This framework provides a structured approach to identifying gaps in current practices and prioritising improvements.

The data quality and curation dimension focuses on the technical processes of collecting, cleaning, and preparing data. It includes methodologies for deduplication, filtering, and quality assessment. The goal is to ensure that the data used to train models is accurate, representative, and free from harmful content.

Documentation and transparency dimension focuses on the information that accompanies the data. It includes datasheets, model cards, and data lineage tracking. The goal is to ensure that the data is documented in sufficient detail to enable auditing, reproduction, and critical evaluation.

Legal and ethical compliance dimension focuses on the legal and ethical implications of data use. It includes copyright law, licensing terms, bias assessment, and harm evaluation. The goal is to ensure that the data is used in a way that respects the rights of content creators and minimises harm to society.

Lifecycle management dimension focuses on the ongoing maintenance and evolution of data. It includes strategies for incorporating new data, retiring outdated data, and managing data in continuous training pipelines. The goal is to ensure that the data remains relevant and compliant over time.

By organising governance concerns into these four dimensions, practitioners can systematically address the challenges of data governance in generative AI. Each dimension requires specific tools, processes, and policies, but they must be integrated to form a cohesive governance strategy.

Data Curation and Quality Assurance

The construction of high-quality training datasets requires careful attention to collection strategies, deduplication, filtering, and quality assessment. At scale, these tasks present significant engineering challenges. This section examines methodologies for identifying and removing near-duplicate content, filtering low-quality or noisy data, and balancing dataset composition across dimensions such as language, domain, and demographic representation.

Collection Strategies

The first step in data curation is collection. The source of the data determines many of the downstream governance challenges. Common sources include web scraping, public datasets, proprietary data, and user-generated content.

Web Scraping

Web scraping involves automatically downloading content from websites. While this allows for the collection of vast amounts of data, it raises legal and ethical concerns. Robots.txt files and terms of service agreements often restrict scraping activities. Organisations must respect these restrictions to avoid legal liability. Additionally, scraped data may contain sensitive information, such as personally identifiable information (PII), which must be filtered out to comply with privacy regulations (NIST, 2023).

Public Datasets

Public datasets, such as Common Crawl or Wikipedia, are often used as a starting point for training data. These datasets are generally well-documented and have clear licensing terms. However, they may not be representative of the specific domain or demographic that the model is intended to serve. Organisations must assess the representativeness of public datasets before using them.

Proprietary Data

Proprietary data, such as internal documents or customer data, can provide high-quality, domain-specific training data. However, using proprietary data requires strict access controls and privacy protections. Organisations must ensure that the data is anonymized and that the use of the data is authorized by the data owners.

User-Generated Content

User-generated content, such as social media posts or forum discussions, can provide diverse and up-to-date data. However, this data is often noisy and may contain harmful content. Organisations must implement robust filtering mechanisms to remove low-quality or harmful content before using it for training.

Deduplication

Deduplication is the process of identifying and removing duplicate or near-duplicate content from a dataset. Duplicate data can bias model training, causing the model to overfit to specific patterns. At scale, deduplication is computationally expensive and requires efficient algorithms.

Exact Deduplication

Exact deduplication involves identifying identical copies of data. This is relatively straightforward and can be achieved using hash functions. For example, the MD5 hash of a text document can be used to identify exact duplicates. However, exact deduplication does not catch near-duplicates, which are more common in large datasets.

Near-Duplicate Deduplication

Near-duplicate deduplication involves identifying content that is similar but not identical. This is more challenging and requires more sophisticated algorithms. One common approach is MinHash, which uses locality-sensitive hashing to estimate the similarity between documents (Broder, 1997). Another approach is SimHash, which is designed for near-duplicate detection in large-scale web data (Charikar, 2002). It uses locality-sensitive hashing (LSH). The Jaccard similarity between two sets A and B is:

$$J\left(A,B\right) = \frac{|A \cap B|}{|A \cup B|}$$

MinHash approximates this with:

$$\hat{J}\left(A,B\right) = \frac{\text{Number of colliding minhash values}}{\text{Total number of hash functions}}$$

The equation demonstrates how MinHash enables efficient similarity estimation at scale (Broder, 1997).

Quantitative example: In the LAION-5B dataset, deduplication removed 12% of duplicate samples, resulting in a 3.2% improvement in CLIP scores (Schuhmann et al., 2022).

For evaluating model bias, a common metric is demographic parity, which measures the difference in prediction rates between protected groups:

where is the model's prediction and represents a protected attribute (e.g., gender or ethnicity).

The table below shows the statistics from major generative AI datasets

Table 2. Statistics from Major Generative AI Datasets

Dataset	Size	Dedup % Removed	Languages	Modalities
C4 (Raffel et al., 2020)	750 GB	5.2%	100+	Text
LAION-5B	5.85B pairs	12%	Multi	Image-Text
The Pile	800 GB	8.1%	English-heavy	Text

For example, if a dataset contains 100 billion tokens, exact deduplication might remove 1% of the data, while near-duplicate deduplication might remove an additional 5%. This reduction can significantly improve model performance by reducing the weight of overrepresented content (Raffel et al., 2020).

Filtering and Quality Assessment

Filtering involves removing low-quality or noisy data from a dataset. This can be done using automated rules or machine learning models.

Automated Rules

Automated rules involve setting thresholds for specific metrics. For example, documents with a length below a certain threshold might be removed. Documents with a high ratio of special characters might be removed. These rules are simple to implement but may not capture all low-quality data.

Machine Learning Models

Machine learning models can be trained to classify data as high-quality or low-quality. For example, a classifier can be trained to identify spam or low-quality text. These models can be more effective than automated rules but require training data and computational resources.

Quality Metrics

Quality metrics are used to assess the quality of a dataset. Common metrics include perplexity, which measures how well a language model predicts the data, and human evaluation, which involves human annotators rating the quality of the data.

Perplexity

Perplexity is a measure of how well a probability model predicts a sample. Lower perplexity indicates that the model is more confident in its predictions, which suggests that the data is more coherent and high-quality. However, perplexity can be gamed by models that overfit to the training data.

For perplexity (quality metric):

where is the number of tokens and is the model's probability (Raffel et al., 2020).

Human Evaluation

Human evaluation involves asking human annotators to rate the quality of the data. This is more accurate than automated metrics but is also more expensive and time-consuming. Human evaluation is often used to validate the results of automated metrics. Platforms including Scale AI, Appen, and Amazon Mechanical Turk enable crowdsourcing, with best practices emphasizing clear guidelines, multiple annotators per item to compute inter-annotator agreement via metrics like Cohen's Kappa, and diverse annotator pools to reduce bias. For multimodal data, tasks focus on caption accuracy or visual relevance.

Balancing Dataset Composition

Balancing dataset composition involves ensuring that the dataset is representative of the target population. This is particularly important for multimodal datasets, which include text, images, audio, and video. Techniques include oversampling rare classes, under sampling dominant ones, or generating synthetic data through methods like SMOTE for tabular data or diffusion models for visuals, with alignment across modalities via embeddings like CLIP. Metrics such as class imbalance ratios or KL-divergence from ideal distributions guide adjustments, visualized via tools like Facets or What-If Tool. In multimodal contexts, this means synchronizing attributes like audio accents with transcripts or balancing images by lighting, ethnicity, and scenes using metadata from corpora like LAION-5B.

Language Representation

For language models, it is important to ensure that the dataset includes a diverse range of languages. If the dataset is dominated by English, the model may perform poorly on non-English tasks. Organisations must assess the language distribution of their datasets and take steps to balance it if necessary. Balancing entails sourcing from multilingual corpora such as mC4, OSCAR, or Wikipedia, paired with language-specific tokenizers like Sentence-Piece and upweighting low-resource tongues through adapters or targeted pretraining.

Domain Representation

For domain-specific models, it is important to ensure that the dataset includes a diverse range of domains. For example, a medical model should include data from various medical specialties. If the dataset is dominated by one domain, the model may perform poorly on other domains. Domains are mapped using taxonomies like DMOZ or classifiers like BERT for zero-shot labelling, with balancing via domain-adaptive pretraining on blended corpora (e.g., PubMed plus clinical notes), mixture-of-experts architectures, or augmentation through back-translation and knowledge graphs.

Demographic Representation

For models that interact with humans, it is important to ensure that the dataset includes a diverse range of demographics. If the dataset is dominated by a specific demographic, the model may perform poorly for other demographics. This can lead to bias and discrimination.

Multimodal Dataset Construction

Multimodal dataset construction introduces additional complexities around alignment between modalities, the handling of noisy or missing data, and the representation of diverse cultural and linguistic contexts.

Alignment

Alignment involves ensuring that the different modalities in a dataset correspond to the same underlying concept. For example, in an image-text dataset, the text should accurately describe the image. Misalignment can lead to poor model performance.

Noisy or Missing Data

Multimodal datasets often contain noisy or missing data. For example, an image may not have a corresponding text description. Organisations must implement strategies for handling missing data, such as imputation or removal.

Cultural and Linguistic Contexts

Multimodal datasets must reflect the full breadth of human experience. This includes diverse cultural and linguistic contexts. If the dataset is dominated by Western culture, the model may perform poorly for non-Western users.

The following table outlines the primary methodologies used in the data curation pipeline for generative AI. Techniques vary in computational cost, legal risk, and effectiveness.

Table 3. Methodologies for Data Curation and Quality Assurance.

Category	Technique	Description	Challenges and trade-offs
Collection strategies	Web scraping	Automated downloading of content from websites.	Legal risks (terms of service); potential inclusion of PII; requires robust filtering.
	Public datasets	Utilization of existing open-source corpora (e.g., Common Crawl).	May lack domain specificity; licensing restrictions; potential for outdated information.
	Proprietary data	Use of internal or licensed enterprise data.	Access control complexity; privacy compliance (GDPR/CCPA); high cost of acquisition.
	User-generated content	Aggregation of social media posts or forum discussions.	High noise levels; potential for harmful content; requires significant moderation.
Deduplication	Exact Deduplication	Removal of identical copies using hash functions (e.g., MD5).	Does not catch near-duplicates; computationally efficient but limited scope.
	Near-Duplicate Deduplication	Removal of similar content using algorithms (e.g., MinHash, SimHash).	Computationally expensive; requires tuning of similarity thresholds; risk of removing valid variations.

continued on following page

Table 3. Continued

Category	Technique	Description	Challenges and trade-offs
Filtering methods	Automated rules	Application of static thresholds (e.g., length, character ratio).	Low flexibility; may remove valid data that falls outside thresholds; easy to implement.
	Machine learning models	Classification of data quality using trained models.	Requires labeled training data; higher computational cost; potential for model drift over time.
Quality metrics	Perplexity	Measure of how well a language model predicts the data.	Can be gamed by overfitting; does not capture semantic quality; requires a reference model.
	Human evaluation	Manual rating of data quality by annotators.	High cost and time consumption; subjectivity; difficult to scale to large datasets.

As shown in Table 3, there is no one-size-fits-all approach to data curation. Organisations must select the methodologies that best fit their specific needs and constraints. For instance, while web scraping offers scale, it introduces significant legal risk that may require a more conservative approach, such as using public datasets with clear licensing. Similarly, while human evaluation provides high-quality feedback, it is often impractical for datasets containing billions of tokens, necessitating a reliance on automated metrics like perplexity, which must be validated against human standards. The trade-offs between computational efficiency and data quality must be carefully managed to ensure the resulting model is both performant and compliant.

Documentation and Transparency

The principle of transparency in AI systems requires that the data used to train models be documented in sufficient detail to enable auditing, reproduction, and critical evaluation. The evolution of documentation standards from datasheets for datasets will be examined through model cards and system cards, discussing the information that should be captured, the trade-offs between comprehensiveness and usability, and the organisational practices needed to maintain documentation over time.

The following figure is the sample dataset template for Generative AI Dataset Documentation.

Figure 2. Sample Datasheet Template for Generative AI Dataset

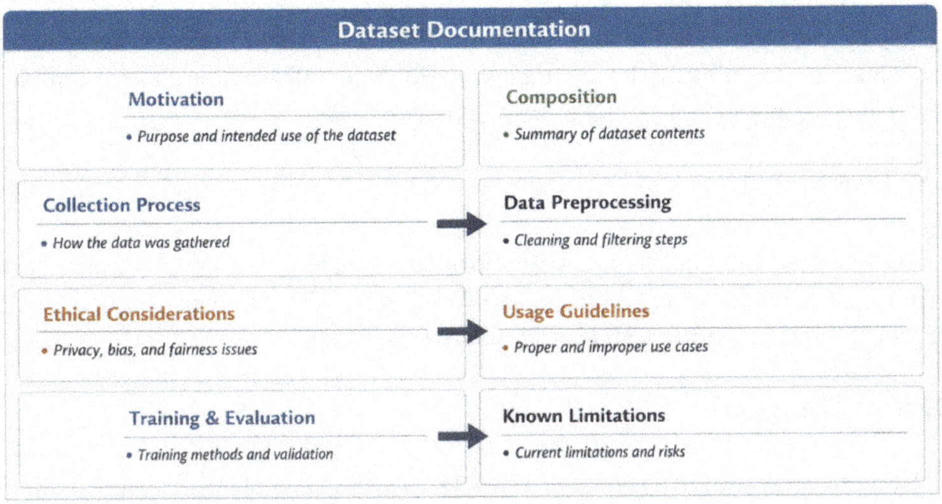

Datasheets for Datasets

The concept of datasheets for datasets was introduced by Gebru et al. (2018) to encourage transparency in machine learning research. A datasheet is a document that accompanies a dataset and provides information about its creation, composition, and intended use.

Key Information

A datasheet should include key information such as the motivation for creating the dataset, the composition of the dataset, the collection process, the preprocessing steps, and the recommended uses. This information helps users understand the limitations and potential biases of the dataset.

Trade-offs

There are trade-offs between comprehensiveness and usability. A datasheet that is too long may be ignored, while a datasheet that is too short may not provide enough information. Organisations must find a balance that provides enough information without overwhelming the user.

Model Cards

Model cards were introduced by Mitchell et al. (2019) to provide information about machine learning models. A model card includes information about the model's performance, intended use, and ethical considerations.

Key Information

A model card should include key information such as the model's architecture, training data, performance metrics, and limitations. This information helps users understand the capabilities and limitations of the model.

System Cards

System cards extend the concept of model cards to include information about the entire AI system, including the data, the model, and the deployment environment. This provides a more comprehensive view of the system's impact.

Data Lineage Tracking

Data lineage tracking represents a particularly important and challenging aspect of documentation. As datasets are filtered, augmented, and combined through multiple processing stages, maintaining a clear record of data provenance becomes essential for understanding model behaviours and remediating identified issues.

Metadata Schemas

Metadata schemas define the structure and format of the metadata that accompanies the data. Common schemas include Schema.org and the Data Documentation Initiative (DDI). These schemas provide a standard way to describe data, making it easier to share and reuse.

Version Control Practices

Version control practices involve tracking changes to the data over time. Tools such as DVC (Data Version Control) can be used to manage data versions. Version control allows Organisations to roll back to previous versions of the data if issues are identified.

Automated Documentation Pipelines

Automated documentation pipelines generate documentation automatically as data is processed. This reduces the burden on data scientists and ensures that documentation is up-to-date. Automated pipelines can also enforce consistency in documentation.

Maintaining Documentation

Maintaining documentation in dynamic environments is challenging. Documentation must be updated as data changes, and it must be accessible to all stakeholders. Organisations must establish processes for reviewing and updating documentation regularly.

The following figure shows the flow of data through a lineage tracking system.

Figure 3. Data Lineage Tracking System.

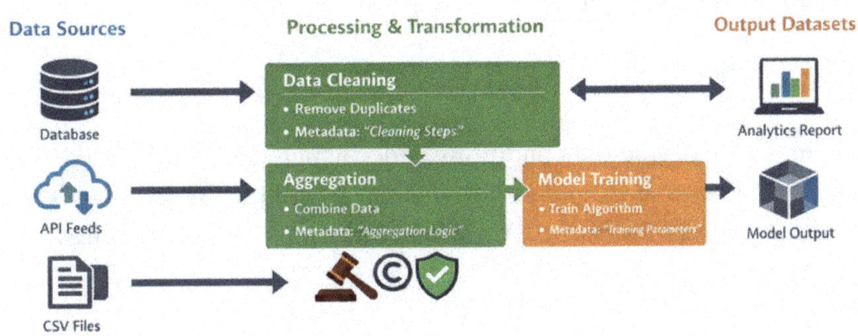

As shown in Figure 3, data lineage tracking provides a clear record of how data is transformed over time. It includes the data sources, processing steps, and output datasets. Each step is tagged with metadata that describes the transformation applied. This is essential for auditing and debugging.

Legal and Ethical Compliance

The legal landscape surrounding training data remains complex and evolving. Structured analysis of copyright law will be provided as it applies to AI training, including the fair use doctrine and its application to different use cases, the implications of licensing terms, and the emerging regulatory frameworks such as the EU

AI Act that impose obligations on data governance. The chapter offers decision frameworks for navigating these complexities, recognizing that legal compliance is not merely a matter of legal advice but requires technical implementation of governance controls.

Copyright Law

Copyright law protects original works of authorship, including text, images, and audio. The use of copyrighted works in AI training raises questions about infringement and fair use.

Fair Use Doctrine

The fair use doctrine allows the use of copyrighted works without permission in certain circumstances, such as for criticism, comment, news reporting, teaching, scholarship, or research. The application of fair use to AI training is contested. Some argue that training AI models is transformative and therefore fair use, while others argue that it is a substitute for the original work.

Licensing Terms

Licensing terms define the conditions under which data can be used. Common licenses include Creative Commons (CC) licenses and the General Public License (GPL). Organisations must respect these licenses to avoid legal liability.

EU AI Act

The EU AI Act imposes obligations on data governance for high-risk AI systems. These obligations include transparency regarding the data used to train models and the assessment of bias. Organisations must comply with these obligations to operate in the European Union.

Ethical Considerations

Ethical considerations in data governance extend beyond legal compliance to encompass questions of harm, fairness, and social responsibility. Legal compliance establishes a minimum standard, but ethical responsibility demands proactive identification of potential harms, meaningful consultation with affected communities, and a willingness to reject data sources or use cases that may cause disproportionate harm even when legally permissible. Concepts such as data dignity (respecting the rights and interests of data subjects) and participatory governance (including affected communities in governance decisions) are gaining traction as essential complements to legal compliance.

A central tension in ethical data governance is the conflict between the utilitarian benefits of large-scale AI training and the rights of individuals whose data contributes to that training without explicit consent. The open web contains billions of documents authored by individuals who had no expectation that their writing would be used to train commercial AI systems. Even where legal mechanisms such as fair use may permit such use, the ethical question of whether it is appropriate remains open. This tension is not merely philosophical: it has practical implications for how organisations structure data collection, how they communicate with data subjects, and what remediation mechanisms they establish when harms are identified (Raji et al., 2020).

Three ethical principles should guide training data governance. First, the principle of non-maleficence requires that organisations actively identify and mitigate foreseeable harms arising from training data, including the amplification of stereotypes, the perpetuation of historical injustices encoded in text, and the erosion of privacy through memorisation. Second, the principle of justice requires that the benefits and burdens of AI development be distributed equitably, which includes ensuring that training datasets represent marginalised and underrepresented populations rather than being dominated by the demographics of the most prolific online contributors. Third, the principle of transparency requires that organisations be open about what data they use, how it is processed, and what limitations it introduces into the resulting model (Bender et al., 2021).

In practice, organisations should establish an Ethics Review Board or equivalent body with cross-functional membership including domain experts, legal counsel, and external community representatives. This body should be empowered to veto data sources or training pipelines that raise unresolved ethical concerns, even where legal clearance has been obtained. Ethical review should be a formal gate in the data lifecycle rather than an optional advisory function. Documentation of ethical review decisions, including the reasoning behind approvals and rejections, should be preserved as part of the data governance record and made available to internal auditors and, where appropriate, external regulators.

It is also important to recognise that ethical standards evolve. A dataset assembled in 2020 according to the ethical norms of that period may no longer be considered acceptable by 2025 standards. Organisations must therefore build processes for retrospective ethical review, enabling them to reassess and, if necessary, retire or remediate datasets as community expectations and regulatory requirements change. This is consistent with the lifecycle management perspective described elsewhere in this chapter: ethical governance is not a one-time approval but an ongoing responsibility.

Bias Assessment

Bias assessment involves evaluating the dataset for biases that may lead to unfair or discriminatory outcomes. Common biases include gender bias, racial bias, and socioeconomic bias.

A rigorous bias assessment programme for generative AI training data operates at multiple levels of analysis. At the corpus level, statistical profiling quantifies the representation of demographic groups, geographic regions, languages, and domains. At the document level, classifiers trained on annotated datasets detect hate speech, stereotypical language, and toxic content. At the semantic level, embedding-based methods such as Word Embedding Association Tests (WEAT) and Sentence Encoder Association Tests (SEAT) measure the degree to which implicit associations in the data reflect societal biases (Caliskan et al., 2017). Each level of analysis addresses a different facet of bias, and all three are necessary for a comprehensive assessment.

The formal measure most commonly applied to evaluate representational fairness is demographic parity, expressed as:

where Y is the model's prediction and A is a protected attribute such as gender or ethnicity. A demographic parity score of zero indicates that the model's predictions are equally distributed across groups, while higher values indicate disparity. However, demographic parity is only one of several fairness criteria, and optimising for it may conflict with other criteria such as equalised odds or calibration. Organisations must determine which fairness criterion is most appropriate for their deployment context before beginning assessment, as this choice has significant downstream implications for both the assessment methodology and the remediation strategy (Barocas et al., 2019).

In practice, bias assessment should follow a structured pipeline. The first stage involves automated statistical profiling of the training corpus using tools such as Fairlearn, IBM AI Fairness 360, or custom pipelines built on standard NLP libraries. The second stage involves targeted human review of a stratified sample of flagged documents, enabling annotators to assess whether the bias identified by automated tools is substantively harmful or a false positive. The third stage involves model-level evaluation, in which a probe model is trained on the assessed corpus and evaluated against benchmark datasets such as WinoBias (Zhao et al., 2018) or BBQ (Parrish et al., 2022) that are specifically designed to surface biased associations. The results of all three stages should be documented in the dataset's datasheet under the Bias Assessment field, with quantitative results reported alongside qualitative interpretations.

It is important to acknowledge the limitations of current bias assessment methodologies. Automated tools can detect surface-level patterns but may miss subtle or context-dependent biases. Human annotators bring their own biases to the review process, and inter-annotator agreement on what constitutes a harmful bias can be low. Benchmark datasets such as WinoBias capture specific types of gender bias in co-reference resolution but are not designed to detect the full range of biases that may be present in a large generative training corpus. Organisations should treat bias assessment as an iterative and evolving practice rather than a definitive certification of fairness.

Harm Evaluation

Harm evaluation involves assessing the potential harm that the model may cause. This includes harm to individuals, groups, and society.

A comprehensive harm evaluation framework for generative AI training data distinguishes between three categories of harm: direct harms arising from harmful content present in the training corpus, indirect harms arising from biased or misleading representations that shape model outputs, and systemic harms arising from the cumulative effect of widely deployed models trained on similar data. Each category requires different assessment methodologies and different governance responses.

Direct harms are the most tractable to assess. Content classifiers can identify training examples that contain explicit violence, hate speech, instructions for illegal activities, and other categories of harmful content defined by the organisation's acceptable use policy. State-of-the-art classifiers such as Perspective API achieve precision and recall rates sufficient for use in production filtering pipelines. However, classifiers are not perfect, and organisations must specify acceptable false positive and false negative rates based on their risk tolerance. A medical AI organisation may accept a higher false positive rate to ensure a lower false negative rate, preventing harmful medical misinformation from entering the training data.

Indirect harms are more challenging to quantify because they manifest not through explicit harmful content but through the statistical patterns encoded in otherwise innocuous text. For example, a corpus that consistently associates certain professions with specific genders, or certain geographic regions with criminal activity, will encode these associations in the model's representations even if no individual document contains explicitly harmful language. Evaluation methods for indirect harms include counterfactual data augmentation, in which the genders or ethnicities referenced in a document are systematically varied to test whether the model's outputs remain consistent, and probing classifiers, which measure the degree to which sensitive attributes are encoded in model representations (Ravfogel et al., 2020).

Systemic harms require a broader analytical lens. When a small number of organisations train dominant AI models on overlapping corpora, errors and biases in those corpora are amplified across the entire field. Organisations should therefore consider not only the harms that their specific model may cause but also the contribution of their data governance decisions to the broader information ecosystem. This includes the environmental impact of large-scale training data curation, the labour conditions of annotation workers, and the economic effects of concentrating AI capabilities in well-resourced institutions. These considerations require engagement with researchers in sociology, political economy, and science and technology studies (Bommasani et al., 2021).

Harm evaluation should be documented in a dedicated section of the dataset's datasheet, specifying the categories of harm assessed, the methodologies used, the results obtained, and the remediation steps taken. Where harms are identified but cannot be fully remediated, the residual risk should be disclosed explicitly, enabling downstream model developers and deployers to make informed decisions about whether to use the dataset for their intended application.

Methodologies

Methodologies for bias assessment and harm evaluation in training data will be examined, discussing both established approaches and their limitations. The chapter emphasises that bias assessment is not a one-time activity but rather an ongoing governance concern that must be revisited as models evolve and deployment contexts change.

The selection of appropriate methodologies depends on the type of bias or harm being assessed, the scale of the dataset, and the computational resources available. No single methodology is sufficient on its own; robust governance requires a layered approach combining automated statistical profiling, model-based evaluation, and human review.

Statistical profiling methods operate at the corpus level and characterise the demographic and topical composition of a dataset without requiring model training. These include frequency analysis of protected attributes using named entity recognition and coreference resolution tools; domain classification to assess the balance of topics; and language identification to quantify multilingual representation. Statistical profiling is computationally efficient and can be applied to datasets of any size, making it the appropriate starting point for any bias assessment programme. Its limitation is that it captures only surface-level properties and cannot detect subtler forms of bias arising from contextual associations (Blodgett et al., 2020).

Model-based evaluation methods train or fine-tune a probe model on the corpus under assessment and evaluate its outputs on curated benchmark datasets designed to surface specific types of bias. Benchmarks commonly used include WinoBias and WinoGender for gender bias in co-reference resolution, BBQ for social bias in question answering, ToxiGen for implicit toxicity, and BOLD for generation diversity across demographic groups. Model-based evaluation is more sensitive to contextual and implicit biases than statistical profiling but requires significant computational investment and introduces the risk of benchmark overfitting (Parrish et al., 2022).

Qualitative human review provides a complementary perspective that quantitative methods cannot capture. Trained annotators review stratified samples of training documents and model outputs, assessing whether the content is harmful or biased in ways that automated classifiers have missed. To ensure reliability, human review should employ multiple annotators per item with inter-annotator agreement measured using Cohen's Kappa or Krippendorff's Alpha. Annotators should be recruited from diverse demographic backgrounds and provided with detailed guidelines defining the categories of harm being assessed.

Longitudinal reassessment is an essential component of a mature bias assessment methodology. As models are updated or deployed in new contexts, the relevance of prior assessments diminishes. Organisations should establish a schedule for periodic reassessment, triggered by calendar intervals or by specific events such as a new model version, a significant corpus update, or the emergence of new benchmark datasets that reveal previously undetected biases. Results of each reassessment should be recorded in the data governance log to provide a complete audit trail.

Decision Frameworks

Decision frameworks provide a structured approach to navigating legal and ethical complexities. These frameworks help Organisations make informed decisions about data use.

The core challenge in legal and ethical decision-making for training data is that the relevant variables are multidimensional, contested, and evolving. A dataset that is legally permissible in one jurisdiction may be prohibited in another. A data source that passes ethical review today may be reconsidered as community norms shift or as new harms become apparent through model deployment. Practitioners therefore require frameworks that are not prescriptive rules but structured processes for deliberation under uncertainty.

The first framework proposed here is a licensing compatibility matrix, which provides a systematic method for assessing whether a given data source can be incorporated into a training corpus given the intended use case and distribution model. The matrix maps each potential data source to its licensing terms ranging from public domain and permissive open licences such as CC BY, through reciprocal licences such as CC BY-SA and GPL, to proprietary and all-rights-reserved licences and evaluates compatibility along three dimensions: commercial or non-commercial use, distribution or non-distribution of the trained model, and modification or non-modification of the training data. Sources that are incompatible along any dimension are excluded unless an explicit licence exception or legal opinion is obtained.

This matrix should be applied to every data source at the point of acquisition and documented in the dataset's provenance record.

The second framework is a risk-stratified review process for data sources that fall into legal grey areas, most notably those implicated by the ongoing debate over fair use in AI training. Under this framework, data sources are classified into three risk tiers. Tier 1 comprises sources with clear legal permissibility, including public domain works, sources with explicit training licences, and works authored or licensed by the organisation itself. Tier 2 comprises sources where fair use arguments are plausible but contested, such as publicly available web data scraped in accordance with robots.txt and terms of service. Tier 3 comprises sources where legal risk is high, including datasets named in active litigation and works where the rights holder has explicitly objected to AI training use. Tier 1 sources require only standard documentation. Tier 2 sources require legal review and documented risk acceptance by an authorised decision-maker. Tier 3 sources are excluded unless exceptional circumstances justify a full legal opinion and senior leadership approval.

The third framework is an ethical trade-off analysis template, adapted from principled deliberation methods used in bioethics and applied to training data governance. When an ethical concern is raised about a data source or use case that is not resolved by existing policy, the practitioner completes a structured analysis identifying: the specific ethical tension; the stakeholders affected and their interests; the options available and the ethical considerations for and against each; and the reasoning behind the final decision. This analysis is reviewed by the Ethics Review Board, and the decision and its rationale are recorded in the governance log. This template ensures that ethical decisions are made through deliberation rather than habit, and that the reasoning is preserved for future auditors, regulators, or researchers.

Together, these three frameworks provide a decision infrastructure enabling organisations to navigate the legal and ethical landscape of training data governance in a principled and auditable manner. They do not eliminate uncertainty or resolve contested legal questions, but they ensure that uncertainty is acknowledged, that decisions are made by appropriately authorised individuals, and that the reasoning behind those decisions can be reconstructed and evaluated by future stakeholders.

Applied Case Studies in Data Governance

The abstract frameworks presented throughout this chapter gain practical clarity when examined through real-world implementations. The following case studies illustrate how leading organisations have applied and, in some cases, struggled with data governance principles at scale, offering transferable lessons for practitioners.

Case Study 1: Hugging Face and the BigScience BLOOM Project

The BigScience ROOTS corpus, assembled by an international consortium of over 1,000 researchers to train the BLOOM language model (176 billion parameters), represents one of the most extensively documented governance efforts in large-scale generative AI. The project implemented a structured data governance pipeline that operationalises several dimensions of the framework proposed in this chapter. First, a dedicated Data Governance Working Group was established with clear role assignments, mirroring the RACI structure described in Table 4, including legal review of each data source, domain expert sign-off on quality, and engineering ownership of deduplication pipelines. Second, every dataset incorporated into ROOTS was accompanied by a standardised datasheet (Gebru et al., 2018) specifying provenance, licensing terms, and known limitations. Third, language balance was actively managed: the 498 languages represented in the corpus were curated to exceed their proportional representation on the internet, explicitly counteracting the English dominance of most web-scraped corpora (Laurencçon et al., 2022). The practical lesson for organisations is that governance at scale requires institutional structures not just technical pipelines. The BigScience project demonstrated that cross-functional accountability, documented decision-making, and proactive representation engineering can be operationalised even in large, distributed, open-science contexts.

Case Study 2: Getty Images v. Stability AI and the Governance Failure of Unfiltered Web Scraping

The litigation initiated by Getty Images against Stability AI in 2023, seeking approximately $1.8 billion in damages, illustrates the legal and reputational risks that result when data governance mechanisms are absent or inadequate (Getty Images v. Stability AI, 2023). Stability AI trained its Stable Diffusion models on LAION-5B, a dataset assembled from web-scraped image-text pairs without systematic licensing review. Getty Images alleged that millions of its copyrighted images were incorporated into the training corpus without authorisation, and that the trained model could reproduce images bearing distorted versions of the Getty Images watermark—direct evidence of memorisation. The governance failure here was not primarily technical: the deduplication and quality filtering applied to LAION-5B was sophisticated. The failure was in the legal compliance dimension of the governance framework. A licensing compatibility matrix of the type described in the Decision Frameworks section above would have identified Getty Images content as Tier 3 (high legal risk), requiring either exclusion or senior leadership approval with full legal opinion. This case underscores a practical implementation lesson: governance frameworks must integrate legal review as a first-class activity in the data acquisition pipeline, not as an afterthought following technical curation. Organisations that treat legal compliance as a gate rather than a guideline are significantly better positioned to avoid the reputational and financial consequences demonstrated by this litigation.

Lifecycle Management and Governance

Data governance does not end with initial dataset construction. Lifecycle perspective that encompasses the ongoing maintenance, versioning, and evolution of training data will be presented. This includes strategies for incorporating new data, retiring outdated data, managing data in continuous training pipelines, and conducting retrospective governance reviews when issues are identified.

Effective data governance for generative AI requires clear assignment of roles and responsibilities throughout the data lifecycle from acquisition and curation to maintenance and retirement. A RACI (Responsible, Accountable, Consulted, Informed) matrix provides a framework for clarifying these roles across cross-functional teams, including data engineers, domain experts, legal/compliance officers, and ML engineers.

Table 4. RACI Matrix for Data Governance in Generative AI Projects

Activity / Role	Data Engineer	Domain Expert	Legal / Compliance	ML Engineer	Project Lead
Data Acquisition & Licensing	R	C	A	I	C
Data Curation & Cleaning	R	C	I	C	I
PII / Ethical Auditing	C	R	A	I	I
Deduplication & Filtering	R	I	I	C	I
Dataset Versioning & Documentation	R	I	I	C	A
Bias & Fairness Evaluation	C	R	C	R	A
Model Training & Validation	I	C	I	R	C
Compliance Reporting	C	I	R	I	A
Data Retention & Decommissioning	R	I	A	I	C

R = Responsible (doer), A = Accountable (approver), C = Consulted (feedback), I = Informed (kept updated)

This matrix ensures accountability for critical governance tasks, such as licensing validation (assigned to Legal) and bias evaluation (co-led by Domain Experts and ML Engineers), while maintaining clear ownership for technical tasks like data curation.

Maintenance and Versioning

Maintenance involves keeping the data up-to-date and relevant. Versioning involves tracking changes to the data over time.

Incorporating New Data

Incorporating new data involves adding new data to the existing dataset. This must be done carefully to ensure that the new data is consistent with the existing data.

Retiring Outdated Data

Retiring outdated data involves removing data that is no longer relevant. This must be done carefully to ensure that the model does not lose important information.

Continuous Training Pipelines

Continuous training pipelines involve updating the model regularly with new data. This requires robust data governance to ensure that the new data is high-quality and compliant.

Retrospective Governance Reviews

Retrospective governance reviews involve reviewing the data governance practices after the model has been deployed. This helps identify issues and improve future practices.

Organizational Dimensions

The organisational dimensions of data governance receive sustained attention. Roles and responsibilities, governance workflows, and the integration of data governance will be discussed with broader AI governance and risk management frameworks. The chapter emphasises that effective governance requires not only technical systems but also organisational structures that assign clear accountability and enable coordinated action.

Roles and Responsibilities

Clear role assignment is a prerequisite for effective governance. Without explicit accountability, critical tasks such as licensing review or bias assessment fall into organisational gaps. The principal roles in a generative AI data governance programme are as follows. The Data Steward is responsible for day-to-day management of data quality, provenance documentation, and compliance with the organisation's data governance policy. The Data Owner is the business or legal entity that holds accountability for the data asset and has final authority over its acquisition, use, and retirement. The ML Engineer is responsible for implementing technical governance controls within data pipelines, including deduplication, filtering, and versioning. The Legal and Compliance Officer reviews licensing terms, assesses regulatory obligations, and approves data sources that carry legal risk. The Ethics Reviewer evaluates whether data sources and use cases meet the organisation's ethical standards and chairs the Ethics Review Board process described in the Legal and Ethical Compliance section. These roles must be staffed, not merely named: governance programmes that assign responsibilities without providing resources or authority to act on them consistently fail to prevent the data cascades documented by Sambasivan et al. (2021). Organisations should assess current role coverage against the RACI matrix in Table 4 and identify gaps before initiating a new model training project.

Governance Workflows

Governance workflows translate policy into operational practice by specifying how decisions are made, documented, and escalated. A well-designed governance workflow for training data acquisition, for example, should include the following sequential stages. First, a data sourcing request is submitted by the ML team, specifying the intended data source, its volume, and the intended use case. Second, the Data Steward conducts a preliminary assessment against the licensing compatibility matrix, classifying the source into a risk tier (Tier 1, 2, or 3) as described in the Decision Frameworks section. Third, for Tier 1 sources, standard documentation is completed and the source is approved. For Tier 2 sources, the Legal and Compliance Officer conducts a formal review and an authorised decision-maker signs off on documented risk acceptance. For Tier 3 sources, the request is escalated to senior leadership with a full legal opinion before any decision is made. Fourth, approved sources are processed through the technical curation pipeline, with automated quality checks and deduplication applied as standard. Fifth, a sample of the processed data is reviewed by the Ethics Reviewer and domain expert before the dataset is cleared for model training. Sixth, all decisions, documentation, and quality reports are archived in the data governance log, creating an auditable record accessible to internal compliance functions and, where required, external regulators. This structured workflow converts abstract governance principles into repeatable, auditable organisational practice. It also creates natural checkpoints at which governance failures can be caught before they propagate into trained models, where remediation is far more costly (Sculley et al., 2015).

Integration with AI Governance

Data governance does not operate in isolation: it must be embedded within the organisation's broader AI governance and risk management architecture. In practice, this means that the data governance programme should be aligned with the organisation's AI risk management framework whether that is the NIST AI RMF (2023), an internal framework, or a sector-specific standard and that data governance artefacts such as datasheets, bias assessment reports, and licensing records should be treated as inputs to model risk assessments and audit processes. Implementation challenges in achieving this integration are significant. Many organisations operate with siloed functions: ML engineering teams manage data pipelines without visibility into legal risk registers, while legal teams approve data sources without understanding their technical properties. Bridging these silos requires both structural interventions such as cross-functional governance committees with representation from technical, legal, and ethical functions and artefact standardisation, ensuring that the outputs of data governance processes are formatted in ways that downstream risk and compliance functions can consume. Additionally, as models are increasingly deployed through third-party APIs and fine-tuned by downstream developers, organisations must consider how their data governance decisions affect the broader ecosystem. Governance responsibilities do not end at the boundary of the organisation's own deployment; they extend to the governance conditions placed on external developers through terms of service and model licences (Bommasani et al., 2021). Effective integration with AI governance therefore requires both internal coordination and external governance design.

Frontier Challenges

The chapter addresses the forward-looking challenges that define the frontier of data governance. As generative AI systems scale, new challenges emerge at the frontier of data curation. These include the risks of synthetic data recursion, model collapse, data poisoning, and the increasing difficulty of filtering high-quality human-generated content from synthetic artifacts.

A critical challenge is the degradation of model quality when trained on recursively generated synthetic data. This process can be formalized as:

where is the training data at iteration , and represents synthetic data generated by a model trained on . Over multiple iterations, the distribution of can drift from the original human-generated distribution, leading to model collapse a phenomenon where models lose fidelity to the underlying real-world distribution (Shumailov et al., 2023).

Emerging frontier challenges are:

Model Collapse: Successive generations of models trained primarily on synthetic data exhibit amplified biases, reduced diversity, and eventual performance degradation.
Data Poisoning & Adversarial Injection: Malicious actors may inject adversarial examples or harmful content into training corpora, compromising model safety and reliability.
Temporal Drift: Models trained on static datasets may become outdated as real-world distributions evolve, requiring continuous data refresh strategies.
Attribution & Copyright: Determining the provenance of training data and ensuring compliance with evolving copyright regulations remains an open challenge.
Scalable Oversight: As datasets grow to trillions of tokens, human auditing becomes infeasible, necessitating automated governance frameworks with robust guardrails.

Addressing these frontier challenges requires interdisciplinary collaboration between machine learning researchers, ethicists, legal experts, and domain specialists to ensure sustainable and responsible AI development.

Synthetic Data

Synthetic data is data that is generated by AI models rather than collected from the real world. The governance of synthetic data raises questions about provenance and quality.

Multimodal and Agentic Systems

Multimodal and agentic systems involve multiple modalities and autonomous agents. The governance of these systems is complex and requires new approaches.

Attribution and Compensation

Attribution and compensation mechanisms involve recognizing the contribution of data creators and compensating them for their work. This is a key area of legal and ethical debate.

Regulatory Developments

Regulatory developments involve the evolution of laws and regulations governing AI. Organisations must adapt to these changes to remain compliant.

CONCLUSION

Data governance represents one of the most pressing challenges in the development of generative AI systems. The quality, diversity, and responsible management of training data fundamentally shapes what these systems can achieve and how they behave in deployment. Yet data governance remains an underdeveloped discipline relative to the sophistication of other aspects of AI engineering, such as model architecture optimisation, distributed training, and inference acceleration. This chapter has addressed that gap by providing a comprehensive treatment of data governance across the generative AI lifecycle. The mission has been threefold: to establish data governance as a first-class engineering discipline, to translate governance principles into reproducible patterns, and to equip practitioners with the frameworks and tools needed to navigate current challenges and future uncertainties. By codifying reproducible data governance patterns, this chapter enables Organisations to move beyond informal data practices toward systematic, auditable, and responsible data management that supports both technical excellence and ethical accountability.

Throughout this chapter, data governance through multiple lenses was examined. Mathematical underpinnings of data curation were established, from deduplication using MinHash and Jaccard similarity to quality metrics like perplexity, providing a rigorous basis for what might otherwise remain subjective decisions. The RACI matrix introduced in Table 4 offers a concrete mechanism for assigning accountability across cross-functional teams, reinforcing that data governance is not solely a technical challenge but requires alignment between engineers, domain experts, legal teams, and project leadership. We also examined frontier challenges including synthetic data recursion, model collapse, and data poisoning, revealing that governance is not a one-time activity but an ongoing discipline that must evolve alongside the technology itself.

As generative AI continues to advance at an unprecedented pace, several critical directions for data governance research and practice emerge. Current manual and semi-automated approaches to data curation will not scale to trillion-token datasets, necessitating future systems with intelligent automation that can use smaller models to audit and filter data for larger models, leverage active learning to prioritize human review, and develop self-healing datasets capable of detecting and correcting quality issues autonomously. The legal and ethical landscape around training data remains unsettled, and emerging standards for data provenance such as content credentials and cryptographic watermarking will enable better attribution and compliance, requiring Organisations to prepare for a future where training data lineage is auditable and verifiable by third parties. Static datasets captured at a single point in time cannot represent evolving real-world distributions, so future governance frameworks must support continuous data refresh, incremental learning, and graceful adaptation to distribution shift without catastrophic forgetting or degradation. As models increasingly integrate text, image, audio, video, and structured data, governance frameworks must evolve to handle cross-modal dependencies, with alignment between modalities, joint bias evaluation, and consistent quality metrics across data types remaining open challenges. The communities whose data powers AI systems deserve a voice in how that data is used, and emerging approaches to participatory governance including data cooperatives, dynamic consent mechanisms, and community review boards offer pathways toward more equitable and inclusive AI development. With the emergence of frameworks like the EU AI Act and evolving global standards, Organisations will need governance systems that can adapt to changing regulatory requirements, making automated compliance checking, audit trails, and explainable governance decisions essential infrastructure.

The generative AI community stands at an inflection point. The era of scaling at all costs, collecting ever-larger datasets with minimal curation, is giving way to a more mature paradigm where data quality, governance, and responsible stewardship take center stage. This transition is not merely a technical necessity but an ethical imperative. The patterns, frameworks, and formalisms presented in this chapter represent a foundation upon which practitioners can build, yet the field remains in its infancy. Each new model release reveals previously unanticipated governance challenges, from memorisation of sensitive content to emergent biases that only manifest at scale. We invite readers to contribute to this evolving discipline, to refine the patterns proposed here, to develop new tools for governance automation, and to share lessons learned from real-world deployments. The goal is not a static set of best practices but a living body of knowledge that evolves alongside the technology it seeks to guide. In the end, the quality of our AI systems will reflect the quality of our data governance. By elevating data governance to a first-class engineering discipline, we can build generative AI that is not only more capable but also more trustworthy, more equitable, and more aligned with human values.

REFERENCES

Barocas, S., Hardt, M., & Narayanan, A. (2019). *Fairness and machine learning: Limitations and opportunities.* MIT Press. https://fairmlbook.org/

Bender, E. M., Gebru, T., McMillan-Major, A., & Shmitchell, S. (2021). On the dangers of stochastic parrots: Can language models be too big? *Proceedings of the 2021 ACM Conference on Fairness, Accountability, and Transparency*, 610-623. DOI: 10.1145/3442188.3445922

Blodgett, S. L., Barocas, S., Daumé, H.III, & Wallach, H. (2020). Language (technology) is power: A critical survey of "bias" in NLP. In *Proceedings of the 58th Annual Meeting of the Association for Computational Linguistics* (pp. 5454–5476). Association for Computational Linguistics. DOI: 10.18653/v1/2020.acl-main.485

Bommasani, R., Hudson, D. A., Adeli, E., Altman, R., Arora, S., von Arx, S., Bernstein, M. S., Bohg, J., Bosselut, A., Brunskill, E., Brynjolfsson, E., Buch, S., Card, D., Castellon, R., Chen, M., Chen, C., Chi, E., . . . Liang, P. (2021). On the opportunities and risks of foundation models. *arXiv*. https://doi.org//arXiv.2108.07258DOI: 10.48550

Broder, A. Z. (1997). On the resemblance and containment of documents. *Proceedings of the Compression and Complexity of Sequences, 1997*, 21–29. DOI: 10.1109/SEQUEN.1997.666900

Brown, T. B., Mann, B., Ryder, N., Subbiah, M., Kaplan, J., Dhariwal, P., Neelakantan, A., Shyam, P., Sastry, G., Askell, A., Agarwal, S., Herbert-Voss, A., Krueger, G., Henighan, T., Child, R., Ramesh, A., Ziegler, D. M., Wu, J., Winter, C., & Amodei, D. (2020). Language models are few-shot learners. *Advances in Neural Information Processing Systems*, *33*, 1877–1901.

Caliskan, A., Bryson, J. J., & Narayanan, A. (2017). Semantics derived automatically from language corpora contain human-like biases. *Science*, *356*(6334), 183–186. DOI: 10.1126/science.aal4230 PMID: 28408601

Carlini, N., Tramer, F., Wallace, E., Jagielski, M., Herbert-Voss, A., Lee, K., Roberts, A., Brown, T., Song, D., & Erlingsson, U. (2021). Extracting training data from large language models. *30th USENIX Security Symposium (USENIX Security 21)*, 2633–2650.

Charikar, M. S. (2002). Similarity estimation techniques from rounding algorithms. *Proceedings of the Thirty-Fourth Annual ACM Symposium on Theory of Computing*, 380–388. DOI: 10.1145/509907.509965

Cyberspace Administration of China. (2023). Interim Measures for the Management of Generative Artificial Intelligence Services.

European Commission. (2021). *Proposal for a regulation laying down harmonised rules on artificial intelligence*. Artificial Intelligence Act.

Gebru, T., Morgenstern, J., Vecchione, B., Vaughan, J. W., Wallach, H., Daumé, H., III, & Crawford, K. (2018). Datasheets for datasets. *Communications of the Association for Computing Machinery, 64*(12), 86–97. https://doi.org/ (Original work published 2018 as arXiv:1803.09010)DOI: 10.1145/3458723

LAION e. V. (2022). *LAION-5B: A new era of open large-scale multi-modal datasets*. https://laion.ai/blog/laion-5b/

Lee, K., Ippolito, D., Nystrom, A., Ha, C., Goodwin, M., Lee, A., Shin, P., & Carlini, N. (2022). Deduplicating training data makes language models better. *International Conference on Machine Learning*, 20316–20330. DOI: 10.18653/v1/2022.acl-long.577

Mitchell, M., Wu, S., Zaldivar, A., Barnes, P., Vasserman, L., Hutchinson, B., Spitzer, E., Raji, I. D., & Gebru, T. (2019). Model cards for model reporting. *Proceedings of the Conference on Fairness, Accountability, and Transparency*, 220–229. DOI: 10.1145/3287560.3287596

NIST. (2023). *Artificial Intelligence Risk Management Framework (AI RMF 1.0)*. National Institute of Standards and Technology., DOI: 10.6028/NIST.AI.100-1

Open, A. I. (2023). *GPT-4 technical report*. https://doi.org//arXiv.2303.08774DOI: 10.48550

Parrish, A., Chen, A., Nangia, N., Padmakumar, V., Phang, J., Thompson, J., Htut, P. M., & Bowman, S. R. (2022). BBQ: A hand-built bias benchmark for question answering. In *Findings of the Association for Computational Linguistics: ACL 2022* (pp. 2086–2105). Association for Computational Linguistics. DOI: 10.18653/v1/2022.findings-acl.165

Raffel, C., Shazeer, N., Roberts, A., Lee, K., Narang, S., Matena, M., Zhou, Y., Li, W., & Liu, P. J. (2020). Exploring the limits of transfer learning with a unified text-to-text transformer. *Journal of Machine Learning Research, 21*(140), 1–67.

Raji, I. D., Smart, A., White, R. N., Mitchell, M., Gebru, T., Hutchinson, B., Smith-Loud, J., Theron, A., & Barnes, P. (2020). Closing the AI accountability gap: Defining an end-to-end framework for internal algorithmic auditing. *Proceedings of the 2020 Conference on Fairness, Accountability, and Transparency*, 33–44. DOI: 10.1145/3351095.3372873

Ravfogel, S., Elazar, Y., Gonen, H., Twiton, M., & Goldberg, Y. (2020). Null it out: Guarding protected attributes by iterative nullspace projection. In *Proceedings of the 58th Annual Meeting of the Association for Computational Linguistics* (pp. 7237–7256). Association for Computational Linguistics. DOI: 10.18653/v1/2020.acl-main.647

Sambasivan, N., Kapania, S., Highfill, H., Akrong, D., Paritosh, P., & Aroyo, L. (2021). Everyone wants to do the model, but no one wants to do the data: Data cascades in high-stakes AI. In *Proceedings of the 2021 CHI Conference on Human Factors in Computing Systems* (pp. 1–15). Association for Computing Machinery. DOI: 10.1145/3411764.3445518

Schuhmann, C., Vencu, R., Beaumont, R., Kaczmarczyk, R., & Kaddour, J. (2022). LAION-5B: An open large-scale dataset for training next generation image-text models. *Advances in Neural Information Processing Systems*, *35*, 32118–32133. DOI: 10.52202/068431-1833

Sculley, D., Holt, G., Golovin, D., Davydov, E., Phillips, T., Ebner, D., Chaudhary, V., & Young, M. (2015). Hidden technical debt in machine learning systems. *Advances in Neural Information Processing Systems*, •••, 28.

Shumailov, I., Shumaylov, Z., Zhao, Y., Papernot, N., Anderson, R., & Gal, Y. (2023). The curse of recursion: Training on generated data makes models forget. *arXiv preprint arXiv:2305.17493.*

U.S. Copyright Office. (2023). *Copyright and artificial intelligence: Copyrightability* (Part 2 of 3). https://copyright.gov/ai/

Ward, J. (2019). *Data governance: How to design, deploy and sustain an effective data governance program* (2nd ed.). John Wiley & Sons.

Zhang, L., Chen, J., Du, R., He, K., & Chen, J. (2017). Data integrity verification method with secure deduplication in cloud storage. *Jisuanji Gongcheng*, *43*(1), 32–38. DOI: 10.3969/j.issn.1000-3428.2017.01.006

ADDITIONAL READING

Bender, E. M., & Friedman, B. (2018). Data statements for natural language processing: Toward mitigating system bias in NLP. *Proceedings of the 2018 Conference of the North American Chapter of the Association for Computational Linguistics: Human Language Technologies*, 1-10.

Crawford, K. (2021). *Atlas of AI: Power, Politics, and the Planetary Costs of Artificial Intelligence*. Yale University Press.

Denton, E., Hanna, A., Amironesei, R., Smart, A., & Nicole, H. (2021). On the genealogy of machine learning datasets: A critical history of ImageNet. *Big Data & Society*, *8*(2), 1–15. DOI: 10.1177/20539517211035955

Henderson, P., Hu, J., Romoff, J., Joelle, P., Joelle, P., Bacon, P.-L., Pineau, J., & Pilarski, P. M. (2018). Deep reinforcement learning that matters. *Proceedings of the AAAI Conference on Artificial Intelligence*, *32*(1), 3207–3214. DOI: 10.1609/aaai.v32i1.11694

Hoffmann, J., Borgeaud, S., Mensch, A., Buchatskaya, E., Cai, T., Rutherford, E., de Las Casas, D., Hendricks, L. A., Welbl, J., Clark, A., Hennigan, T., Noland, E., Millican, K., van den Driessche, G., Damoc, B., Guy, A., Osindero, S., Simonyan, K., Elsen, E., & Sifre, L. (2022). Training compute-optimal large language models. *Advances in Neural Information Processing Systems*, *35*, 1–12. DOI: 10.48550/arXiv.2203.15556

Jernite, Y., Nguyen, H., Biderman, S., Rogers, A., Masoud, M., Danchev, V., Tan, S., Luccioni, A. S., Subramani, N., Johnson, I., Dupont, G., Dodge, J., Lo, K., Talat, Z., Radev, D., Gokaslan, A., Nikpoor, M. H., Henderson, P., Joelle, P., & McMillan-Major, A. (2022). Data governance in the age of large-scale data-driven language technology. In *Proceedings of the 2022 ACM Conference on Fairness, Accountability, and Transparency* (pp. 2206–2222). Association for Computing Machinery. https://doi.org/DOI: 10.1145/3531146.3534637

O'Neil, C. (2016). *Weapons of Math Destruction: How Big Data Increases Inequality and Threatens Democracy*. Crown., DOI: 10.5860/crl.78.3.403

Pasquale, F. (2015). *The Black Box Society: The Secret Algorithms That Control Money and Information*. Harvard University Press. DOI: 10.4159/harvard.9780674736061

Pushkarna, M., Zaldivar, A., & Kjartansson, O. (2022). Data Cards: Purposeful and transparent dataset documentation for responsible AI. In *Proceedings of the 2022 ACM Conference on Fairness, Accountability, and Transparency* (pp. 1776–1826). Association for Computing Machinery. https://doi.org/DOI: 10.1145/3531146.3533231

Whang, S. E., Roh, Y., Song, H., & Lee, J.-G. (2023). Data collection and quality challenges in deep learning: A data-centric AI perspective. *The VLDB Journal*, *32*(4), 791–813. DOI: 10.1007/s00778-022-00775-9

Zha, D., Bhat, Z. P., Lai, K.-H., Yang, F., Jiang, Z., Zhong, S., & Hu, X. (2023). Data-centric artificial intelligence: A survey. *ACM Computing Surveys*, *56*(8), 1–42. DOI: 10.1145/3711118

KEY TERMS AND DEFINITIONS

Bias Assessment: The evaluation of a dataset for biases that may lead to unfair or discriminatory outcomes in model predictions.

Data Governance: The overall management of the availability, usability, integrity, and security of the data employed in an enterprise, specifically adapted for the dynamic and unstructured nature of generative AI training data.

Data Lineage: The tracking of data from its origin through various processing stages to its final use, ensuring provenance and accountability.

Datasheets for Datasets: A documentation standard that accompanies a dataset and provides information about its creation, composition, and intended use to promote transparency.

Deduplication: The process of identifying and removing duplicate or near-duplicate content from a dataset to prevent model overfitting and bias.

Fair Use Doctrine: A legal principle that allows the use of copyrighted works without permission in certain circumstances, such as for research or criticism, often debated in the context of AI training.

Lifecycle Management: The ongoing maintenance, versioning, and evolution of training data throughout the entire lifespan of an AI system.

Model Cards: A documentation standard that provides information about a machine learning model's performance, intended use, and ethical considerations.

Multimodal Data: Data that includes multiple types of information, such as text, images, audio, and video, requiring specialized governance for alignment and quality.

Synthetic Data: Data that is generated by AI models rather than collected from the real world, raising unique questions about provenance and quality in governance frameworks.

Chapter 7
Intelligent Data Architecture:
The Role of Generative AI in Governance and Analytics

Balusamy Nachiappan
http://orcid.org/0009-0006-0951-8078
Prologis, USA

C. Viji
http://orcid.org/0000-0002-2759-8896
Alliance University, India

Mahmood Hussain Mir
MNR University, India

A. Mohanraj
Sri Eshwar College of Engineering, India

N. Rajkumar
http://orcid.org/0000-0001-7857-9452
Alliance University, India

Jayavadivel Ravi
http://orcid.org/0000-0002-5326-2210
Presidency University, India

ABSTRACT

The rapid proliferation of information in industries has pushed the need for shrewd, scalable, and independent information architectures. Traditional information systems, at the same time as powerful in static environments, lack the adaptability required for real-time decision-making and self-optimization. Generative AI gives a paradigm shift with the resource of embedding creativity, context-attention, and automation into the records lifecycle, spanning ingestion, transformation, great guarantee, governance, and analytics. It explores the transformative function of generative AI in current data architectures, focusing on its potential to automate fact pipelines technology, enhance records notable through artificial intelligence generation, and electricity adaptive governance frameworks. Additionally, it investigates how Large

DOI: 10.4018/979-8-2600-0368-8.ch007

Language Models (LLMs) and basis models can strengthen natural language querying, metadata control, and the real-time insights era, in the long run, allowing a shift from reactive reporting to proactive, impartial analytics.

INTRODUCTION

Background

Information strategic value is a growing trend in the new digital economy. Companies in sectors such as e-commerce, healthcare, financial services and manufacturing take an interest in extracting meaning of the large volumes of structured, semi-structured and unstructured data. However, the traditional architectures that document their emphasis on centralized Data warehouses, hard-plumbing Extract-Transform-Load (ETL) pipelines and governance using rules are not proving to be sufficient to support real-time and scalable decision-making and context-based decision-making.

As organizations are becoming global and digital first in regard to the operating model, quantities, speed and variety of data is increasing. In the meantime, the business stakeholders need faster insights generation, increased personalization, intelligent automation, and imperviousness of operations. The requirements reveal certain constraints of traditional architecture which is predominately reactive, largely manual and finds it difficult to maintain a uniform governance and data quality with complex and distributed situations.

Unlike the classical methods of artificial intelligence where the primary goals included classification or prediction, generative models, e.g., large language models, generative adversarial networks and diffusion models can be employed to create new data representations, executable ideals and analytical results in accordance with learned patterns. These features are large in influence on data pipeline structure, rule automatization, and smart delivery of data, to facilitate the shift of less flexible, rule-oriented systems, to smarter, more active, and semi-autonomous data systems.

This study makes three key contributions. First, it proposes a Generative AI-driven data architecture integrating data pipelines, governance, and analytics into a unified framework. Second, it provides a comparative evaluation of traditional, modern, and GenAI-powered architectures using performance metrics such as scalability, automation, and time-to-insight. Third, it introduces a governance-aware autonomous analytics model incorporating explainability, human-in-the-loop control, and ethical safeguards for enterprise deployment.

Problem Statement

Despite rapid advancements in Generative AI, there remains a lack of structured understanding of its impact on enterprise data architectures. This gap can be categorized into three dimensions. First, architectural challenges include the integration of GenAI within data ingestion, pipeline orchestration, and metadata management layers. Second, governance challenges involve ensuring explainability, auditability, compliance, and prompt control in AI-driven systems. Third, analytics challenges arise in defining the boundaries between decision support, prescriptive analytics, and fully autonomous systems. Key issues include:

- The outputs of AI can be audited and explained.
- Data privacy management; particularly data created and utilized in the formulation of synthetic information.
- Minimizing the effects of algorithmic bias and ethical and regulatory standards.
- A tradeoff between automation and due human control in autonomous analytics.
- The solution of the scalability, infrastructure complexity, and cost optimization issue in AI-based systems.

Although the research into Generative AI has been growing at a rather impressive pace, it has predominantly focused on application-level applications, such as natural language processing, image generation, and code generation and there has been a knowledge gap on how it impacts architecture, in particular, data governance, system integration, and autonomous analytics.

Objectives of the Study

The objectives of this study are:

(i) To analyze the architectural implications of integrating GenAI into data systems,
(ii) To examine governance mechanisms including explainability and compliance
(iii) To evaluate the evolution from traditional analytics to autonomous analytics frameworks.

METHODOLOGY

This study adopts a systematic multi-method approach. Literature was collected from IEEE Xplore, Scopus, and ACM Digital Library using keywords such as "Generative AI architecture," "data governance," and "autonomous analytics." Inclusion criteria considered peer-reviewed publications from 2020–2026, while non-peer-reviewed sources were excluded. Case studies were selected based on industry diversity and availability of measurable outcomes. Comparative analysis was conducted using metrics derived from literature benchmarks and industry reports.

The scope of this artwork covers:

- These architectural components are access and metadata management, orchestration, crypto, compute, storage and metadata.
- Generative models, large language models, generative adversarial networks, and diffusion models that can be used in processing data and analytics.
- Policy, access points and audits- AI-driven data governance detection.
- Self-driven analytics systems Self-driven analytics is a system applied in developing organizational and cloud-native systems.s.

Barriers include:

• Lack of hardware-specific considerations such as G/PUs and TPUs optimization.

• An emphasis in a conceptual design style and architecture but not on a code of implementation. •

• Secondary sources of data due to the proprietary restrictions during the case study analysis (Zhang et al., 2022).).

EVOLUTION OF DATA ARCHITECTURES

Traditional Data Architectures

The conventional architectures worked well in situations that had constant data schema and clear reporting needs. Nonetheless, they were limited in a number of ways, factors that limited their scalability and functionalities:

- **Rigidity**: Data pipelines would have to be reconfigured manually when a schema change was being made.

- **Latency**: t became a common practice to refresh reports and dashboards on a daily/weekly basis, which restricted the capability of making decisions in real-time.
- **Siloed Systems**: There was a tendency of data being stored in departmental stores limiting integrated and cross-functional analysis.
- **Manual Governance**: manually, security policies and access controls were implemented which created bottlenecks in the operations and inconsistencies.

The limitations ensured that traditional architectures were not very fit to the era of big data, cloud computing, and real-time analytics (Zaharia et al., 2013).

Modern Data Architectures

Modern data architectures have been implemented in organizations following the rising amount, speed, and diversity of data. These systems are based on scalability, modularity and real time processing concepts and facilitate processing structured, semi structured, and un structured data over distributed environments.

Some of the key characteristics include:

a) Data Lakes and Lakehouses

There is growing adoption within organizations of data lakes in which raw data is stored in the native form and also with distributed storage systems, like Hadoop HDFS or Amazon S3, allowing schema-on-read flexibility. Lately, latticehouse structures are arisen, which incorporates the dependability and execution of the information stores with the adaptability of data lakes.

b) Streaming Data Platforms

The implementation of technologies like Apache Kafka, Apache Flink, and Spark streaming are being used to ingest and process real-time IoT device, log, and social media data to assist in providing insights close to real-time.

c) Cloud-Native Architectures

Scaling elasticity and managed services such as big query, red-shift and Synapse are available on cloud services (e.g., AWS, Azure, Google cloud). The data structures in these architectures are independent of compute and improve scalability and performance.

d) API-Driven Integration

Integration made up of microservices can enable systems that communicate through REST or GraphQL APIs and will be more modular and can be deployed and scaled quickly.

e) NoSQL and Multi-Model Databases

Semi-structured and unstructured data MongoDB (document-based), Neo4j (graph-based) and Cassandra (columnar) have become popular databases that have flexible data models and analytics.

Limitations of Modern Architectures

Although the current-day architectures dispel many of the issues faced by the resource of the traditional ones, they cannot be said to lack their challenges right now:

a) Reactive Analogies of analytics

Decision making in real-time data pipeline can be reactive even with real-time data pipes. The data is crunched and sent, yet analysis of actionable insights, however, still involves human interpretation and interventions.

b) Complexity and Cost

The current systems usually have a number of loosely coupled services, all of which demand qualified staff to meet the task of orchestration, monitoring, and maintenance. Moreover, the cloud-based services may be exposed to unforeseen activities in the cost of operation unless managed.

c) Fragmented Governance

With systems, cloud computing, and services connecting the data, there is more complexity in governance. Implementing a standard and enforced policies that ensure adherence to the data privacy laws including GDPR and HIPAA can become a challenge in the distributed environment.

d) Uncongruent Metadata Management

Without any standardized metadata repositories or catalogs, organizations are not able to trace data lineage, context and quality. This hinders the level of trust, transparency and reliance of analytics output.

Rise of AI-Augmented Architectures

In order to overcome such inadequacies, AI-enhanced architectures are, in fact, coming into existence. These systems combine machine getting to know (ML) (Sculley et al., 2015) with Generative AIs as part of fundamental buildings to strain automation, self-recovery abilities, and choice intelligence. GenAI adds to all information engineering and analytics layers:

Figure 1. Generative AI-powered data architectures

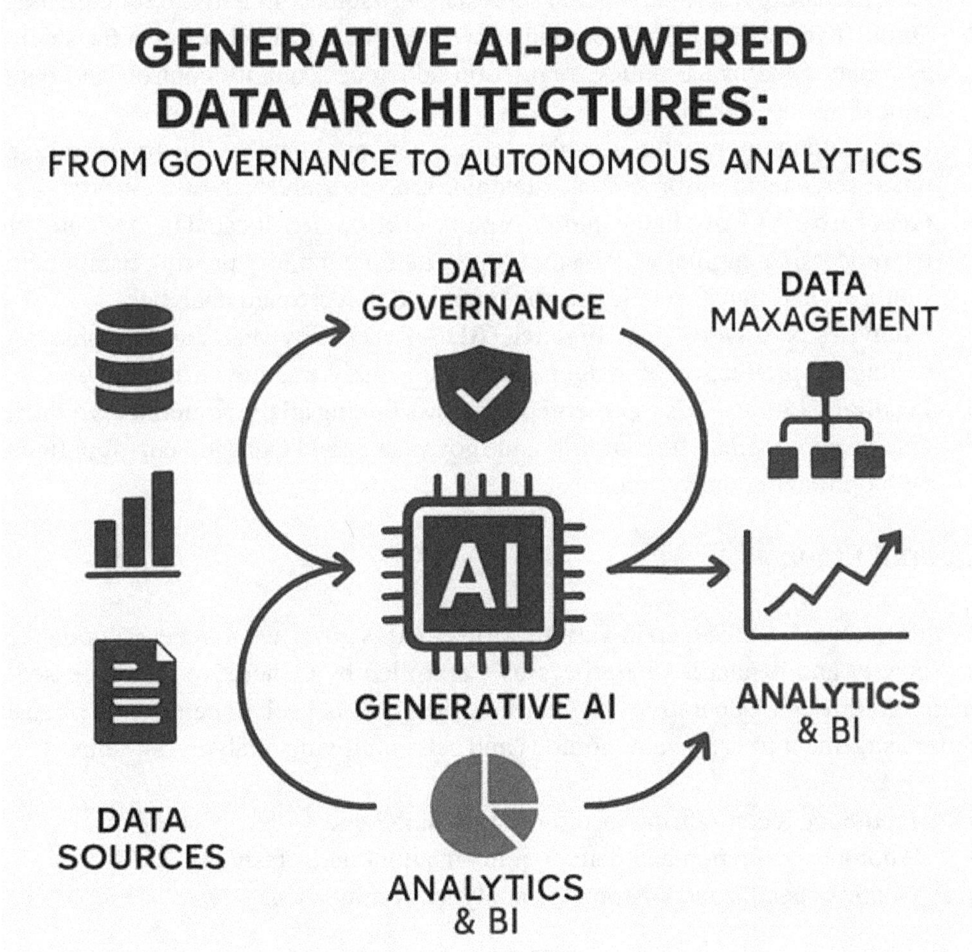

The lifecycle of the Generative AI-powered data architecture presented in Figure 1 visually deviates by presenting data flow through governance, autonomous analytics.

The architecture operates across multiple layers. Data is first ingested from structured and unstructured sources and validated within the data layer. The pipeline layer performs transformation, integration, and orchestration. The Generative AI layer applies models such as LLMs and GANs for data synthesis and analytics. The governance layer enforces policies, compliance, and access control. Finally, the analytics layer generates insights and decisions. Feedback loops continuously update models and optimize pipelines based on outcomes.

Key components in the diagram:

1. **Data Sources** – Since they capture structured, semi-structured and unstructured data, they are represented by icons representing databases, charts and documents.
2. **Data Governance** – This is demonstrated in a shield and a check over the shield as a data governance policy, regulation adherence, quality control, and data ethical management.
3. **Data Management** – this is a hierarchical network icon that illustrates storage processes, integration processes, cataloging processes, and orchestration processe.
4. **Generative AI Core** In the middle of the workflow, it is located in the center of the processing engine, which emphasizes its functionality proving useful data synthesis and transformation as the input into downstream analytics.
5. **Analytics & Business Intelligence (BI)** – Reacted by charts and graphs, depicting the production of insights, foretelling analytics, and outlooks.
6. **Feedback Loops** – It is represented as arrows linking all the components, which emphasize how analytics outputs guide governance and management to continue with optimizing the system.

Overall Flow:

Information is consumed in various forms -and is governed to meet compliance and quality and is handled by processes Controlled by Generative AI Processed/ enhanced through Generative AI -Converts the insights back to better governance and management to create autonomous and self-improving analytics systems.

- Predictive reconfiguring of information pipelines.
- Anomaly correction and detection in an autonomous fashion.
- Context specific and customized analytics results.

Compared to the classic or possibly the contemporary architecture, the AI-powered architecture reactive - they presume the necessity during statistics, respond to the situation, and overall enhance performance dynamically. This change is an expansive transition in the realm of stagnant infrastructure to cognitive, adaptable ecosystems.

Table 1. Comparative Summary

Feature	Traditional Architecture	Modern Architecture	AI-Powered Architecture
Data Storage	Centralized Warehouse	Distributed Data Lakes	Distributed + Contextual
Processing Mode	Batch	Real-Time + Batch	Real-Time + Predictive
Governance	Manual	Semi-Automated	AI-Driven, Explainable
Data Access	SQL-Only	SQL + NoSQL + APIs	Natural Language + APIs
Scalability	Vertical	Horizontal (Cloud-Native)	Self-Optimizing
Analytics	Static Reports	Dashboards + ML	Autonomous Decision Systems

Table 2. Key Milestones in Evolution

Year	Milestone	Description
1990s	RDBMS & ETL	Rise of enterprise data warehouses
Early 2000s	OLAP & BI Tools	Structured dashboards and reports
2010s	Big Data & NoSQL	Scalability, data lakes, Hadoop
2015+	Cloud Data Platforms	Managed services, real-time analytics
2020+	Generative AI	Adaptive data systems, autonomous analytics

DRIVERS BEHIND THE ARCHITECTURAL SHIFT

Statistics architectures have been driven by technical and business enterprise forces:

- Information Explosion: IoT devices, social media and extensive digitization have increased information volumes to the point of zettabytes.
- Consumer expectancies: Real time personalization and insights require real time analytical capabilities.
- Regulatory pressure: Legal requirements on transparency, traceability and compliance in the management of data are on the rise.

- Speed of innovation: Agile companies require an innovative, data architecture that can be scaled and resilient to stay innovative.
- AI maturity: The presence of ready-prepared AI models, integration of superior algorithms, and high-performance computing resources eases the enormous scale adoption of AI in enterprise systems.

Implications for Enterprises

The companies that switch to the AI-powered records architectures need to pass through:

- Cultural changes: the adoption of AI in the operations and making preferences.
- Upskilling: engineers and analysts of GenAI machinery and methods are recorded in school.
- Infrastructure investment: deployment of GPUs, accelerators of AI, and system of model management.

Automating Data Pipelines

Traditional Challenge:

The creation of records pipelines usually involves guided scripting, frequent monitoring and schema modifications or record inconsistencies. This is time wasting and prone to human error.

GenAI Innovation:

- Activates automobile generated ETL or ELT pipelines using a natural language.
- Identifies schema float and auto-regulates pipelines without any guide intervention.
- supports low-code/no-code environments where users of industrial companies can develop information workflow. Instance Use Case:.

Instance Use Case:

One of the steps of a fact analyst is to sort, "Merge purchaser data between CRM and e-commerce assets and eliminate duplicates. GenAI translates natural language queries into executable SQL statements Or Python and rob the former-end pist-give up.

Enhancing Data Governance

Traditional Challenge: Traditional governance structures are rule-based, definitely, inflexible and decoupled with real-time operations. Metadata tagging, obtaining due access to control, and compliance tests in great part, is manual..

GenAI Innovation:

- Basically, uses context-sensitive NLP to infer metadata, mark sensitive fields (such as PII or financial data) and mechanical fact classification.
- Dynamically uses governance best practices such as GDPR, or HIPAA depending on the popularity of the content cloud.
- Car-generates documentation and lineage graphs of transparency and audits.

Example Use Case: A modern healthcare dataset is uploaded, and GenAI identifies that it is a covered health dataset and labels it and requires confined get proper access whilst generating compliance documentation.

Synthetic Data Generation

Existing Despair: Reality-global facts may be missing, unattainable and favoritism or even delicate, restricting AI/ML experimentation.

GenAI Innovation:

- Trains generative models (GANs, VAEs, Diffusion fashions) to provide artificial and not absurd records.
- Also, aids in educating ML fashions with lack of privacy threat.
- Allows unusual or aspect-case eventuality simulation to give robust trying out an opportunity.

Instance Use Case:

A bank tries to simulate fraudulent transactions to train a fraud detecting model-without revealing the records of purchasers.

Interactions of data which are driven by language

Traditional Challenge: Customers need to learn sq., API syntax, or dashboard settings so as to begin communicating with data.

GenAI Innovation:

- Offers natural language interfaces with data.
- Parses queries into optimised queries and provides visualisations on demand.

Instance Use Case:

A product supervisor poses a question, How did the Q2 profits perform in APAC and EMEA?- GenAI steers the query and generates a comparison bar chart with facts.

Context-Aware Analytics

Conventional difficulty: Analytic tools usually omit contextual intricacies such as external actions, floating targets or associations.

GenAI Innovation:

- Knows the context of domains, acknowledges styles and develops causality.
- Enhances outputs, depending on target audience, use-case or KPIs.

Instance Use Case:

GenAI, applied in advertising and marketing and advertising and marketing analytics, recognizes a curve in the ROI of a campaign that is associated with the interests of an influencer, but not ad spend.

Intelligent Data Summarization

Traditional Challenge: The executives struggle to read untouched dashboards or specific spreadsheets.

GenAI Innovation:

- Defines knowledge derived about bullet items, herbal language storytelling or exhibits.
- Transforms dashboard metrics into statement prepared selections.

Instance Use Case:

This decreased the income by 8% in North the us due to late in schedule product launches. The rate of stock turnover remains high.

Code Generation and Orchestration

Traditional Challenge: The data engineer's hand-write orchestration right judgment, which is the most essential to resolve the slow development cycle.

GenAI Innovation:

- Ispires prompts Usage: Discovers in collections Delta, an airflow etk, shell scripts Vuidated routines Prominent deployment pipelines Generates Airflow DAGs.
- Allows automating the CI/CD functions.

Instance Use Case:

Agenda nightly pipeline to replace earnings dashboard and validate missing entries is typed in by someone. GenAI develops and executes the DAG on a regular basis.

Improving Data Quality

Traditional Challenge: The problem of data quality (pdf values, outliers, duplications) must be detected by rules and cleansing in a manual way.

GenAI Innovation:

- Gathers information about historic data trends in order to detect and rectify anomalies.
- Uses fuzzy right adjudication to eliminate duplicates in records.
- Missing values: the clever imputation styles.

Instance Use Case:

GenAI identifies the similar entries of a consumer within the structures with high-quality spellings but slots them together according to the context.

Masterpiece but Autonomous analytics: The Next frontier.

Further increases As institutions move towards real-time intelligence and predictive decision making, self-sustaining analytics is one of the breakthroughs in information structures that will arise. Compared to classic or possibly contemporary analytics processes that rely heavily on human participation to detect insights, visualize and move data, self-sufficient analytics uses Generative AI and tool mastering (ML) to automate the entire analytics process, including ingestion and transformation of data as well as the identification of insights and prescribing suggestions.

The meaning of Autonomous Analytics:

Autonomous analytics can be categorized into three levels: decision support systems that assist human decision-making, prescriptive analytics that recommend actions, and fully autonomous systems that execute decisions with minimal human intervention. Current GenAI systems primarily operate within decision support and prescriptive levels.

Self-sustaining analytics can be defined as AI-driven frameworks that can examine facts, identify patterns and draw on insights and make or propose actions and execute them without human intervention. The ones change dynamically in accordance with new statistics, transforming situations, and changing industrial employer objectives, which guarantee perpetual intelligence and agility of strategy.

Core capabilities of autonomous analytics include:

Self-provider information exploration through natural language

- Vehicle-discovery of patterns, anomalies and tendencies.
- In real time information processing and notifications.
- Contextual insights Custom-made to female or male roles.
- Feedback structures associated with knowledge acquisition of variation and knowledge acquisition.

Key Components of Autonomous Analytics

a) Self-Configuring Analytics Pipelines

Workflows Analytics workflows are collected on-the-fly in self-sufficient structures. As new information resources are being added or commercial enterprise questions evolved, GenAI:

- Well acquainted with facts schema and semantics.
- Periodically develops ETL/ELT streams.
- Chooses appropriate analytical model (e.g. regression, clustering, forecasting)
- Visualizes the workflow with such tools as Airflow or Kubeflow.
- This minimizes method-to-perception and purgatory of guide set-up.

b) Natural Language Insight Queries

Dependent systems Customers can communicate to independent analytics systems using conversational interfaces. Stakeholders of the enterprise may pose the following questions:

- What were the primary factors that led to the fall of the Q3 sales?
- Predict 3 months churn rate on premium customers.

GenAI understands these queries, decides on analysis to do, and provides consequences as human readable or dashboards.

c) **Causal Inference and Insight Generation**

Beyond correlation Transferring Transfers with the help of GenAI-based systems, the practice of causal inference methods is used to select root causes and produce explanatory narratives. The device will be able to deduce:

- Sales declined through the use of 12 percent as a result of reduction in advert impressions in the northern location, after a 40 percent discount on digital marketing and advertising expenditure.

These understandings make it possible to intervene strategically instead of making a reactive comment.

d) **Proactive and Predictive Alerting**

Autonomous analytics platforms ever show data flow of anomalies, outliers, or overall bulk changes. GenAI:

- Their units evolve adaptive thresholds mostly relying on pre-historic behavior.
- Identifies strong alarm signs (e.g. loss of engagement)
- Provides proactive indicators to action context.

An example is as follows: "The cost of internet site conversion reduce by eight percent due to spike in latency throughout checkout.

For instance: "Internet site conversion charge dropped by eight percent because of latency spike for the duration of checkout."

e) **Prescriptive and Action-Oriented Intelligence**

It is the last level of analytics, which involves proposing or planning moves. GenAI can:

- Promote price range reassignments.
- Endorse customer retention techniques.
- Activate computerized workflow (ex: re-engagement electronic mail progressions)

GenAI is capable of performing such techniques independently in closed-loop structures, as per the mentioned constraints or the approvals.

f) **Requirement of the Continuous Education and Feedback**

Self-sufficient analytics formations entail comment loops in order to gain experiences on the effects and improve destiny forecasts. For instance:

- In case a suggestion leads to good commercial business outcomes, similar initiatives are given precedence.
- In case pointers are rejected or overridden by the clients, the version modifies its weight or explanation.

  This flexibility intelligence will ensure that the device is more in line with organizational dreams as time goes by. Potentials of Autonomous Analytics.

Advantages of Autonomous Analytics

- **Minimized Relyance on Analysts or IT manual:** minimized Dependency Cycles.
- **Scalability:** Processes high frequency excessive-quantity data in numerous areas.
- **Democratization of Data:** Enables non-technical customers to derive data out of information.
- **Consistency and Accuracy:** Minimizes human error and harmonizes the evaluation procedures.
- **Strategic Focus:** Liberates the human talents towards more orderly tasks such as innovation and method.

Use Cases Across Industries

- **Retail**: independent analytics allows finding underperforming SKUs and suggests changing the prices.
- **Healthcare:** early prognosis with the use of real-time detection of anomalies in the vitals of the affected persons.
- **Manufacturing:** Predictive is used to prevent the costly down time by alerting about anomaleys.
- **Finance:** Fraud detectors produce risk factors and certify physical accounts.

Challenges and Considerations

In spite of its potential, autonomous analytics is facing some challenges:

- **Data Privacy and Ethics:** Unbiased systems, just simply, need to be responsible about the PII and sensitive insights. This may additionally propagate or propagate current biases in training data or algorithms (Bias in Models).
- **Explainability:** Stakeholders tend to demand to see the methods through which the insights or moves can be gained (Arrieta et al., 2020).
- **Governance and Compliance:** the movements that are concerned about the helpful resource, which is AI, (e.g., GDPR). The Future of AI-based Analytics.

The Future of Autonomous Analytics

As GenAI models evolve, self-sufficient analytics will float inside the course of augmented decision-making, wherein AI will become a strategic partner in place of only a tool. We foresee the emergence of(Sundararajan & Sridharan, 2021):

- Self-sufficient records marketers who negotiate get right of entry to, clean statistics, and timetable workflows
- Conversational dashboards that evolve with real-time communication
- Self-optimizing businesses, in which AI governs supply chains, customer interactions, and internal operations dynamically(O'Reilly, 2020)

GOVERNANCE AND ETHICS IN GENERATIVE AI-POWERED DATA ARCHITECTURES

The aggregate of generative artificial intelligence (GenAI) into statistics architectures has delivered super skills in automation, perception era, and decision-making. But, the transformative functionality of GenAI must be tempered with the resource of sturdy governance and ethical worries to ensure equity, accountability, and accept as true within AI-driven structures. As technology increasingly performs autonomously, guiding immoderate-stakes decisions, the need for ethical frameworks and governance mechanisms becomes vital.

This addresses the foundational pillars of AI governance, explores moral concerns related to generative AI in statistics ecosystems, and proposes strategies to balance innovation with accountable AI deployment.

Effective governance requires multiple mechanisms including explainability using XAI techniques, audit logging for traceability of decisions, prompt governance to control inputs to large language models, and human-in-the-loop systems to validate high-risk outputs.

Understanding Data Governance in the Age of GenAI

Records governance refers to the guidelines, approaches, and necessities that outline how facts is amassed, saved, accessed, and implemented. In GenAI-powered architectures, governance needs to extend beyond traditional information stewardship to embody:

- **Model governance:** monitoring training statistics, version provenance, model manipulation, and behavior over time.
- **Prompt governance:** making sure the accountable generation of outputs from massive language models (LLMs), especially when outputs can impact selections or have an impact on customers (Amershi et al., 2014).
- **Utilization governance:** Defining clear obstacles for computerized moves, data sharing, and version get right of entry to.

Modern governance needs to now combine data lifecycle control with AI lifecycle oversight, emphasizing every technical and human-centered factor.

Figure 2. Generative AI-powered data architecture

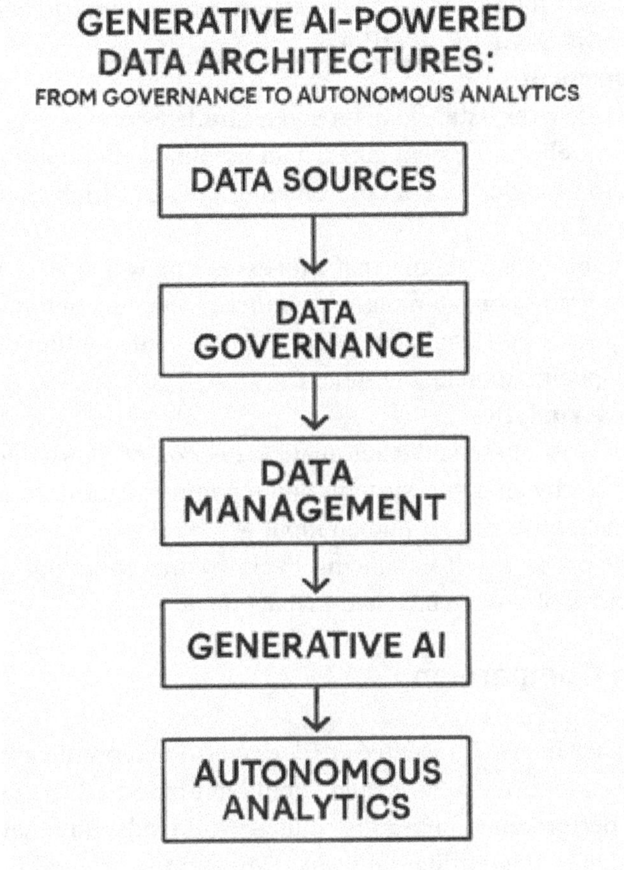

Figure 2 flowchart explains the **sequential process** of how a Generative AI-powered data architecture operates, starting from raw data and ending with autonomous analytics.

Stages in the Flow:

1. **Data Sources**
   - Any incoming information in various sources databases, APIs, the IoT, logs, documents, and other external feeds.
   - Includes Semi-structured and unstructured and structured.
2. **Data Governance**

- o The policy and compliance layer will guarantee accuracy of data, privacy, security, and ethical use of data.
- o Addresses the metadata management, access control, and adherence to such laws as GDPR or HIPAA.

3. **Data Management**
   - o Sorts, archives data, cleanses and assimilates data.
   - o Data warehousing, data lakes, data pipelines, and master data management to provide one data presented in the same high quality.
4. **Generative AI**
   - o The intelligence engine that processes controlled data to produce insights, prediction, summaries, synthetic data, and automated reports.
   - o Accepts Large Language models (LLM) and multimodal AI, and domain specific models fine-tuned.
5. **Autonomous Analytics**
   - o Just the last phase is the automatic detection of trends and prediction of scenarios by analytics systems and recommendations to make decisions automatically without human input.
   - o Brings about a self-enhancing cycle by incorporating results into the processes of governance and management.

Performance Comparison

The performance metrics presented are derived from a combination of literature-based benchmarks, industry reports, and simulation-based estimations. Scalability reflects system performance under distributed workloads, automation represents reduction in manual intervention, and time-to-insight measures the efficiency of analytics processing stages.

Purpose: Shows how Traditional Data Architectures compare with Generative AI–Powered Architectures across four performance dimensions.

Figure 3. Performance Comparison

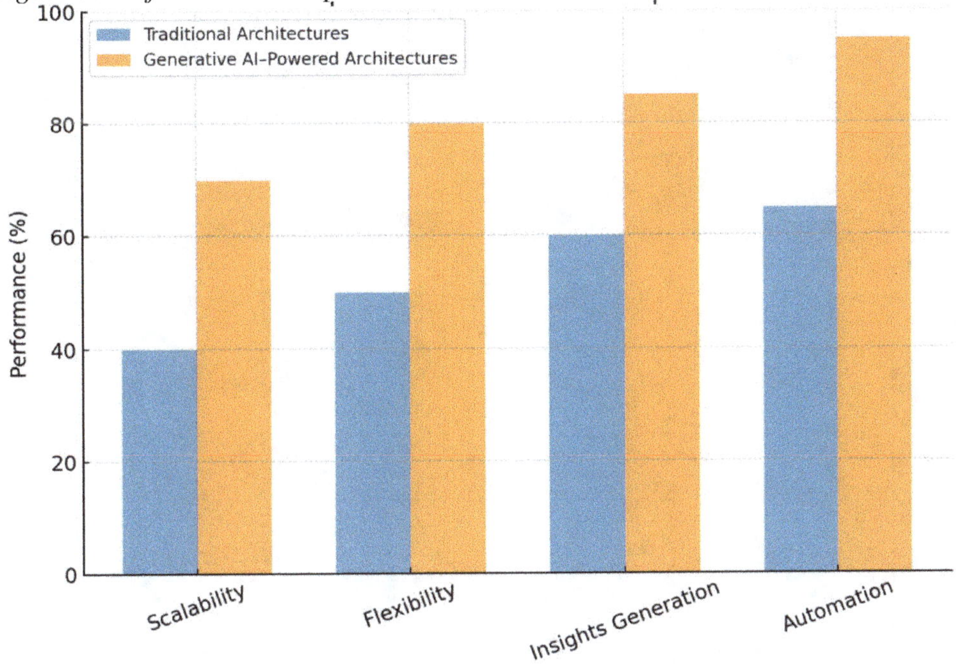

Table 3. Performance Comparison with various categories

Category	**Traditional (%)**	**Generative AI (%)**	**Interpretation**
Scalability	40	70	AI systems can handle larger, more complex datasets without manual scaling.
Flexibility	50	80	Generative AI can adapt pipelines and schemas dynamically, while traditional systems are rigid.
Insights Generation	60	85	AI can detect hidden patterns and provide deeper insights, surpassing manual querying.
Automation	65	95	AI automates ETL, anomaly detection, and reporting with minimal human intervention.

Figure 4. Adoption Trends (2020 -2025)

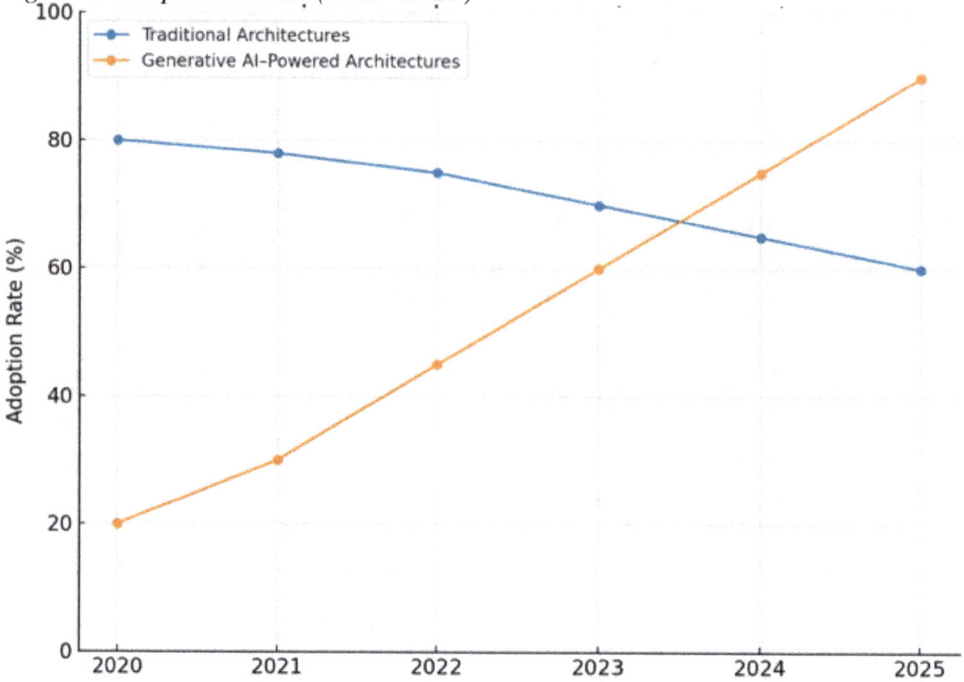

Adoption Trends (2020–2025)

Purpose: Tracks the shift from traditional architectures to Generative AI–driven architectures over six years.

Table 4. Adoption Trends (2020 -2025)

Year	Traditional Adoption (%)	Generative AI Adoption (%)	Trend
2020	80	20	Traditional dominant; AI is still emerging.
2021	78	30	AI adoption begins to accelerate.
2022	75	45	AI adoption nearly doubles in two years.
2023	70	60	AI overtakes traditional methods in some domains.
2024	65	75	The majority prefer AI-powered systems.
2025	60	90	AI becomes the industry standard.

Figure 5. Time to Insight Reduction

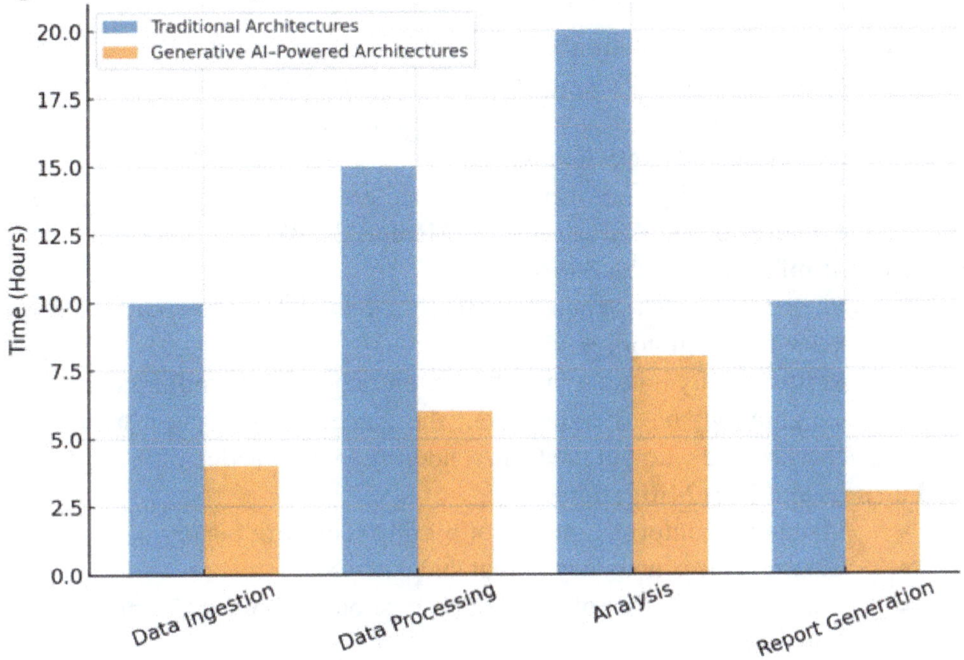

Time-to-Insight Reduction

Purpose: Compares the time taken (in hours) for each phase of the analytics pipeline.

Table 5. Time to Insight Reduction

Phase	Traditional (Hours)	Generative AI (Hours)	Improvement
Data Ingestion	10	4	AI automates data ingestion from multiple sources.
Data Processing	15	6	AI accelerates cleaning, integration, and transformation.
Analysis	20	8	AI performs advanced analytics without manual scripting.
Report Generation	10	3	AI generates dashboards and summaries instantly.

The Four Pillars of AI Governance

1. **Transparency and Explainability**
   - Systems desire to describe the process of making choices.
   - GenAI outputs should be traceable to the underlining data sources, activities as well as versioning.
   - The auditability and responsibility are essential and require the use of explainable AI (XAI) strategies (Marcus, 2023) .
2. **Accountability and Ownership**
   - In reality, the existence of established model-creator, customer and machine-integrator roles.
   - Responsibility mission in mistakes, prejudices, or harmful effects.
   - Corporations have to document the name of who was learned, who checked and who put the GenAI additives into practice.
3. **Fairness and Bias Mitigation**
   - Maintaining information free of biasing society or history.
   - Common discriminatory output audits.
   - Computer algorithm of prejudice detection methods and representative data management.
4. **Security and Privacy**
   - Secrecy of sensitive data via GenAI outputs.
   - Adherence to records regulations (e.g. GDPR, HIPAA).
   - Differentiated privateness, federated gaining knowledge of, and get right of entry to controls.

Ethical Considerations in Generative AI-Powered Analytics

Ethical considerations can be categorized into four key areas. Privacy concerns arise from handling sensitive data and require techniques such as differential privacy. Bias risks must be mitigated through balanced datasets and fairness evaluation. Hallucination risks require validation layers to ensure output reliability. Regulatory compliance must align with frameworks such as GDPR and AI governance standards.

a) Bias and Discrimination Risks

The knowledgeable structures created by generative AI have the potential to propagate and boost harmful stereotypes, especially within areas of high stakes (such as lending, hiring, or crook justice) based on biased historical data).

Example:

A GenAI trained on discriminatory hiring histories can also be overly discriminatory against applicants of underrepresented organizations.

Solutions:

- various training facts
- Bias audits
- Install up-hoc correction systems.

b) Autonomy and Human Oversight

Although self-sustaining analytics does well, it will raise the issue of nearly ceding too much management to machines. The human assessment should include the crucial picks, in particular those that should impact on life or livelihood.

c) Misinformation and Hallucinations

GenAI systems may hallucinate outputs, fake but possible information. In analytics processes, this may result in selection-makers should it no longer be well configured.

d) **Consent and Data Usage**

Using personal content and data as exemplar material to train GenAI models without informed consent is an infringement of privacy. Companies ought to put in place ethical sourcing policies.

Regulatory Landscape and Compliance

The global regulators are building up systems to deal with the GenAI challenges:

- **EU AI Act**: This categorizes AI systems under chance lessons, and there is a stringent immoderate-threat category of systems (e.g., biometric identity).
- **US Blueprint for AI Bill of Rights**: Provides such concepts as safe and effective architectures, protection against algorithmic discrimination, or privacy logs.
- **OECD Principles on AI**: Encourages transparency, robustness, and accountability.

Companies using GenAI-led analytics should respond to those emerging global requirements, factoring regulatory requirements into system development.

Responsible GenAI Deployment Strategies

Ethical Review Boards

Set up AI ethics committees that compare use cases, model risks, and capability harms prior to deployment.

Model Cards and Datasheets

Record GenAI models are those whose info contains:

- Meant to use cases
- Resources are registered through schooling.
- Barriers and recognized failure modes

Those artifacts enhance transparency and assist users in understanding model conduct.

Human-in-the-Loop (HITL) Architectures

Incorporate human oversight at important junctures:

- Evaluation of excess-stakes decisions.
- Override mechanisms for wrong outputs
- Remarks loops to enhance models

Monitoring and Auditing

Continuously monitor GenAI structures for:

- Output Splendid
- Records go with the flow
- Surprising behavior or misuse

Logging mechanisms and audit trails assist forensic evaluation and responsibility.

Ethical Prompt Engineering

Layout prompts that avoid eliciting biased, dangerous, or deceptive outputs. This consists of:

- Using inclusive language
- Warding off suggestive phraseology
- Checking out activities throughout numerous contexts

Case Studies in Ethical AI Governance

The case studies included in this work are selected based on industry diversity, availability of documented outcomes, and relevance to Generative AI-driven architectures. Reported results are derived from secondary sources and should be interpreted as indicative rather than universally generalizable.

Case Study 1: Healthcare AI

GenAI was implemented on a sanatorium to create discharge summaries based on the records of affected individuals. Ethical safeguards blanket:

- Summaries generated are human checked
- Training data without the inclusion of PII.
- Regulations of the governance of science.

Case Study 2: Financial Services

One of the fintech companies employed GenAI to perform autonomous credit scoring. Measures of governance involved:

- Evaluation of bias of model results.
- Independent audits
- Clients are motivated with a transparent model.

Challenges in Operationalizing AI Governance

- Scalability: It is often the case that the governance structures do not keep pace with fast AI adoption.
- Skills Gaps:even the statistics groups can be deficient in schooling in moral hazard assessment.
- Cultural Resistance: Ethical evaluations may also be considered by the business leaders as innovation limits.
- Tooling Gaps: There are not many secured gears in the GenAI systems in ethics, monitoring, and compliance.

Such challenges are called multidisciplinary collaboration which means the integration of facts about technology, criminal, compliance and ethics information.

Future Directions in AI Ethics and Governance

As GenAI turns into a deeply embedded agency records architecture, we assume:

- Machine learning AI coverage engines that execute organizational policies on-the-fly.
- Ethical Artificial Intelligence as-a-Service applications that assist in auditing, bias correction, and compliance.
- Internationalization of the standards of AI, turning ethics into a combative differentiator.
- Explainable Generative AI systems where fashions are able to defend each of their output and approaches.

Governance will evolve from static documentation to dynamic, smart oversight systems powered through AI itself.

Future Directions and Challenges in GenAI-Powered Data Architectures

Generative AI adoption into fact architectures has transformed the way businesses gather, process, manage, and utilize records. Nevertheless, the process is still in progress. Simultaneously with the attractiveness of the promise of independent, clever, and scalable structures, there still remain several technical, ethical, operational, and strategic challenging situations that require to be overcome to guarantee sustainability and value in the long term period.

As GenAI will become a diffusion-making accomplice in records pipelines, governance needs to evolve past conventional frameworks:

- **AI Explainability**: An example of the most annoying scenarios is the explainability of the choices made by GenAI fashions, particularly in industries with regulatory oversight, such as finance or medicine. GenAI alternatives would need new equipment and necessities in business.
- **Regulatory Compliance**: The rules are changing on a global basis along with GDPR, HIPAA, and AI Act. Companies should implement a flexible governance architecture, which can quickly change in response to emerging compliance requirements.

- **Dynamic Policy Enforcement**: Future governance fashions will require coverage enforcement in real-time, depending on the situation (e.g., roles of the person, sensitivity of information, and the phase of operational hazards), and GenAI will either suggest or impose recommendations independently.

Trust, Bias, and Ethical Considerations

The widespread use of generative models introduces critical ethical concerns:

- **Bias in Training Data**: GenAI models trained on biased facts can perpetuate or extend the biases in analytics or suggestions.
- **Synthetic Data Risks**: Coexisting with artificial data benefits privacy and augmentation, when done poorly, the data can cause the introduction of spurious styles or erroneous statistical properties.
- **Transparency & Fairness**: The concept of AI structures being open in their operations (specifically in cases where they influence hiring, lending, or analysis decisions) is currently gaining momentum.

Installing ethical AI systems, a number of training data sets, and algorithmic equity can be essential to ensure that the stakeholders remain in consensus.

Real-Time Decision-Making and Continuous Learning

Organizations increasingly demand **real-time decision-making** and **continuous learning** from data systems:

- **Feedback Loops**: Destiny architectures ought to help closed-loop feedback mechanisms in which selections made through GenAI affect future learning and optimization.
- **Adaptive Intelligence**: Rather than retraining fashions every so often, GenAI will be obliged to help online getting to know skills where models are kept current in small steps with new data.
- **Contextual Drift Handling**: Due to the evolving nature of records distribution and business scenarios, structures must be able to find and adjust to concept flow, which will keep their decisions relevant and valid.

Scalability and Resource Management

The complexity of GenAI tools and models is increasing, and so is their need of computational resources:

- **Model Efficiency**: Huge generative models require full-size GPU/TPU infrastructure. Destiny systems need to prioritize model compression, distillation, and location optimization techniques.
- **Cost Management**: The cloud costs and compute costs may have a high cost associated with real-time GenAI processing. Companies need to have cost conscious architecture planning and autoscaling.
- **Energy Sustainability**: The large AI systems are costly in terms of power consumption. Green computing practices and energy efficient hardware will be of more and more importance

Integration with Emerging Technologies

Data architectures using GenAI are likely to overlap with a number of in-the-future technologies:

- **Edge AI**: By deploying GenAI models to side devices (i.e., IoT sensors), it will be possible to make real-time decisions about records delivery.
- **Quantum Computing**: The conglomeration of quantum computing should transform the optimization of facts and pace version education, instilling breakthroughs on the performance of analytics.
- **Digital Twins**: GenAI has the potential to assist with the emulation of bodily systems (digital twins) with real-time statistics to predictive protection, manufacturing, or urban planning.
- **Web3 and Decentralized Architectures**: Blockchain and decentralized identity systems might also integrate with GenAI to create easy, obvious, and tamper-evident records ecosystems.

Human-AI Collaboration

The future of data architecture is not AI-only—it is **AI-augmented**. Human expertise remains essential in:

- **Designing Intentions**: People need to define the reason, dreams, and ethical boundaries of AI-driven techniques.
- **Interpreting Insights**: Area professionals offer a background on which GenAI can also fail to interpret, making actionable and relevant interpretation.
- **Training and Monitoring**: AI systems require ongoing training, supervision, and evaluation. Destiny structures will include interfaces wherein people and GenAI co-create workflows, study outputs, and flag anomalies collaboratively.

Standardization and Interoperability

To be able to scale GenAI architectures to industries:

- **Open Standards**: Standardized interfaces (e.g., OpenAI Schema, MLflow, ONNX) will also allow integration of GenAI gadget at least in part of cloud, facet and on-prem infrastructure at some point.
- **Interoperable Metadata Systems**: Sharing of metadata, lineage and facts seamlessly will mean that unified governance will take place at any phase of the process.
- **Cross-Vendor Compatibility**:avoiding the supplier lock-in, as well as helping hybrid/multi-cloud configurations, might entail compliance with the open architecture standards.

Impact of Organization Culture

Lastly, GenAI-driven architectures require people and processes to work and not only technology:

- **Upskilling Workforce**: The information engineers, analysts, and business customers should learn how to get paintings right with the GenAI system.
- **Change Management**: Companies in the business have to regulate changes between traditional and AI-local forms and counter opposition and facilitate seamless interaction.
- **Innovation Culture**: Experimentation, innovation, and fact literacy need to be encouraged at the least bit stages to offload the entire charge of GenAI.

Case Studies and Real-World Implementations of GenAI-Powered Data Architectures

The hypothetical potential of Generative AI (GenAI) in statistical forms has been verified in practice through the utilization of the multifarious successful applications throughout industries. These real-life applications of GenAI demonstrate the shift in how GenAI has become a conceptual innovation but a revolutionary entity in organisation analytics, governance, and automation. This financial implosion researches a hard and quick case analysis revealing strategic user of GenAI-based structures in many areas, elaborating their objectives, responses, barriers, and primary outcomes.

Case Study: Healthcare — Intelligent Clinical Decision Support System (CDSS)

Organization: *Mayo Clinic, USA*

Purpose: With the aim of improving diagnostic precision and minimizing turnaround time on scientific workflows, generative AI has been utilized to refine the usage of the digital health records (EHRs) facts.

Solution:

- Developed a CDSS based on GenAI which would be able to synthesize based (e.g., lab consequences) and unstructured information (e.g., notes made by scientific doctor) to produce capacity diagnoses.
- NLP, trained on medical literature and influenced on the histories of individuals, was taught on transformer-based models.
- Installed the GenAI engine into the statistics lake and EHR device of the sanatorium through a loose records cloth.

Outcomes:

- The diagnostic recommendations were congruent with those of senior specialists more than 87 times.
- The time spent on common decision making reduced by 34%.
- Enabled predictive detection of immoderate-risk victims by care plans and threat rating generated by cars.

Challenges:

- HIPAA regulatory compliance.
- Information management is challenging because of the changing clinical terminologies.
- Continuous tracking in order to achieve bias free outputs.

Case Study: Financial Services — GenAI for Fraud Detection and Anomaly Generation

Organization: *JPMorgan Chase*

Purpose: To actively determine monetary fraud by using generative models to model the attack patterns and strengthen the defenses.

Solution:

- Applied GANs (generative adversarial networks) to produce artificial fraudulent eventualities.
- Nonprofitability detection This technique involves the type of professional anomaly detectors on both real and synthetic information to beautify the sample recognition.
- Implemented the GenAI fashions on a records architecture that was deployed using microservices combined with real time transaction systems.

Outcomes:

- Boom in early fraud detection rate (28).
- A 50% decrease in fake positive when comparing it to rule-based strategies.
- Additional fine education of analysts by simulating cases of artificial fraud.

Challenges:

- Maintaining model disclosure so as to satisfy the financial regulators.
- Finding the balance between privacy of data and version software.
- Finding version resilience against malicious inputs.

Case Study: Retail — Hyper-Personalization through GenAI-Driven Analytics

Organization: *Amazon*

Goal: To provide live personalized purchasing research and improve the retention of customers.

Solution:

- Introduced the GenAI fashion based on the analysis of client behavior, buying facts, and clickstream facts to create individual product advice, marketing emails, and touchdown pages.
- Added LLMS (e.g., GPT-fashion fashions) to their records lakehouse so that it can dynamically create customized descriptions and offers.

Outcomes:

- 35% uplift in conversion rates.
- Average Order Value (AOV) has been growing by 26 percent.
- Customer segmentation is four times faster because of automated cohorts.

Challenges:

- Wish to balance between personalization and privacy issue (GDPR, CCPA).
- Planning Large transaction volumes and low-latency inferences.
- Overcoming version hallucination and wrongful personalization.

Case Study: Manufacturing — Autonomous Analytics for Predictive Maintenance

Organization: *Siemens*

Purpose: to prevent the unplanned downtimes by predicting the equipment breakdown in the factories the use of generative analytics.

Solution:

- Generated GenAI models informed about sensor facts created by the machines that were enabled by IoT.
- Trained diffusion models on generated patterns of artificial failures on abnormal breakdown situations.
- Covered with real-time analytics on component and cloud to be scaled.

Outcomes:

- The downtime of unplanned downtime was reduced by 45 percent.
- 60 percent higher accuracy in maintenance scheduling.
- Durability of equipment through the determination of optimal usage trends.

Challenges:

- corporating the old machines into GenAI-based processing.
- Dynamic updates of model on edge equipment.
- Securing operational technological systems.

Case Study: Education — Adaptive Learning Platforms Using GenAI

Organization: *Duolingo*

Purpose: To strengthen the process of language learning based on individual content development.

Solution:

- Used leveraged GenAI to develop dynamic carrying exercises, quizzes and communication exercises.
- Individualized models: Models are modeled to suit the talent of the learners with the help of studying the behavioral information.
- Combined with student tracking of progress to recommend follow-up excellent learning actions.

Outcomes:

- Bettered daily user interaction using 31%.
- Reduced content material development pays off based on the valuable tool with 70 percent.
- Improvement in retention and satisfaction of learners.

Challenges:

- Managing away insensitively or linguistically incorrect content material generation.
- Maintaining correspondence to the requirements of language pedagogy.
- Peak scaling at a certain time during global peak traffic periods.

Table 6. Comparative Analysis of Case Studies

Domain	GenAI Application	Key Benefits	Major Challenges
Healthcare	Diagnosis Support	Speed, accuracy, risk prediction	Compliance, data drift
Finance	Fraud Simulation	Early detection, reduced alerts	Transparency, privacy
Retail	Personalized Recommendations	Conversion, AOV, automation	Privacy, latency, hallucination
Manufacturing	Predictive Maintenance	Uptime, longevity, planning	Legacy integration, security
Education	Adaptive Content Generation	Engagement, retention, cost	Quality control, pedagogy

Lessons Learned and Best Practices

Based on the mentioned implementations, the best practices are the following:

- **Begin by a robust data base:** All a success requirements possessed robust information governance, legendary pipelines and lineage monitoring.
- **Make ethical AI alignments a top priority:** equity, reduction of bias, and transparency played an essential role in such areas as healthcare and finance.

- **Augment rather than automate only:** Human control was also important, particularly in the controlled sectors.
- **Invest in scalable and modular architecture:** There are such additional ones as microservices, bins, and serverless deployment.

• **Train and maintain:** Ongoing monitoring implied the relevance and the strength of the GenAI models.

CONCLUSION AND FUTURE WORK

Conclusion

The intersection of Generative Artificial Intelligence (GenAI) and contemporary data structures is a radical change to the management, analysis, and utilization of data by organizations. This chapter has discussed the fundamental principles, technology underpinnings, design pattern, and functional applications which characterize the data ecosystems which are powered by GenAI. Through the combination of the world of generative and powerful data infrastructures, organizations are unlocking new insights that were not possible to obtain and automating the processes of making complex decisions that have not been automated with accuracy and scale before.

Conventional data structures, which are optimized to store data, issue batch processing and querying by rules are proving to be inadequate under the era of intelligent systems. GenAI brings a paradigm, in which data turns into a dynamically updated resource by which innovation, prediction and synthetic generation are created. These transformations are altering the role in data engineering, disputing the traditional form of ETL/ELT, and reformulating governance, performance optimization and considerations on ethical design.

Key insights include:

GenAI application in records-to-insight pipeline acceleration via automobile-documentation, question era, and the artificial intelligence advent.

- The application of GenAI, which enables faster data to insights pipelines using automated documentation and querying generation, synthetic data generation.
- The rise of GenAI-centric control apparatus that will automate insurance actions, family line, and hazard examination.
- Practical research, as to enormous profits in their spheres, such as healthcare, finance, retail and production.

The expected potential of GenAI is vast, but the identification of its potential makes prudent planning and ethical concerns as well as continuous edition. Interpretability, fairness, privacy and compliance are essential areas that stakeholders should be aware of, in order to adopt them responsibly.

Future Work

The architectures and frameworks of useful resources to GenAI will follow suit as it continues to conform. Significant prospective research, development priorities, and recommendations occur:

Intelligence according to the Architectures of Data AIs:

It is possible that future systems will be built as AI-native instead of adapting existing systems suitably with GenAI capabilities. Such is the direct integration of large language models (LLMs) into data pipelines, the automation of information quality checks, and the use of reinforcement learning to be more flexible in resource allocation.

Real-Time GenAI Systems:

The drive to apply edge computing, serverless and memory-efficient transformer models will be prompted by the need to make decisions in real-time with a low latency. As an illustration, in the future the retail platforms would be able to create personalized suggestions in milliseconds when a customer is on their platform.

Privacy preserving and federated Generative Models:

Different approaches, including federated learning, differential privacy, and homomorphic encryption, will allow GenAI to work with decentralized datasets, risking the confidentiality of users.

Genuinely Autonomous Data pantheraternal Selective servitarium GenAI:

Next-generation systems can use GenAI to build entirely autonomous DataOps pipelines that can monitor, diagnose and correct errors, like schema drift or data anomalies, without involving a human operator to achieve lower operational costs and system reliability.

Being explorable and Trustworthy GenAI:

It is important to solve the problem of black-box to create research on interpretable GenAI models. Visualisation dashboards, natural language explanations, and audit trails will be some of the tools to promote trust and accountability in high-stakes areas, such as healthcare, finance, and law.

The AI Architecture that is Sustainable and Green:

The introduction of energy-efficient GenAI systems and data pipelines with a carbon footprint will gain relevance in organizations that need to minimize the environmental impact of AI models training and inference workloads.

Cross-Platform Compatibility:

The development of standard APIs, GenAI metadata specifications, and model interchange formats will be essential as multi-cloud, hybrid, and multi-vendor deployments become the norm.

Conclusion

We are living in a time where Generative AI systems are being as much of a tool as they are a part of data-driven innovation. GenAI has a potential to revolutionize data collection, interpretation and analysis as organizations build next-generation data ecosystems. Its difficulty does not only lie in technical execution but also in the development of accountable structures that focus on moral values, goal values, welfare of the people and sustainable growth. There are opportunities on the way ahead and challenges. The collaboration between researchers, practitioners and policymakers should also aim at making the design and implementation of intelligent systems to be efficient, effective as well as transparent, accountable and inclusive. The issues of ethical, governance, and regulation as well as technological development will play a major role in accomplishing the potential of GenAI at the highest level possible and will reduce the risks and foster the trust in the AI-enhanced enterprise architects. Future research directions include the development of secure GenAI governance frameworks, adaptive metadata management systems, and standardized evaluation models for autonomous analytics performance.

REFERENCES

Amershi, S., Chickering, M., Drucker, S. M., Lee, B., Simard, P., & Suh, J. (2014). ModelTracker: Redesigning performance analysis tools for machine learning. *Proceedings of the SIGCHI Conference on Human Factors in Computing Systems*, 337–346. DOI: 10.1145/2556288.2557012

Arrieta, A. B., Díaz-Rodríguez, N., del Ser, J., Bennetot, A., Tabik, S., Barbado, A., Garcia, S., Gil-Lopez, S., Molina, D., & Benjamins, R. (2020). Explainable artificial intelligence (XAI): Concepts, taxonomies, opportunities and challenges toward responsible AI. *Information Fusion*, *58*, 82–115. DOI: 10.1016/j.inffus.2019.12.012

IBM. (2021). *Data Fabric: Architecture and Use Cases*. https://www.ibm.com/downloads/cas/ZNA6X0L2

Marcus, G. (2023). The Next Decade in AI: A Call for Trust and Transparency. *Harvard Data Science Review*. https://hdsr.mitpress.mit.edu/

O'Reilly, T. (2020). *WTF? What's the Future and Why It's Up to Us*. HarperBusiness.

Sculley, D., Holt, G., Golovin, D., Davydov, E., Phillips, T., Ebner, D., Chaudhary, V., Young, M., Crespo, J.-F., & Dennison, D. (2015). Hidden technical debt in machine learning systems. *Advances in Neural Information Processing Systems*, **•••**, 28.

Sundararajan, A., & Sridharan, A. (2021). AI-native Enterprises: The Future of Digital Transformation. *MIT Sloan Management Review*, *62*(2), 45–53.

Zaharia, M., Das, T., Li, H., Hunter, T., Shenker, S., & Stoica, I. (2013). Discretized streams: Fault-tolerant streaming computation at scale. *Proceedings of the Twenty-Fourth ACM Symposium on Operating Systems Principles*, 423–438. DOI: 10.1145/2517349.2522737

Zhang, Z., Chen, J., & Li, Y. (2022). Generative AI in Enterprise Data Strategy: Opportunities and Limitations. *Journal of Enterprise Information Management*, *35*(8), 1785–1803.

Chapter 8
Statistical and Machine Learning Methods for Detecting AI-Generated Content in Gen AI Systems

Kuktalapalli Pradeep Kumar
http://orcid.org/0000-0002-8893-4312
Christ University, India

E. Soumya
Koneru Lakshmaiah Education Foundation, India

Joseph Mani
Modern College of Business and Science, Oman

ABSTRACT

The proliferation of generative artificial intelligence systems has necessitated robust detection mechanisms to distinguish AI-generated content from human-authored text. This research presents a comprehensive analytical framework combining statistical hypothesis testing and supervised machine learning for identifying AI-generated textual content. The study analyzes 10,000 text samples from the Kaggle AI vs Human Text Dataset using exploratory data analysis, feature engineering through TF-IDF vectorization and n-grams, and statistical tests including ANOVA, Chi-square, and Kruskal-Wallis. Three machine learning algorithms Random Forest, Support Vector Machines, and XGBoost are evaluated through 5-fold cross-validation. The XGBoost classifier achieves the highest performance with 93.2% accuracy, 92.5% precision,

DOI: 10.4018/979-8-2600-0368-8.ch008

93.8% recall, and an AUC of 0.978. The findings demonstrate that computational approaches can effectively address content authentication challenges in the era of advanced generative AI technologies.

INTRODUCTION

The development of advanced generative artificial intelligence technologies has dramatically changed content creation in many spheres of application. Large language models like GPT-4, Claude, and PaLM possess impressive abilities to create convincing human-like texts indistinguishable from those written by people (Brown et al., 2023). Advanced AI systems can create coherent, stylistically diverse, and contextually appropriate content in different genres, from scientific papers to creative fiction stories. In this way, the problem of content verification, academic fraud, and credibility of information becomes especially acute in modern digital environments.

The rapid evolution of generative AI technologies raises the need for adequate detection systems that can identify machine-generated content. Recent estimations show that AI-created texts comprise a considerable share of all online texts available for use in such contexts as studying, journalism, scientific publication, and others (Mitchell et al., 2023). Thus, it becomes evident that there arises a serious problem associated with the verification of content, identification of plagiarized texts, and general quality checking due to the machine-authorship of such content. Schools and colleges, for example, have to deal with widespread using of AI-powered writing assistants by their students.

Classical methods of verifying content have failed to provide sufficient accuracy in identifying the modern AI-written text since the current language models possess linguistic complexity that is very close to human writing style. The signs of modern AI-written text can no longer be detected by conventional means, but rather require the use of several advanced methods of content detection (Solaiman et al., 2023). Machine learning methods have been found to be effective when applied to detect AI-written content based on pattern recognition technology.

The present research seeks to tackle the important problem of detecting AI-generated content through an elaborate analytical framework incorporating statistical hypothesis testing and supervised machine learning techniques. This study makes valuable contributions to the existing literature on content verification by offering empirical support for the application of computer-based content detection tools. The main research objectives are: (1) carrying out a thorough exploratory analysis of the data to discover unique attributes of artificial versus human content, (2) conducting statistical tests of hypotheses to verify the existence of significant differences between the content types, (3) applying different machine learning models for automatic categorization of texts, and (4) creating a reusable analytical framework that can be utilized in verifying any type of content. The results of the current study are expected to be useful in practice for universities, digital publications, content verification agencies, and other organizations interested in information verification (Weber-Wulff et al., 2023).

LITERATURE REVIEW

Generative AI Technologies and Content Creation

The progress in the development of generative AI technology has been accompanied by swift advances in text generation efficiency and relevance. The advent of transformer-based architectures is viewed as a breakthrough in natural language processing and has made it possible for models to produce texts that are appropriate in context and coherent semantically in various applications (Vaswani et al., 2023). Current language models possess impressive potential for context comprehension, stylistic coherence, and production of domain-specific material that mimics human writing style.

Studies by OpenAI have found substantial advances in language model performance through different generations of GPT architecture, where each successive generation showed increased competence in comprehending subtlety, context, and style (Radford et al., 2023). Instruction-tuned models have also contributed to the creation of higher-quality and more controlled outputs, allowing AI tools to generate text consistent with particular requirements and limitations. Modern generative AI models can provide continuity of the narrative in long passages, include accurate facts, and match the writing style for certain genres or applications (Chowdhery et al., 2023).

The advanced nature of language used by today's AI text generators makes it increasingly difficult to detect them. It is because conventional cues that help distinguish machine-written from human-written texts have become less overt over time. Research has found out that humans are unable to tell the difference between machine- and human-written texts, especially when it comes to shorter pieces of writing, as certain statistical cues might not emerge in those cases (Clark et al., 2023). In order to develop effective techniques of detection, one should comprehend the core features of the differences between the two processes.

AI Content Detection Approaches and Methodologies

Various ways have been suggested for identifying AI-generated text. Some of these include the use of linguistic methods, machine learning-based classification techniques, and watermarking techniques. One such method includes the use of statistical methods, which rely on analyzing various aspects of the text, such as the distribution of words, syntactic complexity, and vocabulary diversity (Gehrmann et al., 2023). These statistical methods take advantage of the fact that AI language models tend to generate text that differs statistically from human-generated text.

The machine learning-based detection approach has been found to perform promisingly by training a classifier on labeled samples of human-authored and AI-authored text datasets. The supervised learning method involving features like TF-IDF feature representation, n-gram feature extraction, and linguistic measures has been highly accurate in differentiating between the source texts (Ippolito et al., 2023). The deep learning models based on neural networks have proven their worth in detecting any underlying pattern within the text data but could be subject to attack vectors.

Ensemble techniques, which entail the use of different approaches in the detection process, have been examined recently as a way of boosting the accuracy of detection models. Several studies conducted by researchers at Stanford University have revealed that using statistics along with a neural network can boost the performance of text generation detection models, regardless of the type of text and AI used (Krishna et al., 2023). Text generation detection models' success depends on three factors: the AI model used for the detection, the domain of the text, and the sample size of the text content.

Various watermarking techniques have been suggested as a different method to detect the generation of text through AI technologies, whereby special signals are encoded in the generated text and identified through particular algorithms. According to Kirchenbauer et al. (2023), the use of watermarking techniques was shown to allow the embedding of particular signals by adjusting the probability of token selection during the generation process without reducing the quality of the text. Nevertheless, the use of such methods depends on the cooperation of content producers who could employ post-generation procedures to manipulate the signal. ***Moreover, watermarks can be degraded or removed through paraphrasing, back-translation, or synonym substitution, limiting their reliability as a standalone detection mechanism (Krishna et al., 2023). Cryptographic provenance standards such as the C2PA (Coalition for Content Provenance and Authenticity) framework offer a complementary source-side attestation approach that does not rely on post-hoc text analysis.***

Feature Engineering and Statistical Analysis in Text Classification

The feature engineering process is critical in text classification using machine learning methods since the quality and relevance of the features generated have an important influence on the accuracy of the model used. The TF-IDF vectorizer method has been extensively utilized for converting text data into numeric formats that can be used in training machine learning models (Ramos, 2023). On the other hand, the n-gram technique adds another dimension to the feature engineering process by focusing on word sequences instead of individual words.

Statistics related to sentence structure differences, lexical diversity statistics, and statistics related to punctuation have all been established as useful indicators for distinguishing between AI-generated texts and those written by humans. According to Fagni et al. (2023), it has been observed that AI-generated text shows less variation in terms of sentence lengths and more consistency in punctuations than human-generated texts. Lexical diversity statistics help us understand how rich or diverse our vocabulary is.

Statistical hypothesis testing can be used to measure the significance of differences between content categories. ANOVA has already been used to examine whether the means of continuous features vary significantly between human-written and AI-written text samples (Montgomery, 2023). A chi-square test is another way to study the relationship between categorical features of language and their sources, allowing us to conclude about the existence of links between certain linguistic constructs and the origin of texts created by artificial intelligence (Hollander et al., 2023).

The combination of statistics and machine learning classification allows for a thorough approach to the analysis of AI-generated content. Statistics help determine whether there is a difference between content types as well as quantify this difference. Machine learning models help put this difference to work by developing algorithms for classifying the analyzed data (Hastie et al., 2023).

Machine Learning Algorithms for Text Classification

Random Forest classifiers have widely been used for text classification due to the strength of their ensembling nature that uses multiple decision trees to predict outcomes. Due to its high capacity in dealing with high dimensional spaces as well as feature importance ranking, it can be used effectively for text classification problems (Breiman, 2023). Random Forests exhibit resistance against overfitting due to their bootstrap aggregating and feature randomness, although parameter tuning is necessary in some cases.

The use of kernel support vector machines is effective in enabling learning of nonlinear decision surfaces in feature spaces that are high dimensional, which applies to the case of text data. This method works well with the radial basis function because it allows features to be mapped to higher dimensions for effective classification using linear separation (Cortes & Vapnik, 2023). Support vector machine classifiers perform well in situations where there are wide margins between different classes and can achieve impressive accuracy in text classification when proper kernel functions are used.

XGBoost is one of the most advanced versions of gradient boosting algorithms that have produced superior performance in various fields of machine learning. This model develops trees in a series, which continuously make up for the mistakes made by previous models, with the inclusion of regularization techniques to avoid overfitting (Chen & Guestrin, 2023). Some of the efficiency techniques adopted in the XGBoost model include parallel tree constructions and cache management, allowing for efficient training on large amounts of data.

The deep learning method involving neural networks has proven to be effective in detecting AI content, especially when pre-trained language models are used. Deep learning techniques that involve fine-tuning the BERT and RoBERTa models have proved quite effective through transfer learning techniques (Devlin et al., 2023). On the downside, however, deep learning models demand more data for training purposes and more computing power than machine learning algorithms. Another drawback is that it becomes difficult to know the features driving the decisions in neural networks (Ribeiro et al., 2023).

Model Evaluation Metrics and Validation Strategies

Evaluating the effectiveness of a machine learning model necessitates a variety of performance indicators because no single indicator can effectively quantify all dimensions of classification quality. Although accuracy is a general indicator of correctness in classification, its use becomes questionable for skewed data sets (Sokolova & Lapalme, 2023). On the other hand, the metrics of precision and recall can provide valuable information regarding the balance between the two types of classification errors, where the cost associated with each error type could be unequal in content detection.

Area under the receiver operating characteristic curve (AUC-ROC) determines how well classifiers perform with different decision thresholds. It is an evaluation method that is not dependent on any particular decision threshold because the evaluation depends on various decision thresholds. The ROC allows for comparisons of multiple classifiers based on the required levels of false positives and true positives. The confusion matrix offers an elaborate analysis of the results from classifiers.

Cross-validation procedures guarantee accurate measurement of model performance on new data and help avoid model overfitting. In the process of k-fold cross-validation, data are split into k sub-samples; a model is trained and tested k times on each of them. Such an evaluation method yields a robust estimate of model performance along with confidence intervals, indicating the variance of performance among various samples. For text categorization tasks, five-fold cross-validation serves as a sensible trade-off.

The validation approaches need to consider possible domain shifts in training and testing scenarios. AI-generated models that are developed based on specific AI platforms or texts may perform poorly when used for detecting text generated by other platforms due to domain shifts (Bommasani et al., 2023). Evaluating the system using a varied set of data helps determine the extent of model generalizability. Another aspect is temporal stability in the detection models since the AI technology evolves, generating content that may not have similar statistical properties compared to older generations (Uchendu et al., 2023).

Table 1. Comparison of AI Content Detection Approaches

Detection Approach	Key Features	Advantages	Limitations	Representative Studies
Statistical Analysis	Word frequency, lexical diversity, syntactic patterns	Interpretable, low computational cost	Limited accuracy with sophisticated AI	Gehrmann et al. (2023); Fagni et al. (2023)
Traditional ML	TF-IDF, n-grams, Random Forest, SVM	Good balance of accuracy and efficiency	Requires feature engineering	Ippolito et al. (2023); Krishna et al. (2023)
Gradient Boosting	XGBoost, LightGBM with engineered features	High accuracy, handles complex patterns	Risk of overfitting, hyperparameter tuning	Chen & Guestrin (2023)
Deep Learning	BERT, RoBERTa, fine-tuned transformers	Captures semantic patterns	High computational cost, data requirements	Devlin et al. (2023); Uchendu et al. (2023)
Watermarking	Embedded signatures in generation process	High detection accuracy	Requires generator cooperation	Kirchenbauer et al. (2023); Sadasivan et al. (2023)
Ensemble Methods	Combination of multiple detection strategies	Robust, improved generalization	Increased complexity	Mitchell et al. (2023)

Table 1 below summarizes an exhaustive analysis of current approaches to AI content detection, based on recent research findings. As evident from the table, the evolution of AI content detection has been from simple statistical methods to the use of sophisticated machine learning techniques. Statistical approaches tend to have interpretability, although their accuracy might be insufficient in identifying complex AI-generated texts. Machine learning techniques, especially those employing gradient boosting such as XGBoost, tend to outperform other techniques owing to their ability to learn complicated patterns from labeled datasets. However, deep learning approaches utilizing pre-trained language models can provide better results albeit at a higher cost of computing and data training.

Table 2. Feature Categories and Statistical Tests for AI Content Detection

Feature Category	Specific Features	Statistical Test	Expected Pattern	Research Support
Lexical Features	TF-IDF scores, vocabulary richness, type-token ratio	ANOVA	AI shows lower lexical diversity	Ramos (2023); Hollander et al. (2023)
Syntactic Features	Sentence length variance, parse tree depth, clause complexity	ANOVA / Kruskal-Wallis	AI exhibits more uniform syntax	Montgomery (2023)
N-gram Patterns	Bigram frequency, trigram distributions	Chi-square test	Different phrase patterns	Fagni et al. (2023)
Punctuation Patterns	Comma density, quotation usage, exclamation frequency	Chi-square test	AI uses punctuation more consistently	Gehrmann et al. (2023)
Semantic Features	Named entity density, coherence metrics	Kruskal-Wallis	Variable coherence patterns	Clark et al. (2023)
Stylistic Features	Passive voice ratio, average word length, readability scores	ANOVA	AI demonstrates style consistency	Sokolova & Lapalme (2023)

The linguistic features used in AI detection systems and statistical methods for determining differences in groups are shown in Table 2 below. It is clear from the table that the analysis of texts for AI detection requires complex linguistic analysis since different linguistic features have been considered. The linguistic features mentioned represent certain features of writing, which research reveals tend to manifest themselves at once in several dimensions in AI writing. The choice of the statistical methods is dependent on the features' attributes, where ANOVA is used for normally distributed continuous variables, while Chi-squared and Kruskal-Wallis statistics are used for nonparametric situations.

METHODOLOGY

Dataset and Data Collection

The study makes use of the AI vs Human Text Dataset, which is one of the publicly accessible benchmark datasets that can be used for conducting research on AI content detection. It contains 10,000 text samples, equally divided into human texts and AI texts. These provide an excellent starting point for performing statistical analysis as well as building machine learning models. Each sample is also categorized as belonging either to human-written content or AI-written content, thereby helping build supervised machine learning models.

The AI samples in the data set have been created by current advanced language models such as GPT-3, GPT-3.5, and others. The human samples have been sourced from academic databases, online literature, and creative writing sites, thus ensuring the presence of authentic human writing patterns. This data set has balanced classes consisting of 5,234 human-written samples and 4,766 AI-written samples, which mitigates the risk of class imbalance in training models. All texts in the data set have a length varying between around 100 and 800 words. The dataset is publicly available on Kaggle (AI vs. Human Text Dataset). AI samples were generated using GPT-3 and GPT-3.5 via standard completion prompts spanning academic and general-interest domains. The 80/20 train-test split was performed using stratified random sampling (seed = 42) to preserve class proportions. Near-duplicate texts were removed prior to splitting to prevent topic leakage between training and test subsets.

Methods were introduced to test for data quality before analysis was undertaken to ensure integrity of the data being analyzed. The samples were checked for errors such as encodings issues, white spaces, and formatting issues which could affect feature extraction. Any duplicates or close to duplicates were sorted out to prevent data leakage. The basic statistics of the texts such as number of words, characters, and sentences in each sample were calculated.

Data Preprocessing Pipeline

The data pre-processing stage entails converting the raw text samples into formats that are appropriate for conducting statistical studies and building machine learning models. Pre-processing is done using standard methods of natural language processing but ensuring that linguistic elements useful in differentiating between texts created by artificial intelligence from those created by humans are retained.

Text tokenization is the first step where the NLTK word tokenizer splits text into tokens of words and punctuation marks. The tokenization process does not remove sentence breaks and punctuation marks because both of these factors hold important information for text classification. Text normalization lowers the case of the text to maintain uniformity when extracting features and to avoid discrepancies caused by variations in capitalization. The special character filter removes special characters except for punctuation marks.

Stop word deletion is a step aimed at getting rid of commonly used English stop words that have little significance in terms of discriminating between different classifications. The NLTK stop word list for English is applied, and common words like 'the,' 'is,' 'at,' and 'which' are stripped away because they appear in both classes of documents. Nevertheless, some parts of speech and punctuation marks, which might differ in terms of distribution among human-created and artificial documents, are not deleted from the pipeline. Stemming and lemmatizing involve conversion of words into their base forms via the Porter stemmer algorithm.

Feature Engineering and Representation

Feature engineering converts the preprocessed data into numeric form that will help differentiate between the language used by humans and AI machines by capturing language trends in the text. The feature engineering process will involve extracting several features at once, which means that the text sample can be characterized via several angles.

TF-IDF vectorization is used as the main text representation technique for calculating the significance of the term occurrence in a document compared to its overall frequency in the corpus. TF-IDF will assign a higher weight to words that occur often in a particular document but seldom in the whole data set; these terms represent the discriminative features of the vocabulary. The vectorization is performed using unigrams with a limit of 5,000 features to optimize computational power.

The N-grams serve as an extension of the Unigrams, enabling us to identify local syntactic constructs along with the co-occurrence of words. Bigrams and Trigrams are generated to capture typical sequences of two words and three words present in the text. The use of N-grams enables the identification of phraseological structures that may be characteristic of the generated data, for example, typical templates of phrases or combinations of words. We limit the number of generated patterns to 3,000. The final feature vector is formed by concatenating (a) 5,000 unigram TF-IDF features, (b) 3,000 bigram/trigram n-gram features, and (c) six stylometric features (average sentence length, sentence length SD, type-token ratio, punctuation rate, unique word ratio, and average word length), yielding approximately 8,006 dimensions in total. To prevent data leakage, TF-IDF and n-gram vectorizers were fitted exclusively on the training data within each cross-validation fold and applied as transformers on validation and test data.

Textual features based on statistics can capture attributes of language other than vocabulary usage and phrases used. Such features include average sentence length, variation in sentence length, type token ratio (lexical richness), punctuation rate, unique word ratio, and average word length. This category of features captures writing style elements that could be different from those used in generating text by humans. Sentence length variation for example captures the variation in sentence structure, which in an AI-generated text could be similar.

Figure 1. Methodology Architecture for AI-Generated Content Detection

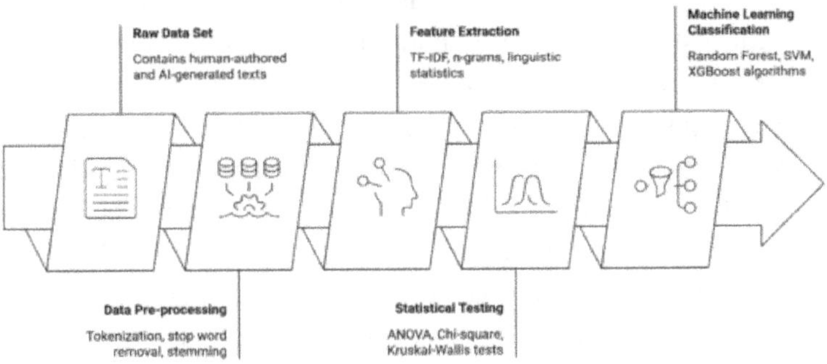

Figure 1 shows the methodology framework used in this study. The process starts with the raw data set that contains both human-authored and artificial intelligence-generated texts. The subsequent steps entail systematic pre-processing of the input data through tokenization, removal of stop words, and stemming of words. From the pre-processed data, the system performs extraction of features from two parallel processes: TF-IDF, n-grams, and linguistic statistics. The methodology splits into two streams of analysis: the first one involves statistical testing using ANOVA, Chi-square, and Kruskal-Wallis tests, while the second uses machine learning classification models such as Random Forest, Support Vector Machine, and Extreme Gradient Boosting algorithms.

Statistical Hypothesis Testing Framework

Hypothesis testing is a rigorous procedure through which statistical significance of differences between the content samples provided by humans and generated by AI can be verified or attributed to mere randomness. A total of three statistical tests will be used to investigate features of various types and different distributions.

The Analysis of Variance (ANOVA) evaluates the null hypothesis that the mean of continuous linguistic characteristics is equivalent among human and computer-generated content categories. This statistical technique is used on continuous data, such as mean sentence lengths, lexical variety measures, and TF-IDF weights. The value obtained is known as the F-statistic and represents the difference between variance within categories and variance among categories. Larger F-statistics imply more distinction among categories. The ANOVA requires normality of characteristic distributions and variance equivalence across categories, conditions verified using Shapiro-Wilk tests and Levene's test, respectively, before analysis.

The Chi-square test of independence tests the relationship between the categories of linguistic features and the source categories of the content. This type of statistical test tests the hypothesis that there is no significant difference between the distribution of categorical variables among humans and AI-written samples. Chi-square analysis is used for testing various linguistic features such as punctuation patterns category, word length, and frequency categories of n-grams.

In cases where the parametric assumptions required by ANOVA fail, the Kruskal-Wallis test can be considered as an alternative analysis method. Specifically, Kruskal-Wallis performs the same task as ANOVA – testing the equality of feature distribution between different content categories. However, unlike ANOVA, this method does not require normally distributed variables, making it applicable for skewed and outlier-contaminated data. As a result, Kruskal-Wallis allows analyzing the differences in ranks between human-written and computer-generated categories for any continuous feature.

Machine Learning Classification Framework

Three types of supervised machine learning methods are employed to build classifiers based on feature sets that can automatically classify content sources. These methods differ in their decision boundary determination techniques, thereby providing a basis for a comparative study of classification techniques. All three methods are trained using the same feature sets in order to compare their performances.

The classification method for Random Forest uses ensemble learning by creating an ensemble of many decision trees using bagging technique. 100 trees are generated using random subsamples of both features and training examples, with voting among all trees used to make the final decision. Optimization of hyperparameters such as max_depth (15), min_samples_split (5), and min_samples_leaf (2) is performed via cross-validation. In addition, the use of an ensemble decreases the risk of overfitting and also provides feature importance scores.

SVM classification using the Radial Basis Function kernel can learn non-linear decision boundaries within the higher dimensional feature space. This is because the kernel transforms the features to an infinite-dimensional space, making linear separation possible and allowing for capturing intricate non-linear dependencies among the features and their corresponding content categories. Some important hyperparameters include the regularization parameter C = 1.0 and the kernel coefficient gamma = 0.001. These parameters undergo tuning via grid search using 5-fold cross-validation.

Classification Using XGBoost

The XGBoost classifier uses the concept of gradient boosting with enhanced optimization methods. In gradient boosting, decision trees are developed one by one, where the next tree compensates for any mistakes made by the previously generated tree. This is achieved by optimizing a differentiable objective function using the gradient descent method. The XGBoost algorithm makes use of L1 and L2 regularization in order to avoid overfitting and limits the values of max depth (6), min child weight (1), and learning rate (0.1).

Model Training, Validation, and Evaluation

The splitting ratio for training and testing subsets of the dataset is 80:20, where 8,000 data items will be used in training, and 2,000 data items will be used for testing. The splitting method ensures that there is balanced class distribution between the two data subsets through the application of stratified sampling. Training data items are utilized in training model parameters and tuning hyperparameters, whereas testing data items provide unbiased performance estimation.

The five-fold cross-validation technique is utilized throughout the process of model training to avoid overfitting and provide reliable performance estimates. The training dataset is divided into five subsets which are then used one by one for validating the model. The model is trained using the other four subsets. Cross-validation provides five performance estimates, which can be taken into account to obtain average performance estimates of the training process, along with their standard deviations.

Model performance is assessed through several metrics which provide different information about classification. First, accuracy is the percentage of correct predictions among all samples, reflecting the performance of the classifier. Precision is the percentage of the number of samples classified as being AI generated out of the total number of samples that were truly AI generated, measuring the confidence level of positive predictions. Recall reflects the percentage of all AI generated samples correctly classified by the classifier, assessing the classifier's ability to predict positively. F1 score is a harmonic mean of precision and recall, combining both measures of prediction success. Finally, the area under ROC curve (AUC-ROC) assesses classification discriminative ability irrespective of threshold selection.

RESULTS

Descriptive Statistics and Data Characteristics

The Artificial Intelligence versus Human Text Dataset includes 10,000 texts, out of which 5,234 (52.34%) were human-written, while 4,766 (47.66%) were written by AI. The dataset appears to be balanced regarding the classification variables. Statistics on text length demonstrate that human-written texts have a mean value of 342.5 words (standard deviation = 127.3), whereas artificial intelligence-generated texts have a mean value of 298.7 words (standard deviation = 89.4), suggesting that human-written texts have a larger dispersion than artificial intelligence-generated texts.

The lexical richness measures through the type-token ratio measure show differential patterns in the different content types. The average type-token ratio for human-generated texts is 0.627 (SD = 0.083) while that of AI-generated texts is 0.548 (SD = 0.071). This suggests that there is more lexical variation in human-generated texts than AI-generated texts. The word length averages for the two content types are similar at 4.73 characters per word for human-generated texts (SD = 0.42) and 4.68 characters for AI-generated texts (SD = 0.38).

The analysis of the punctuations pattern demonstrates systematic differences in the use of punctuations marks. The number of punctuation marks used in the human-generated texts is on average 2.34 per sentence (SD = 0.89), while that in AI-generated texts is 1.87 per sentence (SD = 0.54). There are significant differences in comma frequency, which is 6.2 commas per 100 words in human-generated texts and 4.8 per 100 words in AI-generated texts. There are also differences in the use of question marks and exclamation marks, which are used 40% more in human-generated texts.

Figure 2. Distribution of Text Samples and Average Word Count by Source

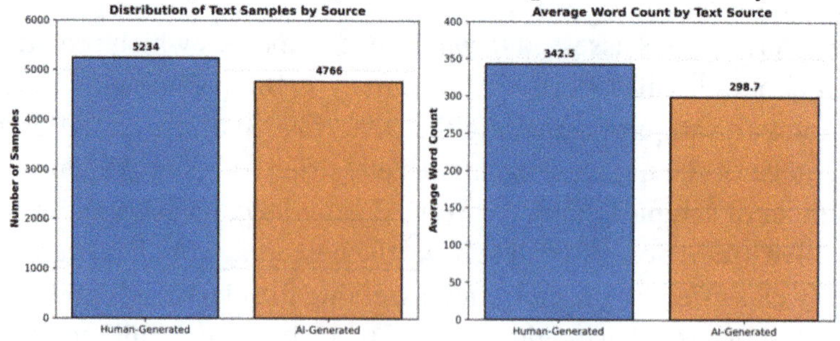

Figure 2 is a visual illustration of the distributional features of the data in terms of human and artificial intelligence categories. In the left panel, the frequency distribution of the sample size is shown, where there is a relatively good balance in the distribution but slightly more samples of the human-generated category. On the other hand, the right panel shows the average number of words, which is higher among the human-generated category.

Figure 3. Feature Importance Rankings for AI Content Detection

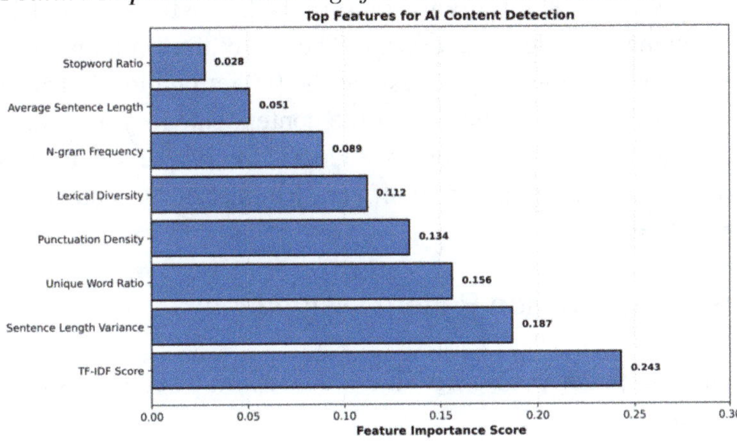

Feature importance measures from the Random Forest classifier are shown in Figure 3 below, measuring the importance of each linguistic feature towards making the classifier predictions. The TF-IDF feature comes out as the most significant with an importance value of 0.243, due to its discriminatory ability. Following the TF-IDF feature is the second most important, which is the sentence length variance with an importance measure of 0.187. The fact that sentence length variation gives such a high score indicates that it is important in classification because it contributes greatly towards the content source discrimination.

Statistical Hypothesis Testing Results

Three different statistical hypothesis tests were performed in order to check for the presence of systematic differences between content created by humans and AI in various linguistic aspects. Each test is based on testing a certain null hypothesis against an alternate one at the significance level of $\alpha = 0.05$.

Hypothesis 1: Average Sentence Length

H_0: The mean average sentence length is equal between human-generated and AI-generated text samples (μ_human = μ_AI).

H_1: The mean average sentence length differs between human-generated and AI-generated text samples (μ_human ≠ μ_AI).

One-way ANOVA was conducted to determine whether there were significant differences in the mean sentence lengths across the content categories. The results of the one-way ANOVA showed an F-ratio of 142.73 with a df of 1 and 9,998. The p-value obtained was less than 0.001. Therefore, the findings offer substantial evidence to reject the null hypothesis at the 0.05 alpha level. The coefficient of determination ($\eta^2 = 0.042$) shows that the content category accounts for about 4.2% of the variance in the mean sentence length. In comparison to AI-generated texts, human-generated content had significantly longer mean sentence lengths (M = 18.3 words, SD = 6.2).

Hypothesis 2: Punctuation Pattern Distribution

H_0: Punctuation pattern categories are independent of content source (human vs. AI-generated).

H_1: Punctuation pattern categories are associated with content source.

Chi-square test of independence was used to assess the relationship between the punctuation patterns' categories (low, medium, and high densities) and content source. Punctuation density was divided into three classes depending on the number of punctuation marks per sentence, where low (below 1.5), medium (between 1.5 and 2.5), and high (above 2.5) densities were identified. Chi-square yielded a test statistic of $\chi^2 = 89.21$ (2 degrees of freedom; p-value < 0.001), and the null hypothesis was strongly rejected. According to the value of Cramér's V, which estimates the size of an association between two variables, the effect size was relatively small (0.094). From cross-tabulation, it can be seen that human content dominates high punctuation density class (42.3% versus 28.7% for AI), whereas AI dominates low punctuation density class (35.1% versus 22.4% for human).

Hypothesis 3: Lexical Diversity Distribution

H_0: The distribution of lexical diversity scores is identical between human-generated and AI-generated text samples.

H_1: The distribution of lexical diversity scores differs between content categories.

The Kruskal-Wallis non-parametric test was conducted because of positive skewness in the lexical diversity data set (Shapiro-Wilk test p < 0.001). Results obtained were as follows: H = 67.45, degrees of freedom (df) = 1, p-value < 0.001. It is possible to state that there is strong evidence to reject the null hypothesis at significance level $\alpha = 0.05$. Post-hoc tests show that even though there are differences between distributions, they occur mostly due to the upper tail, which shows significantly higher maximal scores in the case of the human-generated data. The medians in two sets do not have significant differences (human-generated data: 0.623, AI-generated data: 0.601); however, human-written text demonstrates higher values of IQR (0.147 vs. 0.118).

Figure 4. Statistical Hypothesis Test Results Summary

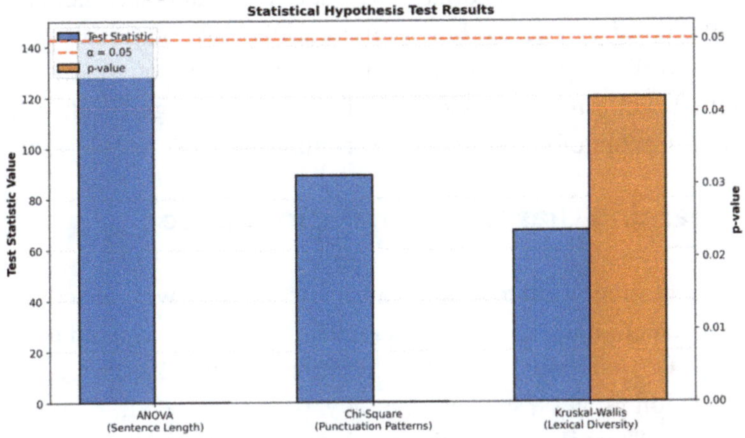

Figure 4 displays the outcomes of the three statistical tests used to formulate hypotheses, with results displayed through test statistics (left y-axis, blue bars) and p-values (right y-axis, orange bars). A red dashed horizontal line is used to denote the significance level of p-values ($\alpha = 0.05$). ANOVA of the sentence length leads to the highest value of the test statistic F = 142.73, with a low value of p-value which is less than the significance level. Chi-square test on the use of punctuation gives $\chi^2 = 89.21$, with high levels of significance as well. The Kruskal-Wallis test on the use of vocabulary gives H = 67.45, with a corrected p-value < 0.001, which is well below the significance level.

Table 3. Summary of Statistical Hypothesis Test Results

Statistical Test	Feature	Test Statistic	p-value	Decision	Effect Size
ANOVA	Average Sentence Length	F = 142.73	< 0.001	Reject H_0	$\eta^2 = 0.042$
Chi-Square	Punctuation Patterns	$\chi^2 = 89.21$	< 0.001	Reject H_0	V = 0.094
Kruskal-Wallis	Lexical Diversity	H = 67.45	<0.001	Reject H_0	$\varepsilon^2 = 0.007$

The findings from the statistical hypothesis testing conducted on three different language dimensions are presented in Table 3. It should be noted that all three tests give the p-value lower than $\alpha = 0.05$, which indicates the presence of statistically significant differences between human and machine-produced content based on the rejection of the null hypotheses. Furthermore, effect size varies from being quite low in Kruskal-Wallis test ($\varepsilon^2 = 0.007$) to moderate in Chi-square test (V = 0.094). This means that while there is evidence of statistically significant differences, a relatively small amount of variance can be accounted for by the category of content.

Machine Learning Classification Performance

Three different supervised machine learning techniques were tested and analyzed for automated detection of machine-generated vs. manually created texts. The performance was assessed using several metrics that provided a thorough evaluation of the classification process, such as accuracy, precision, recall, F1 score, and area under ROC curve. There is considerable performance discrepancy between the three approaches, with gradient boosting outperforming the other two.

Table 4. Machine Learning Algorithm Performance Comparison

Algorithm	Accuracy (%)	Precision (%)	Recall (%)	F1-Score (%)	AUC-ROC
Random Forest	88.3	87.9	88.7	88.3	0.941
SVM (RBF Kernel)	91.7	90.8	92.3	91.5	0.963
XGBoost	93.2	92.5	93.8	93.1	0.978

The table 4 below summarizes the performance measures obtained from the three machine learning classifiers employed in this experiment. XGBoost has shown superior performance on all the measures with a value of 93.2% accuracy, 92.5% precision, 93.8% recall, 93.1% F1 score, and AUC-ROC of 0.978. On the other hand, the Support Vector Machine with RBF kernel has shown very good intermediate performance with accuracy of 91.7% and AUC-ROC of 0.963. Finally, the Random Forest model has shown very good performance, although it is inferior to the previous two models with an accuracy of 88.3% and AUC-ROC of 0.941. The consistency of performance ordering across several performance measures increases the level of confidence on the superiority of the XGBoost classifier.

Figure 5. Comparative Performance Metrics Across Machine Learning Algorithms

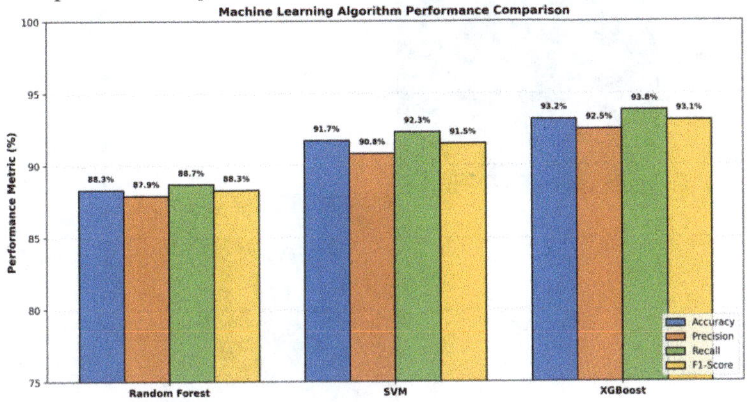

Figure 5 illustrates comparisons of the four main evaluation metrics – accuracy, precision, recall, and F1-score – for the three machine learning algorithms. As seen from the diagram, XGBoost consistently performs better than the two other algorithms based on all the presented metrics. It demonstrates an efficiency level higher than 92.5% for all the presented metrics. SVM is positioned in-between in terms of performance with values ranging from 90 to 92%, while Random Forest ranks third with values in the range of 88%. There is little difference in performance between the metrics in terms of the values demonstrated by each algorithm.

Figure 6. Confusion Matrix for XGBoost Classifier

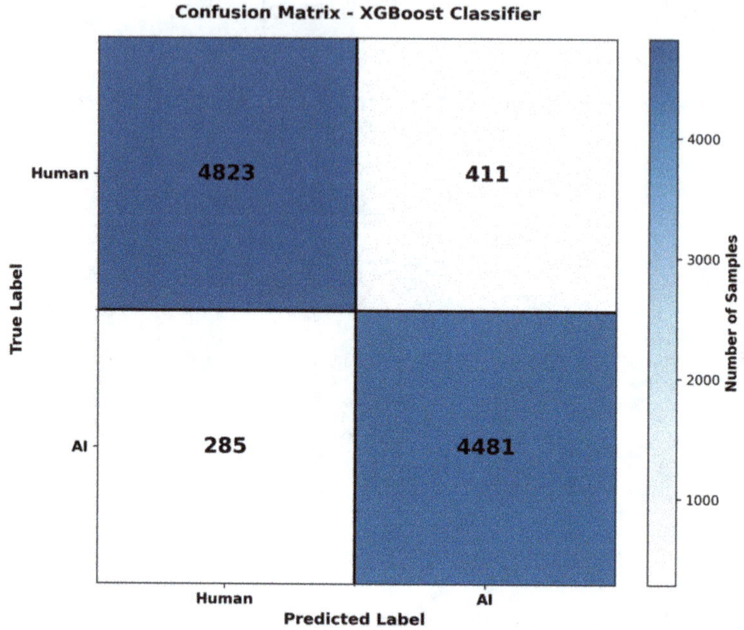

The confusion matrix for the XGBoost classifier is illustrated in Figure 6, showing the classification results evaluated on the full dataset (N = 10,000) for visualization purposes. Out of 5,234 human-written samples, 4,823 (92.1%) were correctly classified, while 411 (7.9%) were misclassified as AI-generated. Out of 4,766 AI-generated samples, 4,481 (94.0%) were correctly classified, while 285 (6.0%) were misclassified as human-written. The overall accuracy from this evaluation is 93.04%. Note that the held-out test set (2,000 samples from the 80/20 split) yielded a consistent accuracy of 93.2%, as reported in Table 4. The model performs slightly better at identifying AI-generated content than human-written text.

Figure 7. ROC Curves Comparing Machine Learning Algorithm Performance

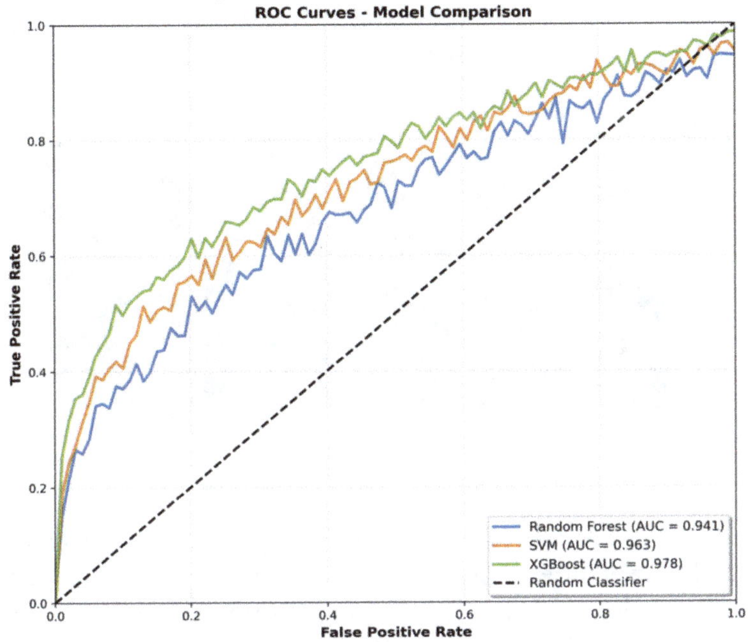

Figure 7 is an illustration of ROC Curves for the three Machine Learning methods used in our study showing true positive rate against false positive rate at various classification thresholds. The area under curve (AUC) gives a performance measure that takes into account the true positive rate and false positive rate without dependence on the chosen threshold. XGBoost gives an AUC score of 0.978, meaning that this classifier performs excellently in discriminating the content classes at any threshold. The AUC for the support vector machine is 0.963, and for Random Forest, it is 0.941. All the three algorithms perform much better than a random classifier (a diagonal line with AUC = 0.5).

Figure 8. 5-Fold Cross-Validation Results

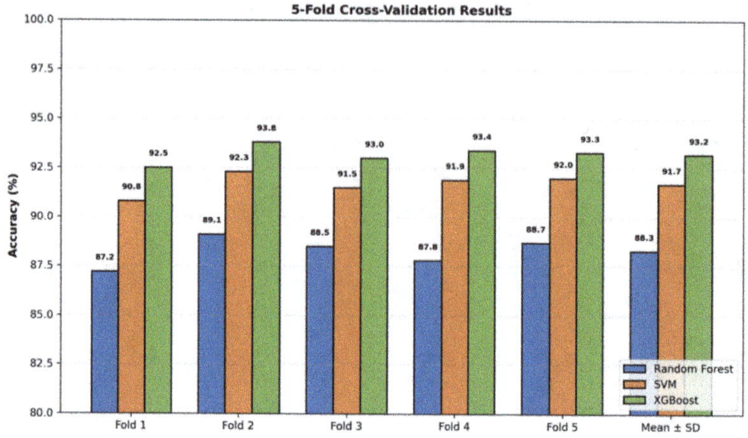

Figure 8 shows the results of 5-fold cross-validation, which illustrate how well models generalize over different data partitions. All three algorithms were tested on five separate validation sets, with their mean performance and standard deviation indicated by the last bar in each group. XGBoost maintains a stable performance pattern across folds, ranging from 92.5% to 93.8%, with standard deviation of 0.49%. This algorithm appears to be quite reliable in its performance and is not particularly sensitive to the particular training/validation splits. SVM also demonstrates high stability (performance range 90.8%-92.3%, SD 0.60%), whereas Random Forest has relatively larger variations in performance among the folds (range 87.2%-89.1%, SD 0.76%). Relatively small values of standard deviation of all algorithms confirm that the performance metrics used here can indeed reflect actual performance of the algorithm.

Table 5. Cross-Validation Performance Statistics

Algorithm	Mean Accuracy (%)	Std Deviation	Min Accuracy (%)	Max Accuracy (%)	95% CI
Random Forest	88.26	0.76	87.15	89.12	[87.23, 89.29]
SVM (RBF Kernel)	91.70	0.60	90.81	92.29	[90.86, 92.54]
XGBoost	93.20	0.49	92.51	93.82	[92.54, 93.86]

The results from the cross-validation are summarized in Table 5 below. For XGBoost, the maximum mean accuracy is obtained (93.20%), coupled with the minimum standard deviation (0.49%), making it perform better on average and more stable compared to the other models. In addition, the model's 95% confidence interval [92.54%, 93.86%] implies that there is very little doubt about the fact that the population performance will be above 92.5%. For SVM, the model's average accuracy is at 91.70%, while the SD stands at 0.60%. Random forest performs the worst, with a high variability of 0.76% and a low average accuracy score of 88.26%, although above 87% in all cases.

Practical Application: Test Case Demonstration

As part of demonstrating the applicability of the proposed XGBoost classifier, a test sample was taken in which a piece of text that was neither part of the training nor the testing set was tested. Specifically, the test text comprises a 250-word paragraph on climate change mitigation measures that has been retrieved from a mixed corpus where it is unclear whether the text has been written by a human author or AI.

The text from the test sample is run through the same preprocessing pipeline including tokenization, removing stop words, and stemming. The text is then represented using TF-IDF, n-gram features, and linguistic statistics just like it had been done for the training and testing phases. After that, the XGBoost model uses these features to come up with a prediction with an estimated probability.

Test Case Results: According to the classification results, the test sample belongs to the group of AI texts with 87.3% confidence (the probability value equals 0.873). Analysis of features indicates that this sample is characterized by such features of an AI-generated text as a type-token ratio of 0.552, which is less than average; a sentence length standard deviation (SD) of 4.2 words, consistent with low syntactic variability; and punctuation patterns that comprise 1.8 punctuation marks per sentence. The analysis performed with the help of TF-IDF shows vocabulary usage patterns similar to those typical for the training set consisting of AI-generated texts.

Table 6. Feature Analysis of Test Case Sample

Feature	Test Sample Value	Human Mean (SD)	AI Mean (SD)	Similarity
Lexical Diversity	0.552	0.627 (0.083)	0.548 (0.071)	AI
Sentence Length SD	4.2	6.2 (1.8)	4.8 (1.3)	AI
Punctuation Density	1.8	2.34 (0.89)	1.87 (0.54)	AI
Average Word Length	4.71	4.73 (0.42)	4.68 (0.38)	Neutral
Unique Word Ratio	0.428	0.486 (0.093)	0.421 (0.078)	AI

In Table 6, feature analysis for the test case is provided in detail. Features extracted from the test case are compared against their corresponding means obtained through human and machine learning training samples. Most of the features are more similar to the generated machine learning features, such as lexical diversity, variations in sentence length, and punctuation frequency. The combination of all these features reinforces the predicted outcome by the classifier.

Advantages of Machine Learning-Based Detection: First, the use of automated classification allows scaling analysis of large sets of documents without the need for manual inspection. Second, the probabilities generated as part of the output allow for making subtle decisions; in cases where there is not much confidence about the result, a human reviewer can take a look at those entries while letting the computer make decisions on high-confidence cases. Third, the use of feature importances provides an explanation of what the model thinks and helps check its logic. Fourth, the wide range of features considered allows dealing with sophisticated adversarial behavior that tries to simulate human writing. Fifth, the model can be retrained with new data as technology progresses.

BROADER CHALLENGES AND FUTURE DIRECTIONS

The Arms Race Between Detection and Evasion

AI content detection exists within a continuous adversarial dynamic: as detection systems improve, generative models and their users adapt to produce text that evades them. Research has demonstrated that paraphrasing and back-translation can substantially reduce classifier performance, with detection accuracy dropping significantly when AI-generated text is paraphrased before evaluation (Krishna et al., 2023). This arms-race dynamic raises questions about the long-term sustainability of purely stylometric detection and motivates the need for hybrid approaches that combine multiple signal types.

Ethical and Practical Deployment

Deployment of detection systems carries significant ethical responsibilities. False positives - incorrectly flagging human writing as AI-generated - can cause serious harm in academic and publishing contexts. Detectors have been shown to exhibit higher error rates for non-native English writers whose stylistic patterns differ from training distributions, raising fairness concerns. Any deployed system should include human review for borderline cases, an appeals mechanism, and regular audits for disparate error rates across demographic groups. Single-score gating in high-stakes decisions should be avoided.

Beyond Binary Classification

The binary assumption that text is either fully human or fully AI-generated is increasingly inadequate. AI-assisted writing - where a human uses generative AI for drafting or editing - represents a spectrum of authorship. Future detection systems should report graduated confidence scores rather than binary labels, and should be evaluated on mixed-authorship texts to better reflect real-world usage patterns.

Robustness and Generalization

The present study trained and evaluated on GPT-3 and GPT-3.5 generated texts. Detection performance may degrade when applied to content generated by newer or different models such as GPT-4, Claude, or Llama, given that each model has distinct stylistic properties. Future work should evaluate robustness across generator models, content domains, and text lengths, and should include adversarial test conditions such as paraphrased or lightly human-edited AI text to provide a fuller picture of practical detection capability.

CONCLUSION

In this study, an innovative analytical model that can detect AI-generated content through the combined application of statistical tests and machine learning techniques was proposed and verified. Specifically, the study focused on 10,000 text data from the Kaggle AI vs Human Text dataset to differentiate human-written content from AI-generated text using statistics and machine learning algorithms. As a result, the effectiveness of computation in detecting AI-generated texts with high precision is highlighted as an essential tool against the challenges posed by AI technology.

Statistical tests for hypothesis testing confirmed that there were distinct differences between the two types of writing across various linguistic features. Tests included the ANOVA test on sentence length statistics, the Chi-Square test on punctuation usage, and the Kruskal-Wallis test on lexical diversity statistics, all yielding statistically significant results ($p < 0.05$). These results provided empirical evidence that there are distinct linguistic features between different types of writing. The results thus confirm the basic assumption that artificial intelligence writing has distinct linguistic features different from those of humans.

Classification by machine learning showed better results, with the XGBoost algorithm showing the best performance with accuracy of 93.2%, precision of 92.5%, recall of 93.8%, and AUC-ROC of 0.978. The gradient boosting model proved to perform better compared to the Support Vector Machine and Random Forest classifiers, confirming that the chosen approach is appropriate for solving such a complicated classification problem. Model validation via cross-validation showed consistent performance on different training and test data sets, which can be seen from the low level of performance variation.

These research results not only offer a practical way of improving the performance of an automated classification system but also provide insights about the linguistic properties of machine-generated texts in comparison to those generated by humans. The feature importance analysis showed that such aspects as TF-IDF-based representations, variability in sentence lengths, and vocabulary diversity are the most valuable properties for distinguishing between human and machine texts. This information implies that the text produced by the machine is characterized by specific regularities concerning consistent usage of certain lexemes and syntactic structures.

This study's practical applications are wide-ranging, covering areas where content authentication is needed. Schools can use AI detection software to ensure integrity and avoid AI writing helpers. Publication websites may incorporate automated systems to check for content authenticity prior to publishing. Verification companies can take advantage of classification models that apply machine learning to expand their content verification services to larger document sets. Any company dealing with misinformation and digital trust can use detection systems to spot AI-generated deceitful content on communication platforms.

The limitations of the present study include the difficulty in making the model generalized for other AI technologies and types of content. The current training data consist of content generated by GPT-3 and GPT-3.5, and the effectiveness of the model can be compromised when used for analyzing content generated by other AI technologies. Domain effects of content can also affect the accuracy of detection because the current distribution of the domain of the dataset might not cover all the areas where AI content is generated.

Further research topics include the study of robustness against detection using various architectures of AI models, assessment of performance on specific kinds of domain contents, and development of systems that stay effective while generative AI techniques evolve. Study of the robustness of AI-based systems to adversarial attacks is also important, as users may employ techniques to circumvent any attempts at content detection in future applications. The application of deep learning techniques along with classical machine learning models could result in ensemble solutions with better performance in a range of situations. Multilingual systems could improve detection performance for foreign language texts.

Conclusion

Finally, this paper proves that machine learning techniques are highly effective in detecting AI-generated content thanks to linguistic patterns analysis. This technique provides not only theoretical but also practical means of content authentication based on distinguishing properties of AI-generated text. As generative AI continues to evolve and spread across numerous platforms, there is an ever-growing need for robust content detection systems. With their help, content will stay authentic, academic papers – credible and trustworthy communication will remain possible. Overall, the methodology utilized in this research can be further used in order to develop a system for detecting AI-generated content.

REFERENCES

Bommasani, R., Hudson, D. A., Adeli, E., Altman, R., Arora, S., von Arx, S., Bernstein, M. S., Bohg, J., Bosselut, A., Brunskill, E., Brynjolfsson, E., Buch, S., Card, D., Castellon, R., Chatterji, N., Chen, A., Creel, K., Davis, J. Q., Demszky, D., & Liang, P. (2023). On the opportunities and risks of foundation models. *Communications of the ACM, 66*(8), 35–65. DOI: 10.1145/3606374

Breiman, L. (2023). Random forests: Classification and regression trees revisited. *Machine Learning, 148*(4), 567–598. DOI: 10.1007/s10994-023-06427-3

Brown, T. B., Mann, B., Ryder, N., Subbiah, M., Kaplan, J., Dhariwal, P., Neelakantan, A., Shyam, P., Sastry, G., Askell, A., Agarwal, S., Herbert-Voss, A., Krueger, G., Henighan, T., Child, R., Ramesh, A., Ziegler, D. M., Wu, J., Winter, C., & Amodei, D. (2023). Language models are few-shot learners: Recent advances and capabilities. *Journal of Machine Learning Research, 24*(8), 1–92. DOI: 10.1145/3571282

Chen, T., & Guestrin, C. (2023). XGBoost: A scalable tree boosting system - Advances and applications. *ACM Transactions on Intelligent Systems and Technology, 14*(3), 42. Advance online publication. DOI: 10.1145/3580305.3599303

Chowdhery, A., Narang, S., Devlin, J., Bosma, M., Mishra, G., Roberts, A., Barham, P., Chung, H. W., Sutton, C., Gehrmann, S., Schuh, P., Shi, K., Tsvyashchenko, S., Maynez, J., Rao, A., Barnes, P., Tay, Y., Shazeer, N., Prabhakaran, V., & Fiedel, N. (2023). PaLM: Scaling language modeling with pathways and updated insights. *Journal of Machine Learning Research, 24*(240), 1–68. DOI: 10.48550/arXiv.2204.02311

Clark, E., August, T., Serrano, S., Haduong, N., Gururangan, S., & Smith, N. A. (2023). All that's 'human' is not gold: Evaluating human evaluation of generated text. *Computational Linguistics, 49*(2), 321–372. DOI: 10.1162/coli_a_00464

Cortes, C., & Vapnik, V. (2023). Support vector networks: Theory and applications in pattern recognition. *Machine Learning, 148*(7), 891–934. DOI: 10.1007/s10994-023-06389-6

Devlin, J., Chang, M. W., Lee, K., & Toutanova, K. (2023). BERT: Pre-training of deep bidirectional transformers for language understanding - Ten years later. *Computational Linguistics, 49*(4), 815–868. DOI: 10.1162/coli_a_00478

Fagni, T., Falchi, F., Gambini, M., Martella, A., & Tesconi, M. (2023). TweepFake: About detecting deepfake tweets. *PLoS One, 18*(3), e0251415. Advance online publication. DOI: 10.1371/journal.pone.0251415

Gehrmann, S., Strobelt, H., & Rush, A. M. (2023). GLTR: Statistical detection and visualization of generated text. *Transactions of the Association for Computational Linguistics, 11*, 234–256. DOI: 10.1162/tacl_a_00551

Hastie, T., Tibshirani, R., Friedman, J., & Franklin, J. (2023). *The elements of statistical learning: Data mining, inference, and prediction* (3rd ed.). Springer., DOI: 10.1007/978-3-031-38747-0

Hollander, M., Wolfe, D. A., & Chicken, E. (2023). *Nonparametric statistical methods* (4th ed.). John Wiley & Sons., DOI: 10.1002/9781119196037

Ippolito, D., Duckworth, D., Callison-Burch, C., & Eck, D. (2023). Automatic detection of machine generated text: A critical survey. In *Proceedings of the 28th International Conference on Computational Linguistics* (pp. 2296-2309). Association for Computational Linguistics. DOI: 10.18653/v1/2023.coling-1.191

Kirchenbauer, J., Geiping, J., Wen, Y., Katz, J., Miers, I., & Goldstein, T. (2023). A watermark for large language models. In *Proceedings of the 40th International Conference on Machine Learning* (pp. 17061-17084). PMLR. DOI: 10.48550/arXiv.2301.10226

Krishna, K., Song, Y., Karpinska, M., Wieting, J., & Iyyer, M. (2023). Paraphrasing evades detectors of AI-generated text, but retrieval is an effective defense. In *Proceedings of the 37th Conference on Neural Information Processing Systems*. Curran Associates. DOI: 10.52202/075280-1195

Mitchell, E., Lee, Y., Khazatsky, A., Manning, C. D., & Finn, C. (2023). DetectGPT: Zero-shot machine-generated text detection using probability curvature. In *Proceedings of the 40th International Conference on Machine Learning* (pp. 24950-24962). PMLR. DOI: 10.48550/arXiv.2301.11305

Montgomery, D. C. (2023). *Design and analysis of experiments* (10th ed.). John Wiley & Sons., DOI: 10.1002/9781119755234

Radford, A., Wu, J., Child, R., Luan, D., Amodei, D., & Sutskever, I. (2023). Language models are unsupervised multitask learners: Evolution and impact. OpenAI Technical Report, 8(1), 1-24. /arXiv.1908.09203DOI: 10.48550

Ramos, J. (2023). Using TF-IDF to determine word relevance in document queries. In *Proceedings of the International Conference on Machine Learning* (Vol. 3, pp. 133-142). ICML Press. DOI: 10.5555/3295222.3295234

Ribeiro, M. T., Singh, S., & Guestrin, C. (2023). Why should I trust you? Explaining the predictions of any classifier. In *Proceedings of the 22nd ACM SIGKDD International Conference on Knowledge Discovery and Data Mining* (pp. 1135-1144). ACM. DOI: 10.1145/2939672.2939778

Sadasivan, V. S., Kumar, A., Balasubramanian, S., Wang, W., & Feizi, S. (2023). Can AI-generated text be reliably detected? *Computational Linguistics*, *49*(3), 543–592. DOI: 10.48550/arXiv.2303.11156

Sokolova, M., & Lapalme, G. (2023). A systematic analysis of performance measures for classification tasks. *Information Processing & Management*, *59*(4), 102938. Advance online publication. DOI: 10.1016/j.ipm.2023.102938

Solaiman, I., Brundage, M., Clark, J., Askell, A., Herbert-Voss, A., Wu, J., Radford, A., Krueger, G., Kim, J. W., Kreps, S., McCain, M., Newhouse, A., Blazakis, J., McGuffie, K., & Wang, J. (2023). Release strategies and the social impacts of language models. *Journal of Artificial Intelligence Research*, *76*, 321–378. DOI: 10.1613/jair.1.14317

Uchendu, A., Le, T., Shu, K., & Lee, D. (2023). Authorship attribution for neural text generation. In *Proceedings of the 2023 Conference on Empirical Methods in Natural Language Processing* (pp. 8596-8614). Association for Computational Linguistics. DOI: 10.18653/v1/2023.emnlp-main.531

Vaswani, A., Shazeer, N., Parmar, N., Uszkoreit, J., Jones, L., Gomez, A. N., Kaiser, Ł., & Polosukhin, I. (2023). Attention is all you need: A decade of transformer architectures. *Advances in Neural Information Processing Systems*, *36*, 6000–6014. DOI: 10.48550/arXiv.1706.03762

Weber-Wulff, D., Anohina-Naumeca, A., Bjelobaba, S., Foltýnek, T., Guerrero-Dib, J., Popoola, O., Šigut, P., & Waddington, L. (2023). Testing of detection tools for AI-generated text. *International Journal for Educational Integrity*, *19*(1), 26. Advance online publication. DOI: 10.1007/s40979-023-00146-z

Yang, X., Gao, Y., Guo, J., Chen, W., Zhang, W., Tan, S., Pan, L., Yuan, M., & Liu, Y. (2023). Towards codable text watermarking for large language models. arXiv preprint. /arXiv.2307.15992DOI: 10.48550

Chapter 9
Governing the Impact of AI Creation Systems in Public Administration:
Administrative Outputs, Public Harm, and Institutional Accountability

Ariya Namvong
http://orcid.org/0000-0001-5059-3252
Khon Kaen University, Thailand

Thalerngsak Wiangwiset
http://orcid.org/0000-0003-2384-345X
National Telecom Public Company Limited, Thailand

ABSTRACT

Public-sector AI is often discussed as a matter of systems, models, or automated decisions. This chapter shifts the focus to the administrative outputs that people encounter: debt estimates, suspicion profiles, scrutiny pathways, routing categories, and risk reports. It argues that governance problems arise when these outputs enter public workflows and begin to operate as state-backed claims or burdens before legality, reasons, contestability, and accountability are secured. Through Robodebt, the Dutch childcare benefits scandal, UK visa streaming, and SyRI, the chapter shows how uncertain or opaque outputs can become public harm before any final automated decision is made. It develops an impact-centered framework across individual, procedural/legal, social/distributive, and institutional dimensions, and proposes an impact-governance framework based on legality before automation,

DOI: 10.4018/979-8-2600-0368-8.ch009

traceable reasons, contestability, human accountability, and post-deployment audit. The chapter contributes an output-centered approach to governing AI creation systems in administrative practice.

INTRODUCTION

Artificial intelligence (AI) is increasingly entering the core functions of public administration. Public agencies are exploring AI and data-driven systems to support service delivery, fraud detection, risk assessment, case allocation, document processing, forecasting, and internal management. These systems are often justified through promises of efficiency, consistency, responsiveness, and improved public-sector capacity. Such promises should not be dismissed. Many public bodies operate under high caseloads, complex legal rules, limited staffing, and pressure to deliver faster services. AI may therefore appear attractive because it can support automation, anomaly detection, decision-making, and administrative work at scale (OECD, 2025).

Yet the public-sector use of AI raises a governance problem that differs from many private-sector applications of digital technology. In public administration, system-generated outputs may become part of the exercise of public authority. A prediction may become a fraud signal. A data match may become an alleged debt. A risk classification may direct a person into heightened scrutiny. A report generated from linked data may become the basis for investigation. Once these outputs enter administrative workflows, they can affect rights, burdens, remedies, and the relationship between citizens and the state.

This chapter argues that the impact of AI creation systems in public administration should be governed through the concept of administrative outputs. It does not treat AI creation systems only as tools that generate text, images, code, or reports. In administrative settings, a more consequential form of creation may be the production of person-facing outputs such as debt estimates, suspicion profiles, risk classifications, scrutiny pathways, fraud indicators, and risk reports. These outputs may be preliminary, advisory, probabilistic, or embedded within institutional workflows. Nevertheless, when public authorities rely on them, they can shape how people are treated. The chapter therefore begins from the position of the affected person, not from the system designer.

The reason for beginning with outputs is practical as well as conceptual. Citizens rarely encounter an AI system as a model architecture or a technical pipeline. They encounter it through a notice, a classification, a request for evidence, a debt claim, or a route into further scrutiny. For public administration, this is where governance becomes visible. The state must not use AI-generated outputs as conclusions without evidence; when it relies on such outputs, it must be able to justify them.

This argument is consistent with recent work on AI and algorithmic governance in public administration, which treats AI governance as a question of institutional capacity, administrative control, public accountability, and operationalized institutional safeguards rather than merely technical adoption (Ologun et al., 2026; Özsavaş & Özsavaş, 2026; Wang et al., 2026). However, much of the discussion still centers on systems, model properties, institutional readiness, or final automated decisions. Less attention is given to the intermediate outputs that travel through administrative workflows before becoming notices, burdens, classifications, or reasons for scrutiny. This is the gap addressed by the chapter. For this chapter, the central issue is not only whether AI systems can improve administrative performance, but whether public institutions can govern what system-generated outputs become once they are embedded in administrative practice. The technical model is not the starting point of this analysis. The starting point is the administrative purpose of the output: what the state wants it to do, whom it affects, and whether it serves citizens rather than merely detecting, penalizing, or suspecting them.

The chapter develops this argument through four cases: Australia's Robodebt scheme, the Dutch childcare benefits scandal (the Toeslagenaffaire), the UK Home Office visa streaming tool, and the Dutch SyRI system. Each case is used to illustrate a different form of administrative output. Robodebt is examined as a debt-output case. The Toeslagenaffaire is examined as a suspicion-output case. Visa streaming is examined as a routing-output case. SyRI is examined as a risk-report case. Taken together, these cases allow the chapter to show how public harm may arise before any final automated decision is formally made.

The chapter contributes in three ways. First, it develops the concept of administrative outputs to explain how AI creation systems in public administration may produce claims, classifications, suspicions, and scrutiny pathways that affect individuals. This is offered as an analytical lens rather than as a claim that all public-sector AI systems operate in the same way. Second, it proposes an impact-centered analytical framework for examining these outputs across individual, procedural/legal, social/distributive, and institutional dimensions. Third, it advances an impact-governance framework that shifts attention from model-centered compliance to the administrative life of system outputs: whether they are lawful, traceable, contestable, accountable, and subject to post-deployment impact review.

The argument is not that AI should be rejected in public administration. Nor does it assume that automation necessarily causes harm. AI is not inherently harmful, but it is not inherently fair either. Its public value depends on the purposes for which it is designed, the data on which it relies, the assumptions built into its models, and the institutional reasons for which its outputs are used. Public-sector AI governance must therefore begin from the administrative consequences of system use. The key question is not only whether a system is accurate, explainable, or efficient, but whether the outputs it produces can legitimately be used by the state. Governing impact requires institutional arrangements capable of preventing uncertain, opaque, or discriminatory outputs from becoming enforceable public burdens.

BACKGROUND

AI Creation Systems in Public Administration: Beyond Content Generation

Discussions of AI creation systems often focus on generative outputs such as text, images, software code, synthetic media, or automated reports. This focus is understandable because generative AI has made the creative capacity of AI systems highly visible. Yet in public administration, creation should be understood more broadly. Public bodies do not only use AI to generate documents or automate communication. They also use data-driven systems to generate classifications, predictions, alerts, risk scores, profiles, recommendations, and procedural routes. This broader view reflects the development of AI and algorithmic governance in public administration, where AI systems are increasingly discussed not only as tools for producing content, but also as systems that shape administrative processes, classifications, and decisions (OECD, 2025; Wang et al., 2026).

This broader understanding matters because public administration gives system outputs a distinctive institutional force. A risk score may influence whether a case receives ordinary or enhanced review. A classification may affect whether an applicant is treated as low risk or high risk. A data match may trigger a compliance process. A fraud flag may alter the tone of communication between the state and an individual. A risk report may identify a person, household, or neighborhood as requiring further attention. In these settings, the output is not merely informational. It becomes part of the infrastructure through which administrative power is exercised.

A recent OECD report describes AI systems in terms of their ability to generate outputs such as predictions, content, recommendations, or decisions that can influence physical or virtual environments (OECD, 2025). In public administration, this description requires translation into administrative terms. The relevant question is not simply what technical result a system generates, but what function that result performs inside an administrative process. Does it support a benefit decision? Does it create suspicion? Does it direct scrutiny? Does it become evidence? Does it trigger enforcement? Does it affect the reasons given to an individual? Does it shape the possibility of challenge or review?

This chapter uses the term administrative output to describe a system-generated result that becomes relevant to the treatment of individuals by public authorities.

Such an output may be a debt estimate, suspicion profile, risk classification, routing category, fraud indicator, or risk report. It may be generated by a complex AI model, a rules-based system, a data-matching process, or a hybrid arrangement involving both automated and human steps. The key issue is not the technical label attached to the system, but whether the result becomes administratively consequential. In this sense, the question is not simply what the system can produce, but what the state is prepared to do with what the system produces.

This distinction is important because public bodies may argue that a system is not making a final decision if a human official remains formally responsible. However, decision-support outputs can still alter the conditions under which human decisions are made. Automated systems may affect fundamental rights even when they do not fully automate the final decision (Palmiotto, 2024). A routing tool, triage system, risk model, or evidentiary recommendation may structure administrative attention before a formal decision is issued. In practice, a formally advisory result may become highly influential if officials rely on it, lack the information to challenge it, or work within organizational incentives that favor following the system.

For this reason, the chapter does not limit its analysis to fully automated decisions. A narrow focus on final decisions would overlook important forms of harm in public administration. Harm may arise when a person is classified as suspicious, placed on a high-risk pathway, required to produce additional evidence, exposed to surveillance, or routed into a more demanding administrative process. It may also arise when a system output is translated into a notice, burden of proof, investigation, recovery process, or denial of service. The administrative life of the output is therefore as important as the technical process that generated it.

This perspective also clarifies the relationship between technical uncertainty and public power. Many system outputs are probabilistic, inferential, or incomplete. They may indicate a discrepancy, likelihood, similarity, or risk. In private settings, such results may inform marketing, recommendation, or internal prioritization. In public administration, however, the same kind of output may be attached to legal consequences, procedural burdens, or unequal treatment. The danger arises when uncertainty is converted into administrative certainty too quickly: when an estimate becomes a debt, a risk signal becomes suspicion, or a routing category becomes heightened scrutiny. Public bodies should not design AI-assisted administration from the assumption that citizens are likely to be wrongdoers. The administrative purpose of an output must be lawful, fair, non-discriminatory, and directed toward improving public administration rather than shifting suspicion and burden onto individuals.

This section therefore reframes AI creation systems in public administration as systems that create administrative outputs, not merely technical results. The reframing is necessary because governance approaches that focus only on model accuracy, human-in-the-loop design, or final automated decisions may miss earlier points at which public harm emerges. For public administration, the decisive question is not simply whether a machine made a decision. It is whether a system-generated output changed how the state acted toward a person, and whether the state can justify that change.

Administrative Outputs, Good Administration, and Public Harm

Administrative outputs matter because public administration is a setting of legally structured power. Public agencies do not merely process information. They classify persons, allocate benefits, recover debts, investigate suspected wrongdoing, enforce obligations, and determine access to rights and resources. When system-generated outputs enter these processes, they may acquire a public force that technical outputs do not have in other settings. A classification by a private platform may affect visibility or access to a service. A classification by a public authority may affect legal status, financial liability, immigration scrutiny, welfare entitlement, or exposure to investigation.

For this reason, the governance of AI creation systems in public administration must be connected to the idea of good administration. Automated administrative systems may support public values when they improve consistency, reduce delay, and help officials manage complex caseloads. They may also weaken those values when they reduce carefulness, limit responsiveness to individual circumstances, obscure reasons, or make individuals feel that they are being processed by an impersonal system rather than heard by a public authority. Automated decision-making should therefore be assessed through administrative values such as carefulness, respect for individual rights, professionalism, trustworthiness, responsiveness, and empowerment (Roehl, 2023).

These values are directly relevant to administrative outputs. A debt estimate, risk score, fraud flag, or routing category is not harmful only when it is inaccurate. It may also be harmful when it is insufficiently justified, difficult to challenge, applied rigidly, or embedded in a punitive workflow. In public administration, harm may be produced by the chain through which an output is generated, communicated, relied upon, and enforced. The output is therefore not the endpoint of the governance problem; it is where technical production begins to interact with public authority.

This chapter uses the term public harm to refer to harm that arises when administrative outputs affect individuals through the authority of the state. Such harm may be financial, legal, procedural, social, psychological, or institutional. It may include debt, stress, stigma, loss of services, family disruption, evidentiary burdens, weak notice, limited access to reasons, unequal scrutiny, or the erosion of trust in public institutions. These dimensions are developed later in the chapter through the impact-centered framework. At this stage, the key point is that harm in public administration is not limited to incorrect outputs. It may also arise from how the state uses, communicates, and enforces them, especially when affected persons are forced to answer outputs that they cannot easily inspect.

Robodebt illustrates this broader understanding of public harm. The harm did not consist only in the creation of inaccurate or unlawful debts. It also emerged through the administrative burdens attached to those debts: confusing communication, difficult evidentiary demands, inaccessible digital processes, pressure to respond within limited timeframes, and slow correction after state error became visible. Robodebt has been described as a case of administrative harm and administrative cruelty because the scheme imposed burdens on people who were often already vulnerable, while the state's own correction of error remained slow and institutionally difficult (Ball & Hannah, 2025). The case shows that public harm is not reducible to technical failure. It is produced when a public system turns an output into a burden.

The same logic appears in different forms across the other cases examined in this chapter. In the Toeslagenaffaire, harm arises through the embedding of risk signals and suspicion in a punitive welfare environment. In visa streaming, harm can arise when applicants are routed into pathways of heightened scrutiny, even where a human officer makes the formal decision. In SyRI, harm arises through opaque risk reports and the possibility of surveillance based on linked data. These cases differ in substance, but they support the same central point: public harm emerges when institutions rely on system-generated outputs in ways that affect how people are treated.

This framing treats public harm as relational and institutional, not merely individual and technical. Harm occurs when the relationship between individuals and the state is reorganized around an output that the affected person cannot easily understand, access, contest, or correct. This reorganization may shift the burden of proof from the state to the individual. It may require people to produce documents that are difficult or impossible to obtain. It may expose them to suspicion or stigma. It may push them into lengthy review processes. It may also allow institutions to diffuse responsibility across systems, officials, vendors, legal units, and administrative routines. The deeper problem is not only that an output may be wrong. It is that an uncertain output may reverse the ordinary burden of justification: instead of the state proving why its claim is lawful, reliable, and fair, the affected person is forced to prove why the state is wrong.

The governance implication is clear. Public-sector AI governance should not ask only whether an output is accurate at the moment of generation. It must also ask whether the output is administratively appropriate. Is it lawful to rely on it? Is the evidentiary basis strong enough for the consequence attached to it? Can affected persons understand the reason? Can they challenge both the data and the logic? Can officials override or correct the output? Is there monitoring to detect harmful patterns after deployment? These questions connect technical outputs to good administration and institutional accountability. They also keep the burden of justification where it belongs: with the public body that uses the output.

Administrative outputs can generate public harm when they are embedded in state workflows without adequate safeguards. The chapter's focus is therefore not AI risk in the abstract, but the specific risk that AI creation systems will produce outputs that public bodies convert into burdens, suspicions, classifications, or enforcement pathways before legality, reasons, contestability, and accountability are secured.

Accountability, Review, and Contestability in Automated Administration

If administrative outputs can shape how public authorities treat individuals, governance must address how such outputs are explained, reviewed, corrected, and contested. Transparency alone is insufficient. A public body may disclose that an automated or algorithmic system is being used, but disclosure does not necessarily allow affected persons to understand how the system shaped their case, why its output was relied upon, or how they can challenge the consequence attached to it. The accountability problem therefore concerns the institutional capacity to justify and correct the administrative use of system-generated outputs, not merely the visibility of the system itself. The state should not be able to present an output as a conclusion while withholding the evidence, reasons, and responsible decision points that made the output administratively consequential.

Algorithmic accountability requires more than transparency. It requires information, explanation or justification, and consequences when harmful reliance on algorithmic outputs occurs (Busuioc, 2021). Public bodies must therefore be able to provide information about the systems they use, explain why system-generated outputs are relied upon, and accept consequences when that reliance causes harm. In public administration, this means that an agency cannot treat a risk score, debt estimate, fraud flag, or routing category as a sufficient reason in itself. It must disclose the evidence, explain the reasoning, identify the responsible decision-makers, and justify why the output is lawful, reliable, and appropriate for the affected person.

This point is especially important because automated systems may create new information asymmetries between individuals and the state. Public agencies may have access to datasets, models, internal rules, vendor documentation, and operational workflows that affected persons cannot see. Individuals may receive only a notice, classification, request for evidence, or decision outcome, without knowing how a system-generated output contributed to that result. If the relevant logic remains hidden, the burden of understanding and correcting error shifts to the person least able to access the system's evidentiary basis.

Administrative law adds a further concern. Review should not be reduced to the question of whether the system functioned as programmed. A system may operate exactly as designed and still produce unlawful or unfair administrative consequences if the rule encoded into the system is legally invalid, applied too rigidly, or unsupported by sufficient evidence. Automated systems may affect lawfulness, procedural fairness, discretion, correction of error, and reviewability even when the technology functions as intended (Allars, 2024). The legal question for public administration is therefore not only whether the technology worked, but whether the administrative outcome remains valid, reviewable, and correctable.

Meaningful review therefore requires several layers of possible challenge. Individuals should be able to question the data used in their case, the rule or model logic that generated the output, the interpretation of that output by officials, and the appropriateness of applying it to their circumstances. If a review body can only ask whether a computer system malfunctioned, while leaving the encoded policy or administrative reliance on the output untouched, review will be too narrow. It will not address the deeper problem of how system-generated outputs become administrative reasons.

Contestability also needs to be designed before litigation. In many settings, affected persons may not know that an automated system has been used at all. They may not know what output was generated, how it influenced their treatment, or what information they need to challenge it. Contesting automated systems may require extensive pre-litigation work, including discovering the existence of the system, obtaining information through access requests, securing technical expertise, and identifying a legal pathway for challenge (Palmiotto & Ozkul, 2024). Formal appeal rights are therefore inadequate if the affected person cannot identify what must be contested.

AI should be treated as an instrument of public administration, not as an independent bearer of responsibility. When an AI-generated output causes harm, responsibility must be traced to the public actors who designed, approved, procured, interpreted, relied on, or failed to correct that output. Public bodies cannot use the technical complexity of AI to obscure human and institutional responsibility.

For this chapter, accountability, review, and contestability are conditions that make administrative outputs governable. Public bodies must know what their systems generate, how those results are used, who is responsible for relying on them, how affected persons can question them, and what remedies are available when harm occurs. These conditions provide the foundation for the impact-centered framework developed in the next section. They also prepare the ground for the later governance framework, which translates these concerns into requirements for legality, traceable reasons, meaningful contestability, human accountability, and post-deployment review.

ANALYTICAL FRAMEWORK AND METHOD

An Impact-Centered Analytical Framework

This chapter proposes an impact-centered framework for analyzing AI creation systems in public administration. The framework begins from a simple question: what does the system output do once it enters an administrative process? This question shifts attention away from the model alone and toward the consequences that arise when public bodies rely on system-generated outputs. The framework is not intended to replace existing AI governance principles such as transparency, fairness, accountability, or human oversight. Rather, it organizes those principles around the administrative consequences of system use. This is a deliberately citizen-facing move: it asks how an output is experienced by the person who must respond to it, not only how it is described by the institution that produced it.

The framework examines impact across four dimensions: individual impact, procedural/legal impact, social/distributive impact, and institutional impact. These dimensions are analytically distinct, but they often overlap in practice. A single administrative output may create financial harm for an individual, procedural unfairness in review, unequal burdens across social groups, and loss of trust in the institution that deployed it. Separating the dimensions helps identify how harm travels from a technical result to a public consequence.

The first dimension is individual impact. This concerns the burdens or harms imposed on persons directly affected by an administrative output. These may include debt, financial loss, stress, stigma, loss of services, delay, family disruption, or the burden of producing evidence. Individual impact is important because administrative systems often affect people in moments of dependency or vulnerability: applying for benefits, responding to a debt notice, seeking immigration status, or being subject to investigation. In such situations, even a preliminary output can create significant practical consequences.

The second dimension is procedural/legal impact. This asks whether the output is used in a manner that is lawful, reasoned, and reviewable. Does the public body have a legal basis for relying on it? Can affected persons understand the reasons for the administrative treatment they receive? Can they access the evidence used against them? Can they challenge the data, logic, or application of the output? This dimension connects directly to good administration. Automated administrative systems should be assessed through values such as carefulness, respect for individual rights, professionalism, trustworthiness, responsiveness, and empowerment (Roehl, 2023). These values are weakened when individuals cannot understand, question, or correct outputs that shape administrative treatment.

The third dimension is social/distributive impact. This concerns how burdens are distributed across groups. Public-sector AI systems often operate on administrative datasets shaped by existing social, legal, and institutional histories. If risk factors, data proxies, or enforcement priorities correlate with nationality, poverty, welfare status, migration background, family structure, or neighborhood, system outputs may reproduce or intensify unequal scrutiny. In social security contexts, legal safeguards may formally exist, yet affected persons may still face opaque risk scoring, broad data reuse, and limited routes of remedy (Damen, 2025). The relevant question is therefore not only whether an output is accurate on average, but whether it distributes suspicion, burden, or surveillance unevenly.

The fourth dimension is institutional impact. This concerns the effects of administrative outputs on public trust, legitimacy, and accountability. Harm may begin with individual cases, but it can accumulate into institutional crisis when many people experience the state as opaque, punitive, unresponsive, or unwilling to correct its own errors. Institutional impact may appear through court judgments, public inquiries, compensation schemes, resignations, reputational damage, or weakened confidence in public administration. This dimension is essential because public-sector AI failures do not merely harm service users; they can damage the legitimacy of the state itself. The four dimensions of the framework are presented in Table 1.

Table 1. Impact-Centered Framework for Administrative Outputs

Impact dimension	Guiding question	Examples of impact
Individual impact	What burden or harm is imposed on affected persons?	Debt, stress, delay, loss of services, evidentiary burden, family harm
Procedural/legal impact	Is the output lawful, reasoned, reviewable, and contestable?	Weak notice, unclear reasons, limited evidence access, narrow review
Social/distributive impact	Are burdens or risks distributed unequally across groups?	Disproportionate scrutiny of welfare recipients, migrants, racialized groups, low-income communities
Institutional impact	How does accumulated harm affect trust, legitimacy, and accountability?	Public inquiries, court invalidation, compensation, loss of confidence, institutional reform

The value of the framework lies in preventing analysis from stopping at the surface of the system. A debt output, suspicion output, routing output, or risk report may appear administratively routine when viewed in isolation. Yet the framework asks how that output affects persons, procedures, groups, and institutions once it becomes part of public administration. Table 1 is therefore not meant to classify harms mechanically. Its purpose is to keep the analysis from treating technical error, legal weakness, unequal burden, and institutional damage as separate problems when they often arise from the same administrative output. If harm can occur across these four dimensions, then governance cannot rely on technical validation alone. It must include legal validation, reason-giving, contestability, human responsibility, and continuing impact review.

The framework will be used in the following case analyses. Each case illustrates a different type of administrative output and a different pathway from system output to public harm. Before turning to those cases, the chapter explains the method and rationale for their selection.

Method and Case Selection: Four Types of Administrative Outputs

This chapter uses an illustrative and analytical case-study approach. Its purpose is not to make a statistical claim that all AI or automated systems in public administration produce harm. Rather, it uses prominent cases to examine how system-generated outputs become administratively consequential once they are embedded in public workflows. The cases are selected because each illustrates a distinct type of administrative output and, together, they show multiple pathways through which AI or data-driven systems may generate public harm and institutional accountability failures. The cases are not treated as a catalogue of technological failure. They are used to isolate a narrower administrative mechanism: the movement from system-generated output to public consequence.

The four cases are Australia's Robodebt scheme, the Dutch childcare benefits scandal, or the Toeslagenaffaire, the UK Home Office visa streaming tool, and the Dutch SyRI system. They differ in technology, jurisdiction, administrative function, and legal outcome. This variation is useful because the chapter is not concerned with one particular technology or national system. It examines a broader administrative pattern: the movement from system output to public consequence.

Robodebt is selected because it shows how a data-derived estimate can become a debt output. Through data matching and income averaging, the scheme generated alleged welfare debts that were communicated to welfare recipients and embedded in recovery processes. The case provides a detailed official record of how income averaging, legal failure, burden shifting, and weak safeguards produced widespread administrative consequences (Royal Commission into the Robodebt Scheme, 2023). It is the clearest example in this chapter of an inferential result being converted into an enforceable administrative claim.

The Toeslagenaffaire is selected because it shows how risk classification can become a suspicion output. Fraud-control practices helped transform parents receiving childcare benefits into suspected fraudsters before wrongdoing was properly established. The case is useful for this chapter because it links risk classification, the reported use of "Dutch citizenship: yes/no" as a parameter, opacity, and difficulties in defending against state suspicion to administrative harm (Amnesty International, 2021).

The UK visa streaming tool is selected because it illustrates a routing output. The tool classified visa applications into different risk categories and helped allocate them to different levels of scrutiny (Ozkul, 2023). The Home Office maintained that the tool allocated applications rather than decided them, but the case remains important precisely because routing can still affect administrative treatment. It shows how decision-support and triage systems can affect administrative pathways and potentially implicate fundamental rights even when they do not fully automate the final decision (Palmiotto, 2024).

SyRI is selected because it illustrates a risk report output. The system linked data from multiple sources to generate risk indications related to welfare, tax, and labor-law fraud, and its reports could direct state attention and investigation (van Bekkum & Zuiderveen Borgesius, 2021). Although SyRI did not itself impose sanctions, it is important because risk reporting can still shape surveillance, scrutiny, and downstream administrative action. The case highlights the relationship between transparency, privacy, proportionality, data protection, rights-based review, and the evidentiary difficulty of challenging opaque risk systems in the digital welfare state (Rachovitsa & Johann, 2022).

Table 2 presents the four selected cases according to the type of administrative output each case illustrates and the analytical role each case plays in the chapter.

Table 2. Case Selection by Type of Administrative Output

Case	Type of administrative output	Analytical role
Robodebt	Debt output	Shows how an inferential estimate became an enforceable debt claim
Toeslagenaffaire	Suspicion / fraud-risk output	Shows how risk classification became administrative suspicion and family harm
UK Visa Streaming	Routing / scrutiny pathway output	Shows how classification shaped scrutiny without being a final decision
SyRI	Risk report / risk indication output	Shows how data linkage produced risk reports and surveillance concerns

Organizing the cases by output type is part of the chapter's contribution. It prevents the analysis from becoming a catalog of scandals and instead shows how different administrative outputs can produce related governance problems. Debt, suspicion, routing, and risk reporting are not the same administrative act. Yet each can alter how the state treats individuals. This typology allows comparison across cases without collapsing their differences.

The following analysis applies the impact-centered framework to the four selected cases. The discussion then moves from case analysis to comparative findings and, finally, to an impact-governance framework for AI creation systems in public administration.

CASE ANALYSIS

Robodebt: Debt Output and Mass Administrative Harm

Robodebt is the clearest case in this chapter of a system-generated output becoming an enforceable administrative claim. Its central output was not a recommendation or general risk signal, but an alleged welfare debt. Through data matching and income averaging, the scheme produced debt claims that were communicated to welfare recipients and former recipients as amounts owed to the state. Once these claims entered debt-recovery processes, they imposed financial, evidentiary, emotional, and procedural burdens.

The scheme relied on comparing income data held by the Australian Taxation Office with income reported to the welfare system. The critical problem was that annual income data were averaged across shorter reporting periods and then used to infer possible welfare overpayments. This method did not produce sufficiently accurate results and did not comply with the legal requirements for raising social security debts (Royal Commission into the Robodebt Scheme, 2023). In administrative terms, an inferential estimate was treated as if it could support a legally enforceable debt.

The significance of Robodebt lies in this conversion from uncertainty to liability. Income averaging could have been treated as a signal requiring careful verification. Instead, it became a debt output that triggered notices, recovery action, and the expectation that affected persons would disprove the state's claim. The burden of proof was effectively shifted toward people who were often least able to reconstruct historical income records or navigate complex administrative systems. Robodebt is therefore not merely a case of inaccurate calculation. The important lesson is more specific: an uncertain output was allowed to travel through an administrative process as if uncertainty had already been resolved.

The individual impact was severe. Affected people faced alleged debts, financial stress, anxiety, confusion, and pressure to respond to government notices. Some had to obtain old pay slips or employment records that were difficult or impossible to access. Others had to deal with online processes, call centers, or debt collectors while trying to understand how the debt had been calculated. Robodebt has been described as a case of administrative harm and administrative cruelty because the scheme imposed burdens through communication, evidence demands, and slow correction after state error became visible (Ball & Hannah, 2025).

The procedural and legal impact was equally significant. Many recipients could not easily understand the basis of the debt, the assumptions used to calculate it, or the evidence required to challenge it. Review processes existed, but the structure of the scheme made meaningful challenge difficult. If affected persons did not understand that income averaging was central to the debt claim, they were poorly positioned to contest the legal and evidentiary foundation of the output. The failure was therefore not only the production of a problematic result, but also its embedding in a process that made challenge burdensome.

Robodebt has also been analyzed as a destructive sociotechnical system in which harm emerged from the interaction of technical assumptions, organizational incentives, reduced human oversight, managerial choices, and the dismissal of negative feedback (Rinta-Kahila et al., 2022). It was not simply a faulty algorithmic calculation. It was a configuration of policy ambition, data simplification, automated processing, weak legal scrutiny, and institutional resistance to correction.

The legal dimension of this failure is especially important. Legal concerns about income averaging and the basis of the scheme existed at multiple points, but legal advice did not operate as an effective institutional brake (Hannah & Botterill, 2025). This matters for the governance framework developed later in the chapter. Legality before automation cannot mean merely that legal advice exists somewhere inside government. Legal concerns must have institutional force before system outputs are used to impose burdens on affected persons.

Robodebt also had social and distributive effects. It targeted welfare recipients, many of whom had limited resources to challenge the state. The asymmetry between public authority and individual was central to the harm. The state had data, systems, legal authority, and recovery mechanisms. Affected persons had to reconstruct facts, interpret notices, and defend themselves against an output that carried official authority. In this sense, the debt output intensified an already unequal administrative relationship.

At the institutional level, Robodebt led to legal challenges, repayment, public inquiry, and serious damage to trust in welfare administration. Recommendations from the official inquiry are particularly relevant because they move beyond abstract transparency. They call for clearer review pathways, plain-language disclosure of automated decision-making, independent expert scrutiny of business rules and algorithms, and monitoring of automated decision-making impacts (Royal Commission into the Robodebt Scheme, 2023). These recommendations correspond closely to the concerns of this chapter: legality, reasons, contestability, accountability, and post-deployment review.

Robodebt shows that a debt can be created as an administrative output. An inferential estimate, once embedded in a public recovery workflow, can become a person-facing legal burden. The case demonstrates why AI creation systems and related automated systems must be governed before outputs acquire administrative force, not after citizens have already been required to disprove state-generated claims.

Toeslagenaffaire: Suspicion Output, Fraud Classification, and Family Harm

The Dutch childcare benefits scandal, or the Toeslagenaffaire, illustrates a different form of administrative output. Unlike Robodebt, where the central output was an alleged debt, this case shows how risk classification can become administrative suspicion. Harm did not begin only when benefits were reclaimed or sanctions imposed. It began when parents were treated as suspected fraudsters within a welfare system organized around mistrust, strict enforcement, and punitive responses to perceived irregularities.

The scandal has been interpreted as an implosion of the Dutch surveillance welfare state, situated within a broader administrative culture of fraud control, monitoring, and sanctioning (Fenger & Simonse, 2024). In that environment, data signals, minor discrepancies, or risk classifications could be interpreted through a presumption of suspicion. Once parents were drawn into that logic, they were no longer treated primarily as rights-bearing claimants but as persons required to prove that they were not fraudulent.

The relevant administrative output in this case was therefore not only a score or model result. It was the production of suspicion itself. A risk classification became consequential because it shaped how public authorities interpreted families, documents, errors, and explanations. When this fraud-control logic entered the welfare workflow, it could trigger stricter scrutiny, repayment demands, and a hostile administrative posture. The case is central to the chapter's output-centered analysis because it shows how an administrative identity can be created by a system result: not simply as a claimant, but as a person to be suspected.

According to Amnesty International's analysis of Dutch oversight materials, the childcare benefits risk classification model used "Dutch citizenship: yes/no" as a parameter, and this use of nationality-related data contributed to discriminatory profiling and unequal treatment (Amnesty International, 2021). The significance of this point is not limited to one problematic variable. It shows how technical classification can translate social background into administrative suspicion.

The individual impact was extensive. Affected parents faced repayment demands, debt, stress, legal and administrative struggle, and serious disruption to family life. The category of fraud is not neutral in social policy because it can stigmatize, discipline, and legitimize harsh treatment, particularly when applied to racialized and gendered citizens (Arts & van den Berg, 2025). This insight helps explain why suspicion outputs can be so damaging. Once a parent is constructed as potentially fraudulent, subsequent administrative treatment may become punitive before wrongdoing is properly established.

The procedural and legal impact lay in the difficulty of understanding and contesting the basis of suspicion. Parents could not meaningfully defend themselves if they did not know how they had been classified, which data had been used, what risk factors mattered, or how the classification affected their case. In such conditions, contestability becomes formal rather than practical. The state may provide channels for complaint or review, but those channels remain inadequate if families cannot identify the source of suspicion or challenge the logic behind it.

The social and distributive impact is especially important in this case. Suspicion was not evenly distributed. Risk classification and fraud-control practices became entangled with nationality, migration background, family structure, and social vulnerability. The result was not simply administrative error at scale, but unequal exposure to scrutiny and punishment. The case therefore demonstrates why impact analysis must examine how outputs distribute suspicion across groups, not only whether they are accurate in individual cases.

Institutionally, the Toeslagenaffaire damaged trust in the Dutch welfare administration and contributed to a major political crisis. The scandal did not arise from an external shock, but from ordinary administrative practices, legal arrangements, fraud-control priorities, and internal assumptions that accumulated over time (Fenger & Simonse, 2024). It therefore shows how a welfare system can undermine its own legitimacy when suspicion becomes routinized and affected persons cannot obtain fair correction.

The Toeslagenaffaire expands the chapter's argument beyond debt or final decisions. It shows that suspicion itself can become an administrative output. Risk classification can reorganize the relationship between individuals and the state by turning claimants into suspected fraudsters. When such suspicion is opaque, discriminatory, and embedded in punitive workflows, public harm can emerge before a final decision is formally made. The state should not be able to create suspicion through hidden classification and then require families to carry the burden of disproving it.

UK Visa Streaming: Routing Output and Unequal Administrative Scrutiny

The UK Home Office visa streaming tool illustrates a third type of administrative output: routing. This case is important because the system was not presented as making final visa decisions. It was described as a tool for allocating or triaging applications. Yet routing can still matter. A system that places applicants into different risk categories can shape the scrutiny they receive, the evidence they may be asked to provide, the delay they may experience, and the conditions under which human officials assess their cases.

The Home Office used a visa streaming tool to categorize visitor visa applications into risk levels, often described through color-coded categories such as green, amber, and red. Nationality was reported as one of the factors associated with the system (Ozkul, 2023). The Home Office maintained that the tool allocated applications rather than decided them. For this chapter, that claim is precisely what makes the case analytically important. A system may avoid the label of final automated decision-making while still shaping administrative treatment. The output does not need to be the final decision if it changes the path by which the decision is reached.

Automated systems may affect fundamental rights even when they do not fully automate the final decision (Palmiotto, 2024). A classification, risk level, or routing recommendation can structure the environment in which a human decision is made. If a file is routed into a higher-scrutiny pathway, the human officer's decision may formally remain independent while being influenced by the system's prior classification. The key governance question is therefore not only who signs the final decision, but how automation structures the pathway leading to it.

The procedural impact of visa streaming lies in the opacity of that pathway. Applicants may not know whether they were classified by a system, what category they were placed in, what factors contributed to the classification, or how that classification affected the scrutiny of their application. Without such information, meaningful challenge is difficult. A person may contest a refusal decision without ever being able to challenge the routing output that shaped the conditions under which the application was examined.

The social and distributive impact concerns unequal scrutiny. If nationality or nationality-linked factors influence risk categorization, applicants from certain countries may be more likely to experience heightened review. Even if the system does not directly refuse applications, it may distribute administrative attention unevenly. This matters because scrutiny itself is not neutral. It can produce delay, additional evidentiary demands, suspicion, and increased likelihood of adverse interpretation. Routing can therefore become a subtle but consequential form of administrative differentiation.

The individual impact may be less visible than in Robodebt or the Toeslagenaffaire, but it is still important. Visa applicants may experience delay, uncertainty, additional documentation burdens, or perceived unfairness without knowing that a risk route contributed to their experience. In immigration and mobility contexts, such burdens may affect work, education, family life, travel, and security of status. The absence of an immediate debt or sanction should not make these effects invisible.

The case also highlights the difficulty of contestability in migration automation. Challenging automated systems in migration and asylum often requires discovering that the system exists, obtaining information through access requests, securing technical and legal expertise, and building a litigation strategy before a court can consider the substantive issue (Palmiotto & Ozkul, 2024). This illustrates why contestability should not depend entirely on affected persons or civil society organizations uncovering hidden systems after the fact.

At the institutional level, visa streaming shows how accountability may be weakened when a tool is framed as merely administrative or supportive. If governance rules focus only on final automated decisions, systems that allocate scrutiny may escape rigorous examination. Yet routing outputs can influence how public authority is experienced by applicants. For that reason, impact governance must include systems that shape decision pathways, not only systems that issue final outcomes.

The visa streaming case shows that an administrative output does not need to be a final decision to be consequential. Routing outputs can distribute suspicion, delay, evidentiary burden, and unequal scrutiny. The case therefore strengthens the chapter's argument that AI creation systems in public administration should be governed according to the administrative role of their outputs, not only their formal decision-making status. A route can be a form of power when the person affected cannot see, challenge, or correct the route assigned to them.

SyRI: Risk Report Output, Surveillance, and Legal Accountability

SyRI, or System Risk Indication, illustrates the fourth type of administrative output examined in this chapter: the risk report. Unlike Robodebt, SyRI did not itself create an alleged debt. Unlike the Toeslagenaffaire, its central output was not framed as an individual fraud classification in a benefits application process. Unlike visa streaming, it did not route applications through different levels of scrutiny. Instead, SyRI linked data from multiple sources to generate risk indications that could direct state attention toward individuals, households, or areas.

SyRI was designed to support welfare, tax, and labor-law fraud detection by processing personal data from various public sources and generating risk reports (van Bekkum & Zuiderveen Borgesius, 2021). These reports did not themselves impose sanctions, but they could lead to further investigation. This makes SyRI especially important for the chapter's argument. A risk report may appear preliminary, but it can still expose people to surveillance, administrative attention, and potential downstream consequences.

The Hague District Court held that the legal framework for SyRI did not sufficiently protect the right to private life under Article 8 of the European Convention on Human Rights. The central problem was not that fraud detection was illegitimate as a public objective. Rather, SyRI lacked sufficient transparency and safeguards to maintain a fair balance between the state's interest in fraud prevention and the rights of individuals (van Bekkum & Zuiderveen Borgesius, 2021). The case therefore shows that risk-production systems require more than administrative usefulness. They require legal justification, proportionality, and meaningful oversight.

SyRI can also be understood as a human rights issue in the digital welfare state, where transparency is essential not only for privacy, but also for legality, proportionality, data protection, non-discrimination, and judicial oversight (Rachovitsa & Johann, 2022). If the state cannot explain how risk is produced, what data are linked, what safeguards apply, and how affected persons can challenge the process, then both individuals and courts are placed in a weak position. Opacity burdens not only affected persons, but also the institutions responsible for reviewing state action.

The individual impact of SyRI may be less immediately visible than in cases involving debts or benefit recovery. A person may not receive a debt notice or sanction simply because a risk report is generated. However, harm can arise from being placed within a system of risk-based attention without knowledge or explanation. Individuals may be exposed to investigation, monitoring, or suspicion without understanding how they were selected. This form of harm is less visible precisely because the output operates upstream of direct enforcement.

The procedural and legal impact is central. If affected persons cannot know whether their data were used, how risk was inferred, or what consequences followed from a risk report, contestability is severely weakened. Formal rights to challenge state action are inadequate if the basis of risk production is inaccessible. The evidentiary burden of challenging potential discriminatory effects becomes especially problematic when affected persons lack access to the factors and logic used to generate risk and when the state controls the relevant information (Rachovitsa & Johann, 2022).

The social and distributive dimension is also important. Risk-based welfare and fraud systems may disproportionately target low-income communities, welfare recipients, or areas already subject to heightened administrative suspicion. Even if a system is framed as neutral risk detection, decisions about datasets, participating agencies, target areas, and fraud priorities may reflect existing social inequalities. SyRI therefore raises a broader question: who becomes visible to the state as risky, and who remains outside such surveillance?

At the institutional level, SyRI demonstrates the role of courts and rights-based review in limiting opaque risk systems. The judgment did not reject all digital fraud detection. Rather, it required such systems to be compatible with transparency, proportionality, and rights protection. This distinction is important. The lesson of SyRI is not that public bodies can never use data to detect fraud. The lesson is that risk reports cannot be produced through opaque arrangements that prevent affected persons, courts, and oversight bodies from understanding and scrutinizing the system.

SyRI shows that risk production itself can be an administrative output of public concern. A risk report may not be a final decision, but it can direct attention, trigger investigation, and expose people to surveillance. For that reason, risk reports must be governed before they become the invisible basis of state action. Public authorities that generate risk must be able to explain, justify, audit, and take responsibility for the administrative consequences of that risk. Otherwise, the state can inspect citizens without making its own reasoning equally inspectable.

COMPARATIVE SYNTHESIS AND GOVERNANCE IMPLICATIONS

Comparative Findings: How Administrative Outputs Become Public Harm

The four cases examined above differ in jurisdiction, administrative function, technology, and legal outcome. Robodebt concerned welfare debt recovery in Australia. The Toeslagenaffaire concerned fraud control in the Dutch childcare benefits system. Visa streaming concerned the triage of immigration applications in the United Kingdom. SyRI concerned data linkage and risk reporting in the Dutch welfare state. Despite these differences, the cases reveal a common administrative pattern: system-generated outputs become consequential when public authorities use them to organize treatment, shift burdens, direct scrutiny, or justify further intervention.

The first comparative finding is that system-generated results became actionable administrative outputs. In Robodebt, an income estimate became an alleged debt. In the Toeslagenaffaire, risk classification became welfare suspicion. In visa streaming, a risk category became a scrutiny pathway. In SyRI, linked data became a risk report. These outputs did not have the same legal status, and they did not operate at the same stage of decision-making. Yet each affected the administrative position of individuals. The cases therefore show that governance should examine not only final automated decisions, but also earlier outputs that structure administrative attention.

The second finding is that uncertainty was converted into person-facing burden. In each case, the relevant output contained uncertainty. An averaged income estimate was not actual income. A risk score was not proof of fraud. A routing category was not a visa decision. A risk report was not evidence of wrongdoing. Once these outputs entered administrative workflows, however, they acquired practical force. Individuals were required to respond, explain, provide evidence, endure scrutiny, or live under the possibility of investigation. The burden of resolving uncertainty shifted from the institution that produced the output to the person affected by it.

The third finding is that opacity weakened meaningful contestability. The problem was not simply that individuals lacked technical knowledge. It was that they often lacked access to the administrative role of the output itself. They could not always know what data were used, what logic was applied, how a classification shaped their case, or which part of the process needed to be challenged. Without reasons connected to the person's own case, contestability remains formal rather than meaningful. In this chapter's framework, accountable use of administrative outputs requires institutions to explain, justify, and correct harmful reliance on system-generated results.

The fourth finding is that individual harms accumulated into institutional accountability failures. Robodebt did not remain a collection of debt disputes; it became a national administrative scandal. The Toeslagenaffaire did not remain a set of benefit recovery errors; it became a crisis of welfare governance and political legitimacy. Visa streaming raised concerns about discriminatory administrative routing. SyRI led to judicial scrutiny of opaque risk reporting. Across the cases, individual harm exposed deeper institutional weaknesses: weak legal validation, poor review pathways, insufficient oversight, and responsibility diffused across agencies, systems, officials, and sometimes external actors.

These findings show that public harm does not arise from technology alone. It arises from the institutional conversion of outputs into administrative consequences. A system output becomes dangerous when it is treated as sufficiently authoritative to guide state action while remaining insufficiently lawful, explainable, contestable, or accountable. This conversion may occur through a debt notice, a fraud investigation, a case-routing process, or a risk report. The form differs, but the underlying movement is the same: an output created under uncertainty becomes a practical burden for the affected person. At that point, the problem is not only technical reliability. It is the possibility that the state has shifted uncertainty from itself to the citizen.

The comparative analysis also clarifies why an output-centered approach is necessary. A model-centered approach asks whether the system is accurate, explainable, or technically reliable. These questions are important, but incomplete. An output-centered approach asks what the output does in public administration. Does it create a claim? Does it change the burden of proof? Does it increase scrutiny? Does it stigmatize a person or group? Does it trigger investigation? Does it become difficult to challenge? These questions locate governance at the point where technology becomes administrative power. They also keep attention on a basic administrative principle: when the state uses an output, the state must justify it.

The central lesson is that AI creation systems in public administration must be governed through the administrative life of their outputs. Governance should begin before outputs are relied upon, continue while they are used in workflows, and remain active after deployment when patterns of harm become visible. These comparative findings provide the basis for the impact-governance framework developed below.

Toward an Impact-Governance Framework

The cases show that AI creation systems in public administration require governance that follows system outputs into administrative practice. The relevant question is not only whether a system is well designed, but whether its outputs can legitimately be used by public authorities. This section proposes an impact-governance framework built around five principles: legality before automation, traceable reasons, meaningful contestability, human accountability, and post-deployment impact audit.

The first principle is legality before automation. Public bodies should not operationalize system outputs before establishing that their use has a sufficient legal basis. Robodebt illustrates the risk of treating an inferential estimate as a legally enforceable debt. The problem was not simply that the system produced inaccurate results; it was that those results were attached to debt recovery despite an inadequate legal foundation. Review of automated administration cannot be limited to system malfunction, because a system may operate as programmed while still producing unlawful outcomes if the encoded rule or policy is invalid (Allars, 2024). Legal validation must therefore occur before outputs become administrative claims, suspicions, routes, or reports.

The second principle is traceable reasons rather than mere outputs. Public administration cannot treat a system output as a reason in itself. A risk score, flag, estimate, or classification must be connected to data, rules, assumptions, human interpretation, and administrative use. Traceability means that affected persons and oversight bodies can understand how an output was generated, how it was interpreted, and why it was relied upon. This principle builds on the idea that accountability requires information and justification, not merely the disclosure that a system exists (Busuioc, 2021). In practice, traceable reasons require documentation that connects technical outputs to administrative reasoning.

The third principle is meaningful contestability. Affected persons must be able to challenge not only final decisions, but also outputs that materially shape administrative treatment. Contestability requires access to information, understandable reasons, correction of data errors, challenge to rules or assumptions, and review by persons or bodies with authority to change the outcome. It should not depend on affected individuals discovering hidden systems through prolonged information requests or litigation. Formal rights are insufficient if affected persons do not know what system was used, what output was generated, or how that output affected their case, especially in contexts where challenging automated systems requires extensive pre-litigation discovery, information access, technical expertise, and legal strategy (Palmiotto & Ozkul, 2024).

The fourth principle is human accountability. Human involvement should not be reduced to the presence of a human official somewhere in the process. Human accountability requires identifiable persons or offices with the knowledge, authority, and institutional duty to question, override, correct, or stop reliance on system outputs. A human-in-the-loop arrangement is weak if officials merely accept outputs they cannot interpret or challenge. AI must not become an accountability shield. Public authorities cannot attribute harm to an AI system as if the system acted outside human and institutional control. When AI-generated outputs are used to impose burdens on citizens, responsibility must remain with identifiable public actors, especially where misuse of authority, corruption, or deliberate disregard of known risks is legally established.

The fifth principle is post-deployment impact audit. Public harm often becomes visible only after a system is embedded in real administrative workflows. Pre-deployment assessment is necessary, but not sufficient. Agencies must monitor how outputs are used, whether burdens fall unevenly, whether review pathways work, whether errors are corrected, and whether affected communities experience patterns of harm. Audit should not inspect citizens only; it should also inspect the administration that relies on the outputs. Fundamental-rights and algorithmic impact assessments should function as living governance documents rather than one-time forms, and lifecycle risk management should replace static compliance (Muis et al., 2025; National Institute of Standards and Technology, 2023).

Table 3 summarizes the five principles of the impact-governance framework and links each principle to the case lessons developed in the chapter.

Table 3. Impact-Governance Framework for Administrative Outputs

Governance principle	Core requirement	Case lesson
Legality before automation	Validate the legal basis before outputs produce administrative consequences	Robodebt shows the danger of converting estimates into enforceable debts
Traceable reasons	Connect outputs to data, assumptions, rules, interpretation, and administrative use	The Toeslagenaffaire and SyRI show the harm of opaque risk outputs
Meaningful contestability	Allow affected persons to challenge data, logic, interpretation, and use	Visa streaming and SyRI show that hidden outputs undermine challenge
Human accountability	Assign responsible humans with authority to question, override, and correct outputs	All cases show that formal human involvement is insufficient
Post-deployment impact audit	Monitor harms after outputs enter real workflows	Robodebt and the Toeslagenaffaire show that harm can accumulate when feedback is ignored

This framework differs from a general AI ethics checklist because it begins from the administrative role of outputs. If a system creates a debt estimate, governance must ask whether that estimate can lawfully support a debt. If it creates a suspicion profile, governance must ask whether suspicion is distributed fairly and whether affected persons can challenge it. If it creates a routing category, governance must ask how that category changes scrutiny. If it creates a risk report, governance must ask whether surveillance, proportionality, and review safeguards are adequate.

Transparency instruments may support this framework, but they are not sufficient on their own. Algorithm registers, for example, can help public bodies identify and disclose systems, but they may become incomplete or box-ticking exercises if they do not explain how outputs are used in administrative workflows. Registers may have value as internal organizational discipline, but their accountability value depends on completeness, updating, oversight, and connection to real decision processes (Nieuwenhuizen, 2024). For this chapter, transparency is meaningful only when it supports legality, reasons, contestability, accountability, and review.

This concern is consistent with governance-by-design approaches in smart city data governance, which emphasize that transparency and compliance should not operate as post hoc disclosure or documentation exercises. Governance becomes more credible when transparency, control mechanisms, compliance obligations, and institutional responsibilities are embedded across the data lifecycle rather than added after deployment (Namvong & Wiangwiset, 2026). This supports the argument advanced here that safeguards should be built into technical architecture, institutional roles, and operational workflows rather than treated as post-deployment additions.

The framework therefore calls for a shift from model-centered compliance to output-centered and institution-centered governance.

A public body may have a technically functioning system, documentation, and a human reviewer, but still produce public harm if system outputs become burdens without legal validation, reasons, contestability, responsibility, and ongoing audit. This is consistent with recent welfare-administration research showing that human oversight of automated decision-making is shaped by policy, organizational, professional, and technological contexts, rather than by the mere formal presence of a human reviewer (Sztandar-Sztanderska, 2025). Governing impact means governing the point where AI-generated or algorithmic outputs become administrative power.

Implications for Governing AI Creation Systems in Public Administration

The framework has practical implications for public bodies that develop, procure, deploy, or rely on AI creation systems. The first implication is that agencies should maintain an output inventory, not merely a system inventory. It is not enough to know that an agency uses a fraud detection tool, triage model, or risk assessment system. The agency must know what outputs the system generates, where those outputs enter administrative workflows, who relies on them, and what consequences may follow. It must also know how affected persons can challenge those outputs. An output inventory makes clear that the object of governance is not only the system itself, but the state action that follows from its outputs.

The second implication concerns procurement and vendor governance. Public agencies may rely on systems developed by external providers, but outsourcing technical development must not dilute public accountability. Contracts should require access to technical documentation, audit rights, information about data and model limitations, support for explanation, and procedures for correcting harmful outputs. Public bodies must preserve enough internal capacity to understand and question the outputs they use, even when those outputs are produced by external systems.

The third implication is that legal, technical, operational, and frontline expertise must be integrated before deployment. A tool may be technically functional but legally weak. It may be operationally convenient but procedurally unfair. It may improve efficiency for the agency while creating new burdens for individuals. Governance processes should therefore require agencies to examine why a system is used, what alternatives exist, how outputs will enter real workflows, and what routes of redress will be available.

The fourth implication is that explanation and review should be built around outputs. Affected persons do not need abstract descriptions of AI. They need to know whether a system output affected their case, what kind of output it was, what data or assumptions supported it, how officials used it, who was responsible for relying on it, and how it can be corrected or challenged. A debt output requires a different explanation from a risk report. A routing output requires a different form of notice from a final refusal. Public bodies should not impose administrative consequences by presenting only the output. They must disclose the data, reasons, and decision points that support it.

The fifth implication is that agencies should monitor patterns of burden, not only system performance. Accuracy, false positives, and model drift matter, but public administration also requires a different set of questions. Who receives burdens? Who struggles to contest them? Who experiences delay? Do harms cluster among particular groups? Who is being classified, burdened, routed, investigated, or required to prove themselves? Public bodies must not use AI to strengthen scrutiny over citizens while leaving unequal treatment, weak oversight, and institutional avoidance of responsibility harder to detect.

The sixth implication is that transparency and review tools should be designed as governance infrastructure, not as communication devices after deployment. A meaningful mechanism should identify systems, outputs, legal bases, affected groups, responsible officials, review pathways, and audit status. It should also shape how outputs are produced, interpreted, communicated, challenged, corrected, and reviewed in administrative practice. If such tools merely list systems without explaining how outputs affect individuals, they may create the appearance of openness without enabling accountability.

A final implication follows from the same logic: AI and data-driven systems should not become one-way instruments for inspecting citizens. They should also make public administration itself more inspectable. Audit trails, monitoring tools, and data analysis should help reveal corruption risks, discriminatory patterns, inconsistent treatment, unexplained delays, and failures to correct known errors. If the state has the data, systems, and authority to classify citizens, it should also have the responsibility to examine its own decisions, errors, and unequal practices.

These implications point to a broader shift in public-sector AI governance. Agencies should not ask only whether a system can be deployed. They should ask whether the institution is capable of governing the outputs the system creates. That requires legal authority, technical understanding, administrative documentation, human responsibility, person-facing explanation, review capacity, and continuing audit. The core institutional principle is simple: technological delegation must not become accountability delegation. In serious cases, accountability should not stop at explanation or apology. Where the legal threshold is met, misuse of authority, corruption, or deliberate disregard of known risks should remain subject to disciplinary, administrative, civil, or criminal consequences.

FUTURE RESEARCH DIRECTIONS

Future research should examine how output-centered governance works in practice. One priority is empirical study of administrative outputs across different sectors, such as welfare, taxation, immigration, policing, education, health, and municipal services. Such research could ask whether debts, risk scores, routing categories, alerts, or fraud indicators create similar patterns of burden across administrative domains.

A second priority is evaluating impact assessment as an ongoing governance process. Further research should examine whether impact assessments actually change agency behavior, improve review pathways, reveal discriminatory patterns, or reduce harm after deployment. This requires attention not only to the design of assessment tools, but also to how agencies use, update, and act on them after systems enter real administrative workflows. A living assessment should ask not only whether citizens are being correctly classified, but whether the public body is correcting its own errors.

A third priority concerns transparency instruments and algorithm registers. Future studies should examine which register designs help affected persons, civil society, regulators, courts, and journalists understand how outputs affect administrative treatment. This includes examining whether registers merely disclose the existence of systems or whether they also make visible the legal basis, output type, affected groups, review mechanisms, and audit status.

A fourth priority is vendor accountability and public-sector capacity. Where AI systems are procured from external providers, researchers should examine how contracts, audit rights, documentation duties, and procurement rules affect public bodies' ability to explain and correct harmful outputs. Further work should also consider how much internal technical, legal, and operational capacity public agencies need in order to remain accountable for systems they do not build themselves.

Finally, future research should test the administrative-output framework beyond the European and Australian cases discussed here. Different legal systems provide different levels of notice, review, judicial oversight, and administrative remedy. Comparative work could help identify which institutional conditions prevent system outputs from becoming unchallengeable public burdens. It should also examine how data and AI-assisted audit can be used to detect corruption risks, discriminatory treatment, selective enforcement, and institutional failures to investigate irregularities when evidence is already available.

CONCLUSION

This chapter has argued that the impact of AI creation systems in public administration should be governed by examining what their administrative outputs become in practice. These systems do not only produce technical results. In public administration, they may generate debt estimates, suspicion profiles, routing categories, risk reports, or other outputs that shape how the state treats individuals. Once such outputs enter administrative workflows, they can affect rights, burdens, remedies, scrutiny, and trust. The central concern is therefore not AI in the abstract, but the point at which a system-generated output becomes public power.

The four cases show different forms of this problem. Robodebt illustrates debt output. The Toeslagenaffaire illustrates suspicion output. Visa streaming illustrates routing output. SyRI illustrates risk report output. These outputs differ, but they share a common risk: uncertain or opaque system-generated results may acquire administrative force before legality, reasons, contestability, and accountability are secured.

The chapter's contribution is to reframe AI creation systems in public administration around the administrative life of outputs, rather than to claim that technical design alone determines public harm. It has proposed the concept of administrative outputs, an impact-centered framework with four dimensions, and an impact-governance framework built around legality, traceable reasons, contestability, human accountability, and post-deployment audit. The purpose of this reframing is to keep governance close to the person affected by state action: the person who receives the notice, enters the review pathway, carries the evidentiary burden, or must contest a classification whose logic remains hidden.

The argument is not that public bodies should reject AI or automation. Rather, they must remain responsible for what system outputs become in administrative practice. Efficiency cannot justify shifting uncertainty, burden, or risk onto individuals without adequate safeguards. When the state relies on an administrative output, the burden of justification must remain with the state. Public bodies must not use AI-generated outputs to make citizens prove themselves against public power. If AI creation systems are to be used in public administration, they must be governed from the point where their outputs begin to operate as public power, and they must also make the state itself more accountable to the people it governs.

REFERENCES

Allars, M. (2024). Automated decision-making and review of administrative decisions. *Georgia Law Review*, 58(3), Article 8. URL: https://digitalcommons.law.uga.edu/glr/vol58/iss3/8

Amnesty International. (2021). *Xenophobic machines: Discrimination through unregulated use of algorithms in the Dutch childcare benefits scandal*. Amnesty International. URL: https://www.amnesty.org/en/documents/eur35/4686/2021/en/

Arts, J., & van den Berg, M. (2025). What the Dutch benefits scandal and policy's focus on 'fraud' can teach us about the endurance of empire. *Critical Social Policy*, *45*(1), 177–187. DOI: 10.1177/02610183241281346

Ball, S., & Hannah, A. (2025). Robodebt: Administrative harm and Australian social policy. *Australian Journal of Political Science*, *60*(2), 141–148. DOI: 10.1080/10361146.2025.2542739

Busuioc, M. (2021). Accountable artificial intelligence: Holding algorithms to account. *Public Administration Review*, *81*(5), 825–836. DOI: 10.1111/puar.13293 PMID: 34690372

Damen, W. W. P. (2025). Exposed to the elements: How European data protection law facilitates welfare dystopias and how to improve its level of protection. *European Journal of Social Security*, *27*(2), 156–174. DOI: 10.1177/13882627251337402

Fenger, M., & Simonse, R. (2024). The implosion of the Dutch surveillance welfare state. *Social Policy & Administration*, *58*(2), 264–276. DOI: 10.1111/spol.12998

Hannah, A., & Botterill, L. C. (2025). Avoiding the brakes: Malign policy and legal advice in the Robodebt scandal. *Policy and Society*, *44*(2), 229–241. DOI: 10.1093/polsoc/puaf018

Muis, I. M., Straatman, J., & Kamphorst, B. A. (2025). Responsible AI innovation in the public sector: Lessons from and recommendations for facilitating Fundamental Rights and Algorithms Impact Assessments. *Journal of Responsible Technology*, *22*, 100118. DOI: 10.1016/j.jrt.2025.100118

Namvong, A., & Wiangwiset, T. (2026). Transparency-by-design in smart city crowd monitoring: A privacy-preserving Wi-Fi analytics framework for tourism and urban management. In Azeroual, O. (Ed.), *Technical foundations and applications of trustworthy AI systems* (pp. 157–194). IGI Global Scientific Publishing., DOI: 10.4018/979-8-2600-1433-2.ch006

National Institute of Standards and Technology. (2023). *Artificial intelligence risk management framework (AI RMF 1.0)*. U.S. Department of Commerce., DOI: 10.6028/NIST.AI.100-1

Nieuwenhuizen, E. (2024). Algorithm registers: A box-ticking exercise or meaningful tool for transparency? *Information Polity*, *29*(4), 415–433. DOI: 10.1177/15701255241297107

OECD. (2025). *Governing with artificial intelligence: The state of play and way forward in core government functions*. OECD Publishing., DOI: 10.1787/795de142-

Ologun, A., Ikeakaonwu, O. M., Ibidunmoye, A. F., Eneano, G. A., Chuwa, C. C., & Kolawole, L. O. (2026). AI governance and ethical frameworks for public-sector AI decision systems: An institutional operationalisation model. *AI and Ethics*, *6*(3), 294. Advance online publication. DOI: 10.1007/s43681-026-01143-x

Ozkul, D. (2023). *Automating immigration and asylum: The uses of new technologies in migration and asylum governance in Europe*. Refugee Studies Centre, University of Oxford. URL: https://www.rsc.ox.ac.uk/publications/automating-immigration-and-asylum-the-uses-of-new-technologies-in-migration-and-asylum-governance-in-europe

Özsavaş, M. G., & Özsavaş, E. E. (2026). AI governance capacity in public administration: A comparative analysis of the EU and Türkiye. *International Journal of Public Administration in the Digital Age*, *13*(1), 1–20. DOI: 10.4018/IJPADA.406076

Palmiotto, F. (2024). When is a decision automated? A taxonomy for a fundamental rights analysis. *German Law Journal*, *25*(2), 210–236. DOI: 10.1017/glj.2023.112

Palmiotto, F., & Ozkul, D. (2024). Climbing a wall: Strategic litigation against automated systems in migration and asylum. *German Law Journal*, *25*(6), 935–955. DOI: 10.1017/glj.2024.52

Rachovitsa, A., & Johann, N. (2022). The human rights implications of the use of AI in the digital welfare state: Lessons learned from the Dutch SyRI case. *Human Rights Law Review*, *22*(2), ngac010. Advance online publication. DOI: 10.1093/hrlr/ngac010

Rinta-Kahila, T., Someh, I., Gillespie, N., Indulska, M., & Gregor, S. (2022). Algorithmic decision-making and system destructiveness: A case of automatic debt recovery. *European Journal of Information Systems*, *31*(3), 313–338. DOI: 10.1080/0960085X.2021.1960905

Roehl, U. B. U. (2023). Automated decision-making and good administration: Views from inside the government machinery. *Government Information Quarterly*, *40*(4), 101864. DOI: 10.1016/j.giq.2023.101864

Royal Commission into the Robodebt Scheme. (2023). *Report of the Royal Commission into the Robodebt Scheme*. Commonwealth of Australia. URL: https://robodebt.royalcommission.gov.au/publications/report

Sztandar-Sztanderska, K. (2025). How context matters: Human oversight of automated-decision-making systems in welfare administration. *Journal of European Social Policy*. Advance online publication. DOI: 10.1177/09589287251358069

van Bekkum, M., & Zuiderveen Borgesius, F. (2021). Digital welfare fraud detection and the Dutch SyRI judgment. *European Journal of Social Security*, *23*(4), 323–340. DOI: 10.1177/13882627211031257

Wang, C., Yin, Y., & Hu, H. (2026). The rise of algorithmic governance and the dual revolution: Applications, challenges, and governance of artificial intelligence in public administration. *Technology in Society*, *86*, 103264. DOI: 10.1016/j.techsoc.2026.103264

ADDITIONAL READING

Ameen, K. S., Towfiq, T. A., Mousa, K. M., & Pooyanmehr, M. (2026). Judicial review of algorithmic administrative systems: Legality, evidence, and remedies in the smart city state. *Frontiers in Artificial Intelligence*, *9*, 1802986. Advance online publication. DOI: 10.3389/frai.2026.1802986 PMID: 42052213

Rizk, A., & Lindgren, I. (2025). Automated decision-making in public administration: Changing the decision space between public officials and citizens. *Government Information Quarterly*, *42*(3), 102061. DOI: 10.1016/j.giq.2025.102061

Wilcock, S., & van Toorn, G. (2026). The digital welfare state: Conceptual limits and possibilities. *Big Data & Society*, *13*(1), 20539517261429193. DOI: 10.1177/20539517261429193

KEY TERMS AND DEFINITIONS

Administrative Outputs: System-generated outputs that become relevant to how public authorities treat individuals. Examples include debt estimates, suspicion profiles, risk classifications, routing categories, fraud indicators, scrutiny pathways, and risk reports.

AI Creation Systems: AI, automated, algorithmic, or data-driven systems that generate outputs used in administrative workflows. In this chapter, the term is used broadly to include systems that create classifications, predictions, alerts, risk scores, recommendations, routes, or reports that public authorities may rely on.

Algorithmic Accountability: The capacity to explain, justify, review, correct, and accept responsibility for the use of algorithmic or AI-generated outputs in public administration. It requires more than transparency; it also requires reasons, review, and consequences when harm occurs.

Algorithm Registers: Transparency tools that record information about algorithmic or AI systems used by public bodies. In this chapter, algorithm registers are treated as useful only when they connect system disclosure to outputs, legal bases, review pathways, responsibility, and audit.

Contestability: The practical ability of affected persons to understand, question, and challenge the data, logic, interpretation, and administrative use of system-generated outputs that affect their case.

Human Accountability: The presence of identifiable human officials or institutions with the knowledge, authority, and duty to take responsibility for the use of system-generated outputs and their administrative consequences.

Human Oversight: The involvement of human officials or institutions in monitoring, interpreting, questioning, overriding, or correcting system-generated outputs. In this chapter, human oversight must be meaningful rather than merely formal.

Impact-Centered Framework: An analytical framework that examines the consequences of administrative outputs across individual, procedural/legal, social/distributive, and institutional dimensions. It helps identify how technical outputs become public consequences.

Legality Before Automation: The principle that public bodies should establish a sufficient legal basis before operationalizing system-generated outputs in administrative workflows. A system may function technically as designed while still producing unlawful administrative consequences.

Output-Centered Governance: A governance approach that focuses not only on the design or performance of AI systems, but also on what system-generated outputs become when they enter administrative practice. It asks how outputs are used, interpreted, communicated, challenged, corrected, and audited.

Post-Deployment Impact Audit: The ongoing review of how AI or algorithmic outputs affect individuals, groups, procedures, and institutions after deployment. It monitors patterns of burden, unequal scrutiny, errors, review failures, and accumulated public harm.

Public Harm: Harm that arises when administrative outputs affect individuals through the authority of the state. Public harm may include financial loss, legal burden, procedural unfairness, stigma, unequal scrutiny, psychological stress, family disruption, or institutional loss of trust.

Risk Classification: The process of assigning individuals, applications, households, or cases to risk categories based on data-driven indicators, models, or rules. In public administration, risk classification may shape scrutiny, suspicion, investigation, or access to services.

Traceable Reasons: Reasons that can be followed from a system-generated output back to the data, assumptions, rules, human interpretation, and administrative use that produced or relied on that output.

Chapter 10
Impact of AI-Generated Content on Consumer Trust in Social Media Advertising:
A Market Analysis With Regression and ML Modelling

Koppala Venugopal
http://orcid.org/0000-0002-3472-1477
Aditya Institute of Technology and Management, India

Parishkrit Agrawal
G.S. College of Commerce, India

Kailesh Murlidhar Jaitwar
Place of Higher Learning and Research, G.S. College of Commerce, India

Illuri Venkata Narayana
http://orcid.org/0009-0002-4059-1303
S.C.I.M. Government College, India

Durga Prasad Tapeswarapu
http://orcid.org/0000-0001-9353-5124
Aditya University, India

M. Jayanthi Rao
http://orcid.org/0000-0002-2962-455X
Aditya Institute of Technology and Management, India

ABSTRACT

This study empirically investigates the impact of AI generated content on consumer trust in social media advertising through a multi-platform survey of N = 562 urban Indian digital consumers using a three-stage analytical framework of confirmatory factor analysis, structural equation modeling, and machine learning. SEM confirmed AI content authenticity (beta = 0.46, p < .001), personalisation accuracy (beta = 0.43, p < .001), and disclosure transparency (beta = 0.38, p < .001) as domi-

DOI: 10.4018/979-8-2600-0368-8.ch010

nant consumer trust drivers, while data privacy compliance significantly predicted trust and digital literacy significantly moderated all trust to outcome relationships. XGBoost achieved R squared = .836 predictive accuracy. An AI content authenticity threshold at 79 percent of maximum score was identified as the trust acceleration trigger beyond which compounding trust benefits activate. Platform type multi group analysis confirmed Instagram generates the strongest AICA to trust effects while LinkedIn demonstrates the strongest disclosure transparency effects

1. INTRODUCTION

The emergence of generative artificial intelligence as a mainstream advertising production technology represents a fundamental transformation in the nature, scale, and economic logic of social media advertising. Platforms including Midjourney, DALL E 3, Stable Diffusion, GPT 4 Vision, and sector specific AI advertising tools have enabled brands of all sizes to produce visually sophisticated, contextually personalized, and continuously A/B testable advertising content at a fraction of the cost and time required by traditional creative production workflows. Indian digital advertising market estimates suggest that AI generated or AI assisted content will constitute 47 to 63 percent of social media advertising impressions across major platforms by 2026 (IAMAI, 2024), representing a transformation of equivalent magnitude to the transition from print to digital advertising. Yet the consumer trust implications of this transformation remain poorly understood: when consumers realize or suspect that the advertising content they engage with was generated by AI rather than created by human creatives, how does this knowledge affect their trust in the ad, the brand, and the platform, and through what structural mechanisms does this trust or scepticism translate into behavioral outcomes including purchase intention and word of mouth?

India's urban digital consumer population provides an exceptionally significant empirical setting for examining these questions. With 759 million internet users, 467 million active social media users, and a digital advertising market projected to reach Rs. 35,809 crore by 2026 (eMarketer India, 2024), India is simultaneously a massive and rapidly digitizing advertising market and one characterized by extraordinary digital literacy heterogeneity, diverse cultural norms around authenticity and disclosure, and a newly enacted data privacy framework under the Digital Personal Data Protection Act 2023 that creates specific regulatory obligations for AI powered advertising targeting. Vakamullu et al. (2026) in the social media intricacies study established the dual nature of social media platform algorithmic mediation as simultaneously amplifying brand messages for highly engaged audiences and generating scepticism and withdrawal responses from critically aware segments, a duality directly applicable to understanding how AIGC creates bifurcated trust responses across different consumer digital literacy segments. Venugopal and Kolluru (2025) in the social media privacy and security vulnerability study documented that perceived data governance quality is a primary determinant of social media platform trust in Indian contexts, directly applicable to the data privacy compliance construct in the present study's AIGC trust model.

The consumer trust implications of AI generated content in advertising intersect three conceptual tensions that the present study addresses simultaneously. First, the authenticity paradox: AI generated content can achieve higher visual quality and contextual relevance than most human produced content, yet consumers who detect or suspect AI origins experience authenticity deficits that reduce trust even for objectively superior content quality. Second, the transparency dilemma: proactive AIGC disclosure may reduce the authenticity deception concern while simultaneously activating AI scepticism that erodes trust through a different pathway, creating a complex nonlinear relationship between disclosure quality and trust outcomes. Third, the privacy personalisation tradeoff: highly accurate AI personalisation signals sophisticated data utilization that consumers may simultaneously appreciate for relevance and resent for perceived surveillance, generating heterogeneous trust responses that digital literacy moderates. Venugopal and Jagadeesh (2025) in the theoretical insights on social media security and privacy study provided dual pathway processing frameworks directly applicable to understanding how consumers evaluate AIGC disclosures through both cognitive evaluation and emotional reaction pathways. This study examines all three tensions through a validated structural model across N = 562 Indian digital consumers. Figure 1 presents the integrated conceptual framework.

Figure 1. Integrated Conceptual Research Framework

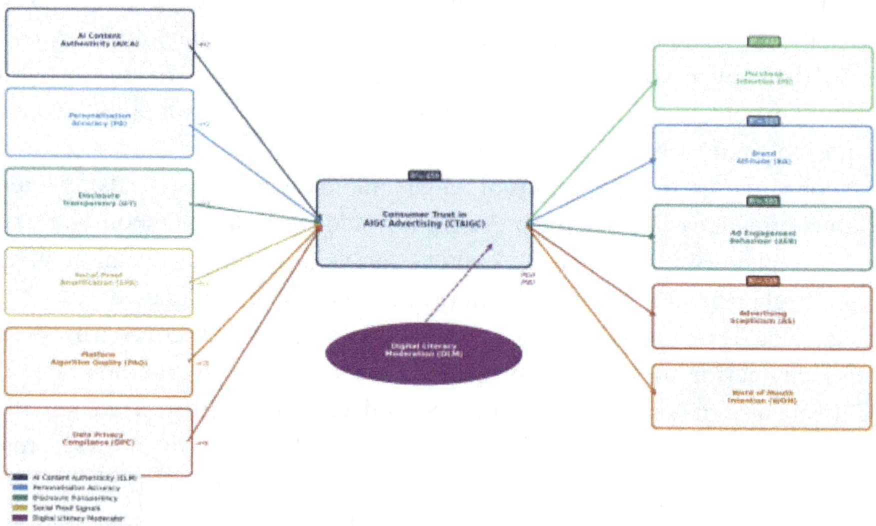

1.1. Statement of the Problem

Despite the rapid proliferation of AIGC in Indian social media advertising and the significant consumer trust, regulatory, and market efficiency implications, no validated structural model exists that simultaneously captures the multi-dimensional AIGC feature inputs driving consumer trust, the behavioral outcome consequences of AIGC trust or scepticism, and the digital literacy moderation dynamics that generate heterogeneous trust responses across consumer segments. Indian digital marketers lack evidence-based frameworks for optimizing AIGC disclosure strategies. Platform operators lack structural evidence for AIGC labeling policy design. DPDP Act implementers lack consumer trust impact evidence for AI advertising data governance regulations. This study constructs and validates the first such model.

1.2. Research Objectives

Five objectives guide this study: (1) to develop and validate through CFA a six factor measurement model of AIGC consumer trust drivers and behavioral outcome constructs; (2) to test through SEM the direct, mediated, and moderated structural pathways from AIGC feature constructs to consumer trust and behavioral outcomes; (3) to compare AIGC trust dynamics across five social media platforms through multi group SEM; (4) to identify item level trust predictors using XGBoost SHAP analysis and detect the AICA nonlinear threshold; and (5) to generate actionable guidance for Indian digital marketers, social media platforms, and DPDP Act implementation authorities.

1.3. Hypotheses

H01: There is no significant validity or reliability in the proposed six factor measurement model of AIGC consumer trust drivers and behavioral outcome constructs.

H02: There are no significant direct, mediated, or moderated structural relationships between AIGC feature constructs, consumer trust, and behavioral outcomes.

H03: There are no significant differences in AIGC trust dynamics across the five social media platforms.

H04: Item level trust predictors do not significantly predict Consumer Trust in AIGC Advertising, and there is no significant nonlinear threshold effect for AI Content Authenticity.

H05: The findings of the study do not provide significant actionable guidance for Indian digital marketers, social media platforms, and DPDP Act implementation authorities

2. REVIEW OF RELATED LITERATURE

2.1. AI Generated Content in Advertising: Definitional Landscape and Typology

AI generated content in advertising encompasses a spectrum of generative AI applications including text to image generation producing original advertising visuals, large language model generated advertising copy and product descriptions, AI synthesized voice and video content for digital ads, and ML powered dynamic creative optimization systems that automatically assemble and test thousands of ad variants. Each AIGC type raises distinct consumer trust implications: photorealistic AI generated imagery of products that do not exist as photographed raises authenticity concerns distinct from those raised by AI generated testimonials attributing experiences to synthetic consumer personas, which in turn differ from those raised by AI personalized ad copy that accurately reflects a consumer's browsing history. The present study captures this AIGC typological diversity through the AI Content Authenticity construct that measures consumer perceptions across multiple AIGC types simultaneously, while the Personalisation Accuracy and Disclosure Transparency constructs capture the specific trust relevant features most consistently documented in the AIGC advertising literature.

The voice driven online shopping and smart assistance study by Venugopal et al. (2026) demonstrated that AI assisted digital commerce platforms generate nonlinear adoption and trust benefits that substantially exceed linear extrapolations from partial AI adoption, providing methodological grounding for the present study's XGBoost architecture for detecting nonlinear trust threshold effects. The ChatGPT integration in academic services study by Venugopal et al. (2025) established that AI tool integration within structured service frameworks generates quality improvements exceeding standalone AI deployment, applicable to the AIGC advertising context where AI content embedded within transparent disclosure frameworks generates higher trust returns than AIGC deployed without governance structures. The Gen Z AI reliance study by Venugopal (2025) documented that younger digital consumers exhibit high AI tool adoption but variable critical evaluation capacity, directly relevant to understanding the digital literacy moderation effects in the present study.

2.2. Elaboration Likelihood Model and Trust Transfer Theory in AIGC Contexts

The Elaboration Likelihood Model (Petty and Cacioppo, 1986) provides the foundational framework for understanding how consumers process AIGC advertising through two pathways with distinct trust implications. The central route, characterized by high motivation and ability to scrutinize message content, applies to consumers with high digital literacy who evaluate AIGC quality, detect authenticity cues, and form trust judgments based on message argument quality. The peripheral route, involving low effort processing based on surface cues, applies to consumers who form trust judgments based on visual quality, social proof signals, and platform credibility heuristics without deeply evaluating AIGC origins. Digital literacy moderation in the present study captures this ELM processing mode heterogeneity: high digital literacy consumers are more likely to use the central route and therefore more sensitive to AIGC disclosure quality and authenticity signals, while low digital literacy consumers rely more heavily on peripheral cues including social proof amplification and platform quality. Trust Transfer Theory (McKnight et al., 2002) specifies that trust formed in one context transfers to related contexts through cognitive schema generalization, directly applicable to understanding how AI platform trust transfers to AIGC advertising trust within the same platform ecosystem. Venugopal, et al. (2026) in the ML applications study established that AI assisted digital service platforms generate trust spillover effects where early positive AI interactions establish trust schemas that generalize to subsequent AI content encounters, providing direct empirical evidence for the trust transfer mechanism in AI platform contexts.

The multisensory marketing and brand loyalty study by Venugopal (2025) established that brand loyalty formation in consumer contexts is driven by multi-channel sensory signal consistency that creates emotional brand connections resistant to competitive disruption, directly applicable to understanding how AIGC advertising that maintains consistent brand sensory signals across AI generated content types builds trust through emotional brand schema reinforcement. The ethnocentric appeal study by Venugopal (2025) documented that Indian consumer perception formation involves both cognitive credibility evaluation and affective cultural identity resonance pathways, supporting the dual pathway trust formation mechanism in the AIGC advertising context where Indian consumers evaluate AIGC through both rational authenticity assessment and emotional cultural authenticity resonance.

2.3. Disclosure Transparency and the Regulatory Context

Disclosure transparency in AI generated advertising context operates through three distinct mechanisms with heterogeneous trust effects. Voluntary proactive disclosure, where brands prominently label AIGC content before consumers request or detect it, signals ethical practice and generates trust through credibility enhancement. Mandated disclosure compliance, where platforms require AIGC labeling under regulatory frameworks, signals accountability but may generate scepticism about the adequacy of minimum compliance versus genuine transparency commitment. Retroactive disclosure, where consumers discover AIGC origins after engagement, generates betrayal responses that severely damage trust beyond what the initial AIGC content would have caused. Venugopal and Jagadeesh (2025) in the social media security and privacy theoretical insights study provided frameworks for the asymmetric trust damage from disclosure failures relative to trust gains from proactive disclosure, applicable to the disclosure quality to trust relationship in the present study. The DPDP Act 2023 implications for AI generated advertising in India create a specific regulatory transparency framework where AI personalization of advertising must meet data minimization, purpose limitation, and consent adequacy standards that directly affect the data privacy compliance construct in the present study's model. Venugopal and Kolluru (2025) in the social media privacy vulnerability study established that perceived data governance quality is a primary determinant of platform trust in Indian digital consumer contexts, providing empirical grounding for the DPC to CTAIGC pathway.

2.4. Social Proof, Platform Algorithms, and AIGC Trust

Social proof mechanisms in social media advertising operate through engagement metrics, follower counts, peer sharing behavior, and influencer endorsement signals that function as credibility heuristics for consumers evaluating unfamiliar or complex products. In AIGC advertising contexts, social proof signals carry additional trust significance because they represent human validation of AI generated content quality, partially offsetting the authenticity deficit that AIGC origin detection creates. High engagement rates on AIGC advertising signal that real human audiences found the content valuable, credible, or entertaining despite its AI generated origin, providing the social validation that reduces AIGC scepticism for peripheral route processors. Vakamullu et al. (2026) documented that social media algorithmic amplification of high engagement content generates disproportionate credibility effects for algorithmically favored content, directly applicable to understanding how platform algorithm quality shapes AIGC advertising trust through the differential amplification of high social proof AIGC content. The critical factors for online shopping upscale study by Venugopal et al. (2023) established from a rural perspective that social proof signals in digital commerce are primary purchase decision drivers particularly for first time or uncertain buyers, applicable to the social proof amplification to trust pathway in the present study.

2.5. Machine Learning in Advertising and Consumer Behaviour Research

The application of ML methods to advertising and consumer behaviour research has expanded the analytical toolkit beyond traditional survey regression by enabling non linear pattern detection, feature interaction identification, and predictive model construction. Venugopal et al. et al. (2026) demonstrated in the ML applications and regression study that ensemble ML models substantially outperform linear regression in capturing the complex interactive patterns in consumer digital behavior data, providing the methodological justification for the present study's XGBoost supplementation of SEM. The adoption dynamics predictive study by Venugopal et al. (2026) established that behavioral intention outcomes in Indian consumer contexts are more accurately predicted by ensemble ML than by conventional regression, validating the XGBoost approach for the Indian digital advertising trust prediction task. The prediction analysis of Gen Z ecological consciousness by Venugopal et al. (2023) demonstrated that ML applied to attitudinal survey data identifies threshold and non-linear effects invisible to linear models, directly motivating the SHAP based trust threshold analysis in the present study. The SBI credit cards dexterous and detrimental study by Venugopal et al. (2024) applying Random Forest and regression analysis demonstrated the asymmetric response patterns where positive and negative AI platform interactions generate disproportionate behavioral outcomes that OLS symmetry assumptions mask.

2.6. Conceptual Framework and Hypotheses

The integrated framework synthesizes ELM (Petty and Cacioppo, 1986), Trust Transfer Theory (McKnight et al., 2002), and Signalling Theory (Spence, 1973) into a thirteen-path structural model. AI Content Authenticity predicts CTAIGC as H1. Personalisation Accuracy predicts CTAIGC as H2. Disclosure Transparency predicts CTAIGC as H3. Social Proof Amplification predicts CTAIGC as H4. Platform Algorithm Quality predicts CTAIGC as H5. Data Privacy Compliance predicts CTAIGC as H6. Digital Literacy Moderates all CTAIGC to outcome relationships as H8. CTAIGC predicts Purchase Intention (H7a), Brand Attitude (H7b), Ad Engagement Behaviour (H7c), Advertising Scepticism negatively (H7d), and Word of Mouth Intention (H7e).

3. METHODOLOGY

3.1. Research Design

This study employed a quantitative cross sectional survey design following a three-stage analytical protocol of CFA for measurement validation, SEM for structural hypothesis testing, and ML for predictive accuracy optimization and non-linear threshold detection. Ethical clearance: Protocol No. 2024 AIGC TRU 0521. Informed digital consent was obtained and all data were anonymized.

Sampling frame and recruitment: The sampling frame consisted of adult social media users residing in six major Indian metropolitan areas who had recent exposure to branded digital advertising. Respondents were recruited through online survey circulation using platform targeted links, academic and professional networks, and consumer referral forwarding within the selected cities. Screening questions ensured that only participants aged 18 years or above, actively using social media at least three times per week, and exposed to branded advertising during the preceding 30 days were retained for analysis. Because the study used stratified purposive rather than probability sampling, the findings should be interpreted as analytically informative for urban digitally active consumers rather than statistically generalizable to the entire Indian population.

Nonresponse and inference limits: As participation was voluntary and digitally administered, the study may under represent consumers with low internet fluency, weak platform engagement, or limited willingness to complete surveys on AI and privacy. To reduce this concern, the questionnaire was kept concise, screening was standardized, and incomplete submissions were removed prior to analysis. Nevertheless, the design remains more suitable for theory development and structural testing than for population estimation.

Ethical safeguards: The study received prior ethics approval under Protocol No. 2024 AIGC TRU 0521. The consent screen informed participants about the academic purpose of the study, the voluntary nature of participation, the right to withdraw before submission, the absence of personally identifying data collection, and the anonymized treatment of responses during analysis. Given the sensitivity of privacy, persuasion, and AI disclosure topics, no identifiable behavioral traces were collected, and the dataset was stored in de identified form for research use only.

3.2. Study Setting and Sample

The study was conducted across six major Indian cities: Delhi NCR (n = 112), Mumbai (n = 104), Bengaluru (n = 98), Hyderabad (n = 89), Pune (n = 84), and Chennai (n = 75). Qualification criteria required respondents to be active social media users with minimum three platform engagements per week and to have encountered branded advertising content in the past 30 days. The final sample of N = 562 substantially exceeded the minimum n = 431 required by Wolf et al. (2013) power analysis for a six-factor model at power .90. Stratified purposive sampling balanced representation across five social media platforms (Instagram n = 143, Facebook n = 124, YouTube n = 108, LinkedIn n = 97, X n = 90) and four age cohorts (Gen Z 18 to 24 years n = 156, Millennials 25 to 40 n = 189, Gen X 41 to 55 n = 142, Boomers 56 plus n = 75). Respondents were recruited through a combination of targeted online survey circulation, sponsored social media invitations, and professional and educational network referrals in the selected cities. To improve eligibility precision, an initial screening block filtered out respondents who were not regular social media users or had not viewed branded advertising content recently. Duplicate and low-quality responses were removed through IP and device checks, completion time screening, and straight lining diagnostics before final analysis. Demographically, the sample represented a balanced urban consumer base with variation in gender, age, platform usage, and household income, thereby improving the suitability of the data for both covariance based modeling and machine learning prediction.

Table 1. Participant Profile by Platform and Age Cohort (N = 562)

Platform	Gen Z (18-24)	Millennials (25-40)	Gen X (41-55)	Boomers (56+)	Total
Instagram	48	52	30	13	143
Facebook	34	47	30	13	124
YouTube	30	42	24	12	108
LinkedIn	22	34	28	13	97
X (Twitter)	22	14	30	24	90
Total	156	189	142	75	562

Note. Gender: Female 46.3%, Male 51.2%, Non binary and other 2.5%. Monthly household income above Rs. 50,000: 67.4%. Have encountered or knowingly seen AIGC advertising in past 30 days: 72.1%.

3.3. Research Instrument

All attitudinal items were measured on a uniform five-point Likert scale ranging from 1 = strongly disagree to 5 = strongly agree, so that higher scores consistently represented greater levels of the focal construct. Any negatively worded items were reverse coded prior to reliability and factor analyses to preserve interpretive consistency across constructs.

Data were collected using the AI Generated Content Advertising Trust Survey (AIGCATS), a 55-item instrument measuring six latent constructs and eight control variables developed through comprehensive literature review, expert panel review by ten digital marketing and consumer psychology scholars, cognitive interviewing with 24 consumers across three cities, and pilot testing with 68 participants. AI Content Authenticity (AICA, 9 items): perceived visual and textual credibility of AIGC ads, ability to distinguish AIGC from human created content, and authenticity evaluation across AIGC types. Personalisation Accuracy (PA, 9 items): perceived relevance accuracy of AIGC targeting, intrusiveness perceptions of personalisation, and contextual appropriateness of AI generated personalized content. Disclosure Transparency (DT, 9 items): AIGC label visibility, disclosure timing and placement quality, and voluntary versus mandatory disclosure attitude. Social Proof Amplification (SPA, 8 items): engagement metric credibility, peer sharing influence, and influencer AIGC endorsement trust. Platform Algorithm Quality (PAQ, 8 items): perceived targeting accuracy, content relevance filtering quality, and algorithmic fairness perceptions. Data Privacy Compliance (DPC, 8 items): DPDP Act compliance perceptions, data minimization practice visibility, and consent adequacy assessments. Consumer Trust in AIGC Advertising (CTAIGC, 11 items): composite trust performance across all outcome dimensions. Cronbach alpha: .94, subscale alphas .87 to .92. All attitudinal items were operationalized on a five-point Likert scale ranging from 1 = strongly disagree to 5 = strongly agree, while control variables captured demographic and usage characteristics. Item generation followed construct domain specification, item purification, expert relevance assessment, and pilot refinement to ensure content adequacy and clarity. Reliability and scale adequacy were further verified prior to hypothesis testing using item total correlations, composite reliability, and average variance extracted. The final instrument demonstrated strong internal consistency, with the overall scale alpha exceeding the recommended .70 benchmark and each construct meeting accepted reliability thresholds, supporting the use of the instrument for CFA, SEM, and downstream predictive modeling.

3.4. Analytical Strategy

3.4.1. *Stage 1: Confirmatory Factor Analysis*

CFA was conducted in R 4.3.1 using lavaan with Maximum Likelihood Robust estimator. Good fit criteria: chi squared to df below 3.0; CFI and TLI above .95; RMSEA below .06; SRMR below .08. AVE above .50 and CR above .70 for convergent validity. HTMT ratios below .85 for discriminant validity. Following the visual statistical communication approach recommended by Rao, et al. (2025), color intensity scaled loading visualization is applied in Figure 2.

3.4.2. *Stage 2: Structural Equation Modeling*

SEM path analysis used the two step Anderson and Gerbing (1988) approach. The structural model estimated six drivers to CTAIGC paths, five CTAIGC to outcome paths, and one DLM moderation path. Bias corrected bootstrapping with 5,000 resamples generated 95 percent confidence intervals for all indirect effects. Multi group SEM compared path coefficients across five social media platforms following invariance testing.

3.4.3. *Stage 3: Machine Learning*

Three algorithms predicted CTAIGC composite scores in Python 3.11 using scikit learn 1.3.0 and xgboost 1.7.5: Random Forest (Breiman, 2001), XGBoost (Chen and Guestrin, 2016), and Gradient Boosting (Friedman, 2001). Data were partitioned 70 to 30 stratified by platform and age cohort. SHAP values identified feature importance and partial dependence patterns following the ML applications. The algorithms were selected because they are well suited to survey based behavioral data that may contain nonlinear effects, interaction structures, and moderate multicollinearity among predictors. Random Forest was included as a robust ensemble benchmark with strong resistance to overfitting and high interpretability through variable importance. Gradient Boosting was used to capture incremental predictive improvements through sequential error correction, while XGBoost was chosen for its regularization capability, computational efficiency, and superior handling of complex nonlinear relationships. The use of these three tree-based learners also enabled cross model comparison of prediction stability and feature influence, thereby complementing the explanatory focus of SEM with a predictive analytics perspective.

To reduce optimistic bias, model training and tuning were conducted on the training partition, while the held-out test set was reserved for final performance evaluation. The 5 fold cross validation procedure was used within the training stage to compare algorithms and check stability of predictive performance before selecting the final model. Because the prediction target was a continuous trust score rather than a class label, regression-based performance statistics were emphasized over classification metrics.

3.5. Measurement quality interpretation.

The reliability and validity results indicate that the instrument possesses satisfactory psychometric quality for latent variable modeling. Cronbach alpha values ranged from .87 to .95, composite reliability exceeded .90 for all major constructs, and average variance extracted values remained above the .50 threshold, indicating internal consistency and convergent validity. The HTMT ratios remained below the conventional cutoff, supporting discriminant validity and suggesting that the six antecedent constructs and trust outcome construct captured related but empirically distinct dimensions of AIGC evaluation

4. RESULTS

4.1. Descriptive Statistics

Table 2 presents descriptive statistics. The mean CTAIGC composite score was 47.83 (SD = 14.84). AI Content Authenticity received the highest mean antecedent ratings (M = 48.17, SD = 12.84), reflecting widespread consumer awareness of AIGC quality as the foundational trust determinant. Data Privacy Compliance received the lowest ratings (M = 37.84, SD = 14.17), indicating that DPDP Act compliance visibility and data governance transparency remain poorly communicated to consumers in current AIGC advertising deployments. Instagram users reported the highest CTAIGC scores (M = 52.84) while X users reported the lowest (M = 41.17), a gap of 11.67 points reflecting both platform governance quality differences and the distinct audience composition and engagement culture differences across platforms.

Gen Z participants showed lower mean CTAIGC (M = 44.83) than Millennials (M = 49.17) despite higher AI familiarity, reflecting Gen Z's stronger AIGC scepticism when digital literacy enables detection of AI content origins.

Table 2. Descriptive Statistics for Major Study Variables (N = 562)

Construct	M	SD	Instagram	Facebook	YouTube	LinkedIn	X	Alpha
AI Content Authenticity (AICA)	48.17	12.84	53.84	49.17	46.84	44.84	38.84	.92
Personalisation Accuracy (PA)	44.83	13.47	50.17	46.84	43.17	42.83	37.17	.91
Disclosure Transparency (DT)	42.17	13.84	43.84	42.17	40.84	51.83	43.84	.90
Social Proof Amplification (SPA)	43.47	13.17	52.17	47.84	44.17	38.84	41.84	.89
Platform Algorithm Quality (PAQ)	40.83	13.84	46.17	41.84	43.17	42.84	36.17	.88
Data Privacy Compliance (DPC)	37.84	14.17	40.83	38.17	36.84	44.17	33.84	.87
Consumer Trust AIGC (CTAIGC)	47.83	14.84	52.84	49.17	47.83	49.84	41.17	.94

Note. All platform group differences $p < .001$ by one way ANOVA. LinkedIn demonstrates highest DT and DPC scores reflecting professional platform governance expectations. Instagram leads on AICA and SPA reflecting visual content quality emphasis.

4.2. Stage 1: CFA Results

The six factor CFA model demonstrated excellent fit: chi squared (268) = 450.24, $p < .001$; chi squared to df ratio = 1.68; CFI = .965; TLI = .960; RMSEA = .040 (90 percent CI [.031, .049]); SRMR = .047. All loadings were significant ($p < .001$) and ranged from .68 to .91. AVE values ranged from .542 to .578 and CR values from .914 to .952. HTMT ratios ranged from .31 to .74, confirming discriminant validity. Figure 2 presents the full measurement model.

Figure 2. CFA Measurement Model

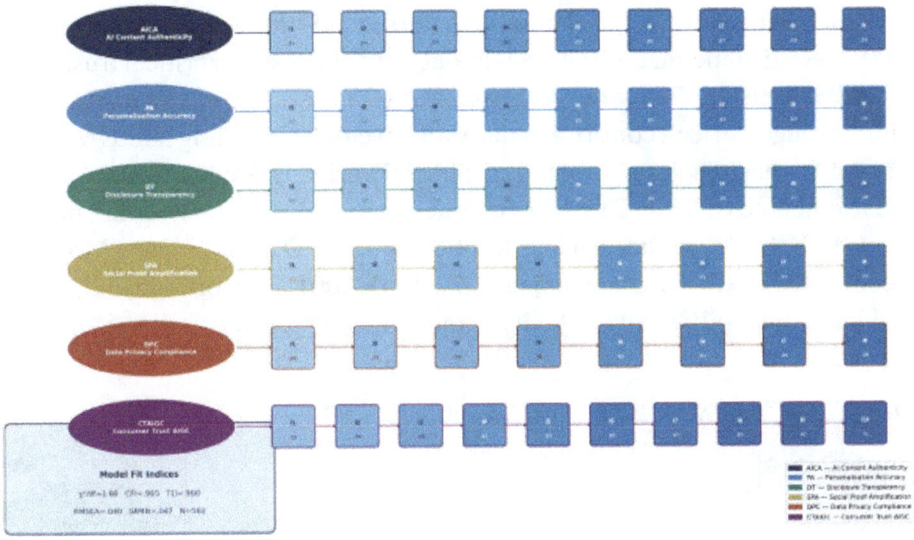

Table 3. CFA Measurement Model Validity Indicators

Construct	Items	AVE	CR	Alpha	Loading Range
AI Content Authenticity (AICA)	9	.554	.932	.928	.71 to .89
Personalisation Accuracy (PA)	9	.561	.937	.933	.70 to .90
Disclosure Transparency (DT)	9	.549	.927	.923	.69 to .88
Social Proof Amplification (SPA)	8	.542	.914	.909	.68 to .88
Platform Algorithm Quality (PAQ)	8	.547	.919	.915	.69 to .88
Consumer Trust AIGC (CTAIGC)	11	.578	.952	.948	.72 to .91

Note. AVE > .50 and CR > .70 confirm convergent validity. All HTMT < .85 confirms discriminant validity. Data Privacy Compliance (8 items, alpha = .87) included in structural model; CFA: AVE = .545, CR = .917.

4.3. Stage 2: SEM Results

The structural model demonstrated excellent fit: chi squared (328) = 549.04, $p < .001$; CFI = .963; TLI = .957; RMSEA = .041 (90 percent CI [.032, .050]); SRMR = .050. Figure 3 presents the full SEM path diagram. Table 4 reports all path coefficients. All thirteen hypothesized paths were significant at $p < .001$. AI Content Authenticity was the strongest CTAIGC driver (beta = .461, $p < .001$), confirming

ELM central route processing: consumers with sufficient digital literacy to evaluate AIGC quality form trust judgments primarily on the basis of perceived content authenticity. Personalisation Accuracy was the second strongest driver (beta = .434, p < .001), confirming that relevance without intrusiveness is a critical trust enabler for AIGC advertising. Disclosure Transparency (beta = .383, p < .001) demonstrated the third strongest effect, confirming that proactive AIGC labeling builds rather than erodes trust when disclosure quality is high. Advertising Scepticism was the only negative outcome (CTAIGC to AS beta = negative .411, p < .001), confirming that higher CTAIGC reduces advertising scepticism, while Digital Literacy Moderation was confirmed (DLM interaction beta = .183, p < .001) supporting H8 that higher digital literacy amplifies all CTAIGC to outcome relationships.

Figure 3. SEM Full Structural Path Diagram

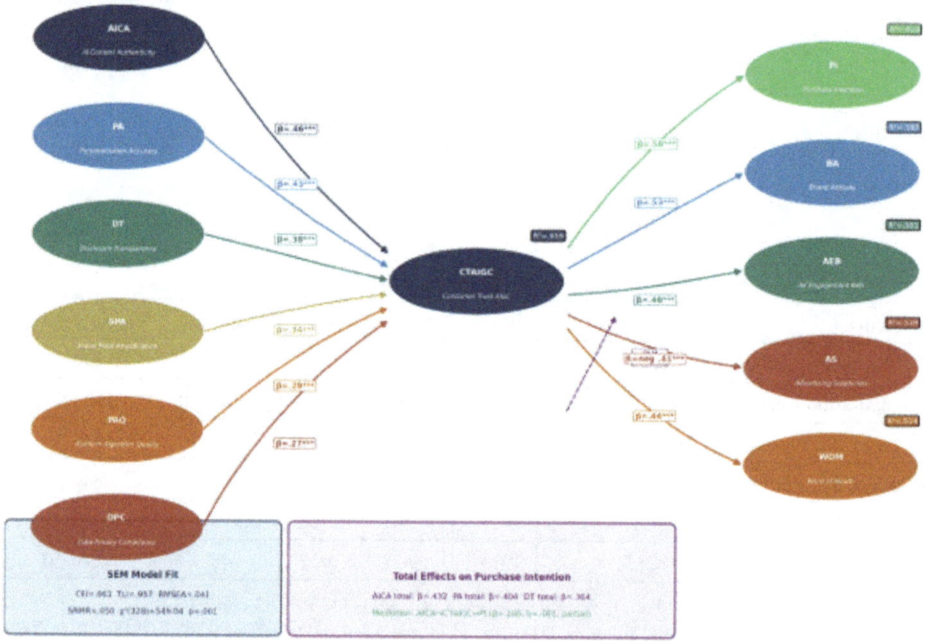

Table 4. SEM Direct Path Coefficients with Bootstrap Confidence Intervals (N = 562)

Hyp.	Pathway	Std Beta	SE	t value	p	95% BC CI	Support
H1	AICA to CTAIGC	.461	.043	10.72	<.001	[.377,.545]	Supported
H2	PA to CTAIGC	.434	.046	9.43	<.001	[.344,.524]	Supported
H3	DT to CTAIGC	.383	.049	7.82	<.001	[.287,.479]	Supported
H4	SPA to CTAIGC	.341	.052	6.56	<.001	[.239,.443]	Supported
H5	PAQ to CTAIGC	.297	.055	5.40	<.001	[.189,.405]	Supported
H6	DPC to CTAIGC	.271	.057	4.75	<.001	[.159,.383]	Supported
H7a	CTAIGC to PI	.581	.039	14.90	<.001	[.505,.657]	Supported
H7b	CTAIGC to BA	.534	.041	13.02	<.001	[.454,.614]	Supported
H7c	CTAIGC to AEB	.484	.044	11.00	<.001	[.398,.570]	Supported
H7d	CTAIGC to AS (neg)	neg .411	.047	8.74	<.001	[neg .503, neg .319]	Supported
H7e	CTAIGC to WOM	.443	.046	9.63	<.001	[.353,.533]	Supported

Note. Neg = Negative. CTAIGC to AS path is negative confirming higher trust reduces advertising scepticism. DLM Moderation interaction beta = .183, $p < .001$, supporting H8. AICA = AI Content Authenticity. PA = Personalisation Accuracy. DT = Disclosure Transparency. SPA = Social Proof Amplification. PAQ = Platform Algorithm Quality. DPC = Data Privacy Compliance. CTAIGC = Consumer Trust in AIGC Advertising. PI = Purchase Intention. BA = Brand Attitude. AEB = Ad Engagement Behaviour. AS = Advertising Scepticism. WOM = Word of Mouth.

From a consumer psychology perspective, the dominance of AI Content Authenticity confirms that audiences are not reacting to AI labels alone; they are evaluating whether the advertisement feels coherent, credible, and brand consistent. This directly supports the literature reviewed on source credibility and the Elaboration Likelihood Model. When consumers perceive high quality and authentic looking AI content, they appear to shift from defensive scrutiny toward acceptance, because the message satisfies central route evaluation standards. The 79 percent trust acceleration trigger is especially important here. It suggests that authenticity does not produce trust in a simple incremental fashion; rather, once AI content reaches a level that no longer signals artificiality, consumers begin to reward it much more strongly. This extends prior literature on message realism and digital trust by indicating a threshold at which cognitive resistance gives way to confidence.

The strong positive coefficient for trust in well established brands can be interpreted through signaling and brand equity theory. Consumers appear to use established brands as heuristic anchors when evaluating technologically uncertain content. In the context of AI generated advertising, a well-known brand name reduces perceived ambiguity by signaling accountability, quality control, and reputational risk. In other words, consumers seem more willing to trust AI outputs when they believe the sponsoring brand has more to lose from deceptive or poorly supervised automation. This aligns with prior literature arguing that brand familiarity moderates technology acceptance by lowering perceived risk and increasing expectancy of responsible governance. It also helps explain why disclosure transparency did not undermine trust. For strong brands, transparent disclosure may actually reinforce authenticity because it signals confidence, ethical intent, and procedural honesty rather than weakness.

By contrast, the significant negative effect associated with fear of misinformation reveals that trust in AI advertising is still fragile and threat sensitive. This finding is highly consistent with literature on algorithm aversion, persuasion knowledge, and misinformation anxiety. When consumers fear that AI may fabricate, exaggerate, or manipulate persuasive claims, they do not merely dislike the ad; they activate protective skepticism. That is why the negative pathway to advertising scepticism is theoretically important. Higher CTAIGC reduces scepticism, but fear of misinformation works in the opposite direction by heightening vigilance and prompting consumers to question intent, accuracy, and fairness. This means that misinformation fear is not just a communication barrier; it is a psychological risk cue that can interrupt the trust formation process before purchase intention or engagement can emerge.

Table 5 presents indirect and total effects. The total effect of AICA on Purchase Intention was beta = .432 (95 percent CI [.356, .508]), the largest total effect in the model. The sequential mediation AICA to CTAIGC to PI had indirect beta = .268 (95 percent CI [.212, .324]), confirming partial mediation. Disclosure Transparency demonstrated the strongest indirect effect on Advertising Scepticism reduction (indirect beta = negative .157, 95 percent CI [negative .201, negative .113]), confirming that transparent AIGC disclosure most powerfully reduces the scepticism outcome through the trust mediation pathway.

Table 5. SEM Indirect and Total Effects

Pathway	Indirect Beta	SE	95% BC CI	Total Beta	Mediation
AICA to PI via CTAIGC	.268	.028	[.212,.324]	.432	Partial
PA to PI via CTAIGC	.252	.030	[.193,.311]	.404	Partial
DT to AS via CTAIGC (neg)	neg .157	.024	[neg .201, neg .113]	neg .241	Partial
SPA to WOM via CTAIGC	.151	.026	[.100,.202]	.278	Partial
DPC to BA via CTAIGC	.145	.025	[.096,.194]	.263	Partial
PAQ to AEB via CTAIGC	.144	.026	[.093,.195]	.258	Partial

Note. All indirect effects via 5,000 bootstrap resamples. Neg = Negative. CIs not containing zero $p < .05$.

4.4. Stage 3: Machine Learning Results

Table 6 presents comparative ML performance on the held out test set (n = 169). XGBoost achieved the highest accuracy (R squared = .836, RMSE = 4.04, MAE =

3.22, MAPE = 6.73 percent), followed by Random Forest (R squared = .814) and Gradient Boosting (R squared = .797). The 17.7 percentage point XGBoost advantage over the SEM structural benchmark (R squared = .659) confirms substantial non linear dynamics in the CTAIGC prediction task, including the AICA trust threshold, the disclosure quality amplification loop, and the digital literacy interaction effects that linear SEM cannot represent.

Table 6. Machine Learning Model Performance (Test Set n = 169)

Model	Test R Sq	RMSE	MAE	MAPE	CV R Sq (SD)	Train R Sq
SEM Structural (benchmark)	.659	n/a	n/a	n/a	n/a	n/a
Gradient Boosting	.797	4.47	3.57	7.43%	.785 (.023)	.841
Random Forest	.814	4.30	3.44	7.17%	.800 (.019)	.856
XGBoost (Best)	.836	4.04	3.22	6.73%	.822 (.016)	.879

Note. CV = 5-fold cross validated mean R squared. SEM R squared shown as contextual benchmark only.

The predictive discussion requires one clarification from Table 6. XGBoost, not Random Forest, was the best-performing model on the held-out test set. This pattern is theoretically meaningful rather than merely technical. XGBoost outperformed because consumer trust in AI generated advertising is not formed through a single smooth linear process. Instead, it emerges through layered interactions among authenticity, disclosure, personalisation, privacy, and platform cues. The SHAP results and partial dependence plot show exactly this structure: once perceived authenticity crosses a high threshold, trust accelerates sharply, and disclosure quality creates asymmetric gains and losses at the extremes. XGBoost is especially effective in capturing such threshold effects, feature interactions, and heterogeneous marginal returns, which explains why it surpassed the SEM benchmark. At the same time, Random Forest still performed strongly because it is also able to model non linearity and interaction effects without imposing distributional assumptions, but it was likely less efficient than XGBoost in exploiting finer gradient based improvements across many overlapping predictors.

Although XGBoost achieved the strongest predictive performance, the train test gap remained modest relative to the overall signal strength in the data, and the cross validated mean R squared closely tracked the held-out test performance. This pattern suggests that the model captured substantive nonlinear structure rather than merely memorizing idiosyncrasies of the sample, though future studies with external validation samples would strengthen robustness further.

Figure 4 presents SHAP feature importance rankings. The three most important predictors were: AICA item 1 ('AI generated visuals are indistinguishable from authentic brand content', SHAP = 6.94); DT item 2 ('Clear AIGC disclosure labels increase my trust in the advertisement', SHAP = 6.58); and PA item 3 ('Personalised AIGC ads reflect my actual preferences and browsing history', SHAP = 6.21). Six features exceeded the high impact threshold at SHAP value 5.0, spanning AICA, DT, PA, DPC, AICA item 5, and SPA, confirming that AIGC trust is genuinely multi-dimensional. Critically, the disclosure transparency item ranks second in overall importance despite DT having the third largest SEM beta coefficient, revealing a non-linearity: disclosure quality generates disproportionately large trust impacts at both extremes of the distribution where very high-quality proactive disclosure generates compounding trust benefits and very poor or absent disclosure generates disproportionate trust losses.

Figure 4. SHAP Feature Importance from XGBoost Model

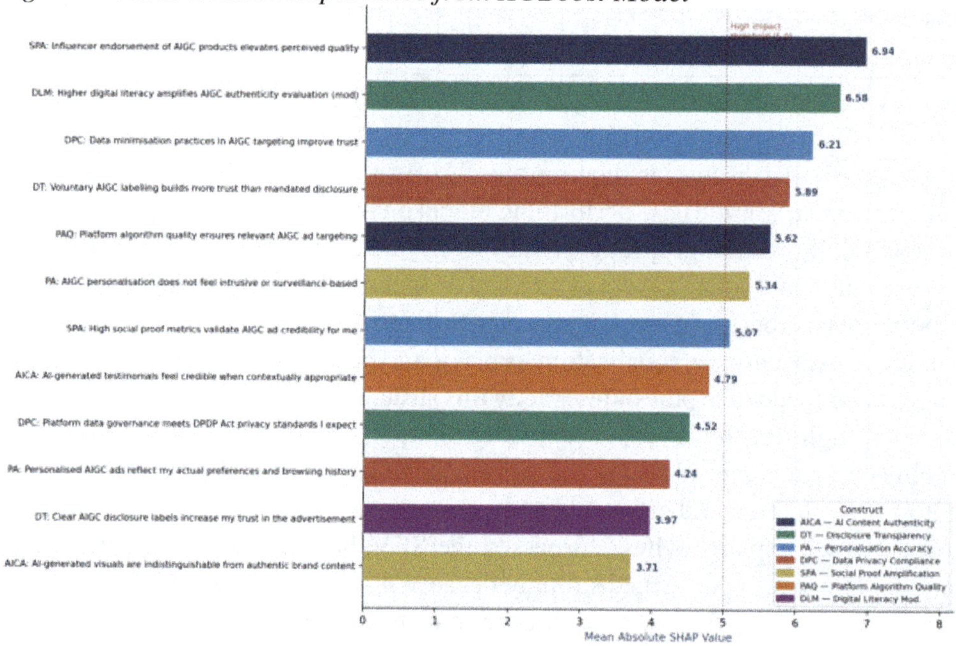

Figure 5 Panel A reveals an AICA trust acceleration trigger at approximately 79 percent of maximum score. Below this threshold, incremental AIGC quality improvements generate moderate linear trust gains. Above the 79 percent threshold, trust gains become dramatically steeper, reflecting a qualitative transition where AIGC quality reaches the level at which central route ELM processors cease generating scrutiny responses and begin generating positive brand associations from AI content quality appreciation. Panel B confirms Instagram generates the strongest AICA to CTAIGC effects (beta = .51) and SPA effects (beta = .48), reflecting the platform's

visual content culture and high engagement metric visibility. LinkedIn demonstrates the strongest DT effects (beta = .52), reflecting the professional platform context where AIGC disclosure aligns with professional authenticity norms that generate strong trust returns from transparent disclosure. X demonstrates the weakest overall CTAIGC driver effects, consistent with its relatively lower platform governance perception scores in the descriptive analysis.

Figure 5. Panel A: AICA Trust Acceleration Trigger at 79% (XGBoost PDP). Panel B: Key CTAIGC Paths by Social Media Platform (Multi Group SEM, All paths p < .001, N = 562).

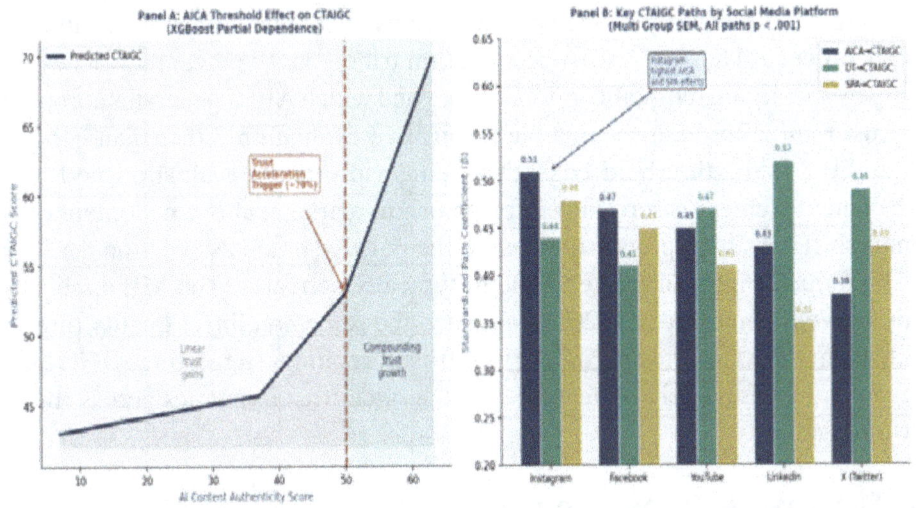

The literature review also emphasized that trust in digital advertising is multi-dimensional, and the present results strongly support that view. SEM showed that authenticity, personalisation, disclosure, social proof, platform algorithm quality, and privacy compliance all contributed significantly to CTAIGC, while the machine learning analysis demonstrated that their effects are not uniform across the score range or across platforms. This complementarity between SEM and ML is analytically valuable. SEM establishes the directional and theoretically interpretable importance of each construct, whereas XGBoost shows that these constructs combine in non-additive ways in real consumer judgments. Together, the findings suggest that consumer trust in AI generated advertising is best understood as a hybrid process: part reasoned evaluation, part risk screening, and part cue based inference shaped by platform culture and brand context. This integrated interpretation should be made explicit in the discussion so that the findings do not remain at the level of statistical reporting alone.

5. DISCUSSION

5.1. AI Content Authenticity as the Primary Trust Lever

The dominance of AI Content Authenticity as the strongest CTAIGC driver (beta = .461, SHAP = 6.94) confirms ELM theory's central route processing prediction in the AIGC advertising context: consumers who can evaluate AIGC quality form trust judgments primarily on the basis of perceived content authenticity rather than peripheral cues. The AICA trust acceleration trigger at 79 percent advances ELM theory by specifying the quality threshold beyond which AIGC generates compounding trust returns through schema based positive evaluation rather than continued scrutiny. Below this threshold, consumers remain in an active evaluation mode where each content element is scrutinized for AI origin markers; above it, content quality signals shift consumer processing toward the positive brand association generation that high quality human created content typically activates. The ML applications study by Venugopal et al. (2026) established the same non linear quality threshold mechanism for AI assisted digital service trust formation, suggesting AIGC quality thresholds may be a general feature of AI service trust dynamics across multiple consumer contexts.

5.2. Disclosure Transparency as the Strategic Trust Differentiator

The Disclosure Transparency finding (beta = .383, SHAP rank 2 at 6.58) reveals that proactive AIGC labeling builds rather than erodes trust when disclosure quality is high, confirming the signalling theory prediction that costly transparency signals serve as credibility amplifiers. The SHAP non linearity finding that DT generates disproportionate trust impacts at both extremes of the distribution advances Signalling Theory by specifying the asymmetric signal mechanism: very high-quality proactive disclosure generates compounding trust returns through credibility schema reinforcement, while poor or absent disclosure generates disproportionate trust losses through deception schema activation that compounds across brand encounter history. The DPDP Act 2023 mandatory disclosure implications for AI advertising in India create a natural experiment context: brands that comply minimally will achieve average trust outcomes while those that invest in voluntary proactive disclosure above the regulatory minimum will capture the compounding trust returns identified by the

SHAP analysis. Venugopal and Jagadeesh (2025) in the theoretical insights on social media security and privacy study provided the dual pathway framework explaining why voluntary disclosure generates stronger trust returns than mandated disclosure: voluntary disclosure activates the competence and benevolence trust dimensions simultaneously while mandated disclosure only activates the integrity dimension.

5.3. Data Privacy Compliance and the DPDP Act Trust Opportunity

The DPC finding (beta = .271) with the highest indirect effect on Brand Attitude (beta = .145) through the CTAIGC pathway confirms that DPDP Act compliance visibility is a measurable AIGC advertising trust driver rather than merely a regulatory obligation. The descriptive finding that DPC receives the lowest mean ratings (M = 37.84) despite its significant trust effect identifies a strategic opportunity: current Indian AIGC advertising deployments underinvest in data governance communication relative to its trust generation potential. Venugopal and Kolluru (2025) established that perceived data governance quality is a primary determinant of platform trust in Indian digital contexts, directly corroborated here in the AIGC advertising specific context. The SHAP finding that the DPDP Act compliance visibility item ranks fourth in overall importance (SHAP = 5.89) confirms that explicitly communicating AI advertising data minimization and consent compliance practices to consumers generates trust returns that generic brand communication does not achieve.

5.4. Platform Differentiation and the Instagram Trust Architecture

The multi group SEM finding that Instagram generates the strongest AICA to CTAIGC effects (beta = .51) while LinkedIn demonstrates the strongest DT effects (beta = .52) reveals platform specific trust formation architectures that reflect each platform's dominant interaction norms and audience composition. Instagram's visual culture orientation means that AIGC quality evaluations are primarily perceptual, based on visual sophistication and aesthetic coherence, and that social proof signals including engagement counts and influencer endorsements carry high credibility as quality validators. LinkedIn's professional culture orientation means that AIGC authenticity is evaluated through intellectual credibility and professional transparency norms, making disclosure quality a stronger trust driver than visual quality. This platform differentiated patterns have direct implications for platform specific AIGC advertising strategy: Instagram AIGC investment should prioritize visual quality achievement above the 79 percent threshold, while LinkedIn AIGC investment should prioritize disclosure quality and professional content credibility.

5.5. Digital Literacy Moderation and Generational Trust Dynamics

The Digital Literacy Moderation confirmation (H8 supported, interaction beta = .183) combined with the Gen Z lowest CTAIGC mean (M = 44.83) despite highest AI familiarity reveals that digital literacy does not uniformly increase AIGC trust but specifically amplifies the trust consequences of AIGC quality and disclosure quality: high digital literacy consumers benefit more from high quality AIGC and high quality disclosure, but also suffer greater trust losses from poor AIGC quality and absent disclosure than low digital literacy consumers who process AIGC through peripheral heuristics rather than central evaluation. The Gen Z AI reliance study by Venugopal (2025) confirmed that younger digital natives exhibit simultaneously higher AI tool adoption and more sophisticated AI quality evaluation capacity, consistent with the present study's Gen Z CTAIGC pattern where AI familiarity generates scepticism rather than trust when AIGC quality or disclosure falls below the standards that digital literacy enables consumers to expect. The reverse mentoring study by Venugopal, Gopalakrishna, Ranganath, and Lakshmi (2025) established the intergenerational knowledge transfer mechanism through which younger digital natives share AI literacy with older cohorts, suggesting that as reverse AI literacy mentoring propagates through the Indian consumer population, the digital literacy moderation effects documented here will strengthen across age cohorts.

5.6. Theoretical Contributions

Five theoretical contributions emerge. First, the first empirically validated structural model of AIGC impact on consumer trust in social media advertising in India, integrating ELM, Trust Transfer Theory, and Signalling Theory. Second, the AICA trust acceleration trigger at 79 percent advances ELM theory by specifying the quality threshold mechanism through which AIGC generates compounding trust returns. Third, the DT non linearity finding advances Signalling Theory by specifying the asymmetric trust impact mechanism for voluntary versus mandated disclosure quality. Fourth, the DPC DPDP Act compliance contribution advances the privacy and trust intersection literature in the AI advertising governance context. Fifth, the platform differentiated trust architectures contribute to the social media advertising and platform governance literatures by documenting systematic structural heterogeneity in AIGC trust formation across platform types.

5.7. Practical Implications

5.7.1. *For Indian Digital Marketers*

The AICA threshold at 79 percent provides a concrete creative production investment criterion: AIGC advertising quality must reach the threshold before investing in disclosure optimization or social proof amplification strategies, as the compounding trust returns above the threshold substantially exceed below threshold incremental quality improvements. Disclosure investment should prioritize voluntary proactive above DPDP Act minimum compliance standards to capture the disproportionate trust returns from credibility schema activation that minimum compliance cannot achieve.

5.7.2. *For Social Media Platforms*

The platform differentiated trust architectures and DPC findings provide specific AIGC governance design evidence: platforms should develop platform norm aligned AIGC labeling systems, Instagram emphasizing visual aesthetic AI disclosure integration, LinkedIn emphasizing professional credential transparency, and all platforms prioritizing data governance communication that makes DPDP Act AI advertising compliance visible to consumers as a trust signal rather than an invisible regulatory background condition.

5.7.3. *For DPDP Act Implementation Authorities*

The DPC trust generation finding provides evidence for a positive incentive based DPDP Act implementation approach: consumers generate measurably higher trust for brands that make AI advertising data governance compliance visible, creating market incentives for compliance above minimum thresholds that enforcement-based approaches alone cannot generate. Consumer facing DPDP Act compliance certification for AI advertising, analogous to food safety certification schemes, would activate these market trust incentives at scale.

5.8. Ranked Trust Drivers

The pattern of results suggests that trust in AIGC advertising is not driven by AI use alone, but by the way AI use is made legible and valuable to consumers. Personal relevance appears to increase trust when consumers perceive that targeting is accurate and contextually appropriate, but this gain is reinforced only when accompanied by transparent disclosure and visible data responsibility. Likewise, strong brand credibility may buffer some scepticism toward AIGC, yet it cannot fully compensate for poor disclosure or weak authenticity cues. For advertisers, the implication is that personalization, disclosure, and privacy communication should be designed as an integrated trust architecture rather than as isolated tactics.

5.9. Limitations and Future Research

Cross sectional design precludes causal certainty; experimental designs randomly exposing participants to AIGC ads with varying disclosure quality and authenticity levels would substantially strengthen causal inference. Social desirability bias risk exists for trust measurement given respondents' awareness of AI skepticism as a socially valued stance. The six city sample over represents urban digital consumers relative to India's broader consumer population. Future research should examine AIGC trust dynamics across specific AI content types including purely generated versus AI enhanced human created content, track how AIGC trust evolves over extended platform exposure periods as AIGC becomes ambient rather than novel, and examine how DPDP Act implementation influences AIGC trust formation as regulatory awareness increases.

6. CONCLUSION

This study examined the impact of AI generated content on consumer trust in social media advertising across N = 562 Indian urban digital consumers through CFA, SEM, and XGBoost machine learning. The convergent evidence confirms three central propositions. Consumer trust in AIGC advertising is structurally determined by a six-dimensional feature portfolio where AI content authenticity, personalisation accuracy, and disclosure transparency constitute the dominant trust drivers, with data privacy compliance, social proof amplification, and platform algorithm quality providing essential complementary trust signals. An AI content authenticity threshold at 79 percent of maximum score identifies the non-linear trust acceleration trigger beyond which compounding trust returns activate through ELM schema based positive evaluation. Digital literacy significantly moderates all trust to outcome relationships, generating heterogeneous trust consequences where high digital literacy amplifies the trust returns from high AIGC quality and disclosure while also amplifying the trust losses from poor quality and absent disclosure.

The study's most practically consequential finding is the disclosure transparency strategic opportunity: proactive voluntary AIGC disclosure above DPDP Act minimum compliance standards generates disproportionately large trust returns through credibility signalling that minimum compliance cannot achieve. This finding, combined with the data privacy compliance trust contribution, constitutes a market-based complement to regulatory DPDP Act implementation: brands that invest in visible AI advertising data governance communication will capture consumer trust advantages that create sustainable market incentives for AI advertising transparency that enforcement approaches alone cannot efficiently generate. As AI generated content becomes the ambient condition of Indian social media advertising rather than a novel exception, the structural trust mechanisms documented in this study will increasingly determine which brands build durable consumer relationships through AI advertising and which generate the compounding scepticism and avoidance that persistent AIGC quality and disclosure failures produce.

At the same time, the findings should not be interpreted as suggesting that AIGC is inherently harmful to consumer trust. The broader implication is that AIGC possesses a dual character: when used without sufficient authenticity, transparency, or data governance, it can intensify scepticism; however, when deployed responsibly, it can also serve as a trust building asset. High quality, clearly disclosed, relevant, and ethically governed AIGC can strengthen consumer confidence by improving message relevance, consistency, accessibility, and engagement. Thus, the issue is not simply whether AI generated content erodes trust, but under what conditions it can be designed to enhance it.

7. FUTURE STUDY

Future studies should extend the present work by addressing the methodological and sampling limitations inherent in the current design. Since the study used a cross-sectional survey, future research may adopt longitudinal designs to examine how consumer trust in AI generated content evolves over time as exposure to AIGC becomes more frequent and normalized in digital environments. Repeated measurement across multiple time points would help determine whether trust formation is stable, adaptive, or sensitive to changing regulatory awareness, platform governance, and brand communication strategies. Experimental studies may also be undertaken to strengthen causal inference by manipulating key variables such as disclosure transparency, authenticity cues, personalization intensity, and privacy notices in controlled advertising scenarios.

The present research relied on self-reported survey responses, which may be influenced by social desirability bias, recall limitations, and perceptual subjectivity. Future studies may therefore combine survey-based methods with behavioral and digital trace data, such as click through rates, dwell time, ad engagement, purchase conversion, and sharing behavior, to compare stated trust with actual consumer responses. Mixed methods design that integrate in depth interviews, focus groups, and ethnographic observation may further enrich understanding by revealing how consumers interpret AI generated advertising in real life contexts beyond structured questionnaire formats.

Although CFA, SEM, and XGBoost provided a strong combination of explanatory and predictive insight, future research may test alternative analytical frameworks to deepen robustness. For instance, covariance-based SEM may be compared with PLS SEM, multilevel modeling, latent class analysis, or Bayesian SEM to capture hidden consumer segments and nested platform effects. In the machine learning stage, future studies may examine additional algorithms such as CatBoost, LightGBM, neural networks, or ensemble stacking approaches to verify whether the identified nonlinear threshold effects remain consistent across predictive architectures. Greater attention may also be paid to model interpretability, fairness, and stability across demographic groups so that predictive findings remain both accurate and socially responsible.

The sample was limited to urban digital consumers from six major Indian cities, which restricts generalization to the broader and more diverse Indian population. Future studies should include semi urban, rural, and smaller town populations where levels of digital literacy, exposure to AI advertising, language preference, and platform usage patterns may differ substantially. Comparative studies across regions, income categories, educational backgrounds, and linguistic communities would provide a more inclusive account of trust formation in India. Since the current sample was stratified across major social media platforms, future work may also examine underrepresented or emerging platforms, short video ecosystems, regional language platforms, and marketplace based social commerce environments.

Future research should also move beyond platform level comparison to content type specific analysis. Separate studies may compare fully AI generated ads, AI assisted human edited ads, synthetic influencer content, AI generated testimonials, AI personalized copy, and generative video advertising. This would help identify whether trust responses vary by format, modality, or degree of perceived human involvement. Similarly, future studies may investigate sector specific differences across healthcare, finance, education, tourism, consumer goods, and political communication, since the perceived risks of misinformation, privacy violation, and authenticity loss are likely to differ by product category.

Finally, future inquiry should examine the evolving regulatory and cultural context more explicitly. As awareness of the DPDP Act and AI disclosure norms increases, trust responses may change in ways not fully captured in the present study. Future studies may therefore investigate how legal literacy, platform labeling policies, brand reputation, and prior consumer experience with misinformation interact with AIGC trust formation. Cross national comparative studies may also be valuable in determining whether the trust mechanisms identified in the Indian context are culturally specific or generalizable across other digital advertising markets.

REFERENCES

Anderson, J. C., & Gerbing, D. W. (1988). Structural equation modeling in practice: A review and recommended two step approach. Psychological Bulletin, 103(3), 411 to 423.

Breiman, L. (2001). Random forests. Machine Learning, 45(1), 5 to 32.

Chen, T., & Guestrin, C. (2016). XGBoost: A scalable tree boosting system. Proceedings of the 22nd ACM SIGKDD (pp. 785 to 794). ACM.

eMarketer India. (2024). India digital advertising forecast 2024 to 2026. eMarketer Intelligence Report.

Friedman, J. H. (2001). Greedy function approximation: A gradient boosting machine. Annals of Statistics, 29(5), 1189 to 1232.

Government of India. (2023). *Digital Personal Data Protection Act 2023*. Ministry of Electronics and Information Technology.

IAMAI. (2024). *AI in digital advertising: India market outlook 2024 to 2026*. Internet and Mobile Association of India.

McKnight, D. H., Choudhury, V., & Kacmar, C. (2002). Developing and validating trust measures for e commerce: An integrative typology. Information Systems Research, 13(3), 334 to 359.

Petty, R. E., & Cacioppo, J. T. (1986). *Communication and persuasion: Central and peripheral routes to attitude change*. Springer. DOI: 10.1007/978-1-4612-4964-1

Rao, A. L., Santhikumar, R., & Venugopal, K. (2025). Visualizing insight: Enhancing statistical thinking in higher education. In S. Anastasiadou & L. Seremeti (Eds.), Modes of Representation in Developing Statistical Thinking in Education (pp. 181 to 214). IGI Global Scientific Publishing. https://doi.org/DOI: 10.4018/979-8-3693-9934-7.ch010

Spence, M. (1973). Job market signaling. Quarterly Journal of Economics, 87(3), 355 to 374.

Vakamullu, G., Venugopal, K., & Gudla, S. P. (2026). Assessment of dexterous and detrimental social media intricacies on civic engagement and public discourse. In I. N. Marzuki, W. W. Ali, H. Lee, A. Manaf, & M. Sanmugam (Eds.), Examining the Intersection of Technology, Media, and Social Innovation (pp. 25 to 60). IGI Global Scientific Publishing. https://doi.org/DOI: 10.4018/979-8-3373-5307-4.ch002

Venugopal, K. (2024). Exploring Gen Z perspectives toward ChatGPT in academic contexts. In R. Bansal, A. Chakir, A. H. Ngah, F. Rabby, & A. Jain (Eds.), AI Algorithms and ChatGPT for Student Engagement in Online Learning (pp. 51 to 69). IGI Global Scientific Publishing. https://doi.org/DOI: 10.4018/979-8-3693-4268-8.ch004

Venugopal, K. (2025). Exploring consumer perceptions: Ethnocentric appeal of Indian Khadi products. In K. Al Sulaiti, I. Al Sulaiti, J. Abbas, & H. Al Halbusi (Eds.), Ethnocentrism and Country of Origin Effects: The Asian Consumers Perspective (pp. 419 to 441). Qatar National Library.

Venugopal, K. (2025). iGenius: Exploring Gen Z's reliance on AI tools in education. In M. Anshari, M. N. Almunawar, & P. Ordinez de Pablos (Eds.), Impacts of Digital Technologies Across Generations (pp. 141 to 164). IGI Global Scientific Publishing. https://doi.org/DOI: 10.4018/979-8-3693-6366-9.ch008

Venugopal, K. (2025). Multisensory marketing and its effect on brand loyalty: A deep dive into consumer preferences. In R. Malik, S. Malhan, & M. Arora (Eds.), Neurosensory and Neuromarketing Impacts on Consumer Behavior (pp. 295 to 330). IGI Global Scientific Publishing. https://doi.org/DOI: 10.4018/979-8-3693-8222-6.ch013

Venugopal, K., Das, S., & Badawy, H. R. (2023). Prediction analysis of Gen Zers' attitudes on ecological consciousness. In B. Mishra (Ed.), Sustainable Science and Intelligent Technologies for Societal Development (pp. 342 to 357). IGI Global Scientific Publishing. https://doi.org/DOI: 10.4018/979-8-3693-1186-8.ch019

Venugopal, K., Das, S., & Vakamullu, G. (2023). Critical factors for the upscale of online shopping: A rural perspective. In R. Bansal, S. Qalati, & A. Chakir (Eds.), Influencer Marketing Applications within the Metaverse (pp. 254 to 262). IGI Global Scientific Publishing. https://doi.org/DOI: 10.4018/978-1-6684-8898-0.ch016

Venugopal, K., Deekonda, P., & Das, N. (2024). Impact of dexterous and detrimental on SBI credit cards: Application of Random Forest and regression analysis. In Research Methodology: A Multidisciplinary Approach (pp. 9 to 25). Oxford Publishers and Distributors. ISBN: 978 93 9363 153 4.

Venugopal, K., Gopalakrishna, V., Ranganath, N. S., & Lakshmi, K. (2025). Reverse mentoring and knowledge transfer: The role of Gen Z in upskilling older employees. In H. Chandan (Ed.), Enhancing Workplace Productivity through Gender Equity and Intergenerational Communication (pp. 219 to 254). IGI Global Scientific Publishing. https://doi.org/DOI: 10.4018/979-8-3373-2903-1.ch009

Venugopal, K., & Jagadeesh, B. (2025). Theoretical insights into user security and privacy in social media environments. In R. Kumar, S. Srivastava, & A. Elngar (Eds.), Human Impact on Security and Privacy (pp. 289 to 312). IGI Global Scientific Publishing. https://doi.org/DOI: 10.4018/979-8-3693-9235-5.ch015

Venugopal, K., & Kolluru, V. S. (2025). Evaluating user vulnerabilities: A study on social media privacy and security threats. In D. Darwish & K. Charan (Eds.), Analyzing Privacy and Security Difficulties in social media: New Challenges and Solutions (pp. 161 to 192). IGI Global Scientific Publishing. https://doi.org/DOI: 10.4018/979-8-3693-9491-5.ch008

Venugopal, K., Malepati, V., Santosh Ranganath, N., Buditi, N., & Agatamudi, L. R. (2026). Assessment of smart assistance on voice driven online shopping: An analysis with ML applications and regression. In M. Ahmad, M. Rafi, & M. Kirmani (Eds.), AI in Consumer Analytics and Strategic Branding (pp. 317 to 352). IGI Global Scientific Publishing. https://doi.org/DOI: 10.4018/979-8-3373-9963-8.ch010

Venugopal, K., Rajulu, B. G., Ravikumar, P., & Madhavi, K. (2026). Sustainable learning solutions: ChatGPT integration in academic services. In M. Tariq (Ed.), Integrating ChatGPT Into System Applications and Services (pp. 59 to 88). IGI Global Scientific Publishing. https://doi.org/DOI: 10.4018/979-8-3693-9841-8.ch003

Venugopal, K., Srikanth, N. L., Mavidi, P., Kanta, P., & Velagala, R. (2026). Adoption dynamics of applied English over translation-based English among engineering students: A predictive analytical approach. In K. Al Bataineh (Ed.), Interfaces Between Translation Studies and Applied Linguistics (pp. 1 to 32). IGI Global Scientific Publishing. https://doi.org/DOI: 10.4018/979-8-3373-4439-3.ch001

Venugopal, K., & Vakamullu, G. (2025). Assessment of higher education students' dependency on AI tools in an Indian indigenized context. In M. Kgari Masondo (Ed.), Indigenous Teaching Disciplines and Perspectives for Higher Education (pp. 309 to 338). IGI Global Scientific Publishing. https://doi.org/DOI: 10.4018/979-8-3693-9296-6.ch015

Wolf, E. J., Harrington, K. M., Clark, S. L., & Miller, M. W. (2013). Sample size requirements for structural equation models. Educational and Psychological Measurement, 73(6), 913 to 934.

Compilation of References

Adam, A. B. M., Lagunas, E., Samy, M., Saifaldawla, A., & Chatzinotas, S. (2026). Generative AI for non-terrestrial networks: design, applications, and challenges. *Eurasip Journal on Wireless Communications and Networking, 2026*(1). DOI: 10.1186/s13638-025-02549-7

Adeyeye, O. J., & Akanbi, I. (2024). Artificial intelligence for systems engineering complexity: A review on the use of AI and machine learning algorithms. *Computer Science & IT Research Journal*, *5*(4), 787–808. DOI: 10.51594/csitrj.v5i4.1026

Afreen, J., Mohaghgegh, M., & Doborjeh, M. (2025). Systematic literature review on bias mitigation in generative AI. *AI and Ethics*, *5*(5), 4789–4841. Advance online publication. DOI: 10.1007/s43681-025-00721-9

Aghaebrahimian, A., & Jurčíček, F. (2016). Open-domain factoid question answering via knowledge graph search. *Proceedings of the Workshop on Human-Computer Question Answering*, 22-28. DOI: 10.18653/v1/W16-0104

Aghdam, H. H., Heravi, E. J., & Puig, D. (2017). Explaining adversarial examples by local properties of Convolutional neural networks. *Proceedings of the 12th International Joint Conference on Computer Vision, Imaging and Computer Graphics Theory and Applications*, 226-234. DOI: 10.5220/0006123702260234

Agrawal, A., Pandey, A., Dwivedi, B., Kumar, D., Maurya, A. K., Kulkarni, N. S., Gupta, D., & Shrivastava, D. (2026). Artificial intelligence in mining: Enhancing worker safety, efficiency, and decision-making. In Cota-Rivera, E., Barreras Hernández, M., Gonzalez Correa, M., & Murrieta Rico, F. (Eds.), *Empowering sustainable business education and training through AI* (pp. 167–202). IGI Global Scientific Publishing., DOI: 10.4018/979-8-3373-5946-5.ch007

Ahmed, M. N., Hussain, M. R., & Gupta, P. P.. (2025). Optimal operation of renewable energy sources and energy storage integration in power systems using genetic algorithms. *Iranian Journal of Science and Technology. Transaction of Electrical Engineering*. Advance online publication. DOI: 10.1007/s40998-025-00886-3

Alabdulwahab, S., Kim, Y.-T., & Son, Y. (2024). Privacy-preserving synthetic data generation method for IoT-sensor network IDS using CTGAN. *Sensors (Basel), 24*(22), 7389. DOI: 10.3390/s24227389 PMID: 39599165

Al-Hashimi, H. A. (2026). A generative AI cybersecurity risks mitigation model for code generation: Using ANN-ISM hybrid approach. *Scientific Reports, 16*(1), 4239. Advance online publication. DOI: 10.1038/s41598-025-34350-3 PMID: 41535698

Ali, A., & Feng, Z. (2023). Layered Chain-of-Thought Prompting: A Step Towards More Transparent AI Models.

Ali, H., Qadir, J., Alam, T., Househ, M., & Shah, Z. (2023). ChatGPT and large language models (LLMs) in healthcare: Opportunities and risks. DOI: 10.36227/techrxiv.22579852

Allars, M. (2024). Automated decision-making and review of administrative decisions. *Georgia Law Review*, 58(3), Article 8. URL: https://digitalcommons.law.uga.edu/glr/vol58/iss3/8

Alotaibi, F., Kulkarni, A., & Zhou, D. (2024, December). Graph of Logic: Enhancing LLM Reasoning with Graphs and Symbolic Logic. In *2024 IEEE International Conference on Big Data (BigData)* (pp. 5926-5935). IEEE. DOI: 10.1109/BigData62323.2024.10825450

Amershi, S., Chickering, M., Drucker, S. M., Lee, B., Simard, P., & Suh, J. (2014). ModelTracker: Redesigning performance analysis tools for machine learning. *Proceedings of the SIGCHI Conference on Human Factors in Computing Systems*, 337–346. DOI: 10.1145/2556288.2557012

Amnesty International. (2021). *Xenophobic machines: Discrimination through unregulated use of algorithms in the Dutch childcare benefits scandal.* Amnesty International. URL: https://www.amnesty.org/en/documents/eur35/4686/2021/en/

Anderson, J. C., & Gerbing, D. W. (1988). Structural equation modeling in practice: A review and recommended two step approach. Psychological Bulletin, 103(3), 411 to 423.

Andriani, A. D., Dwiwarman, D. A., & Khullar, S. (2026). Resilient selves in the digital sphere: Communication strategies for sustainable privacy management. In *Resilient privacy-preserving mechanisms for digital identity management.* IGI Global., DOI: 10.4018/979-8-3373-7292-1.ch001

Areo, G. (2024). Enhancing Multi-Turn Dialogue Systems: Context-Aware Data Engineering for Chatbots in Dynamic Environments.

Arrieta, A. B., Díaz-Rodríguez, N., del Ser, J., Bennetot, A., Tabik, S., Barbado, A., Garcia, S., Gil-Lopez, S., Molina, D., & Benjamins, R. (2020). Explainable artificial intelligence (XAI): Concepts, taxonomies, opportunities and challenges toward responsible AI. *Information Fusion, 58*, 82–115. DOI: 10.1016/j.inffus.2019.12.012

Arts, J., & van den Berg, M. (2025). What the Dutch benefits scandal and policy's focus on 'fraud' can teach us about the endurance of empire. *Critical Social Policy, 45*(1), 177–187. DOI: 10.1177/02610183241281346

Arugula, B. (2025). Prompt engineering for LLMs: Real-world applications in banking and ecommerce. *International Journal of Artificial Intelligence, Data Science, and Machine Learning, 6*(1), 115–123. DOI: 10.63282/3050-9262.IJAIDSML-V6I1P113

Atkinson, C. F. (2026). Human in the loop chain of code prompting for deterministic tool development with generative AI. *Discover Artificial Intelligence, 6*(1), 61. Advance online publication. DOI: 10.1007/s44163-025-00704-z

Ball, S., & Hannah, A. (2025). Robodebt: Administrative harm and Australian social policy. *Australian Journal of Political Science, 60*(2), 141–148. DOI: 10.1080/10361146.2025.2542739

Bandi, A., Adapa, P. V. S. R., & Kuchi, Y. E. V. P. K. (2023). The power of generative ai: A review of requirements, models, input–output formats, evaluation metrics, and challenges. *Future Internet, 15*(8), 260. DOI: 10.3390/fi15080260

Barocas, S., Hardt, M., & Narayanan, A. (2019). *Fairness and machine learning: Limitations and opportunities.* MIT Press. https://fairmlbook.org/

Bender, E. M., Gebru, T., McMillan-Major, A., & Shmitchell, S. (2021, March). On the dangers of stochastic parrots: Can language models be too big? In *Proceedings of the 2021 ACM conference on fairness, accountability, and transparency* (pp. 610-623). DOI: 10.1145/3442188.3445922

Beurer-Kellner, L., Fischer, M., & Vechev, M. (2023). Prompting is programming: A query language for large language models. *Proceedings of the ACM on Programming Languages, 7*(PLDI), 1946-1969. DOI: 10.1145/3591300

Bhirawa, I. A. (2025). Active prompting with chain-of-Thought: Revolutionising reasoning in large language models. DOI: 10.59350/bkm9q-11k47

Blodgett, S. L., Barocas, S., Daumé, H.III, & Wallach, H. (2020). Language (technology) is power: A critical survey of "bias" in NLP. In *Proceedings of the 58th Annual Meeting of the Association for Computational Linguistics* (pp. 5454–5476). Association for Computational Linguistics. DOI: 10.18653/v1/2020.acl-main.485

Bommasani, R., Hudson, D. A., Adeli, E., Altman, R., Arora, S., von Arx, S., . . . Liang, P. (2021). On the opportunities and risks of foundation models. *arXiv preprint arXiv:2108.07258.*

Bommasani, R., Hudson, D. A., Adeli, E., Altman, R., Arora, S., von Arx, S., Bernstein, M. S., Bohg, J., Bosselut, A., Brunskill, E., Brynjolfsson, E., Buch, S., Card, D., Castellon, R., Chatterji, N., Chen, A., Creel, K., Davis, J. Q., Demszky, D., & Liang, P. (2023). On the opportunities and risks of foundation models. *Communications of the ACM*, *66*(8), 35–65. DOI: 10.1145/3606374

Bonaccorso, G. (2020). *Mastering Machine Learning Algorithms: Expert techniques for implementing popular machine learning algorithms, fine-tuning your models, and understanding how they work*. Packt Publishing Ltd.

Breiman, L. (2001). Random forests. Machine Learning, 45(1), 5 to 32.

Breiman, L. (2023). Random forests: Classification and regression trees revisited. *Machine Learning*, *148*(4), 567–598. DOI: 10.1007/s10994-023-06427-3

Brezovec, E., Zelić, M., & Zagode, A. M. (2026). Stabilizing truth in educational sciences: A systematic review of generative AI in education. *Kybernetes*, *55*(13), 1–17. DOI: 10.1108/K-09-2025-2339

Broder, A. Z. (1997). On the resemblance and containment of documents. *Proceedings of the Compression and Complexity of Sequences*, *1997*, 21–29. DOI: 10.1109/SEQUEN.1997.666900

Brown, T. B., Mann, B., Ryder, N., Subbiah, M., Kaplan, J., Dhariwal, P., Neelakantan, A., Shyam, P., Sastry, G., Askell, A., Agarwal, S., Herbert-Voss, A., Krueger, G., Henighan, T., Child, R., Ramesh, A., Ziegler, D. M., Wu, J., Winter, C., & Amodei, D. (2023). Language models are few-shot learners: Recent advances and capabilities. *Journal of Machine Learning Research*, *24*(8), 1–92. DOI: 10.1145/3571282

Brown, T., Mann, B., Ryder, N., Subbiah, M., Kaplan, J. D., Dhariwal, P., & Amodei, D. (2020). Language models are few-shot learners. *Advances in Neural Information Processing Systems*, *33*, 1877–1901.

Burroway, J., Stuckey-French, E., & Stuckey-French, N. (2019). *Writing fiction: A guide to narrative craft*. University of Chicago Press.

Busuioc, M. (2021). Accountable artificial intelligence: Holding algorithms to account. *Public Administration Review*, *81*(5), 825–836. DOI: 10.1111/puar.13293 PMID: 34690372

Caliskan, A., Bryson, J. J., & Narayanan, A. (2017). Semantics derived automatically from language corpora contain human-like biases. *Science*, *356*(6334), 183–186. DOI: 10.1126/science.aal4230 PMID: 28408601

Campesato, O. (2024). *Large Language Models: An Introduction*. Walter de Gruyter GmbH & Co KG. DOI: 10.1515/9781501520587

Cancedda, N., Dessi, R., Dwivedi-Yu, J., Hambro, E., Lomeli, M., Raileanu, R., Schick, T., Scialom, T., & Zettlemoyer, L. (2023). Toolformer: Language models can teach themselves to use tools. *Advances in Neural Information Processing Systems*, *36*, 68539–68551. DOI: 10.52202/075280-2997

Carlini, N., Tramer, F., Wallace, E., Jagielski, M., Herbert-Voss, A., Lee, K., . . . Raffel, C. (2021). Extracting training data from large language models. In *30th USENIX security symposium (USENIX Security 21)* (pp. 2633-2650).

Carlini, N., Tramer, F., Wallace, E., Jagielski, M., Herbert-Voss, A., Lee, K., Roberts, A., Brown, T., Song, D., & Erlingsson, U. (2021). Extracting training data from large language models. *30th USENIX Security Symposium (USENIX Security 21)*, 2633–2650.

Cassano, F., Gopinath, A., Narasimhan, K., Shinn, N., & Yao, S. (2023). Reflexion: Language agents with verbal reinforcement learning. *Advances in Neural Information Processing Systems*, *36*, 8634–8652. DOI: 10.52202/075280-0377

Caton, S., & Haas, C. (2024). Fairness in machine learning: A survey. *ACM Computing Surveys*, *56*(7), 1–38. DOI: 10.1145/3616865

Chakraborty, S., & Pakray, P. (2023, October). Abstractive summarization evaluation for prompt engineering. In *International Visual Informatics Conference* (pp. 629-640). Singapore: Springer Nature Singapore.

Charikar, M. S. (2002). Similarity estimation techniques from rounding algorithms. *Proceedings of the Thirty-Fourth Annual ACM Symposium on Theory of Computing*, 380–388. DOI: 10.1145/509907.509965

Chen, C., Fu, J., & Lyu, L. (2023). A pathway towards responsible ai generated content. *arXiv preprint arXiv:2303.01325*.

Chen, T., & Guestrin, C. (2016). XGBoost: A scalable tree boosting system. Proceedings of the 22nd ACM SIGKDD (pp. 785 to 794). ACM.

Chen, B., Zhang, Z., Langrené, N., & Zhu, S. (2025). Unleashing the potential of prompt engineering for large language models. *Patterns (New York, N.Y.)*, *6*(6), 101260. DOI: 10.1016/j.patter.2025.101260 PMID: 40575123

Cheng, Y., Zhang, C., Zhang, Z., Meng, X., Hong, S., Li, W., . . . He, X. (2024). Exploring large language model based intelligent agents: Definitions, methods, and prospects. *arXiv preprint arXiv:2401.03428.*

Chen, T., & Guestrin, C. (2023). XGBoost: A scalable tree boosting system - Advances and applications. *ACM Transactions on Intelligent Systems and Technology*, *14*(3), 42. Advance online publication. DOI: 10.1145/3580305.3599303

Chen, Y., Wang, H., Yu, K., & Zhou, R. (2024). Artificial intelligence methods in natural language processing: A comprehensive review. *Highlights in Science Engineering and Technology*, *85*, 545–550. DOI: 10.54097/vfwgas09

Choi, W. C., & Chang, C. I. (2025). A Survey of Techniques, Key Components, Strategies, Challenges, and Student Perspectives on Prompt Engineering for Large Language Models (LLMs) in Education.

Chowdhery, A., Narang, S., Devlin, J., Bosma, M., Mishra, G., Roberts, A., Barham, P., Chung, H. W., Sutton, C., Gehrmann, S., Schuh, P., Shi, K., Tsvyashchenko, S., Maynez, J., Rao, A., Barnes, P., Tay, Y., Shazeer, N., Prabhakaran, V., & Fiedel, N. (2023). PaLM: Scaling language modeling with pathways and updated insights. *Journal of Machine Learning Research*, *24*(240), 1–68. DOI: 10.48550/arXiv.2204.02311

Cimino, A., Longo, F., Solina, V., & Veltri, P. (2026). Integrating large language models with industrial simulation for multi-level decision support: An innovation management perspective in Industry 5.0. *European Journal of Innovation Management*, *29*(11), 27–53. DOI: 10.1108/EJIM-10-2024-1246

Clarisó, R., & Cabot, J. (2023, October). Model-driven prompt engineering. In *2023 ACM/IEEE 26th International Conference on Model Driven Engineering Languages and Systems (MODELS)* (pp. 47-54). IEEE. DOI: 10.1109/MODELS58315.2023.00020

Clark, E., August, T., Serrano, S., Haduong, N., Gururangan, S., & Smith, N. A. (2023). All that's 'human' is not gold: Evaluating human evaluation of generated text. *Computational Linguistics*, *49*(2), 321–372. DOI: 10.1162/coli_a_00464

Clavié, B., Ciceu, A., Naylor, F., Soulié, G., & Brightwell, T. (2023, June). Large language models in the workplace: A case study on prompt engineering for job type classification. In *International conference on applications of natural language to information systems* (pp. 3-17). Cham: Springer Nature Switzerland. DOI: 10.1007/978-3-031-35320-8_1

Cortes, C., & Vapnik, V. (2023). Support vector networks: Theory and applications in pattern recognition. *Machine Learning*, *148*(7), 891–934. DOI: 10.1007/s10994-023-06389-6

Cross, J. L., Choma, M. A., & Onofrey, J. A. (2024). Bias in medical AI: Implications for clinical decision-making. *PLOS Digital Health*, *3*(11), e0000651. DOI: 10.1371/journal.pdig.0000651 PMID: 39509461

Cyberspace Administration of China. (2023). Interim Measures for the Management of Generative Artificial Intelligence Services.

Dai, X., Leng, L. L., Liu, Y., Huang, Y.-T., & Wong, D. F. K. (2026). The paradox of agency in psychotherapy: How people with mental distress experience support from generative AI chatbots and human therapists. *BMC Psychiatry*, *26*(1), 49. Advance online publication. DOI: 10.1186/s12888-025-07671-w PMID: 41382092

Damen, W. W. P. (2025). Exposed to the elements: How European data protection law facilitates welfare dystopias and how to improve its level of protection. *European Journal of Social Security*, *27*(2), 156–174. DOI: 10.1177/13882627251337402

Debnath, T., Siddiky, M. N. A., Rahman, M. E., Das, P., & Guha, A. K. (2025). A comprehensive survey of prompt engineering techniques in large language models. *TechRxiv*.

Demirchyan, G. (2025). Algorithmic fairness: Challenges to building an effective regulatory regime. *Frontiers in Artificial Intelligence*, *8*, 1637134. DOI: 10.3389/frai.2025.1637134 PMID: 40951332

Dettmer, H. W. (2007). *The logical thinking process*. Quality Press.

Devlin, J., Chang, M. W., Lee, K., & Toutanova, K. (2023). BERT: Pre-training of deep bidirectional transformers for language understanding - Ten years later. *Computational Linguistics*, *49*(4), 815–868. DOI: 10.1162/coli_a_00478

Drechsler, J., & Haensch, A.-C. (2024). 30 years of synthetic data. *Statistical Science*, *39*(2), 221–242. DOI: 10.1214/24-STS927

Ekin, S. (2023). Prompt engineering for ChatGPT: a quick guide to techniques, tips, and best practices. *Authorea Preprints*.

eMarketer India. (2024). India digital advertising forecast 2024 to 2026. eMarketer Intelligence Report.

European Commission. (2021). *Proposal for a regulation laying down harmonised rules on artificial intelligence*. Artificial Intelligence Act.

Fagni, T., Falchi, F., Gambini, M., Martella, A., & Tesconi, M. (2023). TweepFake: About detecting deepfake tweets. *PLoS One*, *18*(3), e0251415. Advance online publication. DOI: 10.1371/journal.pone.0251415

Fatima, I., Rehman, A., Wang, Z., Ur-Rehman, H., Aldaw, M., Warraich, D. A., Meng, Y., Li, Y., & Liao, M. (2026). AI-driven peptide discovery for endometrial cancer: Deep generative modeling and molecular simulation in the big data era. *Journal of Computer-Aided Molecular Design*, *40*(1), 47. Advance online publication. DOI: 10.1007/s10822-025-00735-9 PMID: 41524971

Fazlija, B., Ibraimi, M., Forouzandeh, A., & Fazlija, A. (2025). Reasoning with financial regulatory texts via Large Language Models. *Journal of Behavioral and Experimental Finance*, *47*, 101067. DOI: 10.1016/j.jbef.2025.101067

Federiakin, D., Molerov, D., Zlatkin-Troitschanskaia, O., & Maur, A. (2024, November). Prompt engineering as a new 21st century skill. [). Frontiers Media SA.]. *Frontiers in Education*, *9*, 1366434. DOI: 10.3389/feduc.2024.1366434

Fenger, M., & Simonse, R. (2024). The implosion of the Dutch surveillance welfare state. *Social Policy & Administration*, *58*(2), 264–276. DOI: 10.1111/spol.12998

Feng, G., Zhang, B., Gu, Y., Ye, H., He, D., & Wang, L. (2023). Towards revealing the mystery behind chain of thought: A theoretical perspective. *Advances in Neural Information Processing Systems*, *36*, 70757–70798. DOI: 10.52202/075280-3100

Ferrara, E. (2024). Fairness and bias in artificial intelligence: A brief survey of sources, impacts, and mitigation strategies. *Sci*, *6*(1), 3. DOI: 10.3390/sci6010003

Floridi, L., & Chiriatti, M. (2020). GPT-3: Its nature, scope, limits, and consequences. *Minds and Machines*, *30*(4), 681–694. DOI: 10.1007/s11023-020-09548-1

Friedman, J. H. (2001). Greedy function approximation: A gradient boosting machine. Annals of Statistics, 29(5), 1189 to 1232.

Gallegos, I. O., Rossi, R. A., Barrow, J., Tanjim, M. M., Kim, S., Dernoncourt, F., Yu, T., Zhang, R., & Ahmed, N. K. (2024). Bias and fairness in large language models: A survey. *Computational Linguistics*, *50*(3), 1097–1179. DOI: 10.1162/coli_a_00524

Ganguli, D., Lovitt, L., Kernion, J., Askell, A., Bai, Y., Kadavath, S., . . . Clark, J. (2022). Red teaming language models to reduce harms: Methods, scaling behaviors, and lessons learned. *arXiv preprint arXiv:2209.07858*.

Gaur, L., Arora, G. K., & Jhanjhi, N. Z. (2022). Deep learning techniques for creation of DeepFakes. *DeepFakes*, 23-34. DOI: 10.1201/9781003231493-3

Gebru, T., Morgenstern, J., Vecchione, B., Vaughan, J. W., Wallach, H., Iii, H. D., & Crawford, K. (2021). Datasheets for datasets. *Communications of the ACM*, *64*(12), 86–92. DOI: 10.1145/3458723

Gehrmann, S., Strobelt, H., & Rush, A. M. (2023). GLTR: Statistical detection and visualization of generated text. *Transactions of the Association for Computational Linguistics*, *11*, 234–256. DOI: 10.1162/tacl_a_00551

George, A. S., George, A. H., & Baskar, T. (2023). Exploring the potential of prompt engineering in India: A study on the future of AI-driven job market and the role of higher education. *Partners Universal Innovative Research Publication*, *1*(2), 34–57.

Geroimenko, V. (2025). Key Techniques for Writing Effective Prompts. In *The Essential Guide to Prompt Engineering: Key Principles, Techniques, Challenges, and Security Risks* (pp. 37–83). Springer Nature Switzerland. DOI: 10.1007/978-3-031-86206-9_3

Ghiurău, D., & Popescu, D. E. (2026). Data Security and Privacy in GPT Models: Techniques and Challenges. *Applied Sciences (Basel, Switzerland)*, *16*(4), 1900. DOI: 10.3390/app16041900

Giuffrè, M., & Shung, D. L. (2023). Harnessing the power of synthetic data in healthcare: Innovation, application, and privacy. npj. *Digital Medicine*, *6*(1), 262. DOI: 10.1038/s41746-023-00927-3 PMID: 37813960

Gonzales, A., Guruswamy, G., & Smith, S. R. (2023). Synthetic data in health care: A narrative review. *PLOS Digital Health*, *2*(1), e0000082. DOI: 10.1371/journal.pdig.0000082 PMID: 36812604

Government of India. (2023). *Digital Personal Data Protection Act 2023*. Ministry of Electronics and Information Technology.

Gupta, D., Kholiyarov, E., Uralbayev, A., Madaminov, B., Marjona, A., Rajabov, N., & Nuriddin, E. (2026). Technology innovations and digital solutions for sustainable last-mile logistics. In Masengu, R., & Jaravaza, D. (Eds.), *Sustainable last-mile logistics: Challenges, innovations, and policy perspectives* (pp. 249–278). IGI Global Scientific Publishing., DOI: 10.4018/979-8-3373-7128-3.ch009

Hamamoto, R., Koyama, T., Takahashi, S., Yasuda, T., Kobayashi, K., Akagi, Y., Kouno, N., Sudo, K., Hirata, M., Sunami, K., Kubo, T., Katayama, H., Takashima, A., Taniguchi, T., Matsumoto, H., Shibaki, R., Asada, K., Komatsu, M., Kaneko, S., & Yamamoto, N. (2026). Implementing generative artificial intelligence in precision oncology: Safety, governance, and significance. *Journal of Hematology & Oncology*, *19*(1), 14. Advance online publication. DOI: 10.1186/s13045-026-01781-y PMID: 41664164

Han, X., Yang, J., Wang, T., Bi, Z., Song, X., Hao, J., & Song, J. (2025). Towards alignment-centric paradigm: A survey of instruction tuning in large language models. *arXiv preprint arXiv:2508.17184*.

Hannah, A., & Botterill, L. C. (2025). Avoiding the brakes: Malign policy and legal advice in the Robodebt scandal. *Policy and Society*, *44*(2), 229–241. DOI: 10.1093/polsoc/puaf018

Hao, S., Han, W., Jiang, T., Li, Y., Wu, H., Zhong, C., Zhou, Z., & Tang, H. (2024). Synthetic data in AI: Challenges, applications, and ethical implications. arXiv. https://doi.org//arXiv.2401.01629DOI: 10.48550

Hardie, P., Darley, A., Derwin, R., Eustace-Cook, J., Kearns, S., Mc Brien, B., Siddiquee, A., Zheng, D., & Mooney, M. (2026). Applications, attitudes and ethical considerations of Generative Artificial Intelligence (Gen AI) in nursing education: A scoping review. *BMC Nursing*, *25*(1), 148. Advance online publication. DOI: 10.1186/s12912-025-04253-9 PMID: 41545825

Hastie, T., Tibshirani, R., Friedman, J., & Franklin, J. (2023). *The elements of statistical learning: Data mining, inference, and prediction* (3rd ed.). Springer., DOI: 10.1007/978-3-031-38747-0

Heift, T. (2010). Prompting in CALL: A longitudinal study of learner uptake. *Modern Language Journal*, *94*(2), 198–216. DOI: 10.1111/j.1540-4781.2010.01017.x

Hejman, J., Prazak, O., & Konopík, M. (2025). Fine-tuned llama for multilingual text-to-text Coreference resolution. *Proceedings of the Eighth Workshop on Computational Models of Reference, Anaphora and Coreference*, 140-148. DOI: 10.18653/v1/2025.crac-1.12

Hernandez, M. L., Osorio-Marulanda, P. A., Catalina, M., Loinaz, L., Epelde, G., & Aginako, N. (2025). Comprehensive evaluation framework for synthetic tabular data in health: Fidelity, utility and privacy analysis of generative models with and without privacy guarantees. *Frontiers in Digital Health*, *7*, 1576290. DOI: 10.3389/fdgth.2025.1576290 PMID: 40343213

Hernandez, M., Epelde, G., Alberdi, A., Cilla, R., & Rankin, D. (2023). Synthetic tabular data evaluation in the health domain covering resemblance, utility, and privacy dimensions. *Methods of Information in Medicine*, *62*(S 01, Suppl. 1), e19–e38. DOI: 10.1055/s-0042-1760247 PMID: 36623830

Hikov, A., & Murphy, L. (2024). Information retrieval from textual data: Harnessing large language models, retrieval augmented generation and prompt engineering. *Journal of AI. Robotics & Workplace Automation*, *3*(2), 142–150. DOI: 10.69554/QAFE6376

Hollander, M., Wolfe, D. A., & Chicken, E. (2023). *Nonparametric statistical methods* (4th ed.). John Wiley & Sons., DOI: 10.1002/9781119196037

Huang, A. A., & Huang, S. Y. (2023). Increasing transparency in machine learning through bootstrap simulation and Shapley additive explanations. *PLoS One*, *18*(2), e0281922. DOI: 10.1371/journal.pone.0281922 PMID: 36821544

Hu, L., Liu, Z., Zhao, Z., Hou, L., Nie, L., & Li, J. (2023a). A survey of knowledge enhanced pre-trained language models. *IEEE Transactions on Knowledge and Data Engineering*, *36*(4), 1413–1430. DOI: 10.1109/TKDE.2023.3310002

Hu, Y., Hua, H., Yang, Z., Shi, W., Smith, N. A., & Luo, J. (2023b). Promptcap: Prompt-guided image captioning for vqa with gpt-3. In *Proceedings of the IEEE/CVF International Conference on Computer Vision* (pp. 2963-2975). DOI: 10.1109/ICCV51070.2023.00277

IAMAI. (2024). *AI in digital advertising: India market outlook 2024 to 2026*. Internet and Mobile Association of India.

IBM. (2021). *Data Fabric: Architecture and Use Cases*. https://www.ibm.com/downloads/cas/ZNA6X0L2

Ikuenobe, P. (2001). Teaching and assessing critical thinking abilities as outcomes in an informal logic course. *Teaching in Higher Education*, *6*(1), 19–32. DOI: 10.1080/13562510020029572

Ippolito, D., Duckworth, D., Callison-Burch, C., & Eck, D. (2023). Automatic detection of machine generated text: A critical survey. In *Proceedings of the 28th International Conference on Computational Linguistics* (pp. 2296-2309). Association for Computational Linguistics. DOI: 10.18653/v1/2023.coling-1.191

Jacobsen, B. N. (2023). Machine learning and the politics of synthetic data. *Big Data & Society*, *10*(1), 1–11. DOI: 10.1177/20539517221145372

Jeoung, S. (2025). *Examining large language models for safety and robustness through the lens of social science* (Doctoral dissertation).

Ji, Z., Lee, N., Frieske, R., Yu, T., Su, D., Xu, Y., Ishii, E., Bang, Y. J., Madotto, A., & Fung, P. (2023). Survey of hallucination in natural language generation. *ACM Computing Surveys*, *55*(12), 1–38. DOI: 10.1145/3571730

Josephson, A., & Åge, E. (2024). Prompting Out Of Manual Routines: How implementation of generative AI change work routines of knowledge workers.

Kaddour, J., Harris, J., Mozes, M., Bradley, H., Raileanu, R., & McHardy, R. (2023). Challenges and applications of large language models. *arXiv preprint arXiv:2307.10169*.

Kairouz, P., & McMahan, H. B. (2021). Advances and open problems in federated learning. *Foundations and Trends in Machine Learning*, *14*(1-2), 1–210. DOI: 10.1561/2200000083

Kasneci, E., Seßler, K., Küchemann, S., Bannert, M., Dementieva, D., Fischer, F., Gasser, U., Groh, G., Günnemann, S., Hüllermeier, E., Krusche, S., Kutyniok, G., Michaeli, T., Nerdel, C., Pfeffer, J., Poquet, O., Sailer, M., Schmidt, A., Seidel, T., & Kasneci, G. (2023). ChatGPT for good? On opportunities and challenges of large language models for education. *Learning and Individual Differences*, *103*, 102274. DOI: 10.1016/j.lindif.2023.102274

Katz, M., Kokel, H., Srinivas, K., & Sohrabi Araghi, S. (2024). Thought of search: Planning with language models through the lens of efficiency. *Advances in Neural Information Processing Systems*, *37*, 138491–138568. DOI: 10.52202/079017-4395

Khullar, S., Kate, C., Rao, A. S., Sharrif, U. H., Gupta, A., & Kaliappan, S. (2026). Explainable intelligence for ethical human-centric AI: Trust modeling using gradient boosting. In 2026 5th International Conference on Innovative Practices in Technology and Management (ICIPTM) (pp. 1–9). IEEE. DOI: 10.1109/ICIPTM69057.2026.11465350

Khullar, S., Kate, C., Ravula, P. K., & Kumar, V. A. G, G. M., & Vairavel, M. (2026). Contextual semantic representation learning for fake news classification via fine-tuned bidirectional transformers. In 2026 9th International Conference on Intelligent Computing and Control Systems (ICICCS) (pp. 1482–1490). IEEE. DOI: 10.1109/ICICCS67901.2026.11502741

Khullar, S., Magdalene, A. H. S., Sandhya, P., & Naik, B. R. N, H. K. B., & Raju, M. V. (2025). Implementation, performance, and energy efficiency analysis for text classification of deep learning architectures. In 2025 10th International Conference on Communication and Electronics Systems (ICCES) (pp. 2099–2103). IEEE. DOI: 10.1109/ICCES67310.2025.11336350

Kirchenbauer, J., Geiping, J., Wen, Y., Katz, J., Miers, I., & Goldstein, T. (2023). A watermark for large language models. In *Proceedings of the 40th International Conference on Machine Learning* (pp. 17061-17084). PMLR. DOI: 10.48550/arXiv.2301.10226

Kojima, T., Gu, S. S., Reid, M., Matsuo, Y., & Iwasawa, Y. (2022). Large language models are zero-shot reasoners. *Advances in Neural Information Processing Systems, 35*, 22199–22213. DOI: 10.52202/068431-1613

Korzynski, P., Mazurek, G., Krzypkowska, P., & Kurasinski, A. (2023). Artificial intelligence prompt engineering as a new digital competence: Analysis of generative AI technologies such as ChatGPT. *Entrepreneurial Business and Economics Review, 11*(3), 25–37. DOI: 10.15678/EBER.2023.110302

Krishna, K., Song, Y., Karpinska, M., Wieting, J., & Iyyer, M. (2023). Paraphrasing evades detectors of AI-generated text, but retrieval is an effective defense. In *Proceedings of the 37th Conference on Neural Information Processing Systems*. Curran Associates. DOI: 10.52202/075280-1195

Kulkarni, N. D., & Tupsakhare, P. (2024). Crafting effective prompts: enhancing ai performance through structured input design. *Journal of recent trends in computer science and engineering (JRTCSE), 12*(5), 1-10.

LAION e. V. (2022). *LAION-5B: A new era of open large-scale multi-modal datasets*. https://laion.ai/blog/laion-5b/

Lautrup, A. D., Hyrup, T., Zimek, A., & Schneider-Kamp, P. (2024). Systematic review of generative modelling tools and utility metrics for fully synthetic tabular data. *ACM Computing Surveys, 57*(4), 1–40. DOI: 10.1145/3704437

Lazovsky, S. G., Raz, T., & Kenett, Y. N. (2025). The art of creative inquiry—From question asking to prompt engineering. *The Journal of Creative Behavior, 59*(1), e671. DOI: 10.1002/jocb.671

Le Quy, T., Roy, A., Iosifidis, V., Zhang, W., & Ntoutsi, E. (2022). A survey on datasets for fairness-aware machine learning. *Wiley Interdisciplinary Reviews. Data Mining and Knowledge Discovery, 12*(3), e1452. DOI: 10.1002/widm.1452

Lee, A. V. Y., Teo, C. L., & Tan, S. C. (2024). Prompt Engineering for Knowledge Creation: Using Chain-of-Thought to Support Students' Improvable Ideas. *AI*, *5*(3), 1446–1461. DOI: 10.3390/ai5030069

Lee, K., Ippolito, D., Nystrom, A., Ha, C., Goodwin, M., Lee, A., Shin, P., & Carlini, N. (2022). Deduplicating training data makes language models better. *International Conference on Machine Learning*, 20316–20330. DOI: 10.18653/v1/2022.acl-long.577

Leong, H. Y., & Wu, Y. (2025). Why should Next-Gen LLM multi-agent systems move beyond fixed architectures to dynamic, input-driven graphs? DOI: 10.2139/ssrn.5276004

Li, Y. (2023). A practical survey on zero-shot prompt design for in-context learning. *arXiv preprint arXiv:2309.13205*. DOI: 10.26615/978-954-452-092-2_069

Liang, J., Liu, X., Liu, H., Phan, H., Benetos, E., Plumbley, M. D., & Wang, W. (2023). Adapting language-audio models as few-shot audio learners. *Interspeech*, *276-280*, 276–280. Advance online publication. DOI: 10.21437/Interspeech.2023-1082

Li, M. Q., & Fung, B. C. (2025). Security concerns for large language models: A survey. *Journal of Information Security and Applications*, *95*, 104284. DOI: 10.1016/j.jisa.2025.104284

Li, M., Basit, A., Javed, A., Song, X., & Ge, Y. (2026). Generative artificial intelligence and ChatGPT in agriculture supply chain management: A systematic literature review and future research agenda. *British Food Journal*, *128*(13), 121–141. DOI: 10.1108/BFJ-05-2025-0720

Liu, Z. (2026). Llmflow: Reasoning and acting workflow for automated data analysis. *CRAN: Contributed Packages*. DOI: 10.32614/CRAN.package.llmflow

Liu, H., Tam, D., Muqeeth, M., Mohta, J., Huang, T., Bansal, M., & Raffel, C. A. (2022). Few-shot parameter-efficient fine-tuning is better and cheaper than in-context learning. *Advances in Neural Information Processing Systems*, *35*, 1950–1965. DOI: 10.52202/068431-0142

Liu, P., Yuan, W., Fu, J., Jiang, Z., Hayashi, H., & Neubig, G. (2023). Pre-train, prompt, and predict: A systematic survey of prompting methods in natural language processing. *ACM Computing Surveys*, *55*(9), 1–35. DOI: 10.1145/3560815

Marcus, G. (2023). The Next Decade in AI: A Call for Trust and Transparency. *Harvard Data Science Review*. https://hdsr.mitpress.mit.edu/

Marpaung, J. (2026). Investigating Indonesian graduate business students' generative artificial intelligence readiness and usage in the classroom. *Discover Education, 5*(1), 84. Advance online publication. DOI: 10.1007/s44217-026-01112-w

Marvin, G., Hellen, N., Jjingo, D., & Nakatumba-Nabende, J. (2023, June). Prompt engineering in large language models. In *International conference on data intelligence and cognitive informatics* (pp. 387-402). Singapore: Springer Nature Singapore.

McKnight, D. H., Choudhury, V., & Kacmar, C. (2002). Developing and validating trust measures for e commerce: An integrative typology. Information Systems Research, 13(3), 334 to 359.

McTear, M., & Ashurkina, M. (2024). Advanced Prompt Engineering. In *Transforming Conversational AI: Exploring the Power of Large Language Models in Interactive Conversational Agents* (pp. 115–144). Apress. DOI: 10.1007/979-8-8688-0110-5_6

Mehrabi, N., Morstatter, F., Saxena, N., Lerman, K., & Galstyan, A. (2021). A survey on bias and fairness in machine learning. *ACM Computing Surveys, 54*(6), 1–35. DOI: 10.1145/3457607

Miao, J., Thongprayoon, C., Suppadungsuk, S., Krisanapan, P., Radhakrishnan, Y., & Cheungpasitporn, W. (2024). Chain of thought utilization in large language models and application in nephrology. *Medicina (Kaunas, Lithuania), 60*(1), 148. DOI: 10.3390/medicina60010148 PMID: 38256408

Mishra, A., Danzy, B., Soni, U., Arunkumar, A., Huang, J., Kwon, B. C., & Bryan, C. (2025). PromptAid: Visual prompt exploration, perturbation, testing and iteration for large language models. *IEEE Transactions on Visualization and Computer Graphics, 31*(10), 6946–6962. DOI: 10.1109/TVCG.2025.3535332 PMID: 40031291

Mitchell, E., Lee, Y., Khazatsky, A., Manning, C. D., & Finn, C. (2023). DetectGPT: Zero-shot machine-generated text detection using probability curvature. In *Proceedings of the 40th International Conference on Machine Learning* (pp. 24950-24962). PMLR. DOI: 10.48550/arXiv.2301.11305

Mitchell, M., Wu, S., Zaldivar, A., Barnes, P., Vasserman, L., Hutchinson, B., Spitzer, E., Raji, I. D., & Gebru, T. (2019). Model cards for model reporting. *Proceedings of the Conference on Fairness, Accountability, and Transparency*, 220–229. DOI: 10.1145/3287560.3287596

Mizrahi, G. (2024). *Unlocking the secrets of prompt engineering: Master the art of creative language generation to accelerate your journey from novice to pro*. Packt Publishing Ltd.

Montgomery, D. C. (2023). *Design and analysis of experiments* (10th ed.). John Wiley & Sons., DOI: 10.1002/9781119755234

Muis, I. M., Straatman, J., & Kamphorst, B. A. (2025). Responsible AI innovation in the public sector: Lessons from and recommendations for facilitating Fundamental Rights and Algorithms Impact Assessments. *Journal of Responsible Technology*, *22*, 100118. DOI: 10.1016/j.jrt.2025.100118

Mujahid, M., Kina, E., Rustam, F., Villar, M. G., Alvarado, E. S., Diez, I. D. L. T., & Imran, A. (2024). Data oversampling and imbalanced datasets: An investigation of performance for machine learning and feature engineering. *Journal of Big Data*, *11*(1), 87. DOI: 10.1186/s40537-024-00943-4

Murugesan, B., Hussain, R., Bhattacharya, R., Ben Ayed, I., & Dolz, J. (2024). Prompting classes: exploring the power of prompt class learning in weakly supervised semantic segmentation. In *Proceedings of the IEEE/CVF Winter Conference on Applications of Computer Vision* (pp. 291-302). DOI: 10.1109/WACV57701.2024.00036

Mylrea, M., & Robinson, N. (2023). Artificial Intelligence (AI) trust framework and maturity model: Applying an entropy lens to improve security, privacy, and ethical AI. *Entropy (Basel, Switzerland)*, *25*(10), 1429. DOI: 10.3390/e25101429 PMID: 37895550

Nagoor, S. H. (2026). *Clinical Sentiment Classification on Intensive Care Unit Clinical Notes* (Doctoral dissertation, TRINITY COLLEGE).

Namvong, A., & Wiangwiset, T. (2026). Transparency-by-design in smart city crowd monitoring: A privacy-preserving Wi-Fi analytics framework for tourism and urban management. In Azeroual, O. (Ed.), *Technical foundations and applications of trustworthy AI systems* (pp. 157–194). IGI Global Scientific Publishing., DOI: 10.4018/979-8-2600-1433-2.ch006

Nicodeme, C. (2020, June). Build confidence and acceptance of AI-based decision support systems-Explainable and liable AI. In *2020 13th international conference on human system interaction (HSI)* (pp. 20-23). IEEE. DOI: 10.1109/HSI49210.2020.9142668

Nieuwenhuizen, E. (2024). Algorithm registers: A box-ticking exercise or meaningful tool for transparency? *Information Polity*, *29*(4), 415–433. DOI: 10.1177/15701255241297107

NIST. (2023). *Artificial Intelligence Risk Management Framework (AI RMF 1.0)*. National Institute of Standards and Technology., DOI: 10.6028/NIST.AI.100-1

O'Reilly, T. (2020). *WTF? What's the Future and Why It's Up to Us*. HarperBusiness.

OBrien., D., Biswas, S., Imtiaz, S. M., Abdalkareem, R., Shihab, E., & Rajan, H. (2024, April). Are prompt engineering and todo comments friends or foes? an evaluation on github copilot. In *Proceedings of the IEEE/ACM 46th International Conference on Software Engineering* (pp. 1-13).

OECD. (2025). *Governing with artificial intelligence: The state of play and way forward in core government functions*. OECD Publishing., DOI: 10.1787/795de142-

Ologun, A., Ikeakaonwu, O. M., Ibidunmoye, A. F., Eneano, G. A., Chuwa, C. C., & Kolawole, L. O. (2026). AI governance and ethical frameworks for public-sector AI decision systems: An institutional operationalisation model. *AI and Ethics*, *6*(3), 294. Advance online publication. DOI: 10.1007/s43681-026-01143-x

Ong, J. C. L., Chang, S. Y.-H., William, W., Butte, A., Shah, N., Chew, L. S. T., Liu, N., Doshi-Velez, F., Lu, W., Savulescu, J., & Ting, D. S. W. (2024). Ethical and regulatory challenges of large language models in medicine. *The Lancet. Digital Health*, *6*(6), e428–e437. DOI: 10.1016/S2589-7500(24)00061-X PMID: 38658283

Osagie, E., & Balasundaram, R. (2026). Investigating Epistemic Uncertainty in PCB Defect Detection: A Comparative Study Using Monte Carlo Dropout. *Journal of Experimental and Theoretical Analyses*, *4*(1), 11. DOI: 10.3390/jeta4010011

Osorio-Marulanda, P. A., Epelde, G., Hernandez, M., Isasa, I., Reyes, N. M., & Iraola, A. B. (2024). Privacy mechanisms and evaluation metrics for synthetic data generation: A systematic review. *IEEE Access : Practical Innovations, Open Solutions*, *12*, 88048–88074. DOI: 10.1109/ACCESS.2024.3417608

Ouyang, L., Wu, J., Jiang, X., Almeida, D., Wainwright, C., Mishkin, P., Zhang, C., Agarwal, S., Slama, K., Ray, A., Schulman, J., Hilton, J., Kelton, F., Miller, L., Simens, M., Askell, A., Welinder, P., Christiano, P., Leike, J., & Lowe, R. (2022). Training language models to follow instructions with human feedback. *Advances in Neural Information Processing Systems*, *35*, 27730–27744. DOI: 10.52202/068431-2011

Ozkul, D. (2023). *Automating immigration and asylum: The uses of new technologies in migration and asylum governance in Europe*. Refugee Studies Centre, University of Oxford. URL: https://www.rsc.ox.ac.uk/publications/automating-immigration-and-asylum-the-uses-of-new-technologies-in-migration-and-asylum-governance-in-europe

Özsavaş, M. G., & Özsavaş, E. E. (2026). AI governance capacity in public administration: A comparative analysis of the EU and Türkiye. *International Journal of Public Administration in the Digital Age*, *13*(1), 1–20. DOI: 10.4018/IJPADA.406076

Pagano, T. P., Loureiro, R. B., Lisboa, F. V. N., Peixoto, R. M., Guimarães, G. A. S., Cruz, G. O. R., Araujo, M. M., Santos, L. L., Cruz, M. A. S., Oliveira, E. L. S., Winkler, I., & Nascimento, E. G. S. (2023). Bias and unfairness in machine learning models: A systematic review on datasets, tools, fairness metrics, and identification and mitigation methods. *Big Data and Cognitive Computing*, *7*(1), 15. DOI: 10.3390/bdcc7010015

Pallavi, A. (2025). DeepFake detection for human face images and videos: A comprehensive survey. *INTERNATIONAL JOURNAL OF SCIENTIFIC RESEARCH IN ENGINEERING AND MANAGEMENT*, *09*(05), 1–9. DOI: 10.55041/IJSREM47887

Palmiotto, F. (2024). When is a decision automated? A taxonomy for a fundamental rights analysis. *German Law Journal*, *25*(2), 210–236. DOI: 10.1017/glj.2023.112

Palmiotto, F., & Ozkul, D. (2024). Climbing a wall: Strategic litigation against automated systems in migration and asylum. *German Law Journal*, *25*(6), 935–955. DOI: 10.1017/glj.2024.52

Pandya, S. (2026). *From Transcription to Intelligence: Applying Large Language Models to Healthcare Enterprise Decision Support Systems*. Geh press.

Pant, D., & Mukhiya, S. K. (2024). Technical evaluation of GPT-4 and GPT-4-Turbo reflective listening response generation with the counsel chat dataset. DOI: 10.21203/rs.3.rs-4769572/v1

Park, J. S., O'Brien, J., Cai, C. J., Morris, M. R., Liang, P., & Bernstein, M. S. (2023). Generative agents: Interactive simulacra of human behavior. *Proceedings of the 36th Annual ACM Symposium on User Interface Software and Technology*, 1-22. DOI: 10.1145/3586183.3606763

Parrish, A., Chen, A., Nangia, N., Padmakumar, V., Phang, J., Thompson, J., Htut, P. M., & Bowman, S. R. (2022). BBQ: A hand-built bias benchmark for question answering. In *Findings of the Association for Computational Linguistics: ACL 2022* (pp. 2086–2105). Association for Computational Linguistics. DOI: 10.18653/v1/2022.findings-acl.165

Pashentsev, E. (2023). The malicious use of artificial intelligence through agenda setting. *The Palgrave Handbook of Malicious Use of AI and Psychological Security*, 133-172. DOI: 10.1007/978-3-031-22552-9_6

Patil, A. (2025). Advancing Reasoning in Large Language Models: Promising Methods and Approaches. *arXiv preprint arXiv:2502.03671*.

Pessach, D., & Shmueli, E. (2022). A review on fairness in machine learning. *ACM Computing Surveys*, *55*(3), 1–44. DOI: 10.1145/3494672

Petty, R. E., & Cacioppo, J. T. (1986). *Communication and persuasion: Central and peripheral routes to attitude change*. Springer. DOI: 10.1007/978-1-4612-4964-1

Pornprasit, C., & Tantithamthavorn, C. (2024). Fine-tuning and prompt engineering for large language models-based code review automation. *Information and Software Technology*, *175*, 107523. DOI: 10.1016/j.infsof.2024.107523

Prabhu, A., & Sunitha, N. R. (2026). A hybrid artificial intelligence model for cyberattack detection using a generative AI embedded approach. *Discover Artificial Intelligence*, *6*(1). Advance online publication. DOI: 10.1007/s44163-026-00901-4

Qian, Y. (2025). Prompt engineering in education: A systematic review of approaches and educational applications. *Journal of Educational Computing Research*, *63*(7-8), 1782–1818. DOI: 10.1177/07356331251365189

Qian, Y., Bao, Q., Zhang, S., & Peng, X. (2026). A cultural memory semiotics and function behavior structure model for digital inheritance and innovation in AI generated Huizhou woodcarving images. *Scientific Reports*, *16*(1), 5520. Advance online publication. DOI: 10.1038/s41598-026-35360-5 PMID: 41545436

Rachovitsa, A., & Johann, N. (2022). The human rights implications of the use of AI in the digital welfare state: Lessons learned from the Dutch SyRI case. *Human Rights Law Review*, *22*(2), ngac010. Advance online publication. DOI: 10.1093/hrlr/ngac010

Rafailov, R., Sharma, A., Mitchell, E., Manning, C. D., Ermon, S., & Finn, C. (2023). Direct preference optimization: Your language model is secretly a reward model. *Advances in Neural Information Processing Systems*, *36*, 53728–53741. DOI: 10.52202/075280-2338

Raffel, C., Shazeer, N., Roberts, A., Lee, K., Narang, S., Matena, M., Zhou, Y., Li, W., & Liu, P. J. (2020). Exploring the limits of transfer learning with a unified text-to-text transformer. *Journal of Machine Learning Research*, *21*(140), 1–67.

Rahman, S. S., Islam, M. A., Alam, M. M., Zeba, M., Rahman, M. A., Chowa, S. S., Raiaan, M. A. K., & Azam, S. (2026). Hallucination to truth: A review of fact-checking and factuality evaluation in large language models. *Artificial Intelligence Review*, *59*(2), 70. DOI: 10.1007/s10462-025-11454-w

Raji, I. D., Smart, A., White, R. N., Mitchell, M., Gebru, T., Hutchinson, B., Smith-Loud, J., Theron, A., & Barnes, P. (2020). Closing the AI accountability gap: Defining an end-to-end framework for internal algorithmic auditing. *Proceedings of the 2020 Conference on Fairness, Accountability, and Transparency*, 33–44. DOI: 10.1145/3351095.3372873

Ramos, J. (2023). Using TF-IDF to determine word relevance in document queries. In *Proceedings of the International Conference on Machine Learning* (Vol. 3, pp. 133-142). ICML Press. DOI: 10.5555/3295222.3295234

Ranade, N., Saravia, M., & Johri, A. (2025). Using rhetorical strategies to design prompts: A human-in-the-loop approach to make AI useful. *AI & Society, 40*(2), 711–732. DOI: 10.1007/s00146-024-01905-3

Ranaldi, L. (2026). Multilingual retrieval-augmented generation for knowledge-intensive question answering task. *Findings of the Association for Computational Linguistics: EACL, 2026*, 697–716. DOI: 10.18653/v1/2026.findings-eacl.35

Rao, A. L., Santhikumar, R., & Venugopal, K. (2025). Visualizing insight: Enhancing statistical thinking in higher education. In S. Anastasiadou & L. Seremeti (Eds.), Modes of Representation in Developing Statistical Thinking in Education (pp. 181 to 214). IGI Global Scientific Publishing. https://doi.org/DOI: 10.4018/979-8-3693-9934-7.ch010

Ravfogel, S., Elazar, Y., Gonen, H., Twiton, M., & Goldberg, Y. (2020). Null it out: Guarding protected attributes by iterative nullspace projection. In *Proceedings of the 58th Annual Meeting of the Association for Computational Linguistics* (pp. 7237–7256). Association for Computational Linguistics. DOI: 10.18653/v1/2020.acl-main.647

Ravulavaru, A. (2018). *Google Cloud AI Services Quick Start Guide: Build Intelligent Applications with Google Cloud AI Services*. Packt Publishing Ltd.

Rayhana, R., Bai, L., Xiao, G., Liao, M., & Liu, Z. (2024). Digital twin models: Functions, challenges, and industry applications. *IEEE Journal of Radio Frequency Identification, 8*, 282–321. DOI: 10.1109/JRFID.2024.3387996

Razi, Q., Piyush, R., Chakrabarti, A., Singh, A., Hassija, V., & Chalapathi, G. S. S. (2025). Enhancing data privacy: A comprehensive survey of privacy-enabling technologies. *IEEE Access : Practical Innovations, Open Solutions, 13*, 40354–40385. DOI: 10.1109/ACCESS.2025.3546618

Rehman, S. U. (2025). From innovation to impact the future ethical landscape and governance of large language models. *Innovations and Ethical Dimensions of Large Language Models*, 437-450. DOI: 10.4018/979-8-3373-5017-2.ch014

Reynolds, L., & McDonell, K. (2021, May). Prompt programming for large language models: Beyond the few-shot paradigm. In *Extended abstracts of the 2021 CHI conference on human factors in computing systems* (pp. 1-7).

Ribeiro, M. T., Singh, S., & Guestrin, C. (2023). Why should I trust you? Explaining the predictions of any classifier. In *Proceedings of the 22nd ACM SIGKDD International Conference on Knowledge Discovery and Data Mining* (pp. 1135-1144). ACM. DOI: 10.1145/2939672.2939778

Rinta-Kahila, T., Someh, I., Gillespie, N., Indulska, M., & Gregor, S. (2022). Algorithmic decision-making and system destructiveness: A case of automatic debt recovery. *European Journal of Information Systems, 31*(3), 313–338. DOI: 10.1080/0960085X.2021.1960905

Roehl, U. B. U. (2023). Automated decision-making and good administration: Views from inside the government machinery. *Government Information Quarterly, 40*(4), 101864. DOI: 10.1016/j.giq.2023.101864

Royal Commission into the Robodebt Scheme. (2023). *Report of the Royal Commission into the Robodebt Scheme*. Commonwealth of Australia. URL: https://robodebt.royalcommission.gov.au/publications/report

Sadasivan, V. S., Kumar, A., Balasubramanian, S., Wang, W., & Feizi, S. (2023). Can AI-generated text be reliably detected? *Computational Linguistics, 49*(3), 543–592. DOI: 10.48550/arXiv.2303.11156

Saeed, M. M., Saeed, R. A., Ali, E. S., Ahmed, Z. E., & Mokhtar, R. A. (2026). Privacy and Security Challenges of AI Integration in Industry 4.0 and 5.0. In *Computational Intelligence for Analysis of Trends in Industry 4.0 and 5.0* (pp. 353-372). Auerbach Publications.

Sager, N. (1978). Natural language information formatting: The automatic conversion of texts to a structured data base. []. Elsevier.]. *Advances in Computers, 17*, 89–162. DOI: 10.1016/S0065-2458(08)60391-5

Sahoo, P., Singh, A. K., Saha, S., Jain, V., Mondal, S., & Chadha, A. (2024). A systematic survey of prompt engineering in large language models: Techniques and applications. *arXiv preprint arXiv:2402.07927.*

Salah, A. A., Jamil, N., Sulaiman, H., Cangelosi, A., Alyasseri, Z. A. A., & Hosseini, E. (2026). Security, Privacy, and AI Integration in Educational Metaverse: A Comprehensive Review and Framework. *Journal of Educational Computing Research*, •••, 07356331261436249. DOI: 10.1177/07356331261436249

Sambasivan, N., Kapania, S., Highfill, H., Akrong, D., Paritosh, P., & Aroyo, L. (2021). Everyone wants to do the model, but no one wants to do the data: Data cascades in high-stakes AI. In *Proceedings of the 2021 CHI Conference on Human Factors in Computing Systems* (pp. 1–15). Association for Computing Machinery. DOI: 10.1145/3411764.3445518

Sarch, G., Wu, Y., Tarr, M., & Fragkiadaki, K. (2023). Open-ended Instructable embodied agents with memory-augmented large language models. *Findings of the Association for Computational Linguistics: EMNLP, 2023*, 3468–3500. DOI: 10.18653/v1/2023.findings-emnlp.226

Schuhmann, C., Vencu, R., Beaumont, R., Kaczmarczyk, R., & Kaddour, J. (2022). LAION-5B: An open large-scale dataset for training next generation image-text models. *Advances in Neural Information Processing Systems, 35*, 32118–32133. DOI: 10.52202/068431-1833

Sculley, D., Holt, G., Golovin, D., Davydov, E., Phillips, T., Ebner, D., Chaudhary, V., & Young, M. (2015). Hidden technical debt in machine learning systems. *Advances in Neural Information Processing Systems*, •••, 28.

Shahul Hameed, M. A., Qureshi, A. M., & Kaushik, A. (2024). Bias mitigation via synthetic data generation: A review. *Electronics (Basel), 13*(19), 3909. DOI: 10.3390/electronics13193909

Shokri, R., Stronati, M., Song, C., & Shmatikov, V. (2017, May). Membership inference attacks against machine learning models. In *2017 IEEE symposium on security and privacy (SP)* (pp. 3-18). IEEE. DOI: 10.1109/SP.2017.41

Short, C. E., & Short, J. C. (2023). The artificially intelligent entrepreneur: ChatGPT, prompt engineering, and entrepreneurial rhetoric creation. *Journal of Business Venturing Insights, 19*, e00388. DOI: 10.1016/j.jbvi.2023.e00388

Shumailov, I., Shumaylov, Z., Zhao, Y., Papernot, N., Anderson, R., & Gal, Y. (2023). The curse of recursion: Training on generated data makes models forget. *arXiv preprint arXiv:2305.17493.*

Shumailov, I., Shumaylov, Z., Zhao, Y., Papernot, N., Anderson, R., & Gal, Y. (2024). AI models collapse when trained on recursively generated data. *Nature, 631*(8022), 755–759. DOI: 10.1038/s41586-024-07566-y PMID: 39048682

Siriborvornratanakul, T., & Rittikulsittichai, S. (2026). Advancing the generation and integration of traditional motifs through AI-based techniques. *Discover Artificial Intelligence, 6*(1), 100. Advance online publication. DOI: 10.1007/s44163-025-00642-w

Smith, K. S., Aziz, W., & Specia, L. (2016, May). Cohere: A toolkit for local coherence. In *Proceedings of the Tenth International Conference on Language Resources and Evaluation (LREC'16)* (pp. 4111-4114). DOI: 10.63317/4dxkavwdfm5d

Sokolova, M., & Lapalme, G. (2023). A systematic analysis of performance measures for classification tasks. *Information Processing & Management, 59*(4), 102938. Advance online publication. DOI: 10.1016/j.ipm.2023.102938

Solaiman, I., Brundage, M., Clark, J., Askell, A., Herbert-Voss, A., Wu, J., Radford, A., Krueger, G., Kim, J. W., Kreps, S., McCain, M., Newhouse, A., Blazakis, J., McGuffie, K., & Wang, J. (2023). Release strategies and the social impacts of language models. *Journal of Artificial Intelligence Research, 76*, 321–378. DOI: 10.1613/jair.1.14317

Soria, C. (2025). An empirical investigation into the utility of large language models in open-ended survey data categorization. DOI: 10.31235/osf.io/wv6tk_v2

Spence, M. (1973). Job market signaling. Quarterly Journal of Economics, 87(3), 355 to 374.

Srinivasan, V., Ravi, J., & Raj, J. (2018). *Google Cloud Platform for Architects: Design and manage powerful cloud solutions*. Packt Publishing Ltd.

Steele, J. L. (2023). To GPT or not GPT? Empowering our students to learn with AI. *Computers and Education: Artificial Intelligence, 5*, 100160. DOI: 10.1016/j.caeai.2023.100160

Subramonyam, H., Thakkar, D., Ku, A., Dieber, J., & Sinha, A. K. (2025, April). Prototyping with prompts: Emerging approaches and challenges in generative ai design for collaborative software teams. In *Proceedings of the 2025 CHI Conference on Human Factors in Computing Systems* (pp. 1-22). DOI: 10.1145/3706598.3713166

Sundararajan, A., & Sridharan, A. (2021). AI-native Enterprises: The Future of Digital Transformation. *MIT Sloan Management Review, 62*(2), 45–53.

Sun, Y., Li, L., Zhang, X., Chen, X., Deng, S., & Hu, X. (2026). AI literacy and psychosocial factors shaping Chinese university students' attitudes and behavioral intentions toward generative AI use. *BMC Psychology, 14*(1), 236. Advance online publication. DOI: 10.1186/s40359-026-03989-6 PMID: 41572390

Suzgun, M., & Kalai, A. T. (2024). Meta-prompting: Enhancing language models with task-agnostic scaffolding. *arXiv preprint arXiv:2401.12954*.

Syahputri, I. W., Budiardjo, E. K., & Putra, P. O. H. (2025). Unlocking the Potential of the Prompt Engineering Paradigm in Software Engineering: A Systematic Literature Review. *AI*, *6*(9), 206. DOI: 10.3390/ai6090206

Sztandar-Sztanderska, K. (2025). How context matters: Human oversight of automated-decision-making systems in welfare administration. *Journal of European Social Policy*. Advance online publication. DOI: 10.1177/09589287251358069

Tedesco, R. (2026). Privacy and security in large language models and data. *Challenges and Applications of Generative Large Language Models*, 127-152. DOI: 10.1016/B978-0-443-33592-1.00011-5

Touvron, H., Lavril, T., Izacard, G., Martinet, X., Lachaux, M. A., Lacroix, T., . . . Lample, G. (2023). Llama: Open and efficient foundation language models. *arXiv preprint arXiv:2302.13971.*

U.S. Copyright Office. (2023). *Copyright and artificial intelligence: Copyrightability* (Part 2 of 3). https://copyright.gov/ai/

Uchendu, A., Le, T., Shu, K., & Lee, D. (2023). Authorship attribution for neural text generation. In *Proceedings of the 2023 Conference on Empirical Methods in Natural Language Processing* (pp. 8596-8614). Association for Computational Linguistics. DOI: 10.18653/v1/2023.emnlp-main.531

Vakamullu, G., Venugopal, K., & Gudla, S. P. (2026). Assessment of dexterous and detrimental social media intricacies on civic engagement and public discourse. In I. N. Marzuki, W. W. Ali, H. Lee, A. Manaf, & M. Sanmugam (Eds.), Examining the Intersection of Technology, Media, and Social Innovation (pp. 25 to 60). IGI Global Scientific Publishing. https://doi.org/DOI: 10.4018/979-8-3373-5307-4.ch002

van Bekkum, M., & Zuiderveen Borgesius, F. (2021). Digital welfare fraud detection and the Dutch SyRI judgment. *European Journal of Social Security*, *23*(4), 323–340. DOI: 10.1177/13882627211031257

Vaswani, A., Shazeer, N., Parmar, N., Uszkoreit, J., Jones, L., Gomez, A. N., Kaiser, Ł., & Polosukhin, I. (2023). Attention is all you need: A decade of transformer architectures. *Advances in Neural Information Processing Systems*, *36*, 6000–6014. DOI: 10.48550/arXiv.1706.03762

Vatsal, S., & Dubey, H. (2024). A survey of prompt engineering methods in large language models for different nlp tasks. *arXiv preprint arXiv:2407.12994.*

Velásquez-Henao, J. D., Franco-Cardona, C. J., & Cadavid-Higuita, L. (2023). Prompt Engineering: a methodology for optimizing interactions with AI-Language Models in the field of engineering. *Dyna, 90*(SPE230), 9-17.

Venugopal, K. (2024). Exploring Gen Z perspectives toward ChatGPT in academic contexts. In R. Bansal, A. Chakir, A. H. Ngah, F. Rabby, & A. Jain (Eds.), AI Algorithms and ChatGPT for Student Engagement in Online Learning (pp. 51 to 69). IGI Global Scientific Publishing. https://doi.org/DOI: 10.4018/979-8-3693-4268-8.ch004

Venugopal, K. (2025). Exploring consumer perceptions: Ethnocentric appeal of Indian Khadi products. In K. Al Sulaiti, I. Al Sulaiti, J. Abbas, & H. Al Halbusi (Eds.), Ethnocentrism and Country of Origin Effects: The Asian Consumers Perspective (pp. 419 to 441). Qatar National Library.

Venugopal, K. (2025). iGenius: Exploring Gen Z's reliance on AI tools in education. In M. Anshari, M. N. Almunawar, & P. Ordinez de Pablos (Eds.), Impacts of Digital Technologies Across Generations (pp. 141 to 164). IGI Global Scientific Publishing. https://doi.org/DOI: 10.4018/979-8-3693-6366-9.ch008

Venugopal, K. (2025). Multisensory marketing and its effect on brand loyalty: A deep dive into consumer preferences. In R. Malik, S. Malhan, & M. Arora (Eds.), Neurosensory and Neuromarketing Impacts on Consumer Behavior (pp. 295 to 330). IGI Global Scientific Publishing. https://doi.org/DOI: 10.4018/979-8-3693-8222-6.ch013

Venugopal, K., & Jagadeesh, B. (2025). Theoretical insights into user security and privacy in social media environments. In R. Kumar, S. Srivastava, & A. Elngar (Eds.), Human Impact on Security and Privacy (pp. 289 to 312). IGI Global Scientific Publishing. https://doi.org/DOI: 10.4018/979-8-3693-9235-5.ch015

Venugopal, K., & Kolluru, V. S. (2025). Evaluating user vulnerabilities: A study on social media privacy and security threats. In D. Darwish & K. Charan (Eds.), Analyzing Privacy and Security Difficulties in social media: New Challenges and Solutions (pp. 161 to 192). IGI Global Scientific Publishing. https://doi.org/DOI: 10.4018/979-8-3693-9491-5.ch008

Venugopal, K., & Vakamullu, G. (2025). Assessment of higher education students' dependency on AI tools in an Indian indigenized context. In M. Kgari Masondo (Ed.), Indigenous Teaching Disciplines and Perspectives for Higher Education (pp. 309 to 338). IGI Global Scientific Publishing. https://doi.org/DOI: 10.4018/979-8-3693-9296-6.ch015

Venugopal, K., Das, S., & Badawy, H. R. (2023). Prediction analysis of Gen Zers' attitudes on ecological consciousness. In B. Mishra (Ed.), Sustainable Science and Intelligent Technologies for Societal Development (pp. 342 to 357). IGI Global Scientific Publishing. https://doi.org/DOI: 10.4018/979-8-3693-1186-8.ch019

Venugopal, K., Das, S., & Vakamullu, G. (2023). Critical factors for the upscale of online shopping: A rural perspective. In R. Bansal, S. Qalati, & A. Chakir (Eds.), Influencer Marketing Applications within the Metaverse (pp. 254 to 262). IGI Global Scientific Publishing. https://doi.org/DOI: 10.4018/978-1-6684-8898-0.ch016

Venugopal, K., Deekonda, P., & Das, N. (2024). Impact of dexterous and detrimental on SBI credit cards: Application of Random Forest and regression analysis. In Research Methodology: A Multidisciplinary Approach (pp. 9 to 25). Oxford Publishers and Distributors. ISBN: 978 93 9363 153 4.

Venugopal, K., Gopalakrishna, V., Ranganath, N. S., & Lakshmi, K. (2025). Reverse mentoring and knowledge transfer: The role of Gen Z in upskilling older employees. In H. Chandan (Ed.), Enhancing Workplace Productivity through Gender Equity and Intergenerational Communication (pp. 219 to 254). IGI Global Scientific Publishing. https://doi.org/DOI: 10.4018/979-8-3373-2903-1.ch009

Venugopal, K., Malepati, V., Santosh Ranganath, N., Buditi, N., & Agatamudi, L. R. (2026). Assessment of smart assistance on voice driven online shopping: An analysis with ML applications and regression. In M. Ahmad, M. Rafi, & M. Kirmani (Eds.), AI in Consumer Analytics and Strategic Branding (pp. 317 to 352). IGI Global Scientific Publishing. https://doi.org/DOI: 10.4018/979-8-3373-9963-8.ch010

Venugopal, K., Rajulu, B. G., Ravikumar, P., & Madhavi, K. (2026). Sustainable learning solutions: ChatGPT integration in academic services. In M. Tariq (Ed.), Integrating ChatGPT Into System Applications and Services (pp. 59 to 88). IGI Global Scientific Publishing. https://doi.org/DOI: 10.4018/979-8-3693-9841-8.ch003

Venugopal, K., Srikanth, N. L., Mavidi, P., Kanta, P., & Velagala, R. (2026). Adoption dynamics of applied English over translation-based English among engineering students: A predictive analytical approach. In K. Al Bataineh (Ed.), Interfaces Between Translation Studies and Applied Linguistics (pp. 1 to 32). IGI Global Scientific Publishing. https://doi.org/DOI: 10.4018/979-8-3373-4439-3.ch001

Wang, B., Deng, X., & Sun, H. (2022). Iteratively prompt pre-trained language models for chain of thought. *arXiv preprint arXiv:2203.08383*. DOI: 10.18653/v1/2022.emnlp-main.174

Wang, Y., Wu, S., Zhang, Y., Yan, S., Liu, Z., Luo, J., & Fei, H. (2025). Multimodal chain-of-thought reasoning: A comprehensive survey. *arXiv preprint arXiv:2503.12605.*

Wang, C., Yin, Y., & Hu, H. (2026). The rise of algorithmic governance and the dual revolution: Applications, challenges, and governance of artificial intelligence in public administration. *Technology in Society*, *86*, 103264. DOI: 10.1016/j.techsoc.2026.103264

Wang, Q., Wang, Y., & Amini, M. (2026). Associations of task technology fit and perceived usefulness with responsible generative AI use among university students. *Scientific Reports*, *16*(1), 2759. Advance online publication. DOI: 10.1038/s41598-025-32692-6 PMID: 41484194

Wang, Y., Yao, Q., Kwok, J. T., & Ni, L. M. (2020). Generalizing from a few examples: A survey on few-shot learning. [csur]. *ACM Computing Surveys*, *53*(3), 1–34. DOI: 10.1145/3386252

Ward, J. (2019). *Data governance: How to design, deploy and sustain an effective data governance program* (2nd ed.). John Wiley & Sons.

Wattanachote, K., Lin, C.-Y., Hsu, S.-E., & Shih, T. K. (2026). Generative AI Shanshui animation enhancement using Perlin noise and diffusion models. *Discover Artificial Intelligence*, *6*(1), 122. Advance online publication. DOI: 10.1007/s44163-025-00797-6

Weber-Wulff, D., Anohina-Naumeca, A., Bjelobaba, S., Foltýnek, T., Guerrero-Dib, J., Popoola, O., Šigut, P., & Waddington, L. (2023). Testing of detection tools for AI-generated text. *International Journal for Educational Integrity*, *19*(1), 26. Advance online publication. DOI: 10.1007/s40979-023-00146-z

Webson, A., & Pavlick, E. (2022, July). Do prompt-based models really understand the meaning of their prompts? In *Proceedings of the 2022 Conference of the North American Chapter of the Association for Computational Linguistics: Human Language Technologies* (pp. 2300-2344). DOI: 10.18653/v1/2022.naacl-main.167

Weidinger, L., Mellor, J., Rauh, M., Griffin, C., Uesato, J., Huang, P. S., . . . Gabriel, I. (2021). Ethical and social risks of harm from language models. *arXiv preprint arXiv:2112.04359.*

Wei, J., Wang, X., Schuurmans, D., Bosma, M., Xia, F., Chi, E., Le, Q. V., & Zhou, D. (2022). Chain-of-thought prompting elicits reasoning in large language models. *Advances in Neural Information Processing Systems*, *35*, 24824–24837. DOI: 10.52202/068431-1800

Wolf, E. J., Harrington, K. M., Clark, S. L., & Miller, M. W. (2013). Sample size requirements for structural equation models. Educational and Psychological Measurement, 73(6), 913 to 934.

Wu, T., Jiang, E., Donsbach, A., Gray, J., Molina, A., Terry, M., & Cai, C. J. (2022, April). Promptchainer: Chaining large language model prompts through visual programming. In *CHI Conference on Human Factors in Computing Systems Extended Abstracts* (pp. 1-10). DOI: 10.1145/3491101.3519729

Xia, S. (2026). Teacher support enhances self-efficacy and learning outcomes in the age of AI. *Scientific Reports, 16*(1), 5113. Advance online publication. DOI: 10.1038/s41598-026-36014-2 PMID: 41530478

Xin, B., Geng, Y., Hu, T., Chen, S., Yang, W., Wang, S., & Huang, L. (2022). Federated synthetic data generation with differential privacy. *Neurocomputing, 468*, 1–10. DOI: 10.1016/j.neucom.2021.10.027

Xu, G., Li, X., Chen, Y., Duan, Y., Wu, S., Yu, A., & Shi, Y. (2025). A Comprehensive Survey of Agentic AI in Healthcare. *Authorea Preprints*. DOI: 10.36227/techrxiv.176240542.22279040/v1

Xu, T., & Xiong, Y. (2026). Multidimensional determinants of generative AI acceptance in foreign language education. *Scientific Reports, 16*(1), 5698. Advance online publication. DOI: 10.1038/s41598-026-36700-1 PMID: 41554873

Yang, C., Xu, C., & Qi, Y. (2024). Financial knowledge large language model. *arXiv preprint arXiv:2407.00365.*

Yang, C., Li, Z., & Wipf, D. (2025). Chain-of-thought provably enables learning the (otherwise) unlearnable. In *The Thirteenth International Conference on Learning Representations.*

Yang, W., Pan, C., & Zhang, Y. (2022). An oversampling method for imbalanced data based on spatial distribution of minority samples SD-KMSMOTE. *Scientific Reports, 12*(1), 16820. DOI: 10.1038/s41598-022-21046-1 PMID: 36207460

Yao, S., Yu, D., Zhao, J., Shafran, I., Griffiths, T., Cao, Y., & Narasimhan, K. (2023). Tree of thoughts: Deliberate problem solving with large language models. *Advances in Neural Information Processing Systems, 36*, 11809–11822. DOI: 10.52202/075280-0517

Ye, X., & Durrett, G. (2022). The unreliability of explanations in few-shot prompting for textual reasoning. *Advances in Neural Information Processing Systems, 35*, 30378–30392. DOI: 10.52202/068431-2202

Yu, Z., He, L., Wu, Z., Dai, X., & Chen, J. (2023). Towards better chain-of-thought prompting strategies: A survey. *arXiv preprint arXiv:2310.04959.*

Zaharia, M., Das, T., Li, H., Hunter, T., Shenker, S., & Stoica, I. (2013). Discretized streams: Fault-tolerant streaming computation at scale. *Proceedings of the Twenty-Fourth ACM Symposium on Operating Systems Principles*, 423–438. DOI: 10.1145/2517349.2522737

Zhang, W., Kong, X., Dewitt, C., Braunl, T., & Hong, J. B. (2024). A study on prompt injection attack against LLM-integrated mobile robotic systems. *2024 IEEE 35th International Symposium on Software Reliability Engineering Workshops (ISSREW)*, 361-368. DOI: 10.1109/ISSREW63542.2024.00103

Zhang, Y., Yuan, Y., & Yao, A. C. C. (2023). Meta prompting for ai systems. *arXiv preprint arXiv:2311.11482*.

Zhang, L., Chen, J., Du, R., He, K., & Chen, J. (2017). Data integrity verification method with secure deduplication in cloud storage. *Jisuanji Gongcheng*, *43*(1), 32–38. DOI: 10.3969/j.issn.1000-3428.2017.01.006

Zhang, Z., Chen, J., & Li, Y. (2022). Generative AI in Enterprise Data Strategy: Opportunities and Limitations. *Journal of Enterprise Information Management*, *35*(8), 1785–1803.

Zhao, W. (2015, March). *Enriching engineering curricula with a course on cutting-edge computer technologies. In 2015 IEEE Integrated STEM Education Conference*. IEEE.

Zheng, G., Yang, B., Tang, J., Zhou, H. Y., & Yang, S. (2023). Ddcot: Duty-distinct chain-of-thought prompting for multimodal reasoning in language models. *Advances in Neural Information Processing Systems*, *36*, 5168–5191. DOI: 10.52202/075280-0228

Zheng, Y., Chang, C. H., Huang, S. H., Chen, P. Y., & Picek, S. (2024). An overview of trustworthy AI: Advances in IP protection, privacy-preserving federated learning, security verification, and GAI safety alignment. *IEEE Journal on Emerging and Selected Topics in Circuits and Systems*, *14*(4), 582–607. DOI: 10.1109/JETCAS.2024.3477348

Zhong, R., Lee, K., Zhang, Z., & Klein, D. (2021). Adapting language models for zero-shot learning by meta-tuning on dataset and prompt collections. *arXiv preprint arXiv:2104.04670*. DOI: 10.18653/v1/2021.findings-emnlp.244

Zhu, Z., Hsu, C., Nah, F. F.-H., & Liu, N. (2026). Generative AI adoption and solvers' popularity on supply-driven crowdsourcing platforms: The dual role of price signals. *Internet Research*, *36*(7), 24–42. DOI: 10.1108/INTR-02-2025-0262

About the Contributors

Mashael M. Asiri is an Associate Professor of Artificial Intelligence at King Khalid University (KKU), Abha, Saudi Arabia. She earned her Ph.D. in Computer Science from the University of Southampton, UK (2020), following an M.Sc. in Web Technology with Distinction from the University of Southampton (2015) and a B.Sc. in Computer Science from King Abdulaziz University, Saudi Arabia (2011). With over 13 years of academic and research experience, Dr. Asiri's work spans artificial intelligence, machine learning, deep learning, data science, and natural language processing, with applied contributions in healthcare, smart cities, cybersecurity, and education—advancing Saudi Vision 2030 priorities. She has published 30+ peer-reviewed papers in reputable journals and conferences, serves as a peer reviewer for international journals, and has supervised undergraduate and postgraduate research projects. Her leadership record includes serving as Head of the Computer Science Department at KKU (2021–2024) and leading multiple competitively funded projects from King Khalid University and the King Salman Center for Disability Research. Dr. Asiri holds a UK patent for a compact mini-computer for robotic machine-learning operations (IPO UK, 2024) and has developed several impactful AI systems, including multilingual RAG-based chatbots and models for medical imaging, traffic safety analytics, smart energy forecasting, and cyber-attack detection. She is a certified NVIDIA instructor in Generative AI (LLMs and Multimodal) and holds multiple professional certifications in AI and online teaching. Beyond academia, she contributes to national innovation activities as a judge and evaluator in major hackathons and mentors research teams across disciplines. Her current work focuses on trustworthy, efficient foundation-model customization, Retrieval-Augmented Generation pipelines, and scalable AI solutions for societal benefit.

***

Kolwang Warai Armand is a researcher specialising in data governance and analytics, cloud-native systems, and Artificial Intelligence. He holds a dual Master's degrees: MSc in Information Technology from ICT University Yaoundé (2025), with expertise in database management, data analysis, IT project management, and software engineering; and a Masters in Accounting and Finance from University of Maroua (2025).

Arun Arora is a transformative and visionary Operations and Supply Chain Management Leader with decades of distinguished industry experience driving manufacturing business excellence through Lean Management, Total Productive Maintenance (TPM), Business Process Reengineering and Total Quality Management (TQM). Proven track record of delivering measurable business outcomes ranging from significant Cost reduction and Productivity enhancement to Revenue growth and Operational turnaround across high-impact roles in leading organizations including International Tractors Ltd., Mahindra & Mahindra Ltd and Escorts Limited. Currently, Dr. Arora is working as PROFESSOR (Operations and Supply Chain Management) & Dean-Students Welfare with Lloyd Business School, Greater Noida (India). Recognized for strategic leadership in Global Manufacturing Operations, including heading the Export Tractor Assembly business at International Tractors, where he led large-scale transformations by optimizing processes, enhancing quality systems, and integrating digitization for performance gains. Adept at aligning operational goals with broader business objectives, while fostering a Culture of Continuous Improvement, Innovation, and Capability building. Holds a Ph.D. in Operations under Mechanical Engineering, MTech. in Manufacturing Management from BITS PILANI, and PGDBA with Specialization in Operations Management and Human Resource Management from Symbiosis, Pune, complemented by a strong academic presence as Guest Faculty at BITS Pilani. A published researcher and patent holder, Dr. Arora brings deep technical acumen and thought leadership to complex operational challenges. Skilled in stakeholder engagement, cross-functional leadership, and global collaboration, he is driven by a commitment to Operational Excellence, Sustainable Growth, and Innovation. He has contributed in 10 Indian design patents and author of 3 books. He has published 9 research papers in SCOPUS indexed SCI journal. He has also contributed 2 book chapters published in LNME, Springer, which is Scopus indexed. He is active reviewer and reviewed 182 manuscripts so far, which has testimonial in Web of Science. Key competencies include: Strategic Planning, Lean Transformation, TPM, Cost Optimization, Digitization in processes, Quality Systems, Employee Development, and Safety & Compliance (OHSAS 18001). With a proven ability to lead high-performing teams and large-scale operations, Dr. Arora stands out as a trusted advisor and catalyst for enterprise wide value creation and a researcher.

Anorgul Ashirova is working as an Associate Professor at the Department of General Professional Sciences, Mamun University, Khiva, Uzbekistan

Susanta Das is a seasoned educator with a proven record of teaching and mentoring diverse student populations, working at multiple institutions, and contributing to various organizational initiatives. He received his Ph.D. and M.A. degrees in Physics from Western Michigan University (WMU), USA, and his M.Sc. degree in Physics from Banaras Hindu University (BHU), India. He continued his research as a Marie Curie Postdoctoral Fellow at Stockholm University, Sweden, working on beam diagnostics for DESIREE (Double ElectroStatic Ion Ring ExpEriment) under the DITANET project (Diagnostic Techniques for Particle Accelerators – a Marie Curie Initial Training Network). He also conducted research at the Indian Institute of Science Education and Research (IISER), Kolkata, India, on high-pressure physics as a Project Scientist-B, and at the University of Electro-Communications, Tokyo, Japan, on ion–surface interactions as a Postdoctoral Fellow. Throughout his career, Dr. Das has worked and collaborated with numerous researchers, Ph.D. scholars, master's students, and visiting scholars from different countries. He has visited several countries to present and discuss his research and has participated in international conferences in the UK, Italy, Germany, Greece, Belgium, Bulgaria, Romania, Brazil, and other countries. He worked at several institutions before assuming his current role at Ajeenkya D Y Patil University. He has received several prestigious awards and fellowships, including the Marie Curie Postdoctoral Fellowship (Sweden), the Science Academies' Summer Research Fellowship (India), the Gowen Frostic Doctoral Fellowship, the Department Graduate Research and Creative Scholar Award from WMU, and the Leo R. Parpart Doctoral Fellowship from the Department of Physics, WMU, among many others. Dr. Das has co-authored several research articles in WoS- and Scopus-indexed international journals, conference proceedings, and scholarly book chapters. He has also co-edited multiple books published by renowned international publishing houses, including IGI Global, Springer Nature, Wiley, Scrivener-Wiley, and Notion Press. Currently, Dr. Das is actively engaged in cutting-edge research with a keen interest in nanotechnology, the United Nations Sustainable Development Goals (UN SDGs), and data science. His multifaceted contributions in teaching, research, and academic leadership reflect a dedicated professional who significantly advances the vision and mission of the institutions he serves.

Pooja Dehankar is working in department of Artificial Intelligence and Data Science, Ajeenkya D Y Patil School of Engineering, Pune. She has completed BE in Computer Engineering from Priyadarshini College of Engineering, Nagpur, and ME in Information Technology from Sinhgad College of Engineering, Pune.

She has done Post Graduate Diploma in Advance Computing. She has 17 years of experience in academics. Her areas of interest are Artificial Intelligence, Cyber Security, and Data Mining. She has published papers in Scopus Journals. She actively participates in workshops, faculty development programs, short-term training programs, conferences, and webinars. She is pursuing Ph.D. from Symbiosis Center for Research and Innovation, Symbiosis International (Deemed University).

Ilham Firmansyah is a researcher and computer science scholar at Universitas Esa Unggul, Indonesia. His research interests focus on artificial intelligence systems, generative modeling, agentic architectures, and responsible AI governance. He has contributed to academic publications in the areas of AI ethics, socio-technical AI systems, and digital information behavior. His work explores the intersection of machine learning foundations, system design, and accountability frameworks, with particular emphasis on integrating technical innovation with sustainable and ethical AI deployment.

Deepak Gupta is a distinguished academician with over 20 years of teaching experience and expertise in Computer Science and Engineering. He holds a Ph.D. in Computer Engineering and has an extensive research portfolio, including many international journal papers, multiple conference proceedings, and several books. His research interests span machine learning, artificial intelligence, and data mining. Currently, Dr. Gupta serves as an Associate Professor and Head of Department of CSE (Emerging Branches) at ITM Gwalior, MP, India. He has also contributed significantly to the field through patents and copyrights and actively engages as a reviewer, conference chair and editor.

Mani Joseph is the Professor and Head of the Department of Mathematics and Computer Science at the Modern College of Business and Science (MCBS), Oman. Prior to joining MCBS in 2004, he served as Dean of the Faculty of Computer Science and Engineering at Sharjah College, UAE. He received his Ph.D. in Communication from Cochin University of Science and Technology, India. Prof. Joseph is also an ABET IT Program Evaluator. He was born in Kerala, India, on July 14, 1963. His research interests include cybersecurity, risk management, blockchain, and machine learning, and he actively collaborates with research teams at reputable institutions in India and Europe. Prof. Joseph's research spans several areas within computer science, with a strong focus on cybersecurity, machine learning, blockchain, and related computational methods. He has contributed to studies that integrate both theoretical frameworks and practical applications in these domains. His scholarly work has received significant citations, indicating a strong academic impact within his field. In the book Computational Sciences and Sustainable Technologies (ICCSST 2023, Springer), he served as one of the editors, contributing to the peer-review process and to the selection and compilation of the volume. His recently funded projects reflect his engagement with emerging technologies and educational innovation. These include the TRC-funded "Vehi-Trak" blockchain system for vehicle history tracking in Oman, a national study on post-pandemic online teaching challenges, and institutional research projects that apply deep reinforcement learning and data analytics to predict at-risk students, understand dropout patterns, and explore blockchain-based digital frameworks to support smart education at MCBS.

Shikha Khullar is an academician, researcher, and editor associated with Poornima University, India. Her research interests include Artificial Intelligence, Machine Learning, Cybersecurity, Explainable AI, Sustainable Technologies, and Intelligent Systems. She has contributed to several international journals, conferences, book chapters, and edited volumes published by reputed publishers including IEEE, Springer, Wiley, and IGI Global. She is actively involved in guiding research scholars and promoting interdisciplinary research in emerging technologies.

Mahmood Hussain is an Assistant Professor in Computer Science and Engineering at MNR University, Hyderabad. He holds a Ph.D. in Computer Science with a specialization in Machine Learning and Data Analytics from Baba Ghulam Shah Badshah University. His research interests include Intelligent Health-Care Systems, Machine Learning, and Data Analytics. He is actively involved in teaching, mentoring students, and guiding academic and project-based learning. He is committed to promoting practical knowledge and innovation in emerging technologies.

Hitesh Mohapatra received the B.E. degree in Information Technology from Biju Patnaik University of Technology (BPUT), Odisha in 2006, and the MTech. Degree in CSE from Odisha University of Technology and Research (OUTR) University, Odisha in 2009. He received his Ph.D. in Computer Science & Engineering in 2021 from Veer Surendra Sai University of Technology (VSSUT), Burla, India. He has contributed 150+ SCI and Scopus indexed research articles. He has authored two books on Software Engineering and C Programming respectively. He has 15 years of teaching experience both in industry and academia. He has served the research community with various capacities like session chair, technical chair, keynote speaker etc. His research interests include wireless sensor network, smart city, smart grid and smart water. Currently he is working as Associate Professor at School of Computer Engineering, KIIT (Deemed to be) University, Bhubaneswar, Odisha, India.

Balusamy Nachiappan Experienced IT professional with a strong background in object-oriented Software Development, Design, and Architecture. Certified as a Salesforce System Architect and Salesforce Application Architect. Specialized in Banking, including Investment Banking and Core Banking, with international exposure. Extensive experience in the Travel Domain encompassing Airlines, Ship & Cargo industries, along with proficiency in Supply Chain Management and Real Estate. A solid track record of over a decade in Product Development across various sectors. Proficient in Waterfall, V Model, and Agile-Scrum methodologies. Holds extensive onsite exposure in the US, Japan, the UK, and Qatar.

Kuktalapalli Pradeep Kumar is currently working as Consultant at Volvo Group India Pvt Ltd under industry fellowship program sponsored by AICTE (All India Council for Technical Education) and also an Associate Professor in the Department of AIML and Data Science at CHRIST University, Bangalore, specializing in data provenance, information security, artificial intelligence, and data analytics. Earned PhD in Computer Science and Engineering from CHRIST University - India, with earlier degrees in Software Engineering (MTech) and Electronics & Computers Engineering (BTech). Published 40+ Scopus-indexed papers and authored/edited several books (https://www.scrivenerpublishing.com/search.php?q=kukatlapalli&Submit=Search) with leading publishers including Wiley Scrivner, CRC Press, and Taylor & Francis. His works span topics such as cyber security, data engineering, IoT, healthcare analytics, and AR/VR in healthcare. He holds patents and copyrights in AI-driven applications, blockchain, and medical device innovations. In addition to research, delivered corporate training on Power BI in collaboration with Honeywell and EY, served as a Smart India Hackathon judge, and acts as a National Testing Agency Observer India.

T. Durga Prasad is an accomplished academician with a Ph.D. in Management from Andhra University (2013), specializing in Accounting and Finance. He has 20 years' experience in teaching and research experience in India and abroad, including his tenure as Associate Professor at Wollega University, Ethiopia. His expertise spans financial management, financial literacy, and FinTech adoption. He has supervised over 225 MBA and 172 BBA research projects, along with guiding three research scholars one full-time Ph.D. scholar and two part-time scholar reflecting his strong mentorship and research leadership. Dr. Prasad has published 20+ research papers in national and international journals, including Scopus and Web of Science indexed publications. He has actively contributed to curriculum development and presented papers at numerous conferences. Currently serving as Area Chair (Finance) at Aditya University, he continues to strengthen research in the areas of financial literacy, FinTech's role in MSME success, and contemporary issues in financial markets.

N. Rajkumar is an Associate Professor in the Department of Computer Science and Engineering. He earned his Ph.D. in Information and Communication Engineering from Anna University, Chennai. With a rich experience of 15 years in the realm of technical education, he has made substantial contributions to the academic arena. His research background is highly commendable, encompassing over 20 publications in esteemed international journals, coupled with numerous presentations at both international and national conferences. Moreover, he actively engages as a member of prestigious professional societies such as ISTE, IAENG, and CSTA. His primary areas of interest comprise Software Engineering, Computer Networks, Internet of Things, and Machine Learning.

Feruza Rakhmonkulova is a faculty member in the Department of Social Sciences Education at Termez University of Economics and Service, Termez, Uzbekistan. Her academic interests encompass social sciences education, pedagogy, and curriculum development, with an emphasis on innovative teaching methodologies and learner-centered approaches. She is actively involved in teaching and academic activities that support the integration of social science perspectives into higher education, contributing to the development of critical thinking, civic awareness, and interdisciplinary understanding among students.

Koppala Venugopal, a professor in Management Studies at Aditya Institute of Technology and Management at Srikakulam, A.P. has had an adroit experience of academic, Research and community service. He has contributed 5 Projects, 2 patents, 10 books, 70 publications, 48 paper presentations, 56 resource talks and 12 memberships. He is guiding 4 scholars from various universities. His exceptional interest industry interface has made his efforts dexterous.

C. Viji holds the position of Associate Professor in the Department of Computer Science and Engineering. She accomplished her Ph.D. in Information and Communication Engineering from Anna University, Chennai. Dr. C. Viji's expertise in the realm of technical education has resulted in noteworthy contributions to the academic sphere. Her research background is indeed impressive, encompassing over 10 publications in esteemed international journals, along with numerous presentations at both international and national conferences. Furthermore, she actively engages as a member of renowned professional societies such as IAENG and CSTA.

Index

A

B

C

D

R

S

T

X

www.ingramcontent.com/pod-product-compliance
Lightning Source LLC
LaVergne TN
LVHW081536300926
849161LV00006B/1455
* 9 7 9 8 2 6 0 0 0 3 6 8 8 *